Meaning

"Betty Birner's new book is an ideal guide for students' magical mystery tour of the fascinating intricacies of pragmatics and semantics. Professor Birner clearly introduces landmark research in linguistics, philosophy, and other relevant disciplines, inspiring and helping students begin exploring meaning–language connections for themselves."

Sally McConnell-Ginet, *Linguistics, Cornell University, USA*

Meaning addresses the fundamental question of human language interaction: what it is to mean, and how we communicate our meanings to others. Experienced textbook writer and eminent researcher Betty J. Birner gives balanced coverage to semantics and pragmatics, emphasizing interactions between the two, and discusses other fields of language study such as syntax, neurology, philosophy of language, and artificial intelligence in terms of their interfaces with linguistic meaning.

Comics and diagrams appear throughout to keep the reader engaged, and end-of-chapter quizzes, data-collection exercises, and opinion questions are employed along with more traditional exercises and discussion questions. In addition, the book features copious examples from real life and current events, along with boxes describing linguistic issues in the news and interesting and accessible research on topics like swearing, politics, and animal communication. Students will emerge ready for deeper study in semantics and pragmatics – and, more importantly, with an understanding of how all of these fields serve the fundamental purpose of human language: the communication of meaning. *Meaning* is an ideal textbook for courses in linguistic meaning that focus on both semantics and pragmatics in equal parts, with special attention given to philosophical questions, related subfields of linguistics, and interfaces among these various areas.

Appropriate for both undergraduate and graduate-level courses in semantics, pragmatics, and general linguistics, *Meaning* is essential reading for all students of linguistic meaning.

Betty J. Birner is Professor of Linguistics and Cognitive Science in the Department of English at Northern Illinois University, DeKalb, IL. She received her Ph.D. in 1992 from Northwestern University, and has written extensively on pragmatics, the semantics/pragmatics interface, and information structure.

Meaning
Semantics, Pragmatics, Cognition

Betty J. Birner

LONDON AND NEW YORK

Designed cover image: Getty Images | MichałBogacz

First published 2023
by Routledge
4 Park Square, Milton Park, Abingdon, Oxon OX14 4RN

and by Routledge
605 Third Avenue, New York, NY 10158

Routledge is an imprint of the Taylor & Francis Group, an informa business

© 2023 Betty J. Birner

The right of Betty J. Birner to be identified as author of this work has been asserted in accordance with sections 77 and 78 of the Copyright, Designs and Patents Act 1988.

All rights reserved. No part of this book may be reprinted or reproduced or utilised in any form or by any electronic, mechanical, or other means, now known or hereafter invented, including photocopying and recording, or in any information storage or retrieval system, without permission in writing from the publishers.

Trademark notice: Product or corporate names may be trademarks or registered trademarks, and are used only for identification and explanation without intent to infringe.

British Library Cataloguing-in-Publication Data
A catalogue record for this book is available from the British Library

Library of Congress Cataloging-in-Publication Data
Names: Birner, Betty J., author.
Title: Meaning : semantics, pragmatics, cognition / Betty J. Birner.
Description: Abingdon, Oxon ; New York, NY : Routledge, 2023. |
Includes bibliographical references and index.
Identifiers: LCCN 2022041975 (print) | LCCN 2022041976 (ebook)
Subjects: LCSH: Semantics. | Pragmatics.
Classification: LCC P325 .B474 2023 (print) | LCC P325 (ebook) |
DDC 401/.43–dc23/eng/20221018
LC record available at https://lccn.loc.gov/2022041975
LC ebook record available at https://lccn.loc.gov/2022041976

ISBN: 978-0-367-02880-0 (hbk)
ISBN: 978-0-367-02884-8 (pbk)
ISBN: 978-1-003-35121-4 (ebk)

DOI: 10.4324/9781003351214

Typeset in Bembo
by Newgen Publishing UK

Dedication

In memory of my parents,
Richard and Pearl Buikema,
who by giving me an education
gave me the world.

Contents

List of boxes	xii
List of figures	xiii
List of truth tables	xv
Preface	xvii
Acknowledgments	xix

1	**What is language?**	**1**
	Linguistics	2
	The rules of language	4
	Language change	6
	Research in linguistics	8
	Philosophy of language: How meaning works	9
	Types of meaning	10
	Where is meaning located?	13
	The philosophers weigh in, beginning with: Frege	15
	Russell	16
	Strawson	17
	Donnellan	18
	The upshot	19
	Semantics and pragmatics	19
	Discourse models and possible worlds	20
	Exercises	23

2 Semantics I: Word meaning — 27

What is a word? — 28
Where words come from — 30
    Historical descent — 30
    Other sources of new words — 31
    Lexical relations — 36
Approaches to word meaning — 40
    Componential analysis — 40
    Other primitive-based approaches — 41
    Prototype theory and The Great Sandwich Controversy — 42
Exercises — 46

3 Semantics II: Sentence meaning — 50

Truth and meaning — 53
Sentential relations — 55
Logical operators — 61
    Negation — 61
    Conjunction — 62
    Disjunction — 63
    The conditional — 64
    The biconditional — 65
Propositional logic — 66
    Analytic statements — 66
    Synthetic statements — 67
Predicate logic — 70
    Predicates and constants — 70
    Variables — 72
    Quantifiers — 72
    Ambiguity and scope — 74
Exercises — 76

4 Pragmatics I: The Cooperative Principle — 82

Reprise: Semantics vs. pragmatics — 84
The Cooperative Principle — 84
    The maxims — 85
    The maxim of Quantity — 87
    The maxim of Quality — 91
    The maxim of Relation — 93
    The maxim of Manner — 96
    Revisiting Grice's problem — 97
    Tests for conversational implicature — 100

	Implicature and pragmatic theory	*102*
	Conventional implicature	*102*
	The Gricean world view	*104*
	Pragmatics after Grice	*105*
	Explicature	*105*
	Impliciture	*106*
	Neo-Gricean theory	*107*
	Relevance theory	*110*
	Boundary disputes	*112*
	Exercises	*114*
5	**Pragmatics II: Speech acts**	**119**
	Speech acts	*120*
	Performatives	*120*
	Constatives	*121*
	Types of speech acts: first pass	*122*
	Indirect speech acts	*124*
	Felicity conditions	*126*
	Felicity conditions, speech acts, and the Cooperative Principle	*129*
	Types of speech acts: second pass	*133*
	Politeness theory	*136*
	Exercises	*140*
6	**Language structure**	**144**
	The Chomskyan revolution	*145*
	Sound structure	*147*
	Word structure	*150*
	Morphemes	*150*
	Allomorphs	*151*
	Words: a review	*152*
	Parts of speech	*153*
	Structure and function	*156*
	Representing word structure	*157*
	Other ways of building words	*159*
	Sentence structure	*161*
	Ambiguity and constituency	*161*
	Representing sentence structure	*165*
	Expanding our grammar	*169*
	Structural ambiguity	*175*
	So what's the point?	*177*
	Exercises	*178*

7 Interfaces I: Semantics, pragmatics, and philosophy — 183

- Reference and the semantics/pragmatics boundary — 184
  - What do we refer to when we refer? — 185
- Deixis and anaphora — 187
  - Indexicals — 187
  - Deixis — 188
  - Personal deixis — 188
  - Spatial deixis — 190
  - Temporal deixis — 191
  - Discourse deixis — 192
  - Anaphora — 192
  - Reference resolution — 193
  - Cataphora — 194
  - Anaphora and phrase types — 195
- Definiteness — 196
  - Definiteness as uniqueness — 197
  - Definiteness as familiarity — 199
- Presupposition — 202
  - Testing for presupposition — 202
  - Presupposition triggers — 204
  - Theories of presupposition — 206
  - Accommodation — 209
- Exercises — 212

8 Interfaces II: Structure and meaning — 216

- Semantic roles — 217
  - Argument-structure alternations — 219
- Information structure — 220
  - Preposing — 222
  - Postposing — 225
  - Argument reversal — 228
  - Inference — 229
  - Open propositions — 232
  - Constructions — 235
  - The type/token distinction — 237
- Exercises — 238

9 Meaning and human cognition — 243

- Language and the brain — 244
  - Brain structure — 244
  - Neurons — 247
  - Aphasia — 248

	Language and thought	250
	Does the language I speak affect my view of reality?	250
	Language use and world view	256
	Advertising	256
	Politics and public policy	257
	Language and prejudice	262
	Connecting the dots	265
	Exercises	266
10	**Meaning, minds, and machines**	**270**
	The nuts and bolts	271
	Natural-language processing	272
	Artificial intelligence	274
	Data mining	276
	Deep learning	277
	Meaning and the self	280
	Bodies and minds	281
	Language and consciousness	282
	Exercises	286
References		289
Index		294

Boxes

1.1	Animal 'language'	5
1.2	Positive *anymore*	7
1.3	Art and meaning	11
2.1	Infixes!	32
2.2	I'm my own opposite	37
2.3	What is a lie?	45
3.1	Lost in translation	51
3.2	Fake news!	56
3.3	"Hospitals named after sandwiches kill five"	59
4.1	"I like beer"	89
4.2	What the meaning of the word *is* is	95
4.3	"I would like you to do us a favor though"	99
5.1	What can you 'hereby' order?	128
5.2	It's hard for me to say I'm sorry	132
5.3	"You made me an offer that I accepted"	135
6.1	Hooray for *they*!	154
6.2	Language invention	163
6.3	Different dialects, different rules	173
7.1	Here's something being discussed by the linguists	196
7.2	Messing with people's memories	210
8.1	Pragmatic borrowing	223
8.2	There's the silliest claim going around	227
8.3	Mutual knowledge and writing	234
9.1	Whorf in fiction: From *1984* to chatting with aliens	253
9.2	Forbidden language	259
9.3	Would you rather be someone's master or their mistress?	263
10.1	Learners of all kinds	279
10.2	Our new overlords?	284

Figures

1.1	Quotative 'like' comic	2
1.2	Magritte, 'The Human Condition'	12
1.3	Discourse model	21
1.4	Embedded discourse models	22
2.1	Infix comic	34
2.2	Partial taxonomy of animals	39
2.3	Sandwich	43
2.4	Fuzzy set for the word *sandwich*	44
3.1	Garden path comic	60
4.1	Conditionals comic	83
4.2	Gricean world view	104
4.3	Gricean world view	112
4.4	Neo-Gricean world view	113
4.5	Relevance theory world view	113
5.1	'How to make friends' comic	126
6.1	Tower of Babel comic	152
6.2	*undesirable* tree, option 1	158
6.3	*undesirable* tree, option 2	158
6.4	*undesirable* tree, option 3	158
6.5	*unbuttonable* tree, option 1	159
6.6	*unbuttonable* tree, option 2	159
6.7	Classical Hebrew morphology	160
6.8	Ambiguity	162
6.9	Phrase structure tree for *mountains*	166
6.10	Phrase structure tree for *around mountains*	167
6.11	Phrase structure tree for *lots of authors of books on management of societies of researchers into origins of species of whale*	168
6.12	S → XP VP	173
6.13	Phrase structure tree for *the problem with our plan is the issue of funding*	173
6.14	Phrase structure tree for *I read a book on the couch*, option 1	177
6.15	Phrase structure tree for *I read a book on the couch*, option 2	177

8.1	Partial taxonomy of animals	237
9.1	The human brain	245
9.2	MRI of human brain	246
9.3	Neuron	247
9.4	Synapse	248
9.5	Sapir-Whorf comic	255
10.1	Hidden layers	272
10.2	Robot	286

Truth tables

3.1	Negation	61
3.2	Conjunction	62
3.3	Disjunction	63
3.4	Conditional	64
3.5	Biconditional	65
3.6	Contradiction	67
3.7	Conjunction	67
3.8	Synthetic statement	68
3.9	$p \wedge (q \to r)$	68
3.10	$(p \wedge q) \to r$	69

Preface

There are excellent textbooks out there on semantics, and excellent textbooks on pragmatics – but until now there hasn't been a book that covers them both, in roughly equal measure. And there certainly hasn't been a textbook that focuses on linguistic meaning itself, in all of its various aspects: semantic, pragmatic, philosophical, neurological, structural, and computational. What I've attempted to do in this book is to weave together all of these strands and their interrelationships for a comprehensive look at meaning in human language.

In doing so, I've chosen to cover areas that are rarely discussed in other books on linguistic meaning, such as neurology, cognition, and the structural correlates of meaning (phonology, morphology, syntax). But of course all of these are relevant to how linguistic meaning arises and how it is interpreted. And the questions tackled at the end of the book regarding human consciousness and artificial intelligence are foundational to the question of where linguistic meaning will go from here.

As an educator, I find that my biggest problem with textbooks is that students don't read them. And the reason they don't read them is that textbooks all too often simply aren't interesting. For this reason, my goal has been to write an interesting, engaging textbook on linguistic meaning that students are actually excited to read. Each chapter includes two or three boxes on topics that students find inherently interesting – things like animal communication, forbidden words, and gender-neutral *they*. I draw examples from real life and current events. There are comics and illustrations, and I've tried to keep the sections short to keep the reader moving along.

At the end of each chapter you'll find five sets of exercises: First, there is a ten-question multiple-choice 'self-test', with the answers given at the end of the exercises; this allows students to check for themselves whether they've understood what they've read. Then come open-ended comprehension questions, which again test understanding and which generally have a correct answer. Following these are a set of opinion questions, for which there is no one correct answer but which give students a chance to think about where they stand in light of what they've learned. Next come discussion questions, deeper questions designed for in-class discussion or more thoughtful essay answers. And finally there are data collection and analysis questions, which serve both to teach basic research skills and to emphasize the importance of looking at actual language use in doing linguistics research.

With this range of question types, it would be possible for the instructor to create exams by drawing questions entirely from the end-of-chapter exercises. If the students know in advance that the exam questions will come from the exercises, it motivates them to work through the exercises in advance, which is an excellent way to solidify their understanding of the material. I've found that even having the self-test answers listed at the end of the chapter isn't a hindrance to using the self-test questions on exams, since if the students choose to memorize the question-answer pairs in advance, well – that's learning.

I have had great fun writing this book. I hope that you, whether you are an instructor or a student, will have great fun reading it.

Acknowledgments

I am grateful to many people for helping to bring this book to completion. Jeff Kaplan read every chapter in draft form and provided a wealth of comments that vastly improved the book; I am grateful for his help, insight, and expertise. I am also indebted to Barbara Abbott, Elizabeth Coppock, Larry Horn, Polly Jacobson, Shahrzad Mahootian, and Gregory Ward for helpful discussion and examples. I thank my colleagues at NIU for their support, and especially Jeff Einboden for many helpful and fascinating conversations.

I thank Shelby Tomassini for her assistance with manuscript preparation, Ed McGarrigle for helping me pull together the discipline to finish, and Mother Hildegard Dubnick OSB for help with German honorifics. I thank Lee Hutchinson of *Ars Technica* for a fun discussion that informed my thoughts on alien communication.

I thank Northern Illinois University for a valuable sabbatical year that gave me the space to get this done during a pandemic.

I am grateful to Ingrid Lundgren and the Artists Rights Society for permission to use the Magritte image. I am also grateful to the following for permission to use images from their absolutely wonderful web comic/humor series:

- Randall Munroe and his assistant Casey Blair, xkcd (www.xkcd.com)
- Ryan North, Dinosaur Comics (www.qwantz.com)
- Zach Weinersmith, Saturday Morning Breakfast Cereal (www.smbc-comics.com)
- Sad and Useless (www.sadanduseless.com)

And, always and forever, I thank Andrew Birner and Suzanne Birner, my husband and daughter, for being everything to me.

CHAPTER 1

What is language?

> **KEY CONCEPTS**
>
> - prescriptive vs. descriptive approaches to language
> - competence vs. performance
> - rule-governed behavior
> - natural vs. nonnatural meaning
> - sentence meaning vs. speaker meaning
> - mentalism vs. referentialism
> - propositional attitudes/opaque contexts
> - sense and reference
> - referential vs. attributive readings
> - semantics vs. pragmatics
> - possible world
> - discourse model
> - proposition/sentence/utterance
> - truth-conditions, truth-value

If there's one word that ought to have a clear meaning, it's the word *meaning*. But it turns out that it's not at all clear what the word *meaning* means. First off, *meaning* and its root, *mean,* mean altogether too many unrelated things. There's the meaning of life, there's an arithmetic mean, there's what I mean to do, people can be mean in the sense of nasty, and they can also be mean in the sense of stingy. What does it all mean?

In this book, we'll look at **linguistic** meaning – the way in which words and sentences describe the world, and in which one person uses language to express their meaning to another. But that definition is already circular, so let's try again. We're going to look at how people use language intentionally to affect what other people think and do – how I get you to understand what I want you to understand, and maybe to act on it. We'll look at the philosophy of language, the structure of language, the difference between a statement's literal meaning and the speaker's intended meaning, how listeners use their knowledge of linguistic rules to figure out

DOI: 10.4324/9781003351214-1

what the speaker meant, and what we know about how the brain interprets and produces language. We'll finish up with a discussion about meaning, machines, and artificial intelligence, and what all of this means for our view of ourselves as human beings.

We'll be doing this using the tools of linguistics, which is where our journey begins.

LINGUISTICS

Linguistics is the **scientific study of language**. And the word *scientific* is very important here. Plenty of people are interested in language in a nonscientific way: People learn foreign languages, or get grumpy when they hear people speaking another language or using what they consider 'ungrammatical' language (we'll get back to that), or simply when they hear someone using *like* or *y'know* too often. But for linguists, language is an object of scientific study. Linguists study language the way botanists study plants or geologists study rocks. And one thing that means is that, just as a geologist would never tell a rock that it contains too much quartz and a botanist would never tell a daisy that it has too many petals, a linguist would never tell a speaker that their sentence contains too many instances of *like*. We just, like, don't do that.

There are two ways to approach the study of language – or really, the study of anything. You can go at it from a **prescriptive** point of view or a **descriptive** point of view. A prescriptive approach, as the word suggests, prescribes how someone ought to behave. A prescriptive grammarian might tell you not to use a double negative (like *He didn't do nothing*) or not to end a sentence with a preposition (often noted to be a rule *up with which I will not put*; see Ben Zimmer's wonderful Language Log post at http://itre.cis.upenn.edu/~myl/languagelog/archives/001715.html regarding the origin of this phrase and its subsequent and persistent misattribution to Winston Churchill). A prescriptive grammarian might tell you not to use the words *ain't* and *irregardless*, or not to introduce a quote with the word *like* (as in *She was like, "That's*

FIGURE 1.1 Courtesy of xkcd.com.

terrible"). And until recently, prescriptive grammarians fought to prevent people from using sentence-initial *hopefully* (as in *Hopefully, it won't rain*) and split infinitives (as in *to boldly go*) – though more recently these last two have mostly been abandoned.

A descriptivist, on the other hand, simply describes how people do in fact behave – and linguists are descriptivists. So for a linguist, the question isn't whether these uses are or aren't okay; linguists aren't in the business of telling people what they should do with their language. Instead, the linguist studies how people actually use language, and tries to work out the rules they're following. Those rules are called a **grammar**. So when someone regularly uses double negatives, they're not speaking ungrammatically; it simply means that their grammar allows double negatives. And since every grammar is as good, useful, and systematic as every other grammar, that's just fine. (And if you're tempted to complain that two negatives make a positive, ask yourself whether you'd be fine with three negatives – as in *I didn't tell nobody nothing* – on the grounds that three negatives make a negative. You're likely to see that your objection isn't really based on logic or math.)

When you tell a new acquaintance that you're a linguist, usually the first thing they'll say is, "I'd better be careful how I talk!" But there's no danger that the linguist you're speaking with will 'correct' you; anything you say is fine with them. (The only real danger is that they'll whip out a pencil and paper and write down what you've said so that they can study it later.)

Now, it's true that not everything you say will be grammatical, even by the rules of your own grammar. Sometimes people make errors. So it's useful to distinguish between, say, (1) and (2):

(1) I didn't tell nobody nothing.

(2) Right now in America, we have seniors, who every day – millions of seniors are going into the Medicare system and they are getting full coverage and the kind of coverage they need.

(Kamala Harris, 7/31/19; cited in *Washington Post* 2019)

Although a prescriptive grammarian would bristle at (1) and let (2) go past without notice, (2) is in fact the 'ungrammatical' example. The speaker in (1) is following a grammar that allows double (and triple) negatives, and by the rules of that grammar, (1) is completely grammatical. But the speaker in (2) stops mid-sentence, shifts direction, and finishes in such a way that the whole thing doesn't end up being a strictly grammatical sentence by the rules of her own grammar. This is what linguists call a **performance** error, and every speaker commits such 'errors' many times a day (again, linguists observe the phenomenon but don't judge it as either good or bad).

Linguists study speakers' performance, but mostly as a way of getting at what we're really interested in, which is speakers' **competence** – that implicit understanding of the rules of their language that they follow every time they speak but of which they're mostly unaware. Your competence in English tells you to say *The cat is adorable* rather than *Cat the adorable is*, but you'd be hard-pressed to explain why. Your grammar allows the first (i.e., it's grammatical), but not the second (i.e., it's ungrammatical). The linguist's job is to figure out what that grammar is, how it works, how you use it, and how you came to have it.

The rules of language

Every version, every dialect, of every language is **rule-governed**. That means that every time anyone on earth speaks, they're relying on a mental grammar – a set of rules that tells them what is and isn't a word, phrase, or sentence of their language. The grammar generates the sentences of the language, and the sentences of the language are grammatical if they're generated by the grammar. So a linguist will never tell someone that they're speaking wrongly, or ungrammatically, or improperly. By definition, if a person's grammar generates a sentence (meaning it's not a performance error), that sentence is proper and grammatical in the dialect they're speaking – which is to say, according to the grammar that they're using.

These rules constitute your **competence** in your native language, and they're implicit, which means you haven't formulated them consciously. They're rules you know without knowing that you know them. (So now you know you know things you didn't know you knew, you know?) Consider a few examples:

(3) a Gilda told Murray a really silly joke.
    b Gilda told a really silly joke to Murray.

(4) a Gilda told Murray that Jane annoyed her.
    b *Gilda told that Jane annoyed her to Murray.

I'm guessing that you found both examples in (3) to be fine, but that (4b) was completely out. (That's what the asterisk means.) But why? What's the difference between the two?

Or consider these:

(5) a I ran down the stairs.
    b I chopped down the tree.

(6) a Down the stairs I ran.
    b *Down the tree I chopped.

(7) a I chopped the tree down.
    b *I ran the stairs down.

The sentences in (5a) and (5b) look parallel in their structure – but while you can move the phrase *down the stairs* to the beginning of the sentence in (6a), you can't do the same thing with *down the tree* in (6b). And while you can move *down* to the end of the sentence in (7a), you can't do the same thing in (7b). What gives?

Clearly you know something implicitly about what you can and can't do with the English language – but you don't know it explicitly, because unless you've been studying linguistics, you've probably never given a moment's thought to pairs of sentences like these and why you can move words or phrases in one case but not another. Nonetheless, you follow these rules all the time, and you share them with most other speakers of English.

BOX 1.1

Animal 'language'

Every so often the news buzzes with word of some animal mastering human language, such as the gorilla Koko supposedly learning American Sign Language (ASL). Or you'll hear that some species, such as dolphins or whales, has its 'own language'. These stories are touching, and there's something deeply compelling about the prospect of being able to talk with another species and get a little closer to understanding what it's like to be them. Unfortunately, most linguists remain unconvinced. Yes, bees and whales and plenty of other species have communication systems, but these generally lack some of what Charles Hockett called the 'design features' of human language.

For instance, language is made up of discrete units (distinct sounds, words, etc.) that can be swapped to make new meanings: change its first sound, and *lip* becomes *rip*. And related to that is the fact that you can put together novel sentences – sentences you've never heard before (i.e., language is **productive**). And related to both of these is the fact that language has syntax: For instance, *Larry loves Lenny* means something different from *Lenny loves Larry,* and you can embed chunks inside each other to get a hierarchical structure, as when you embed one sentence inside another: *Lucy told Laura that Larry loves Lenny.* The question is whether animal communication systems have these features, and so far it appears that they don't. You may be convinced by Koko's use of signs (and I'll admit it's pretty impressive), and certainly her trainer, linguist Penny Patterson, believes she was using language, but others argue that Koko lacked real syntax and productivity – in essence, that she was stringing together individual words without much structure, and that even then her utterances were subject to Patterson's interpretation.

If you're curious, the web is full of fascinating videos and articles on the communicative systems of animals like Koko, Washoe (a chimpanzee), Alex (a parrot), and many others. Decide for yourself – but be sure to investigate both sides. (See, for example, the videos at www.koko.org/ and compare with the withering analysis by linguist Geoff Pullum at www.chronicle.com/blogs/linguafranca/2018/06/27/koko-is-dead-but-the-myth-of-her-linguistic-skills-lives-on/.) And remember that when your dog scratches at the back door and barks, she might be **communicating** with you – but that doesn't mean she's using language.

But you don't share **all** of the rules with **all** other speakers of English, because there's variation among dialects. All my life I've said things like (8):

(8) I'm going to the store. Do you want to come with?

Then at some point I went off to college and discovered that for lots of Americans, *Do you want to come with?* is ungrammatical. For those speakers, it's okay to *come with me* or to *come with us*, but it's not okay to simply *come with*. But for speakers in much of the upper Midwest, it's perfectly all right to *come with*. This is an example of variation in **syntax** (sentence structure), but there's also variation in other areas of the language, such as **phonology** (sound systems) and the **lexicon** (your mental 'dictionary'). For example, some people pronounce the words *cot* and *caught* identically, and (for the same reason) pronounce the names *Don* and *Dawn* identically (so beware if you were planning to name your twins *Don* and *Dawn*); others, like me, pronounce those words very differently. And as we all know, for some people a bubbly soft drink is called a *soda*, for others it's a *Coke* (regardless of flavor), and for folks like me it's *pop*. And as you can already guess, for a linguist there's no 'right' answer.

Language change

In case you're wondering where all these dialects came from, the answer is that language is always changing. All languages, everywhere. So if you have a group of speakers speaking the same language, and half of them wander off to, say, a whole different continent, the language of the group that stayed will continue to change, and the language of the group that left will continue to change – but they'll no longer change in sync, because the groups are no longer speaking to each other very much. And the next thing you know, you've got people in America talking about *trucks* and *elevators* while people in England are talking about *lorries* and *lifts*.

Needless to say, linguists don't see any problem with language change. There always seem to be older people complaining about how younger people are ruining the language – and that makes sense, because language is always changing, so younger people are always speaking differently from older people. And since prescriptivists have been telling these older people all their lives that there's a right and a wrong way to speak, it's perfectly natural for them to draw the conclusion that the way the younger folks are speaking is just wrong. But compare (9) and (10):

(9)   Barbara said, "I can't believe it!"

(10)   a Barbara went, "I can't believe it!"
         b Barbara was like, "I can't believe it!"
         c Barbara was all, "I can't believe it!"

In (9), the speaker is reporting Barbara's actual words – and this is also the case in (10a). But in (10b), Barbara needn't have actually uttered those words; it's enough that she was **like** that – i.e., that she had the general demeanor of someone who couldn't believe it. Similarly for (10c), but here there's an additional requirement, which is that there be heightened affect or emotion to justify the use of *all*: So Barbara can **be like**, "It's 4:15", but she can't **be all**, "It's 4:15" – unless there's something HUGELY important that happens at 4:15.

What this means is that a speaker whose dialect includes the options in (10) is able to make useful distinctions that are denied to a speaker who has only (9) at their disposal. Which, in turn, means that if your grandparents give you grief over saying *he was like… and then she was like…*, you can confidently explain to them that your dialect offers an objective improvement over the prescriptive dictates of Standard English. (But be nice about it.)

BOX 1.2

Positive *anymore*

Language change is happening all the time, in every language – and here's an example of language change that's happening right here, right now: the spread of positive *anymore*. To see which side of this change you're on, ask yourself how you feel about the following sentence:

(i) I eat a lot of chocolate anymore.

Many English speakers would say that this sentence is terrible; for them, to use the word *anymore* you need to have a negative element somewhere in the sentence, as in:

(ii) I don't eat a lot of chocolate anymore.

For plenty of people (including me), this is still the rule; I couldn't say (i) and feel okay about it. But for lots of others, that constraint is loosening, and usages like (i) are increasing. Some usages are intermediate; for example, a friend recently said this to me in conversation:

(iii) It's very, very difficult to find that kind of skill set anymore.

If you're one of the people who finds (i) to be terrible, does the word *difficult* here count as negative enough to make (iii) okay? What about this:

(iv) It's very, very easy to find that kind of skill set anymore.

Whoa – for me, (iii) is sort of middling-okay, but (iv) is absolutely dreadful. Nonetheless, I hear examples like this all the time. If you check out the Yale Grammatical Diversity Project (Maher and McCoy 2011, https://ygdp.yale.edu/phenomena/positive-anymore), you'll discover not only real-life examples of positive *anymore*, but also information about the construction itself and where it occurs. The examples listed there include:

(v) a You stay in your office too late anymore. (Krumpelmann 1939)
    b Anymore, John smokes. (Punske and Barss 2010)
    c Even in the small towns anymore, it's getting like that. (Wolfram and Christian 1976)

When I present examples like these to classes, there are always students who absolutely refuse to believe anyone would say anything like that, and many who can't quite imagine what the speaker even meant. The cool thing is that, in

> many uses, its meaning is the flip side of the negative *anymore* exemplified in (ii): Whereas *I don't eat a lot of chocolate anymore* means 'I used to eat a lot of chocolate but now I don't', *I eat a lot of chocolate anymore* means 'I didn't used to eat a lot of chocolate but now I do'. In any case, if you're a 'positive *anymore*' speaker, you may be puzzled to learn that anybody finds this surprising – but if you're one of those who just don't believe it occurs, keep your eyes and ears open, and I promise you'll start to notice it.
>
> And remember, it's neither good nor bad; it's just language changing, as it always does.

Research in linguistics

Since linguists focus on how language is really used (as opposed to how someone thinks it should be used), it would seem that the best way to get at the linguistic competence of an individual would be to see how they actually use language. But it's a little tricky, because you can't just follow a person around throughout their life, noting everything they say. (Actually, you can, at least for a while; this is called a case study. But it takes a ton of time, and results only in a snapshot of one person's language.) Instead, we usually look at a representative sample of an entire linguistic community – speakers of a single language or dialect – and try to get at the grammar they share. This is an idealization, though, since no two people share the exact same set of words and rules and pronunciations. So one thing we always need to keep in mind is that the mere fact that I disagree with your judgments about what is and isn't okay in English doesn't mean either of us is wrong. It doesn't matter how many linguistics degrees I have; I'm no better a speaker of English than you are. If your reaction to (8) above (*Do you want to come with?*) is frank disbelief that anyone could ever say that, it simply means that our two grammars differ on this point. Neither one of us is wrong; in fact, it's hard to imagine how someone could be 'wrong' about what their own individual grammar allows and disallows.

So, keeping in mind that we want to get at the implicit grammar that accounts for a person's linguistic competence, there are a number of ways linguists approach the problem: They gather **native-speaker intuitions** (either by thinking about what sounds right to them or surveying other speakers for their opinions); they run **empirical studies** that might test, for example, word recognition or reading speed; or they look at **naturally occurring data** – either by examining a **corpus** of collected speech or writing, or by **eliciting** a particular word or phrase (e.g., getting people to say it by asking carefully worded questions), or through **natural observation**. These methods all have strengths and weaknesses; for example, an obvious weakness in a researcher relying on their own intuitions is that they'll be biased toward judgments that support their own theories. And empirical studies are great, but often require expensive equipment or specialized software. In this book, we're going to make use of naturally occurring data, frequently using the internet as our corpus. At the end of each chapter, you'll have the opportunity to look at real-life data (e.g., language used on the internet), collect a mini-corpus, and/or consider what the data suggest with respect to some hypothesis or other. A strength of corpus studies is that we're looking at actual data use, which seems like a pretty good way to get at how people actually use language. A drawback is that natural language, as we saw above, contains performance errors. For this reason, we try to get as many examples (called **tokens**) in our corpus as possible, so that the patterns will be clear.

PHILOSOPHY OF LANGUAGE: HOW MEANING WORKS

So far we've seen that each person has an implicit knowledge of their own personal language system (called an **idiolect** when we're talking about the language system that's unique to a specific individual), and that this knowledge constitutes their linguistic **competence**. Each of these systems is as 'right', useful, and communicative as any other, and because linguists are scientists, we take a **descriptive** approach to studying them. Linguists have found that all linguistic systems are **rule-governed** and also that every linguistic system changes over time. There's nothing wrong with this; languages evolve in ways that are sometimes arbitrary (giving us one group that drinks *soda* and another that drinks *pop*) and sometimes a useful response to a changing world (how could we talk about computers today if the English language hadn't changed since the time of Shakespeare?).

This still doesn't quite answer the question of how language works, and specifically how meaning works. How does meaning get from one person to another?

Good question – by which I mean, bad question. Because meaning doesn't actually 'get from one person to another' at all, at least not literally. As Michael Reddy (1979) noticed, the English language contains a great number of expressions that treat language as a conduit through which meaning travels – expressions like these:

(11) a I couldn't convey my meaning to him.
 b Can you give me that again?
 c His words were full of meaning.
 d I didn't catch that.
 e Did you get my idea?
 f I put my thoughts down in words.

These and many more expressions use what Reddy calls the Conduit Metaphor, which has essentially two parts – first, that linguistic units like words and sentences are containers into which we put meanings, thoughts, ideas, etc., and second, that once we've packaged up our ideas into these containers, we convey them to our listener. But this metaphor is an illusion, because nothing really gets transferred from my head to yours when I talk to you. At best, I encode my meanings into a complex pattern of disruptions in the air – sound waves – that you then decode into speech sounds and try to interpret. But this whole process of encoding, decoding, and interpretation holds endless potential for miscommunication, partly because we can never know how similar our mental worlds are: I can't saw open your skull and look into your brain and see the full range of preexisting beliefs, memories, and dispositions that will influence the way you interpret what I say, and I can't check afterward to see whether your interpretation precisely matched my intent. There are countless ways in which communication can fail, and – here's the descriptive bit again – it's nobody's fault. Virtually nobody is actually trying to misunderstand each other. But miscommunication happens all the time, in big ways and also in small ways that go completely unnoticed. One of the goals of this book is to explain the many ways in which miscommunication happens.

Types of meaning

As we saw above, the word *mean* has many meanings. Some of them are obviously irrelevant to our purposes here: *mean* as in 'cruel', *mean* as in 'arithmetic average', and *mean* as in 'stingy', for example. But there are a lot of uses of the word *mean* that are clearly related, although not quite identical:

(12) a   I didn't mean to step on your toe.
 b   *Inflammable* means 'easily ignited'.
 c   When I said it was getting late, I meant that I wanted to go home.
 d   I meant exactly what I said.
 e   When the door is closed, it means she doesn't want to be bothered.
 f   That thunder means a storm is imminent.
 g   That flashing clock display means the power went out.

In (12a), the meaning in question is pure intent: I didn't intend to step on your toe. It has nothing to do with language. In (12b), on the other hand, the relationship between a word and its meaning involves very little intent. Granted, the person using the word intends to be in sync with the rest of the English-speaking world by using the word the same way others use it, but in most cases there's no one person or group of people who initially intended for a given word to have a given meaning; linguistic meaning just evolves naturally. In (12c), however, language and intent combine: The speaker said it was getting late, but had an additional meaning they wished to convey. In (12d), there's another confluence: The speaker specifically wants to note that their linguistic meaning (as in (12b)) and their intended meaning (as in (12c)) match up in some sense. In (12e), we're again out of linguistic territory, yet the person has used a symbolic act (closing the door) to indicate an intent (don't disturb me), much as is the case in language use. In (12f), the relationship between the thunder and the storm has nothing whatsoever to do with anyone's intent. Thunder doesn't mean to indicate a storm; it's just the way the world works. The 'meaning' here is natural and automatic. And finally, in (12g), the relationship between intent and meaning is a bit removed; someone initially intended that a flashing display would indicate a power outage, but this particular flashing display is an automatic result of the way the clock is constructed.

Whew! So we can pull apart a few distinctions here. First, there is a difference between linguistic and nonlinguistic meaning, distinguishing between, say, (12c) and (12e). Then there's a difference between what H.P. Grice called **natural** and **nonnatural** meaning: Natural meaning is automatic and unintended, as with the thunder in (12f) (and similarly for *smoke means fire, a fever means illness*, etc.), whereas nonnatural meaning is arbitrary and thus depends on a shared convention, as in (12b) and (12c). Sometimes that convention is shared by an entire community, as in (12b); sometimes it's shared between just two people, as may be the case in (12c), and sometimes it can be misunderstood, as seems to be perhaps the case in (12c). It can also be a tricky distinction: In (12e), is the closed door a case of natural meaning (by directly obstructing entry) or nonnatural meaning (by indicating someone's intent to be left undisturbed)? Is (12g) a case of natural meaning or nonnatural meaning?

According to H.P. Grice (and that's a name you'll be seeing a lot of), saying that a person nonnaturally 'meant' something means they spoke "with the intention of inducing a belief by means of the recognition of this intention" (Grice 1957: 384). A little circular? Maybe – a point that was not lost on Grice's critics. (If you want to dig into the criticisms and Grice's responses to them, a couple of good places to start are https://plato.stanford.edu/entries/grice/ and Morris 2007, chapter 13, 'Grice on meaning'.) Still, for me to **mean** I want to go home in (12c), I not only want you to believe I want to go home, but I want you to believe it by virtue of recognizing that I want you to believe it – by recognizing that that's what I intended when I said it was getting late. If I merely ponder how badly I want to go home but don't say anything, that doesn't count as meaning it – and if I say it's getting late but don't actually expect you to get my intent, that doesn't count either – and if I just stand around hoping you'll suddenly realize it's late and I probably want to go home, that doesn't count either. For me to **mean** I want to go home when I say it's getting late, I have to say it, expect you to understand it, expect you to understand what I intend it to mean, and based on all that, expect you to believe that I do in fact want to go home.

A final distinction to be made is between **word** or **sentence meaning** and **speaker meaning**. Speaker meaning is what we just described in the previous paragraph – a speaker's nonnatural meaning in saying something using human language. Sentence meaning, in turn, is a convention – so sentence meaning grows out of speaker meaning, in the sense that conventions grow out of repeated individual uses (see McGinn 2015:199). But the two can diverge: In (12b) the meaning of the word is a shared convention among the speakers of the language, but in (12c) the speaker specifically points out a distinction between the statement's conventional meaning and what was actually intended – that is, a distinction between the **sentence meaning** of what was said and the **speaker meaning** of that same utterance. Much of this book will concern itself with this distinction – the difference between what someone says literally (using the conventions of language) and what they actually mean by it, which can be very different.

BOX 1.3

Art and meaning

Linguists aren't the only people worrying about what it means for one thing to stand for another. (For one thing, there's a whole field of **semiotics,** the study of symbols.) Consider, for example, René Magritte's famous painting 'The Treachery of Images'. (If you're unfamiliar with it, take a look at it online.) In it, the viewer sees an image of a pipe; underneath is written *Ceci n'est pas une pipe* (French for 'this is not a pipe'). Initially, a viewer might think, "But of course it is!" And then they might decide it's a joke: It's not actually a pipe; it's simply paint arranged to look like a pipe. It's paint that **represents** a pipe. And to take it one level further, the vast majority of people never actually see the paint in person; more often, they see an image of the painting either in a book or on a screen – so they're seeing either ink or pixels representing the paint that represents a pipe.

But it's not a joke; instead it gets at a deeper question: What exactly is this relationship of one thing 'representing' another? When we look at the painting, do we see a pipe? Is there a pipe on the canvas, or only in our mind – or neither? If neither, what does it mean to say 'that's a pipe'?

Consider another Magritte painting, 'The Human Condition' (Figure 1.2). Here we see an image of an easel; on the easel is a painting of a landscape, and the easel stands before a window such that the painted landscape's edges match up perfectly with the scene extending beyond it in the window. And in the painting on the easel is depicted a tree. Now: Is there a tree in the scene outside the window

FIGURE 1.2 René Magritte, *La Condition Humaine* ('The Human Condition'), 1933. © 2022 C. Herscovici/Artists Rights Society (ARS), New York.

behind the easel? Certainly not, since there's no window and no easel and no 'behind'. There's only paint on a flat surface. And though we perceive a tree in the painting on the easel, it's of course not a tree – it's an arrangement of paint that represents a tree that in turn represents another tree that doesn't exist (the one 'behind' the painting-within-the-painting). And yet those two trees fail to exist in very different ways: One is a nonexistent tree represented by a pattern of paint; the other is a nonexistent inferred tree of which we still feel that we can talk about whether it's there, outside the window, or not.

These images address the question of how we encounter the world in art, and they raise questions eerily similar to those we run up against in the philosophy of language: Do we encounter reality immediately (i.e., directly)? Or do we experience it only as mediated by language? When I refer to a tree, do I refer to some real-world tree, or only to a tree in my mental world, with language as the paint on the canvas that represents what might or might not actually exist, or whose 'real-world' existence is somehow beside the point? If you and I both perceive a pipe and we both refer to it as a pipe, does the fact that it's not an actual pipe matter?

Where is meaning located?

You would not believe the amount of ink that has been spilled in the pursuit of the answer to this question. In its simplest form, it seems obvious: If I say *I ate the orange*, what I mean is that I ate some particular orange, right? And by *the orange*, I'm referring to some real-world actual orange that I actually really ate.

Needless to say, if it were that simple, there'd be no point in your reading (or my having written) the rest of this book, and we could all go home. But (also needless to say) it's not nearly that simple.

For one thing, we can be wrong about reality. Suppose I actually ate a tangerine, but for some reason I never really learned the difference between a tangerine and an orange. So now my phrase *the orange* doesn't refer to an actual orange, but rather a tangerine. Does that mean that *the orange* **means** 'the tangerine'?

Let's make it worse. Consider this real-world example:

(13) **Constabulary Notes from All Over**
From the Winchester (Mass.) Star.
Police responded to Winchester Place for a report of a suspicious person. Police spoke to a resident of the building who said a bald man dressed in maroon was standing outside her door and appeared to be waiting for the elevator. She said the man had been standing in one spot for nearly 20 minutes. The woman said she saw the man through a peephole. When police brought the woman into the hall she was embarrassed to find the man in question was her neighbor's Christmas wreath.
(*New Yorker* 2017; thanks to Larry Horn for bringing this marvelous example to my attention)

Yup, that really happened. So when the woman used the phrase *a bald man dressed in maroon* in describing him to the police, who or what was she referring to? For that matter, what does the word *him* in my last sentence refer to? A man? A wreath? Some mistaken belief in the woman's head?

We call a thing that's being referred to the **referent**, and it's not so clear what the woman's referent was when she uttered the phrase *a bald man dressed in maroon*. The two top contenders would probably be:

1 the real-world wreath
2 a bald man dressed in maroon who existed only in the woman's head

So, which is it? Do we refer to things in the real world (the **referentialist** view), or just in our heads (the **mentalist**, or **cognitivist**, view)? We certainly **intend** to refer to things in the real world, but can we ever get directly at the real world, or do our beliefs always stand in the way? What if the woman had been hallucinating, and there had been nothing there at all? Can we still say she was referring to something in the real world? But if she was really just referring to something in her head, that doesn't quite work either, since she definitely didn't intend to be saying that something in her head was standing outside her door.

And then there's another little problem, which has vexed philosophers for more than a century. If two phrases refer to the same thing in the world, then you ought to be able to swap them without changing whether the sentence is true or false, right? So:

(14) a Abraham Lincoln signed the Emancipation Proclamation in 1863.
      b The 16th President of the U.S. signed the Emancipation Proclamation in 1863.

Since Abraham Lincoln was the 16th President of the U.S., anything that's true of Abe is true of the 16th president, and vice versa, right? But suppose our friend Molly mistakenly thinks Abraham Lincoln was the 15th president. So Molly thinks (14a) is true but (14b) is false. And that means that (15a) is true but (15b), under one reading, is false:

(15) a Molly believes that Abraham Lincoln signed the Emancipation Proclamation in 1863.
      b Molly believes that the 16th President of the U.S. signed the Emancipation Proclamation in 1863.

There are two readings for (15b): One is that Molly's belief can be described as 'the 16th President of the U.S. signed the Emancipation Proclamation in 1986'. This reading is false, because Molly doesn't believe that. The other reading is that Molly has a certain belief about the person who was the 16th President, and that belief is that he signed the Emancipation Proclamation in 1863. This reading is true, because the 16th President was Abe Lincoln, and Molly's belief about Abe Lincoln's signing the Emancipation Proclamation in 1863 is true.

But wait – that means it's not necessarily true that you can swap **coreferential** phrases (i.e., phrases that refer to the same thing) and retain the truth (or falsity) of a sentence, because the same swap we made successfully in (14) doesn't work (or at least doesn't preserve truth) in (15): Molly can believe something is true of Abe Lincoln but false of the 16th President. And that's a problem for the notion that the meaning of a phrase is its real-world referent, because in (15a) and (15b) *Abraham Lincoln* and *the 16th President of the U.S.* have the same real-world referent but putting them in the same sentence can result in truth in one case and falsity in the other because of poor muddled Molly's incorrect belief.

Sentences like those in (15) are called **propositional-attitude contexts**. That means that the sentence reports someone's attitude toward a proposition (like Molly's belief about the proposition that Abe signed the EP in 1863). These are also called **opaque contexts**, because the context that the proposition appears in (embedded in that larger sentence) is 'opaque' to truth; it doesn't let it 'shine through', so to speak.

So it would seem that there's more to the meaning of an expression than just what it refers to in the world – but what else is there? Time to bring in the philosophers.

The philosophers weigh in, beginning with: Frege

We could spend books and books covering the history of the philosophy of language, but we'll just dip our toe in the water, starting around the end of the 19th century.

First, allow me to introduce Gottlob Frege (1848-1925). Frege believed that meaning is **compositional** – so the reference of a sentence is determined by the reference of its parts (this is sometimes called 'Frege's Principle'). Seems reasonable enough. And what that means is that if you replace one expression in a sentence with a coreferential expression, the reference of the whole thing should stay the same. But now you're probably wondering what on earth the 'referent' of a sentence is. Well, since what stays the same is whether the sentence is true or false, Frege said that the referent of a sentence is either 'the True' or 'the False'. (Yeah, I know; this notion will not turn out to be flawless.)

But as we saw above in (15), you can't always swap in a coreferential phrase and preserve the truth of the whole sentence. This was a problem for Frege and compositionality, but he solved it by distinguishing between **sense** and **reference**. So consider:

(16) a *Inflammable* means 'easily ignited'.
   b In 1700, the phrase *the King of France* meant Louis XIV.

The meaning in (16a) is what Frege called sense: It's the conventional linguistic meaning of an expression. The meaning in (16b) is what he called reference: It's what the expression picks out in the world.

The sense helps to determine the reference, since you can't very well go around referring to a river as *that mountain over there* and expect to be understood, but the two differ in important ways. For one thing, sense is relatively constant from one use to another, but reference can change depending on the context. It's true that the meaning of a word might change over a long stretch of time – and indeed, the word *inflammable* was so often mistaken as meaning 'not flammable' that it gave rise to a new word *flammable*, resulting in the amusing situation we're now in, where *flammable* and *inflammable* mean the same thing. (In case you're wondering, *inflammable* comes from the root word *inflame*, so something that's inflammable is easily inflamed.) But in general, sense is conventional, and therefore pretty stable.

In contrast, reference can change from one use to the next. The reference of the phrase *the King of France* can change from one decade to the next (and a lot more on that topic is coming shortly). Frege came to his sense/reference distinction by thinking of the morning star and the evening star: The two phrases have quite different senses (*morning* obviously means something different from *evening*), but they refer to exactly the same object, the planet Venus. (Actually, he used the two names for these senses, Phosphorus (the morning star) and Hesperus (the evening star). But the discussion is clearer, frankly, without them.)

So back to our friend Molly:

(17) a The morning star is the morning star.
     b The morning star is the evening star.
     c Molly believes the morning star is the morning star.
     d Molly believes the morning star is the evening star.

In (17a), we have an obvious truth. Of **course**, the morning star is the morning star. And if you swap in a coreferential phrase, as in (17b), it's still true. In (17c), we have Molly believing the obvious truth – she's not **that** irrational, after all – but in (17d), swapping in a coreferential phrase, we have a sentence that might very well be false. The reason, according to Frege, is that sameness of sense, rather than sameness of reference, is what's needed in order to preserve truth when swapping expressions in an opaque context.

Another important point is that for Frege, a definite expression like *the dog* or *that guy in the corner* refers to an object. And the principle of compositionality means that if there's no such object – that is, no referent – the sentence containing it also has no referent – that is, no truth-value; it's neither true nor false. Nonetheless, the expression and the sentence both have sense: I can use a phrase like *the first Albanian schnauzer to read the Pledge of Allegiance aloud in a crowded bus*, and you know precisely what it means even though you also know there's no such referent. And according to Frege, since there's no such referent, any sentence that says something about it – like *The first Albanian schnauzer to read the Pledge of Allegiance aloud in a crowded bus was owned by Barack Obama* – is neither true nor false. That's because the referent of a sentence is either the True or the False, and its reference is built up from the reference of its parts, and here one of its parts has no reference at all, and so neither does the sentence.

Russell

But others were quite certain that such a sentence was flat-out false – including, most famously, Bertrand Russell (1872-1970). And here we can abandon our Albanian schnauzer in favor of the King of France, who – despite not actually existing, since France has no king – has played a remarkably important role in the philosophy of language. Russell argued that sentences refer not to truth-values but rather to facts or situations. And he held a **referential** view of meaning, which is to say that he believed the meaning of an expression is its referent.

But here's the tricky part: He said that a complex expression doesn't simply refer to some real-world object; instead, it has a complex meaning. A definite phrase like *the King of France* doesn't have a meaning outside of its contribution to the meaning of the whole sentence – and what it contributes to the meaning of the whole sentence includes existence and uniqueness. So, for Russell, the sentence in (18) means three things, listed in (19):

(18)   The King of France is bald.

(19)   a   There is a King of France.
       b   There is only one King of France.
       c   He is bald.

From Russell's perspective, this analysis solves a nagging problem, which is that under Frege's account, if there's no King of France, (18) is neither true nor false. Russell disagrees; he believes that for every sentence, either that sentence or its negation must be true. This is his 'Law of the Excluded Middle'. Under Russell's analysis, if there's no King of France, (18) is false because (19a) is false, so the Law of the Excluded Middle is preserved and we don't have to worry about sentences that are neither true nor false.

Russell also solves another problem: Under Frege's account, if there's no King of France (18) and its negation both lack a truth-value:

(20)   a   The King of France is bald.
       b   The King of France is not bald.

But for Russell, (20b) is essentially ambiguous between two readings:

(21)   a   There is a King of France, and only one, and he is not bald.
       b   It is not the case that there is a King of France, and only one, and he is not bald.

That is, in (21a), the word *not* applies to only the baldness, whereas in (21b) it applies to the entire trio of assertions in (19). And on that latter reading, (20b) is perfectly true.

Strawson

Russell's account, however, was strongly criticized by P.F. Strawson (1919-2006), who felt that it was odd to say that *The King of France is bald* is false. And certainly if I asked you whether the King of France is bald and you responded 'no', I'd think there was a hairy king in France, not that there was no king. That means at the very least that the three assertions in (19) don't have quite the same status; (19c) seems to be, in some sense, the main assertion of someone uttering (18).

Strawson followed Frege in arguing that (18) is neither true nor false, and that it doesn't assert the existence of a King of France (or that there's only one). Instead, he said, it **presupposes** the existence of a unique King of France, and **asserts** that this individual is bald. For Strawson, if the presupposition doesn't hold, then the sentence isn't true and it's not false; it's just plain weird. According to Strawson, if there's no such person, then the question of whether he's bald or not simply doesn't arise.

Strawson also believed that it's not a **sentence** that's true or false, but rather a given **use** of that sentence. After all, there was a King of France once upon a time, and at that time someone uttering (18) would indeed have said something either true or false. (Frankly, I don't know which.) And only a particular use of an expression refers; or, to be more accurate, a speaker refers, by using the expression.

Donnellan

But then along came Keith Donnellan (1931-2015), who argued that the same definite description (i.e., a definite as opposed to indefinite noun phrase) in the same sentence can have two distinctly different uses, which he called the **referential** and **attributive** uses (Donnellan 1966). To use his example, suppose you are a detective arriving at a crime scene. A guy named Smith has been murdered, and in light of the brutality of the murder, you say:

(22)   Smith's murderer is insane.

What you mean is that whoever murdered Smith, you judge that person to be insane. That's Donnellan's attributive use. But now imagine instead that you've arrived on the scene and recognized the murderous handiwork of Jones, whom you know to be criminally insane. Someone standing by asks why anyone would commit so foul an act, and you respond:

(23)   Smith's murderer is insane.

Same sentence, but very different meaning – because here what you mean is that Jones is insane, which Donnellan argued was distinct from the meaning in (22). Donnellan argued that both Russell and Strawson failed to account for this referential use, and in fact that the same sentence could have different uses on different occasions. In short, Donnellan feels that no one account of definite descriptions can be adequate if it fails to take into account the intent of the speaker, because a given sentence might be true on one use and false on the other.

To see this, consider again poor murdered Smith. Suppose again, as in (23), that you believe Jones to be the murderer, but you're wrong: In actual fact, Anderson is the murderer, and Anderson is sane. But you're right about Jones, who is insane. In this case, according to Donnellan, by uttering (23) you've said something that's true: Jones, your intended referent, is indeed insane. But the same sentence uttered attributively, in the same circumstances, is false: Whoever murdered Smith (i.e., Anderson) is perfectly sane.

According to Donnellan, neither Russell nor Strawson can accommodate this distinction. Consider again poor old Smith – only this time, there was no murderer at all. Smith simply slipped on a banana peel, but in such a way that it appeared to be a murder. (Use your imagination here.) Since there's no murderer, this is much like the King of France situation: For Russell, *Smith's murderer is insane* is false because Smith's murderer doesn't exist, and for Strawson, it has no truth-value, for the same reason. For Donnellan, it's true on the referential reading, if the person you intended to refer to (Jones) is insane – regardless of the fact that Jones didn't actually murder Smith (and neither did anybody else).

One problem with Donnellan's account is that both uses are actually referential in the sense of 'referring' to some entity (even if it's just 'whoever killed Smith'). Another problem is that in many cases the distinction is much less clear: In the banana-peel scenario, suppose the banana peel itself is long gone, but a residual smear of banana pulp on the pavement gives away what actually happened. You now utter *The banana peel that killed this man is missing*. Is the noun phrase now referential or attributive? If you're like me, it seems a whole lot less clear because there's much less to distinguish between one nonpresent banana peel and another, so 'whichever peel it was' and 'the particular peel I'm thinking of' come down to the same thing.

A final problem with Donnellan's account is that it conflates **semantics** and **pragmatics** – two concepts that will form the backbone of our discussion of meaning throughout this book. Donnellan is treating the difference between the literal meaning of a phrase and the speaker's use of that phrase as though they are two distinct readings of the expression – not, he says, an ambiguity in the structure of the sentence or the meaning of its words, but rather, he suggests tentatively, a pragmatic ambiguity, an ambiguity in speaker meaning. But according to Donnellan's critics, *Smith's murderer* is no more ambiguous between the meanings 'person who murdered Smith' and 'Jones' than *It's getting late* is ambiguous between the meanings 'time has advanced to a point that counts as late' and 'I want to go home'. In short, we don't want to have to say that every time we use language nonliterally, it points to an ambiguity between the literal and the nonliteral meaning.

The upshot

We could obviously go on with more and more philosophers and their reactions to each other, but these are a handful of the most influential views. Recall that the original question was where meaning is located, with the top two possibilities being (a) that the meaning of an expression is what it refers to in the world and (b) that its meaning is located in the mind of a speaker. Under the latter view, we have the problem that people intend to refer to things in the real world, not things in their minds. But under a referential view, where the meaning of an expression is its real-world referent, we have the problem that coreferential phrases should be able to be swapped without affecting meaning, but they can't.

Frege tried to solve this second problem by distinguishing between sense and reference, with the side effect that if some expression has no reference, then neither does the sentence it's in (so the sentence is neither true nor false). Russell wanted to exclude such a neither-true-nor-false option; he countered that such a sentence is actually just false, and that a sentence like *The King of France is bald* means that there is a (single) King of France and that he is bald. Strawson argued that those two meanings don't have the same status in the sentence, but rather that it presupposes the existence of the king while asserting his baldness; his account returns to the Fregean notion that in the absence of such a king, the sentence is neither true nor false. Donnellan then showed up and said the problem was that everyone was missing a crucial distinction between two distinct readings of a definite description, the referential and the attributive reading; but this distinction turns out to be less than clear-cut and moreover has been criticized as applying a pragmatic solution to a semantic problem.

That brings us back around to Grice and his distinction between sentence meaning and speaker meaning, and more generally to the distinction between semantics and pragmatics.

SEMANTICS AND PRAGMATICS

You may have noticed that we neatly sidestepped any conclusion on the question of where meaning is located, and we'll do pretty much the same thing on the question of where to draw the distinction between semantics and pragmatics. We'll look at the question in more detail in Chapter 4, but for now we'll try to get at least a general understanding of the difference and its importance.

Suppose you and I are watching some relatives play tennis, and I say to you:

(24)   Your brother is the worst tennis player on the face of the earth.

What I've said literally and what I actually mean are obviously two different things; I don't really mean that there's no other person on the planet who is a worse tennis player, but rather just that your brother is a bad player. And to take the classic example from every Intro to Linguistics class:

(25)   Can you pass the salt?

If we're at dinner and I utter (25), I really don't want you to tell me about your salt-passing abilities (whether your arms are currently in working order, for example); I simply want you to pass it.

The literal meaning of what I've said is its **semantic** meaning. The semantic meaning is the conventional (i.e., societally shared) meaning, the meaning you'll find in dictionaries, the meaning that tends not to vary from one use to another. The **pragmatic** meaning is the speaker's intended meaning, the one that depends on the context of utterance (things like who said it and when and where), and the one that can vary from one use to another. In general, the difference between semantic meaning and pragmatic meaning is the difference between **conventional** and **intentional** meaning, between **sentence** meaning and **speaker** meaning, between **literal** and **figurative** meaning, between **context-independent** and **context-dependent** meaning, between what is **said** and what is **meant**, and between **truth-conditional** and **non-truth-conditional** meaning (fear not; I'll explain that last one in a little while, but it boils down to whether the meaning affects the truth of the sentence).

In general, these dichotomies all cut the pie into the same two pieces – but not always, and that's a problem that we'll talk about in more detail in Chapter 4. But this should give you a sense of the distinction I'm getting at. And it's worth noting that there's a corresponding difference between a **sentence** and an **utterance**. A sentence is an abstract entity, whereas an utterance is an instance of someone actually using that sentence (or any other linguistic expression, such as a single word or phrase). So there are an infinite number of sentences that have never actually been uttered. Here's one that I'm pretty certain has never been uttered before now:

(26)   If the mustard has turned into mushrooms, then Pearl needs to polish some porcelain.

Of course, this has now been uttered (since being written counts), but you can also now imagine the vast range of sentences that have never been uttered – and that doesn't mean they're not sentences. And a sentence has a semantic meaning whether it's been uttered or not, since semantic meaning doesn't depend on context. Only when it is uttered does that utterance have pragmatic meaning, because pragmatic meaning is influenced by context.

Discourse models and possible worlds

Every conversation you have, every article you read, every lecture you attend is a **discourse**, a connected string of utterances (or occasionally even a single stand-alone utterance) that make up a coherent unit. A story is a discourse. So is saying hi to a friend you pass in the hall.

Two or more people participating together in a discourse (as in, say, a conversation) are called **interlocutors**, which is just a fancy way of saying 'people talking to each other'.

Now, remember that when I talk to you, no meaning actually gets 'conveyed'; all that passes between us is a phenomenally complex pattern of sound waves. (And even saying that a wave 'passes between us' is a bit misleading; it's more like I use my mouth to disrupt nearby air, which in turn disrupts nearby air, which disrupts nearby air, and so on, until the air adjacent to your ear has been disrupted.)

Instead, what happens in linguistic communication is that I have some notion in my head, and I try to use language to get you to understand that notion – which means that I'm trying to change what's going on inside your head. Each of us has, in our own mental world, a 'model' of what our shared discourse contains – what we call a **discourse model**. So if John tells you he has a cat, your discourse model now contains John's cat and you can refer to it later with phrases like *the cat* because you assume you both know which cat you're talking about. And if you then tell John that you have a goldfish, John will dutifully add your goldfish to his discourse model.

And attached to the cat in your model is the fact that it's owned by John – and attached to the goldfish in your model is the fact that John knows about it, as well as the fact that John knows that you know he knows about it. And yes, this all gets very complicated very quickly. For now, it's sufficient to realize that each of us has a model of the discourse, and that that model includes information about what information we do and don't share. It goes without saying that you can be wrong about what is and isn't shared, which just means that although we'll sometimes sloppily talk about a shared discourse model, it's never literally shared; mine is stuck in my skull and yours is stuck in yours.

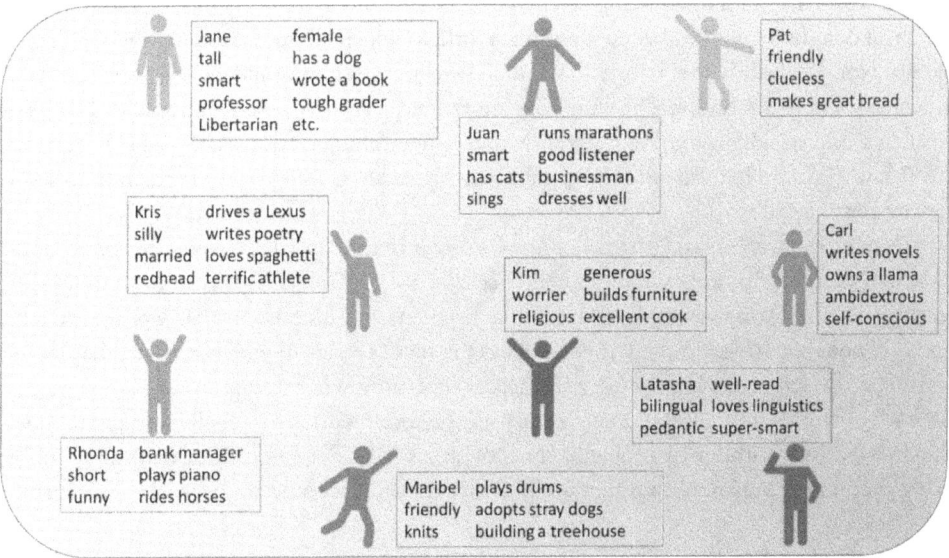

FIGURE 1.3 Discourse models obviously include more than just people, but this gives you the general idea. Adapted from an image by Alex Ghidan/Shutterstock.com.

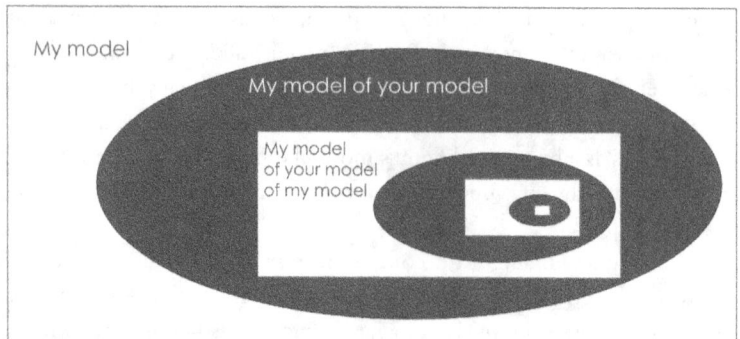

FIGURE 1.4 My discourse model includes a model of your discourse model, along with what I think your model includes as a model of MY model, and so on, *ad infinitum*. Image by the author.

Related to the fact that we can never truly know what's in someone else's discourse model is the fact that we can never be dead certain about the nature of the world. We have our beliefs, of course, and usually there's a pretty good chance that those beliefs are accurate: I believe I'm sitting here writing a linguistics textbook, and chances are good that that's actually what's happening. But maybe I'm dreaming, or deluded, or having a hallucination.

Recall the woman who was sure there was a man outside her door, when it turned out to be a wreath. Logically speaking, it could have been the case that it was a man. Since the man-outside-the-door scenario and the wreath scenario were both logical possibilities, we say that each of them represents a different **possible world**. A possible world is one way that a world could be. There's a possible world in which I'm merely dreaming about writing a book, and a possible world in which I'm writing in a park instead of in my house. There's a possible world in which all dogs have two heads, and a possible world in which all frogs are vampires. And there's the real world, which is also a possible world. There are also impossible worlds, such as a world in which six frogs are vampires and no frogs are vampires; that's logically impossible. There's no possible world in which the Washington Monument is simultaneously taller and shorter than the White House. There are an infinite number of possible worlds, most of which (needless to say) are not the real world.

In some theories, in fact, the meaning of a sentence is essentially the set of possible worlds in which it's true. So, for example, a sentence like *All frogs are green* is true in some possible world if, in that world, every frog that exists is green, and it's false in that world if you can find one nongreen frog. So then, if you collect the set of worlds in which it's true, that set tells you what the sentence *All frogs are green* means – because what distinguishes the *All frogs are green* set of worlds from all the others is that it's the set of worlds in which all frogs are green. This notion isn't without its problems, but the point is that the notion of truth is central to many theories of semantic meaning, and for that reason it'll come up over and over again in this book.

Recall when I said one way of distinguishing between semantic and pragmatic meaning is that semantic meaning is **truth-conditional** and pragmatic meaning is **non-truth-conditional**. Suppose I describe someone to you as follows:

(27) Kyle is a banker but he's nice.

You are likely to feel that I've suggested in some way that bankers aren't generally nice. But does this contribute to the truth or falsity of (27)? Surely if Kyle is actually a gas station attendant and not a banker, (27) is false. And if Kyle is a banker but he's actually a jerk and not at all nice, (27) is false. So 'Kyle is a banker' and 'Kyle is nice' are both **entailed** by (27); that is, in any world in which (27) is true, both of those things must be true. But if there are plenty of bankers who are nice, that in itself doesn't render (27) false. What this means is that (28a) and (28b) are part of the truth-conditional meaning of (27), and (28c) isn't:

(28) a Kyle is a banker.
     b Kyle is nice.
     c Bankers aren't generally nice.

Each of these is called a **proposition**. A proposition is something that can be true or false. It's not the same as a sentence, since sometimes a single proposition can be expressed by more than one sentence:

(29) a Kyle denied the loan.
     b The loan was denied by Kyle.

These two sentences express the same proposition. And the meaning of a sentence, under a **truth-conditional semantics** (i.e., a semantic theory based on truth-conditions), is the set of necessary and sufficient conditions for the proposition it expresses to be true. The conditions under which a proposition is true are (not surprisingly) called its **truth-conditions**; whether a given proposition is true or false in a particular world is its **truth-value** in that world. All of this will become important in Chapter 3, when we consider in much greater detail the semantics of a sentence (and I'll repeat these distinctions at that point). But before we wade into that relatively deep water, let's begin with the semantics of individual words, which will be our focus in Chapter 2.

EXERCISES

Self-test:

1 Because linguistics is a science, it
    a takes a prescriptive approach.
    b takes a descriptive approach.
    c takes a competence-based approach.
    d takes multivitamins.

2 Sally used a double negative when she said *I ain't done nothing wrong*. A linguist would say
    a this is probably grammatical in her dialect.
    b this is probably ungrammatical in her dialect.
    c this is just plain wrong.
    d this technically means 'I have done something wrong'.

3. Most of the time, semantic meaning is
    a. context-dependent and non-truth-conditional.
    b. context-independent and truth-conditional.
    c. context-dependent and truth-conditional.
    d. context-independent and non-truth-conditional.
4. An example of nonnatural meaning is
    a. clouds
    b. thunder
    c. lightning
    d. the sentence *It's raining.*
5. Which of the following is not a possible world?
    a. a world in which all dogs are blue.
    b. a world in which all dogs that chase cats are blue.
    c. a world in which a blue dog is not a dog.
    d. a world in which no blue dogs chase cats.
6. The truth-conditions of a sentence are
    a. the same as its truth-value.
    b. the number of propositions required to make it true.
    c. the number of propositions required to make it false.
    d. the conditions under which it's true (duh).
7. If you're a native speaker of a language,
    a. you have acquired a system of grammatical rules.
    b. you can list the syntactic rules of the language.
    c. you have memorized all of the grammatical sentences of that language.
    d. you will not make performance errors.
8. A descriptive approach to language is one that
    a. describes how people actually speak.
    b. describes how experts believe people should speak.
    c. tells speakers how to speak properly.
    d. describes language as it is used by those who speak most correctly.
9. A referentialist approach to meaning is one that
    a. takes referents to be in the minds of speakers.
    b. distinguishes between sense and reference.
    c. takes referents to be real-world objects.
    d. distinguishes between referential and attributive readings.
10. One way you know that language is rule-governed is that
    a. you can produce and understand sentences you've never encountered before.
    b. most sentences are ambiguous in one way or another.
    c. prescriptive rules govern our linguistic utterances.
    d. your performance includes offensive words, but you suppress them in your competence.

Comprehension questions:

1. Briefly describe each of the following distinctions:
   a. competence/performance
   b. descriptive/prescriptive approaches
   c. sense/reference
   d. natural/nonnatural meaning
   e. sentence meaning/speaker meaning
   f. referential/attributive
   g. semantics/pragmatics
   h. presupposition/assertion
   i. truth-conditions/truth-value
   j. sentence/utterance
   k. sentence/proposition
   l. mentalism/referentialism
2. What does it mean when a linguist says language is rule-governed? How do these rules differ from those you may have learned in grade school, like 'never end a sentence with a preposition' or 'don't say *ain't*'?
3. How do you know language is rule-governed and that children don't simply learn a list of all of the acceptable sentences of their language? Is this a claim that can be proved?
4. Donald Trump in 2017 said he had met with "the President of the Virgin Islands" – apparently not realizing that since the Virgin Islands are a U.S. territory, he himself was their president. He presumably was referring to their governor, with whom he had in fact met. Describe the situation in terms of Frege's distinction between sense and reference; then describe it in terms of Donnellan's distinction between referential and attributive readings of a noun phrase. How do the two distinctions differ?

Opinion questions:

1. Is a discourse model a possible world? Why or why not?
2. At this point, would you say you're a mentalist or a referentialist? Give your reasons.
3. Of the philosophers discussed in this chapter (Frege, Strawson, Donnellan, Russell, Grice), whose account makes the most sense to you so far? Why?
4. Is it possible to talk about communication in English without using the Conduit Metaphor? Should speakers try to avoid it?

Discussion questions:

1. This chapter has spent a lot of time discussing distinctions like those in Comprehension Question 1 above. Which of them seem the most or least important? Do they all make useful distinctions, or are there some we could do without?
2. Have class members play the roles of two or more (or all) of the philosophers discussed in this chapter and have them debate the question of how to describe meaning. Other class members can participate by asking questions and tossing out challenging arguments.

3   Have any of our philosophers successfully solved the problem of opaque contexts?
4   Philosopher Hilary Putnam said that since his concepts for 'beech' and 'elm' were identical (he knew they were distinct types of trees but had no idea how they differed), this argued against the notion that meanings are in the speaker's mind, since these two concepts were in no way distinguished in his mind. Argue for or against this claim.

Data collection and analysis:

For these questions (and those in subsequent chapters), unless otherwise specified, you can find data by searching for utterances online using a search tool (e.g. Google), or you can use data you encounter in your own life (things you overhear people saying, things you read in books or hear on TV, etc.), or a combination thereof. Oral and written utterances are both fine. You can't make it up, rely on vague memories of what you think people have said or written, or use something you yourself have said or written.

1   Search online for examples of 'positive *anymore*'. Rather than simply searching for the word *anymore*, you may find it easier to think of likely phrases it might occur in, like *I… a lot anymore* or *Anymore, I…* Compile a list of 10-15 instances that you find, and describe what the speaker or writer means in each case.
2   Collect at least six instances of opaque contexts concerning a nonexistent entity, such as *Sally believes unicorns exist*.
3   Collect 25 instances of the Conduit Metaphor. Choose five and rewrite them so that they say essentially the same thing without using this metaphor.
4   Collect six examples of performance errors, and rewrite them to say essentially the same thing without the error.

Answers to self-test:

1   b
2   a
3   b
4   d
5   c
6   d
7   a
8   a
9   c
10 a

CHAPTER 2

Semantics I: Word meaning

> **KEY CONCEPTS**
>
> - morpheme
> - lexicon
> - Proto-Indo-European
> - sources of new words: descent, coinage, onomatopoeia, clipping, acronyms, blends, backformation, eponyms, borrowings, conversion, derivation, inflection, compounding
> - language as arbitary but conventional
> - lexical relations: synonymy, antonymy, hyponymy, homonymy, homography, homophony, polysemy
> - types of antonyms: gradable, complementary, relational
> - marked vs. unmarked terms
> - taxonomy
> - componential analysis
> - semantic primitives
> - prototype
> - fuzzy set

Now we're just arguing semantics. You've probably heard people say that before, and usually what they mean is that the argument has become trivial and not worth your time. But if you're truly arguing semantics (much of the time when that phrase is used, you're really not), it's probably not trivial at all: Since we use words to have arguments, agreeing on the meanings of those words is pretty important if we ever want to reach agreement.

So in this chapter we'll be talking about what words mean, how they come to have those meanings, and how those meanings relate to each other. This last point is important: According to many people, words only have meaning in relation to each other. *Purple* begins where *blue* ends (unless you speak one of the many languages that have no word for purple; see Chapter 9), and *dog* ends where *wolf* begins. *Sad* is defined to some extent by its opposition to *happy*; after all, what would count as sadness in a world where there was no such thing as happiness?

DOI: 10.4324/9781003351214-2

Is *chess* a *sport*? In thinking about that, you'll probably immediately go in one of two directions – or both: You'll consider other indisputable sports, like baseball, soccer, and basketball, and think about what chess does and doesn't have in common with them; or you'll think about sports vs. games, and what properties do or don't distinguish them (e.g., competition, action, scoring). That is, you'll either compare *chess* with the meanings of related terms (*basketball, soccer*), or you'll compare *sport* with the meanings of related terms (*game, competition*). And maybe that will lead you down other semantic alleys: Chess is a game, but not all games are sports (*Monopoly*, for example, clearly isn't). On the other hand, are all sports games? Initially you might say 'of course' – but then consider someone who engages in long-distance running noncompetitively, for health and enjoyment; or someone who has been taking horseback riding lessons for years but never participates in a horse show. Would you say they're not engaging in sports? They're certainly not engaging in games. Now suppose the horseback rider begins to compete in shows; it's not at all clear that adding the competitive aspect into the equation has turned their horseback riding into a game. Figure skaters compete in the Olympic Games – but is competitive figure skating a game?

At this point you might be ready to throw the book across the room on the grounds that we're 'just arguing semantics'. Indeed, we are – but I take issue with the word *just*. Semantics matters: Court cases, laws, reputations, and civil rights have hinged on the definitions of words like *person, health, fetus, race,* and (yes) *sex*. (Consider, for example, Bill Clinton's famous claim *I did not have sexual relations with that woman!* Whether he was telling the truth or not depends entirely on how you define *sexual relations*.) What counts as a sport may seem trivial, but what counts as a person isn't. The meanings of words can be a very serious business indeed.

WHAT IS A WORD?

What is a word? That might seem like the silliest question ever, but it's not always clear how to define the word *word*. What takes several words to say in English can often be said with a single word in another language:

(1) a He will like them.
 b Atawapenda.

What takes four words to say in English takes only one in Swahili (OSU Dept. of Linguistics 2016). The first *a-* corresponds to English *he, ta* to English *will* (or, strictly speaking, future tense), *wa* to English *them*, and *penda* to English *like*. So, *atawapenda* corresponds to *he future them like*. Aha, you say – so it really IS four words, even if it's not written with spaces. But no: Linguistically speaking, it's four **morphemes**, which is to say four units of meaning. A morpheme is the smallest unit that has a conventional meaning or grammatical function (so, the word *the* doesn't so much have an obvious 'meaning' as it does a grammatical function, the function of indicating definiteness, which is more of a grammatical category than something you can point to in the world).

But how do we know that (1a) is four words, while (1b) is one? What is a word?

A **word** is defined as the smallest 'free form' in a language – the smallest bit of language that doesn't need to be attached to something else. Well, that's the theory, anyway, but to be honest, very few people go around uttering the word *the* all by itself. But there are other ways of determining where the breaks are between words.

First, let's all agree that it's not about spaces. Spoken language, after all, doesn't have spaces (or even pauses between words, which becomes clear if you look at a spectrogram of someone speaking). And even in written language, the presence or absence of spaces doesn't help:

(2)   a   I'll make up your make-up exam after I put on my makeup.
       b   The White House is a big white house.
       c   Would you rather attend a clambake or a pig roast?

In (2a), you might argue that *make up* is two words, while *make-up* and *makeup* are each one word, based on the lack of a space, but would you also argue that *a first floor apartment* and *a first-floor apartment* differ in the number of words each contains? In (2b), a linguist would argue that *White House* is a single, **compound** word (a word composed of two or more other words), whereas *white house* is two words, despite both containing a space. And there's no sound reason for considering *clambake* to be one word and *pig roast* two words based on the fact that one is spelled with a space and the other not – especially if you consider that there are plenty of people who have no idea whether to put a space in them or not. And of course there are plenty of words that are equally fine with or without a space: *lightbulb/light bulb, smartphone/smart phone, farmhouse/farm house, ballgame/ball game*, etc. We wouldn't want to say that *lightbulb* is one word while *light bulb* is two.

Instead, we say that a word acts as an **island** – essentially a coherent, distinct unit within the sentence. It can't be rearranged or have parts pulled out, for example: *Dogs* can be pulled to the beginning of the sentence, but neither the root word *dog* nor the plural *–s* can:

(3)   a   I love dogs.
       b   Dogs I love.
       c   ★Dog I love s.
       d   ★s I love dog.

And it can't be broken up by other words:

(4)   a   I love cute dogs.
       b   ★I love dog cute s.

You can see, then, that *white house* is a combination of two words that can act independently or be broken up, but not so for *White House*:

(5)   a   I live in a white house.
       b   I live in a white two-story house.
       c   The house I live in is white.

(6)   a   The President lives in the White House.
       b   ★The President lives in the White two-story House.
       c   ★The House the President lives in is White.

Now, (6b) and (6c) are fine on the noncompound reading, in which case they wouldn't be capitalized, but not on the reading where we're using *White House* as the official title of the

President's home. And similarly, I can *make up a test* or I can *make a test up*, suggesting that *make* and *up* are two separate words here; but when I create a *make-up* exam, there's no separating the *make* from the *up*, which in turn suggests that we're dealing here with a single word. And likewise for *clambake* and *pig roast*, each of which behaves as a single unit regardless of spacing. Finally, note that there's frequently a difference in stress between a single compound word and two separate words: When I *make up* a exam, each of the two words in *make up* gets its own stress, but the compounds *make-up* (as in a *make-up* exam) and *makeup* (as in *putting on makeup*) take stress only on the first syllable. Likewise, the compound word *White House* takes stress only on *White*, whereas if I live in a *white house*, each word gets its own stress.

WHERE WORDS COME FROM

Historical descent

Plenty of words in the English **lexicon** (essentially, its word list) have come down to us through earlier forms of the language, with various changes in sound and/or meaning having occurred along the way. Modern English is a descendant of Middle English, which descended from Old English, which descended from Germanic, which descended from Indo-European – often called **Proto-Indo-European (PIE)**, with the 'proto' indicating that we don't have any direct records of this language, but rather have inferred what it must have been like based on what its descendants have in common, along with, for example, sound changes that we already know occurred.

One of my favorite examples of this involves our current words *guest* and *host*, which are opposites and yet come from the same PIE source, *ghostis* (meaning 'stranger') – which is also, obviously, the ancestor of *ghost*. There are two well-known sound shifts that affected it along the way: First is what's known as the First Germanic Consonant Shift, also known as Grimm's Law, named for – no kidding – Jacob Grimm, who not only wrote fairy tales along with his brother Wilhelm, but also was a professor of philology in Göttingen, Germany.

Grimm discovered a series of sound changes that occurred in the Germanic language (so, later than PIE but earlier than Old English) involving a whole bunch of consonants. If you put your hand in front of your mouth and say the words *pooh, coo,* and *two*, you'll feel a little puff of air escape that you don't get with the consonants at the beginning of, say, *boo, goo,* and *do*. But back in Proto-Indo-European, you did get that little puff of air after *b, d,* and *g* in certain words – which is why we put that *h* in *ghostis*, and why we still spell *ghost* with it, and why you still get, for example, *dh* in a word like *jodhpurs*, which comes from the name of an area in India.

Meanwhile, just as Sanskrit formed a separate branch of language from Germanic, so did Latin: All three descended from PIE, but they split into three different languages before that consonant shift took place. But Latin developed into French, and underwent its own consonant change, in which the *gh* combination of sounds became simply *h*. And then, at the time of the Norman Conquest, English borrowed a whole pile of words from French.

So for the English words that descended from *ghostis*, the *gh* sound became a *g* sound, and for those that were borrowed in from Latin, the *gh* sound had become an *h* sound. So what Modern English words were affected by all this? A whole lot of them: *guest, host, ghost, hostel, hospice, hospital, hospitality, hostage, ghastly,* and *hostile*, for starters (and you can see how the original meaning of 'stranger' developed and changed in all of these different words). And the German word for 'inn' is *Gasthaus*, because, since German also descended from Germanic, it too was subject to Grimm's Law. (If you find this as interesting as I do, look up Grimm's Law online; it's just wonderful.)

Other sources of new words

As much fun as it is to trace the historical descent of words from Proto-Indo-European, other words have come to us from a wide range of other sources. We've already seen two: **compounding** (e.g., making one word out of two or more individual words, as in *makeup* and *paperclip*) and **borrowing** from another language, such as a word like *hostile* being borrowed from French.

We borrow words from other languages all the time, and in fact English is notorious for this. James Nicoll famously said, "We don't just borrow words; on occasion, English has pursued other languages down alleyways to beat them unconscious and rifle their pockets for new vocabulary." Words borrowed into English from other languages include *sushi, chutzpah, mosquito, bikini, gesundheit, kindergarten, ninja, ballet, beef, slalom, sari, blitz, espresso*, and a boatload of others (including, speaking of boatloads, *canoe*).

Other new words arise from changes to existing words. For example, the process of **conversion** changes a word's part of speech – e.g., from noun to verb or vice versa – while sometimes also changing its stress pattern. So from the noun *butter* comes the verb *butter* as in *to butter your toast*, while from the verb *play* (as in *to play a game*) we get the noun *play* (as in *Shakespeare's plays*). Among conversions involving a stress shift are *convict* (to *conVICT* someone causes them to become a *CONvict*), and, similarly, *present, refuse, reject*, and many more.

Two obvious ways in which English makes new words from old ones are **derivation** and **inflection**. Derivation is a matter of adding prefixes and suffixes (collectively known as **affixes**) to root words – for example, everyone's favorite (with each new affix shown in bold):

(7)   a   establish   (as in, to establish a national church)
       b   **dis**establish   (to take away the status in (a))
       c   disestablish**ment**   (noun form of (b))
       d   **anti**disestablishment   (in opposition to (c))
       e   antidisestablishment**ary**   (adjective form of (d))
       f   antidisestablishmentari**an**   (someone who can be described as (e))
       g   antidisestablishmentarian**ism**   (the position of those in (f))

Inflection also involves the addition of prefixes and suffixes to a root, but here the affixes serve a grammatical function, and often appear in paradigms such as those that you learn in foreign-language classes, such as this example from German (again, with the affixes in bold):

(8)   a   Ich spiel**e**.   I play.
       b   Du spiel**st**.   You (informal) play.
       c   Er/sie/es spiel**t**.   He/she/it plays.
       d   Wir spiel**en**.   We play.
       e   Ihr spiel**t**.   You (plural) play.

f Sie spiel**en**.   They play.
g Sie spiel**en**.   You (formal; singular or plural) play.

Many languages work this way, with the verb taking a different form depending on whether the subject is first, second, or third person; singular or plural; informal or formal; etc. (depending on the language). English, as it happens, has very little inflection. For example, if you look at the English paradigm in the right-hand column in (8), you'll see that the only suffix on the verb *play* shows up as the little *–s* in *plays* in (8c), indicating third-person singular. Everywhere else, it's just plain *play*.

In fact, English is generally considered to have only eight inflectional affixes:

(9) a *-s*   third-person singular   *sing* → *sings*
     b *-s*   plural   *book* → *books*
     c *-ed*   past tense   *love* → *loved*
     d *-ing*   progressive   *run* → *running*
     e *-en, -ed*   past participle   *eat* → *eaten*
     f *-'s*   possessive   *Jane* → *Jane's*
     g *-er*   comparative   *tall* → *taller*
     h *-est*   superlative   *tall* → *tallest*

So in this way, at least, people learning English as a second language get a bit of a break. (Which is only fair, given the huge number of idioms they have to deal with.)

One of the basic claims of linguistics is that language is by its nature **arbitrary** but **conventional**. We saw in Chapter 1 that the relationship between most words and what they mean is arbitrary; this was one way in which nonnatural meaning differs from natural meaning. (The relationship between thunder and rain isn't at all arbitrary, which is why it's natural.) The object called a *house* could just as easily have been named by some other string of English sounds – which is why it's perfectly all right for it to be called *casa* in Spanish. In fact, if there were a necessary connection between the object and the word *house*, and likewise for all the other words of the language, it's hard to imagine how there could be any other languages. But despite its being arbitrary, it's also conventional, which means it's shared by the speakers of the language, by convention.

BOX 2.1

Infixes!

The best argument I know of for the rule-governed nature of language comes from **infixes.** We've seen that English has both prefixes (attached at the beginning of a word) and suffixes (attached at the end); but lots of languages, such as Tagalog, also have infixes, which attach in the middle. English has only a tiny handful of infixes, almost all of which are taboo words used as intensifiers. Consider what you might insert in these words to add emphasis:

(a) fantastic   fan- -tastic
(b) absolutely   abso- -lutely
(c) incredible   in- -credible

Yup; it's that wonderful all-purpose intensifier, *fuckin*:

(d) fan-fuckin-tastic
(e) abso-fuckin-lutely
(f) in-fuckin-credible

In British English, you also get *bloody* and *bloomin*:

(g) abso-bloody-lutely
(h) abso-bloomin-lutely

And a very recent American English use, particularly among rap/hip-hop artists, involves the infix *iz(n)*:

(i) play / plizay
(j) shit / shiznit

So how do these infixes serve as evidence for the rule-governed nature of language? Well, it's because they're **productive,** meaning they can be inserted into a wide range of different words, not just the 'usual suspects' given above. So imagine you're being dragged along on some tedious trip to a place you don't want to go; where would you insert the infix in these place names?

(k) Alabama
(l) Kentucky
(m) Massachusetts

If you survey your 20 closest friends, you're likely to find 100% agreement on where the infix goes in each of these words: Everyone will say *Alafuckinbama*; you will never, ever, get a native speaker saying *I have to go to Afuckinlabama* or *I have to go to Alabamfuckina*.

Why is that? Your parents certainly never sat you down as a toddler and discussed where the infix belongs in these words (unless you had the world's coolest parents), and you probably didn't even encounter infixes until you were in your teens. Instead, you know a **rule** that tells you where infixes are allowed. The rule appears to be roughly that the infix can appear before stressed syllables, or (similarly but not identically) between metrical feet (McCarthy 1982). (A 'metrical foot' is a pair or trio of syllables forming a unit of rhythm, like the iamb in iambic pentameter: toDAY the DOCtor ATE her LUNCH – daDA daDA daDA daDA; each daDA is a metrical foot.) For this reason, then, *fuckin* is impossible in *Texas* – because the word *Texas* is a single metrical foot.

FIGURE 2.1 Courtesy of xkcd.com.

There's also an interesting interaction between expletive infixation and other linguistic processes: For example, the prefix *in-* changes to *im-* before the 'bilabial' consonants *p, b,* and *m* (i.e., the consonants that bring your two lips together); this is a case of what linguists call **assimilation**: a sound changing to be more like another sound it's near. So, for example, you get words like *inflexible* and *infeasible* when *in-* comes before an *f*, but you get words like *impossible* and *impregnable* when it comes before a *p*.

So what happens when you insert *fuckin* into a word like *impossible*? Do you get *in-fuckin-possible*, retaining the *n* on the prefix before the *f* of the infix, or do you get *im-fuckin-possible*, with the *m* still assimilating to the *p* that it's no longer next to, resulting in a bit of a mismatch between the adjacent *m* and *f* sounds? People differ. (Ask your friends!) Which is, in a sense, a case of the exception proving the rule, as people find themselves trying to decide which rule takes priority when the two clash.

So appreciate your infixes; even the lowliest of taboo words can teach us valuable lessons about how our linguistic competence functions – even if they're not lessons your third-grade English teacher would have approved of.

Nonetheless, there are some words that aren't quite as arbitrary – cases of **onomatopoeia**, in which a word sounds a bit like what it means. Examples in English include words describing animal sounds (*chirp, bow-wow, hee-haw*), sounds of things smashing together *(crash, bang, boom)*, sounds of liquids (*fizz, splash, gurgle*), and many others. It's hard to imagine a language having, say, *ting* as its word for the sound of thunder.

Languages also create new words from old ones by means of **clipping** and **blends**. Clipping involves shortening an existing word to make a new one, as with *piano* (from *pianoforte*), *gym* (from *gymnasium*), and *typo* (from *typographical error*). One interesting pair are *taxi* and *cab*, both of which are clippings of *taxicab*. Meanwhile, **blends** are just what you'd expect – two words blended together to make a new one. Obvious examples are *brunch* (from *breakfast* and *lunch*) and *smog* (from *smoke* and *fog*), but more recent additions to the language include *infotainment* (from *information* and *entertainment*), *blog* (from *web* and *log*), and *spork* (from *spoon* and *fork*).

My personal favorite way in which new words are formed from old ones is **back-formation**, which is when the users of the language flat-out misunderstand the structure of the original word. Remember *inflammable* from Chapter 1? It comes from *inflame* + *-able*, but so many people took the *in* at the beginning to be a prefix meaning 'not' (as in *incapable*, 'not capable'), and hence assumed that the structure of *inflammable* was *in-* + *flammable*, that it gave rise to the new word *flammable*.

This sort of thing has happened a surprising number of times; if you recall the nursery rhyme 'Pease Porridge Hot', you may be amused to learn that *pease* used to be the word for a pile of a particular sort of food in the same way that *rice* today is the word for a pile of a different food, but enough people misunderstood *pease* as being the plural of *pea* (a word that didn't actually exist yet) that it ultimately gave birth to the new word *pea*. Each of the words in (10) is the result of backformation due to a similar misanalysis:

(10) a *edit*   from *editor*
      b *scavenge*   from *scavenger*
      c *diagnose*   from *diagnosis*
      d *administrate* from *administration*
      e *enthuse*   from *enthusiasm*

And I recently saw a newsletter with this wonderful example:

(11) Additionally, we were able to volunteer at Miracle league, Camp Sunshine, and fundraise for Siempre Para Los Ninos.

(Sigma Iota Beta 2018)

Clearly, *fundraise* here is a backformation of *fundraising*, which itself comes from *fund* + *raising* but is here misanalyzed as *fundraise* + *ing*. Watch for more instances of people who decide to 'fundraise' in the future!

Acronyms are a more familiar source of new words, where the initial letters of a string of words become a pronounceable word in their own right; examples include *AWOL* ('absent without leave'), *scuba* ('self-contained underwater breathing apparatus'), *lol* ('laughing out loud'), *POTUS* ('president of the U.S.'), and good old *snafu* ('situation normal, all fucked up'). People disagree about whether to include unpronounceable strings of such letters in the category of acronyms (e.g., *IIRC* for 'if I recall correctly' or *ADHD* for 'attention deficit hyperactivity disorder'); they're often considered to constitute a distinct category of 'initialisms' or 'alphabetisms'. As you can imagine, absolutely nothing hinges on this.

Eponyms are words formed from names: A fairly well-known example is *sandwich* from the Earl of Sandwich, who wanted a meal he could hold in his hand since he couldn't be bothered to come to the dining room. Another is *levis*, from Levi Strauss. Others that are less well known include *watt, fahrenheit, boycott, gerrymander,* and probably – believe it or not – *nachos.*

Finally, occasionally new words are simply made up, a process known as **coinage**. Often a company will coin a name for a new invention, sometimes taking the same invented name for the company itself, as with *Kleenex* and *Google*. Other coinages include *quark, nylon,* and *muggle.*

Lexical relations

At the beginning of this chapter, I argued that relations among words in a language are important to understanding the meanings of the words: *Blue* ends where *purple* begins, for example, and *sad* is understood largely by its opposition to *happy*. In this section – at the risk of loading you down with even more terms – I'll run through a list of lexical relation (relations among words) that linguists find useful in thinking about word meaning.

The first one is easy: **synonymy**. Synonyms are words that mean the same thing – *bucket / pail, car/automobile, mad/angry, couch/sofa/davenport, big/large,* etc. Some linguists have argued that there's no such thing as perfect synonymy, since if two words were identical in meaning, function, dialect, and register (i.e., formality), there would be no need to have both of them and one or the other would fade out of the language. And it's true that there's usually – maybe always – some small difference in meaning or use: For example, *my big brother* means something quite different from *my large brother*, and people who regularly use the word *couch* are unlikely to also use *sofa* or *davenport* for the same object. And if pressed, most people see a difference between a *bucket* and a *pail*, in terms of size and/or material.

Whereas synonymy is identity of meaning, **antonymy** involves difference of meaning – but in a specific sense (since after all *water* and *sofa* mean very different things, but they're not antonyms). Antonymy is **opposition** of meaning. But meanings can be 'in opposition' in a bunch of ways, so linguists talk about various subtypes of antonyms. We'll look at three types here: **gradable** antonyms, **complementary** antonyms, and **relational** antonyms.

Probably the largest category is gradable antonyms. These are cases in which two words are on the same scale but at opposite ends: *big/small, young/old, ugly/beautiful, dark/light, tall/short, loud/soft,* etc. They're considered gradable because they fall at ends of a continuum that ranges from one to the other; and it's possible for the things being described to fall anywhere on the continuum. So if you're not *young*, that doesn't mean you're necessarily *old*; you might be in the middle – or you might be *kind of young*, or *young-ish*. You might be *older* than your friend, and even the *oldest* of your siblings, but that still doesn't mean you're *old*. Gradable adjectives like these can be modified with adverbs like *very* and *most*, and can be made comparative (*older*) or superlative (*oldest*).

Also, interestingly, often one or the other member of the pair is the **unmarked** member while the other is **marked**. To be unmarked means to be the default or basic use. An example will help here. Imagine someone asks you how tall you are – no big deal, right? But now imagine someone asks you how short you are: That's weird, and you might even feel offended, since the question seems to suggest you're remarkably short. That's because *tall* is the **unmarked** member of the pair *tall/short*, and *short* is the **marked** member – the one that is 'marked' as having some additional function, suggestion, or meaning; i.e., the nondefault case.

Complementary antonyms work very differently. Here, it is indeed the case that for a pair of antonyms A and B, if you're not A you're necessarily B (unless the distinction doesn't apply at all). Again, examples will help: If you're not alive, you're dead; there's no in-between (although a paperclip is neither because the concept of life and death doesn't apply at all). So *dead* and *alive* are complementary antonyms. *True* and *false* are probably another pair, although we could happily spend a couple of hours arguing over when and whether it's possible for a proposition to be partially true – but at least given the binary truth-conditional semantics I introduced in the last chapter, there's no third option beyond *true* and *false*. *Black* and *white* aren't complementary antonyms, since something can be purple, but *pass* and *fail* are, since if you haven't passed the test, you've failed it, and vice versa. (Notice that antonyms needn't always be adjectives!)

Relational antonyms are an interesting case: Here, if A is in a certain relation to B, it means that B is necessarily in some other relation to A. *Buy* and *sell* are relational antonyms because if you've bought something from me, I've sold it to you. Likewise for *teacher/student* or *parent/child*: If I'm your teacher, you are necessarily my student, and if I'm your parent, you are necessarily my child. Notice that the necessity goes both ways: If you're my child, I am necessarily your parent. So that means that *parent/daughter* isn't a pair of relational antonyms: If you're my daughter, I'm necessarily your parent – but if I'm your parent, you aren't necessarily my daughter; you could be my son (or, for that matter, nonbinary).

> ### BOX 2.2
>
> ### I'm my own opposite
>
> Fun fact: Some words are their own antonyms! These are called **contranyms**. For example, I can *rent* a bicycle from you while you *rent* it to me, and likewise you *lease* an apartment to me when I *lease* it from you. A few other examples:
>
> (a) You can *cleave* to me or *cleave* something in half – hence, either joining two things or separating them. Marriage vows traditionally have included a phrase about *cleaving* to the other, which would be weird if it meant separating from them (but would make for an interesting wedding).
> (b) To *sanction* something can be to either approve or disapprove it. One country imposes *sanctions* on another as a punishment when it's unhappy with them, but an organization can also *sanction* a particular behavior, which essentially promises that it won't be punished.
> (c) To *dust* something can mean either to apply dust or to remove it. So if you're baking bread, you may have to *dust* your work surface liberally with flour – but if your roommate asks you to *dust* the living room and you scatter flour all over everything, you're going to be in trouble.
> (d) *Oversight* can mean either being watchful or failing to be. The first is a noun form of *oversee*, while the second is a noun form of *overlook*. The United

States House of Representatives, for example, has a House Committee on Oversight and Reform, and regardless of how you feel about government, it's fair to say that their intent, at least, is for the committee to oversee things, not to overlook them.

(e) Interestingly, though, *overlook* itself is a contranym: To overlook can mean to fail to keep an eye on something, or it can mean to look at it from above, as in a scenic *overlook*. I almost forgot to include this one, which would have of course been an *oversight*.

A related situation is found with *raise* and *raze*, where the two are pronounced the same but are spelled differently and have opposing meanings. In a sense, the difference between *dust* and *raise/raze* as contranyms parallels the difference between *bat* (flying animal vs. baseball implement) and *sea/see* as homonyms vs. homophones. Perhaps *raise* and *raze* should be called 'contraphones'? Hm, maybe not. I think we're all terminology-ed out at this point.

Whereas synonyms are words with different forms but the same meaning, **homonyms** are words with the same form but different meanings – for example, *light* ('not heavy') and *light* ('not dark'), or *mean* ('intend') and *mean* ('unkind'). Sometimes people use the word **homophones** for this, but there's a slight difference, as seen in the words *homonym* ('same name') and *homophone* ('same sound'): Homophones are words that are pronounced the same regardless of spelling (e.g., *sea* and *see*), whereas homonyms have both the same sound and the same spelling. So while all homonyms are homophones, not all homophones are homonyms. And just to round out the paradigm, there are also **homographs** ('same writing'), which have the same spelling regardless of their pronunciation (e.g., *read* (present tense) and *read* (past tense)). And just as all sets of homonyms are homophones, all sets of homonyms are homographs; in fact, you could define *homonyms* as 'any pair of words which are both homophones and homographs'. Here are a bunch of examples to help clarify the difference:

(12) a **homophones:** *two/too/to, they're/their/there, pale/pail, reed/read, doe/dough*
 b **homographs:** *lead/lead* ('to conduct' vs. 'metal'), *bow/bow* ('bend at the waist' vs. 'decoratively tied ribbon'), *affect/affect* ('influence' vs. 'demeanor')
 c **homonyms:** *stump* ('confuse' vs. 'remains of a tree'), *state* ('say' vs. 'geographic/political unit'), *date* ('fruit' vs. 'day')

There's a subtle and not always clear-cut distinction between homonymy and **polysemy**, which is a case of a single word with two related meanings, as in *glass* (the material vs. the drinking vessel), *diamond* (the shape vs. the gem), and *hand* (body part vs. to hand someone something). You wouldn't want to say that these are cases of homonymy, because the two related senses of, say, *hand* aren't really two different words in the sense that *mean* ('unkind') and *mean* ('intend') are. Most dictionaries indicate the difference between homonymy and polysemy by giving two homonyms their own entries (e.g., for *bat* the flying critter and *bat* the baseball implement), but treating polysemy (e.g., the various meanings of *hand*) as a string of related meanings listed under a single entry.

But it gets blurry in the middle, because very often what we consider two words today started out as one; for example, did you know that the *pupil* of your eye and a *pupil* in school have the same source? (The connection is the tiny reflection of yourself that you see in another's eye, as a teacher might see their own tiny image in the pupil of their pupil.) So would you now want to say that these are the same word? Not really, because we as linguists want to describe an individual's competence in language, not just esoteric details of how it got that way. But what do we do with the fact of different people's different linguistic competence – the fact that one person might say that *ruler* (something that measures length) and *ruler* (e.g., a king or queen) are two different words, while another might argue that they're related meanings of the same word (since each 'rules' or determines something)? As always, one person's 'English' is rarely if ever identical to another's, and in some cases there's just no single right or wrong answer.

The tally so far:

- same form, different words: homonymy
- same pronunciation, different words: homophony
- same spelling, different words: homography
- same word, different meanings: polysemy
- same meaning, different words: synonymy
- different words, opposing meanings: antonymy

But we're not quite done yet (and I apologize for the flood of terms in this chapter). **Hyponymy** is a case of meaning inclusion – that is, when one word's meaning includes that of another. The meaning of the word *daisy*, for example, includes the meaning of the word *flower*, because a daisy is a kind of flower (hence all daisies are flowers). As a general rule, if you can phrase the relationship as 'A is a kind of B', you've got hyponymy, and in fact these relationships are often called 'isa' relationships (as in 'a daisy is a flower'). So we say *daisy* is a hyponym of *flower*, *poodle* is a hyponym of *dog*, and *dog* in turn is a hyponym of *animal* – and these relationships are transitive, so if *poodle* is a hyponym of *dog*, and *dog* is a hyponym of

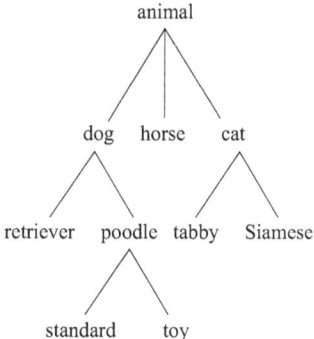

FIGURE 2.2 A simple, and very incomplete, taxonomy.

animal, then *poodle* is a hyponym of *animal*. And that makes sense: If a dog is an animal, then anything that's a dog is necessarily an animal. Meanwhile, we say that *animal* is a **hypernym** or **superordinate** of *dog* (and, naturally, *poodle*). And you can show all these relationships in a **taxonomy**, as in the tree in Figure 2.2.

Obviously I've left out loads of additional animals at each level, but you get the idea. And you can see why *cat* is simultaneously a hyponym of *animal* and a superordinate of *tabby*.

APPROACHES TO WORD MEANING

Componential analysis

So we've seen a bit about where words come from, and we've seen a bit about how they relate to each other semantically. The question, then, is what kind of theory can best account for these relationships, and for word meaning in general.

Let's first be clear about the question we're asking. Does knowing the meaning of the word *dog* involve knowing that it's a synonym for *canine* and that it's got *poodle, schnauzer,* etc., as hyponyms, or does it involve knowing where *dog* ends and *wolf* begins, or does it involve being able to say what it takes for something to count as a dog? Does it require us to be able to list all and only the properties of dog-ness – and if so, does that involve, say, four legs and a tail? If we have a three-legged, tail-less dog, is it no longer a dog? When a child learns the 'meaning' of a word, what sort of thing is it that they have learned?

Let's start with the plausible assumption that to know the meaning of the word *dog* or *cat* or *bird* is to know what it takes for something to count as a dog or a cat or a bird. We know the difference between a dog and a bird: A dog has four legs, a bird has two; a dog has fur, a bird has feathers; a dog is a mammal and a bird is, well, a bird. But these aren't necessary and sufficient conditions: Not all dogs have four legs, although of course the vast majority do; and not all dogs have fur. All dogs are mammals, but not all mammals are dogs. And it's even trickier to distinguish between dogs and cats: Both typically have four legs, fur, a tail, and whiskers. One is tempted to resolve the problem by saying that dogs are canines and cats are felines, but that's hardly helpful, and sort of circular: A dog is a canine because a canine is a dog.

A theory that analyzes the meanings of words in terms of a set of necessary and sufficient conditions is a theory of **componential analysis** – breaking the meaning of a word down into its component parts, often by means of a set of +/- properties:

(13)   a   *dog*: +canine
         b   *puppy*: +canine, -adult
         c   *bitch*: +canine, +female, +adult

And so on. The nice thing is that this could help to explain many of our lexical relations: Synonyms share their componential features, and the features of a hyponym will include the features of its superordinate (so *puppy* has all the features of *dog* and then some).

The problem is that this doesn't take us very far. What are the component features of, say, *human*? A human is sometimes said to be a featherless biped, so okay:

(14) a *human*: +biped, -feathers
  b *bird*: +biped, +feathers

Well, that's not very satisfying, since this doesn't seem to capture the real difference between a human and a bird. But of course I'm cheating by taking the 'featherless biped' definition seriously.

What about something simpler – say, *house*? What does an object require in order to count as a house? Walls and a roof and a floor? Well, no, since an office isn't a house. But is every building that someone lives in a house? No; some of them are apartment buildings. What's the difference between, say, an apartment and a townhouse? Townhouses are connected to each other in a row; does each count as a separate house? What about a duplex, where two homes are attached to each other and together constitute a single building? Is each one a house, is the whole thing a house, or is neither a house? What **is** a house?

Other primitive-based approaches

Componential analysis is based on the notion of **semantic primitives** – smaller units of meaning that are built up into larger units. To say that the meaning of *bitch* is +canine, +female, +adult is to treat concepts like 'female' and 'adult' as more basic units of meaning out of which more complex words like *woman* (+human, +female, +adult) or *girl* (+human, +female, -adult) are built. And there are theories that are based on that notion – that we have a small number of semantic primitives out of which larger meanings are built. Wierzbicka's 'Natural Semantic Metalanguage', for example, analyzes Jesus's injunction to 'love your enemies' as:

(15) if someone wants to do bad things to you
  it will be good if you don't want to do bad things to this person because of this
  it will be good if you want to do good things for this person

(Wierzbicka 2001)

I will leave it to you to decide whether this really captures the notion of 'love', or even of 'enemy'. (For a much more entertaining – and much less serious – take on a similar theme, see Randall Munroe's terrific book *Thing Explainer: Complicated Stuff in Simple Words*, which illustrates and explains complicated concepts – such as cells, 'tiny bags of water you're made of' – using only the thousand most common English words.)

But at some point primitive-based approaches to word meaning run aground on the issue of what constitutes a primitive: The word *red*, for example, would obviously have as one component of its meaning 'color' – but what's the other semantic primitive that distinguishes it from other colors? In short, the question is, which color IS it, and the answer is, circularly, 'the red one'. Similarly, assuming 'featherless biped' isn't really a good set of primitives for defining *human* (I think we can agree that 'featherless' wouldn't be one of our small number of primitives), what would be? And if *human* is itself a primitive, what about *dog, cat, cow, horse, pig, wolf*….? How many primitives do we need in order to distinguish between such subtly similar concepts as *dog, wolf*, and *coyote*?

Another take on primitives is Fodor's 'Language of Thought' hypothesis, which proposes that there is a universal set of cognitive semantic concepts that all humans share, and from which languages choose in constructing their form-meaning pairs. The notion is that the 'language of thought' has a sort of syntax, with more complex meanings being built up out of simpler meanings to allow complex thoughts – which can then be put into linguistic form (or not). One question, then, is whether our thoughts are formed in a particular language such as English, or whether our thoughts themselves are independent of the particular language in which they are expressed, and this is a topic on which researchers disagree.

Prototype theory and The Great Sandwich Controversy

The approaches to word meaning that we've looked at so far take semantic primitives as essentially necessary and sufficient conditions for the applicability of that word – which in turn left us oddly confused as to what exactly a *house* is. It suddenly felt as though the words we use every day might actually be words whose meaning we can't quite pin down.

Needless to say, this leads us into the bizarrely contentious area of what constitutes a *sandwich*, and specifically into the also bizarrely contentious area of whether a hot dog is a sandwich. And once you've decided whether you think a hot dog is a sandwich, you may as well keep right on going: What about a hamburger? A sub? A taco? A gyro? A wrap?

The Atlantic jumped into the fray in 2015, presenting what is essentially a componential analysis of sandwich-hood. According to *The Atlantic*, the following four features are necessary and sufficient for being a sandwich:

(16)   +exterior pieces
        +carb-based
        +horizontal orientation
        +portable

You can find this rather amusing article online at www.theatlantic.com, under the headline "It's Not a Sandwich." The article argues that burgers and Oreos meet the requirements of sandwich-hood, but that a hot dog does not, because its orientation is vertical (i.e., perpendicular to the plate rather than parallel to it). I'm not convinced, though: A sub sandwich or an Italian beef sandwich can be held either vertically or horizontally; that can't possibly change their status as being either a sandwich or not a sandwich.

The problem is of course that there's just no clear-cut boundary between 'is a sandwich' and 'is not a sandwich'; rather, there are all sorts of things that are kind of a sandwich and kind of not. And even when you've got a category in which there's a clear boundary between what's in and what's not – as in a category like *bird* – there are some birds that are more prototypical, just plain *better* birds, than others. A sparrow is a prototypical bird; an emu is not. Just last week, a friend was showing me photos of her trip to South America, and in explaining that the creatures in one photo were cormorants, she said:

(17)   They look like penguins, but they're birds.

Now, of course she knows that penguins are birds – but what she meant was that these were closer to the prototypical bird.

SEMANTICS I: WORD MEANING 43

FIGURE 2.3 A prototypical sandwich (for me). Gowithstock/Shutterstock.com.

What all of this suggests is that many words are defined not by a list of necessary and sufficient conditions, but rather by resemblance to some prototype, and with a possibly fuzzy boundary between what is and isn't a member of the category (that whole sandwich/hot dog problem). This view is called **prototype theory** (Rosch 1973, 1975), which is essentially a subtype of **fuzzy logic**. Fuzzy logic is used in lots of other disciplines, but we'll stick here to its use in lexical semantics, which is all about defining words in terms of prototypes – hence prototype theory.

So under this view the word *sandwich* is defined by the prototypical sandwich, which (at least for many Americans) looks something like the image in Figure 2.3.

This is a classic meat and cheese sandwich – although what you consider a prototypical sandwich might be peanut butter and jelly or a bologna sandwich. But the truly prototypical sandwich needs to have two distinct horizontal slices of bread with a cold, protein-based filling in between: lunchmeat and/or cheese; tuna (or egg or chicken) salad; PBJ.

But all of these are likely to be pretty close to the prototype of a sandwich, hence close to the center of the **fuzzy set** that defines a sandwich, with less 'sandwich-y' objects falling farther from the central prototype, as seen in Figure 2.4. If you change these parameters – swap the bread for a roll, baguette, wrap, pizza crust, or tortilla; change the orientation; make the filling hot; etc. – you've made it a less prototypical sandwich.

The crucial thing to realize is that we're not talking about where the word *sandwich* fits in Figure 2.4; rather, the entire figure is the definition of the word *sandwich*. This nicely fits with a child's process of acquiring the meaning of a word. After all, nobody sits little Suzy down and explains to her the necessary and sufficient conditions for sandwich-hood. Instead, she sees the sorts of things that people refer to with the word *sandwich*: definitely PBJs, bologna and cheese, etc.; frequently subs; occasionally burgers, dogs, or wraps. And so she develops a sense

44 SEMANTICS I: WORD MEANING

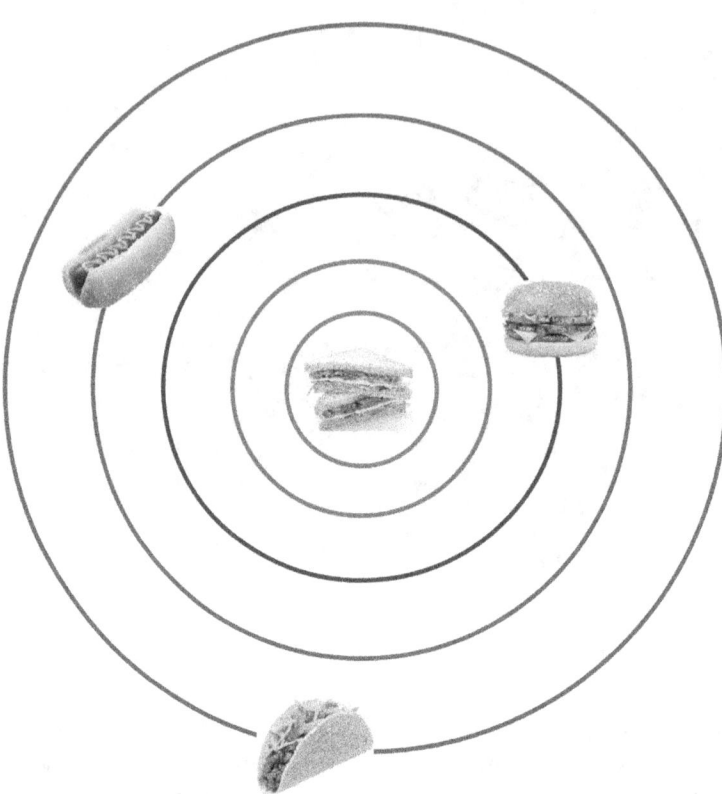

FIGURE 2.4 A fuzzy-set definition of the word *sandwich*. Image by the author; small images from Shutterstock.com: Gowithstock (sandwich prototype), Brenda Carson (hot dog), Hurst Photo (taco), and Andrei Kuzmik (hamburger).

of what counts as a sandwich and observes what those things have in common, and therefore might, upon thinking about it, consider a taco to be a 'sort of' sandwich on the grounds of its having some of those same properties, even though she may never have heard anyone call a taco a sandwich.

The burning issue of what does and doesn't count as a sandwich, surprisingly, has had real-world consequences: In 2006, a Massachusetts judge had to rule on the question of whether a burrito was a sandwich. The problem was that a Qdoba outlet had opened in the same shopping center as a Panera, but the Panera's lease had a stipulation that no other sandwich shop would be permitted in the same shopping center. And of course Qdoba sells burritos – so is it selling sandwiches? The court case hinged on whether a burrito is a sandwich. Panera said it was; the owner of the shopping center said it wasn't. Before reading the next sentence, what do you think? Well, the judge decided – drum roll – that a burrito is **not** a sandwich.

The difference between prototype theory and componential semantics is the status of the properties defining a word. In componential semantics, those properties are considered necessary and sufficient: A sandwich isn't a sandwich unless it has (if you believe *The Atlantic*) exterior carb-based pieces and is both portable and horizontal. According to prototype theory, those properties may describe the prototypical sandwich, but not all sandwiches; it's just that if an object lacks one or more of those properties, it will be a less prototypical sandwich – farther from the center of the fuzzy set, which is considered 'fuzzy' because not all members of the set have equal status as members. This not only better accounts for our sense that not all sandwiches are equally 'sandwich-y' (and not all houses are equally 'house-y', etc.), but also better accords with how we come to develop these meanings for words when we acquire them as children.

BOX 2.3

What is a lie?

So let's say your best friend has asked you that terrible, terrible question: *Do these pants make me look fat?* And rather than explain how beautiful your friend is, independently of culturally defined and ultimately arbitrary norms of body weight (which, while true, probably won't help), you say *nope* – even though you think they kinda do. Have you lied? Well, yeah, even if it's for a good cause. Now suppose you're a kid who's broken your mom's prize vase, and you go to her and say *The cat was running around and your vase got broken.* And suppose the cat *was* running around, but it had nothing to do with the fact that you bumped the table the vase was on and sent it crashing. Have you lied? This one's trickier, because you've told the literal truth: The cat was running around, and the vase got broken.

Coleman and Kay (1981) analyze the word *lie* using prototype theory. In their analysis, a prototypical lie has the following three properties:

(a) It is false.
(b) The speaker believes it is false.
(c) The speaker intends to deceive the hearer.

Any utterance with those three properties (e.g., your saying *nope* to your friend above) is a prototypical lie. Utterances lacking one or more of them are less prototypical, and reasonable people will disagree about whether they are lies. In Coleman and Kay's study, speakers treated (b) as the most important property for an utterance to count as a lie – that is, it was most likely to be considered a lie if the speaker believed it to be false. As for you and your mom above, it's less clear: Your statement is technically true, and you know it, but you do intend to deceive mom – so only (c) is satisfied; and, as predicted, people are torn about whether it's a lie.

Meanwhile, Coleman and Kay also distinguish between prototypicality and mere 'typicality', and one of the features of a 'typical' lie, they say, is 'reprehensibility'. A typical lie is reprehensible; but a nonreprehensible lie is no less a lie, and plenty of clear lies are not reprehensible. So cheer up: You may be lying to your friend above, but it's not a reprehensible lie; the lie is atypical, and you're still a good person.

EXERCISES

Self-test:

1. A word
   a. is the smallest unit of sound in a language.
   b. is the smallest unit of reference in a language.
   c. is a linguistic unit bounded by a space on each side.
   d. acts as an island.
2. Proto-Indo-European is
   a. a reconstructed language from which English is descended.
   b. the newest dialect in the English family.
   c. a now-dead language that descended from Latin.
   d. a Germanic variant spoken by the early Saxons.
3. Which of these modern words is the result of backformation?
   a. *ketchup*, borrowed from Chinese.
   b. *peddle*, a misanalysis of *peddler*.
   c. *exam*, from *examination*.
   d. *bathroom*, a combination of *bath* and *room*.
4. *Homonym* is
   a. a synonym of *antonym*.
   b. a homograph of *polysemy*.
   c. a hyponym of *homophone*.
   d. an antonym of *homograph*.
5. Which of the following are relational antonyms?
   a. *above/below*.
   b. *high/low*.
   c. *tall/short*.
   d. *tallest/shortest*.
6. A componential analysis gives
   a. a list of member entities of a category by which a term is defined.
   b. a fuzzy set with a central prototype by which a term is defined.
   c. a set of semantic primitives by which a term is defined.
   d. a set of necessary but insufficient properties by which a term is defined.
7. A prototype is
   a. a member whose properties are necessary and sufficient for membership in a fuzzy set.
   b. a term being defined by a fuzzy set.
   c. a member at the boundary of a fuzzy set.
   d. the most characteristic member of a fuzzy set.
8. Semantic primitives are
   a. the smallest units of sound in a language.
   b. smaller units of meaning that are combined to form larger meanings.
   c. a linguistic unit bounded by a space on each side.
   d. the smallest free form in a language.

9   The string *–ment*, as in *requirement*, is
    a   an inflectional suffix.
    b   a derivational suffix.
    c   an infix.
    d   a word.
10 So is a hot dog a sandwich?
    a   Yes.
    b   No.
    c   It's impossible to say, since *sandwich* is defined by a fuzzy set and people's lexicons vary.
    d   I'm not sure, but it's vitally important to keep arguing about it.

Comprehension questions:

1   For each of the following gradable-antonym pairs, identify the unmarked member and give an example to show why you chose it:
    a   long/short
    b   young/old
    c   wide/narrow
    d   big/small
    e   soft/loud
    f   happy/sad
    g   comfortable/uncomfortable
2   Give the source words for each of the following recent blends, looking them up if necessary: *bromance, chocoholic, chillax, cyborg, malware,* and *frenemy*.
3   Of the words listed in this chapter as descending from PIE *ghostis*, which descended through Germanic, and which were borrowed in from French? How do you know? To what extent did each of them keep or alter the original PIE sense of 'stranger'?
4   Based on the information given in this chapter, draw a partial family tree for the PIE family of languages, including Proto-Indo-European, French, Old English, Middle English, Germanic, Latin, German, and Sanskrit. Look up the history of Greek online and decide where to fit it into the tree.
5   Pretend you're inventing a language, and create ten onomatopoeic word/meaning pairs. Now create ten other pairs that are so clearly NOT onomatopoeic that they're unlikely to appear in any language (like the text's example of *ting* for the sound of thunder).
6   Draw a fuzzy set for one of the following words: *pet, house, chair, furniture*. (You don't have to use images for the set members; you can use words.)

Opinion questions:

1   Attempt to define the terms *sport* and *game*. First, try to do it with componential semantics, then with prototype theory. Which works better? What are the strengths and weaknesses of the two approaches?
2   Linguists differ on the question of whether there are any true synonyms, on the grounds that there is always **some** slight meaning in difference or usage. What do you think, and

why? Can you come up with a pair of truly swappable synonyms? Would you count the same word in two regional dialects (such as *pop* and *soda*) as synonyms? And how does your answer to that question affect your decision as to whether true synonyms exist?

3   Our current word *bird* descends from Old English *brid*, but nobody complains that the modern pronunciation is incorrect. Meanwhile, our current word *ask* descends from Old English *ascian/acsian* – which is to say, in old English both orderings of the *s* and *k* sounds were acceptable. But today a lot of people object to the *aks* pronunciation. What's your opinion, and why? Do the facts about *bird* and *brid* influence your view? What do you imagine a linguist would say, given that linguistics is a descriptive science? And finally, what ramifications do you see for telling a group of people that the way they speak is right or wrong?

4   Is the distinction between homonymy and polysemy a useful one, in your view? How about the distinction between homonymy and homophony? Explain your reasoning.

5   Is it more helpful to define the word *homonym* in terms of a componential analysis or a fuzzy set? Explain your reasoning.

Discussion questions:

1   Is chess a sport? Give evidence for both sides, weigh the evidence, and come to a conclusion.

2   Is a corporation a person? Many people viewed the Supreme Court's decision in Citizens United (2010) as saying exactly that, though technically it didn't (rather, it extended to corporations certain rights that were already held by persons). Look up the decision in Citizens United and familiarize yourself with its history, and likewise for the concept of 'corporate personhood'. With this background in hand, evaluate the claim 'a corporation is a person' using one or more of the semantic theories from this chapter.

3   See if you can come up with a set of semantic primitives to distinguish the following words: *salad, casserole, stew, soup, chili, lasagna*. What's the smallest number of primitives that fully distinguishes them? Do your primitives correctly categorize *tuna salad, potato salad,* and *vegetarian chili*?

4   Is *ice cream* a compound word, by the criteria in this chapter? How about *hot fudge*? How about *ice cream sundae*? And finally, what about *hot fudge ice cream sundae*?

Data collection and analysis:

1   In January 1998, President Bill Clinton famously asserted, *I did not have sexual relations with that woman*, referring to Monica Lewinsky. (If you're unfamiliar with the details of what did and didn't happen between them, they're easy to find online.) Survey your friends regarding whether he in fact did or did not 'have sexual relations with that woman'. Ask each person to define the term *sexual relations*. Include the broadest demographic range possible among your informants: old, young, women, men, gay, straight, transgender, cisgender, nonbinary, conservative, progressive, etc. What do you learn about the semantics of this term – and what does it say about lexical semantics in general?

2   Look up the borrowings listed in this chapter, and identify the language each one comes from. Then go to the Google Books Ngram Viewer at https://books.google.com/ngrams, type the words into the top box in small groups (separating the words by commas), and click on "Search lots of books" at the right. The resulting graph shows for each word how frequently it appears in books published in the years listed at the bottom. Which words have joined the language since 1800? How can you tell? Search for *beef, sushi, slalom, blitz* and see what the chart looks like; then try the search again, omitting *beef*. What happens, and why? What can you learn about the words *blitz* and *sushi* that gets masked when you include *beef*? Repeat the experiment with *ninja, ballet, slalom*, both with and without including *ballet*. Fiddle around with entering individual words instead of groups, or entering pairs and trios of words, and changing the date range, and note what you learn about when these words seem to have entered the language. (Keep in mind that these data come entirely from books, so they present a much better idea of what people were writing about in a given year than what they were talking about.)

3   The web can be a great corpus for doing linguistics research. (See Chapter 1 for a quick explanation of what a corpus is.) Google the phrases *my little sister* and *my small sister* (separately, and putting each phrase within quotation marks when you search for it to make sure you get only that exact phrase). Before the list of results, Google notes the rough number of results, or 'hits', that it found. How many hits does each phrase get? Why do you think that is? What does it suggest about the status of *little* and *small* as synonyms? **Collocation** is the phenomenon of certain words appearing together more frequently than one would expect by chance. Google the phrases *powerful speakers, strong speakers, powerful smell*, and *strong smell*, and note the number of hits for each. Now go to the Ngram Viewer (described in the previous question) and check, for the years 1950–2000, the pair *powerful speakers, strong speakers*, and then (separately) the pair *powerful smell, strong smell*. What do you learn about the potential synonyms *strong* and *powerful*?

Answers to self-test:

1   d
2   a
3   b
4   c
5   a
6   c
7   d
8   b
9   b
10 c

Semantics II: Sentence meaning

KEY CONCEPTS

- tautology, contradiction, analytic, synthetic
- sentential relations: entailment, paraphrase, redundancy, anomaly
- lexical, sentential, and structural ambiguity
- logical operators, truth-functional operators, logical connectives
- truth table
- predicate, arguments
- negation, conjunction, disjunction, conditional, biconditional
- antecedent, consequent
- inclusive vs. exclusive *or*
- variable, constant
- open and closed propositions
- universal and existential quantifiers
- bound variable, free variable
- existential commitment
- scope, wide vs. narrow scope

The English language, like every language, is full of ambiguity. Consider these examples:

(1) a Microsoft wants to update my hard drive and I find myself questioning seriously if I want to install something called "Malicious Software Removal Tool."

(Maleckar 2019)

    b We love hurting people.

(church sign image posted on Facebook, July 2019)

    c In response, one constituent in the audience exclaimed, "We're short congresspeople that take action!"

(fund-raising solicitation letter; example courtesy of Larry Horn)

One might want to install a tool for removing malicious software – but if it's a software removal tool that's malicious, that's another thing altogether. And it's great if a church loves people who are hurting – but again, if what they love is to hurt people, that's not so great. And perhaps the country has insufficient congresspeople who take action – but if what is meant is that the speaker is part of a group of short congresspeople who take action, well, that's just weird.

The thing is, language is full of ambiguity, but in studying semantics we need to be able to represent meanings unambiguously. If our semantic representations are just as ambiguous as what they represent, then they're not actually representing meanings; instead, we've just traded one code (English) for another. We want a way to represent **propositions** that's independent of all the messiness and ambiguity of natural language. For example, the following two sentences represent the same proposition:

(2) a Harold haunted the house.
    b The house was haunted by Harold.

Now, since these sentences mean the same thing, then if we want to examine sentence meaning, it would be handy to have a scheme that represents them identically – while offering two different representations for each of the ambiguous expressions in (1). We want, as much as possible, for our representational scheme to show what the underlying meanings are like, not just what the English sentences are like. Any representational scheme that represents (2a-b) differently is probably representing the structure of the **sentences**, not the single **proposition** (i.e., meaning) that they share.

So in order to represent meanings in unambiguous terms, we're going to need an unambiguous **metalanguage**: a language for use in talking about language. And using English to describe English clearly isn't going to do the trick.

In this chapter we'll work our way toward a metalanguage for describing linguistic meaning unambiguously. Along the way, we'll consider the sentence-level analogs of lexical relations, and we'll consider in greater depth the relationship between meaning and truth – which is to say, we'll be revisiting some of the concepts we examined in the first two chapters.

BOX 3.1

Lost in translation

If you're translating a passage from one language to another, how do you make sure the meaning is the same in both cases? It's a surprisingly complicated problem, and mistranslation can have severe consequences. In 1956, for example, Soviet leader Nikita Khrushchev told a group of Western ambassadors, *My vas pokhoronim!*, which the translator rendered as 'We will bury you', which some took as a nuclear threat – but an equally possible translation for the phrase is 'We will outlast you', which is much less threatening (Polizzotti 2018). You can imagine the potential consequences in the context of the Cold War.

Similarly, in 1969 Japanese Prime Minister Eisaku Sato was visiting Washington, and President Richard Nixon asked for Japanese restraint in exports. As the *New York Times* later described it, "Mr. Sato replied as he looked ceilingward, 'Zensho shimasu'. Literally, the phrase means, 'I will do my best', and that's how the interpreter translated it. What it really means to most Japanese is, 'No way'. Mr. Nixon thought that he had an agreement, however, and when Japan continued on its merry export way, he reportedly called Mr. Sato a liar" (Haberman 1988).

Every language has ambiguities, so every translator has to make decisions about how to translate an ambiguous text. And at the same time, they have to decide how 'closely' to translate – whether to render the word-for-word 'literal' translation (as Sato's interpreter did) or a much looser translation that might better convey what was meant.

A great example of the problem comes from an English translation of the Bible. The New Revised Standard Version renders Isaiah 40:3 as:

A voice cries out: "In the wilderness prepare the way of the Lord...."

And it renders Matthew 3:3 as:

This is the one of whom the prophet Isaiah spoke when he said, "The voice of one crying out in the wilderness: 'Prepare the way of the Lord....'"

So, what gives? Is the wilderness where we're supposed to prepare the way, as in Isaiah? Or is the wilderness where the voice is, as in Matthew? Is Matthew mis-quoting Isaiah?

The answer is a bit complicated. Isaiah was written in Hebrew, and Matthew in Greek. The Hebrew is completely ambiguous: In essence (factoring out irrelevant grammatical details) it says:

A voice crying out in the wilderness prepare the way of the Lord

This can be interpreted either as 'a voice', which is crying out, 'in the wilderness prepare the way of the Lord'; or it can be interpreted as 'a voice crying out in the wilderness', which is crying out, 'prepare the way of the Lord'. Different translations of the Bible make different decisions about which way to go. What makes the New Revised Standard Version interesting is that it went with an inconsistent, but probably correct, set of translations. Initially, Matthew (like all of the New Testament) was written in Greek, without punctuation. By the time punctuation was added, people had pretty much settled on the 'voice crying in the wilderness' reading for Isaiah, and since the guy Matthew was introducing in his passage, John the Baptist, did indeed live in the wilderness, the Isaiah passage was pertinent.

But in light of modern scholarship, there's good reason to think the Isaiah passage actually was originally intended to be read the other way. So the

> translators rendered Isaiah as it was probably intended (the wilderness is where to prepare), and rendered Matthew as **it** was probably intended (the wilderness is where the voice is). In short, the translators here are making the implicit claim that the second-century Christians who added punctuation to Matthew were reading Isaiah wrong – and that maybe the writer of Matthew was, too!
>
> In short, keep in mind that every time you're reading a translation of **anything,** what you're reading is the translator's best guess at what was meant by the original author – and the translator may have had to make a choice between two (or more!) equally valid translations.

TRUTH AND MEANING

Let's first return to a couple of notions from Chapter 1 – specifically, **possible worlds** and **truth**. Recall that a possible world is simply one way that things could logically be (or that any world could logically be). So possible worlds run the gamut from our own actual world to worlds that are just like ours except for some tiny difference (e.g., one possible world is exactly like the real world except that ants are purple), all the way to worlds that are still perfectly possible but differ wildly from our own (such as a world in which rocks and water are sentient, there are no animals, and clouds are made of cotton candy; the actual physics necessary for such a world to exist will be left as an exercise for the reader).

The reason we care about possible worlds is that they help us create the bridge between truth and meaning. So, let's take a very simple sentence:

(3) All chairs have four legs.

Now, as good semanticists we want to know what this sentence means. And just as one approach to word meaning is to ask what it would take for something to count as, say, a *chair*, one approach to sentence meaning is to ask what it would take for, say, *all chairs have four legs* to be true. You can see the parallel: In lexical semantics, we're asking what an object would have to be like in order for the word *chair* to apply to it; in sentential semantics, we're asking what a world would have to be like in order for the sentence *all chairs have four legs* to apply to it.

To turn it around, you could say that if you want to know what *all chairs have four legs* means, you can simply look at every world in which that sentence is true and see what they share. If you throw all the worlds in which the sentence *all chairs have four legs* is true into a big infinitely large pile (since of course there's an infinite number of such possible worlds), and look through them, you'll see that the one and only thing that they share – which is shared by none of the other worlds – is the fact that all chairs have four legs in these worlds.

Okay, I get that this seems screamingly obvious and pointless – but wait. This is where we're getting tripped up by the fact that we're using English for our language of meaning as well as for the language we're discussing. (Hence, the usefulness of a metalanguage.) If, instead, you keep in mind that what's true or false in (3) isn't really an English sentence but rather a language-independent proposition, it makes a little more sense to say that we can distinguish the worlds in which that proposition is true from those in which it isn't – and then we can talk about which English sentences express that proposition.

So *The book is blue* in English and *Das Buch ist blau* in German express the same proposition, so every world in which *The book is blue* is true is a world in which *Das Buch ist blau* is true. And of course an ambiguous sentence expresses more than one distinct proposition, while two distinct sentences in English can express the same proposition. Now, despite there being an infinite number of possible worlds, there are some propositions that are true in every single one of them, such as this one:

(4) Either it is the case that all chairs have four legs, or it is not the case that all chairs have four legs.

Notice that we're still using English to represent propositions, which we've seen is a problem – and we'll work on that problem shortly. And strictly speaking, (4) isn't a single proposition, or at least not a simple proposition but rather two propositions connected by *or* – that is, it's a **complex** proposition. But in any case, there's no possible world in which (4) is false – which is identical to saying that (4) could never be false, regardless of what the world is like. It's a **tautology** – a sentence that is true in every possible world. And needless to say, there are also propositions that are false in every possible world:

(5) Chairs exist, and all chairs have four legs, and no chairs have four legs.

Again, this is a complex proposition, but it's impossible for it ever to be true, regardless of what the world is like. The sentence in (5) is a **contradiction** – a sentence that is false in every possible world. Tautologies and contradictions whose form alone tells you whether they're true or false (or, more technically, the form of the proposition they represent tells you whether they're true or false) make up the class of **analytic** sentences. Since you can figure out their truth or falsity simply by analyzing their form, it just doesn't matter at all what the world is like; they're either true in all possible worlds (tautologies) or false in all possible worlds (contradictions). All other sentences are **synthetic**, which means that they're true in some worlds and false in others, so in order to figure out whether the sentence is true in some particular world, you need to look at the world itself. *All chairs have four legs* is synthetic; there are some worlds in which all chairs have four legs and others in which some chairs don't have four legs, and to determine the **truth-value** of that sentence in a particular world, you need to check the world and look at the chairs (which also requires us to know what counts as a chair, a problem we dealt with in the last chapter).

The **truth-value** of a proposition, then, is relative to a particular world; it's whether that proposition is true or false in that world. So the truth-value of *all chairs have four legs* in the actual world is **false**, because there are chairs in the actual world that don't have four legs. It's important to distinguish **truth-values** from **truth-conditions**: The truth-conditions of a proposition are the conditions under which it is true – that is, what a world would have to be like in order for that proposition to be true. The truth-conditions of *all chairs have four legs* is that every chair in the world must have four legs. These are its truth-conditions regardless of what world we're looking it – but whether those conditions are satisfied or not (i.e., its truth-value) will vary from one world to another.

SENTENTIAL RELATIONS

We've seen that the meaning of a sentence is analogous to the meaning of a word: For the meaning of a word, we're asking 'What does something have to be like for this word to apply to it?', and for the meaning of a sentence, we're asking, 'What does a world have to be like for this sentence to apply to it?'. So it will come as no surprise to learn that many of the lexical relations we discussed in Chapter 2 have analogs at the sentence level – that is, in the area of **sentential relations**.

You'll recall, for example, that two words are synonymous if they mean the same thing – that is, if they apply to the same set of objects. Likewise, two sentences are **paraphrases** if they mean the same thing – that is, if they apply to the same set of worlds. So, *couch* and *sofa* are synonyms if the exact same set of objects count equally as a *couch* or a *sofa;* and (6a) and (6b) are paraphrases if they are true in the exact same set of worlds:

(6) a Hilda is taller than Fred.
    b Fred is shorter than Hilda.

(In all such examples, we'll assume that there's only one Hilda and only one Fred in the world, to save ourselves the tedium of specifying, say, 'Hilda Johnson of 234 Chestnut St., Philadelphia PA, on 3/19/2019'.)

The sentential analog for hyponymy is **entailment**. Just as we've seen that in hyponymy, anything that satisfies one description necessarily satisfies the other (so, for example, anything that is a daisy is necessarily a flower), in entailment any world in which one sentence is true is necessarily a world in which the other is true. So consider (7):

(7) a John ran into the room.
    b John moved into the room.

Any world in which (7a) is true is also a world in which (7b) is true. It's impossible for John to run into a room without moving into it, since *run* includes the meaning of *move* – which is to say, *run* is a hyponym of *move*. So by replacing a hyponym with its superordinate, you'll get a pair of sentences in which the first entails the second:

(8) a Carol drew a daisy.
    b Carol drew a flower.

Again, any world in which (8a) is true is a world in which (8b) is true (though not vice versa), which means that (8a) entails (8b).

And there's another parallel: Mutual hyponymy is synonymy, and mutual entailment is paraphrase. What I mean is that a pair of synonyms will be hyponyms of each other, and likewise paraphrases will entail each other:

(9) a car
    b automobile

(10) a Greta held a sign.
     b A sign was held by Greta.

In (9), *car* and *automobile* are synonyms – but it's also the case that *car* is a hyponym of *automobile* and vice versa, because the meaning of *car* includes the meaning of *automobile* (and, as it happens, nothing else). It is impossible to be a car without also being an automobile, and it's impossible to be an automobile without being a car. And in just the same way, (10a) and (10b) are paraphrases, but they also entail each other. There's no world in which (10a) is true but (10b) isn't (and vice versa). One could simply define synonymy as mutual hyponymy, and paraphrase as mutual entailment.

> **BOX 3.2**
>
> ## Fake news!
>
> Not all adjectives are created equal. A *rectangular purple block,* for example, is rectangular, and it's purple, and it's a block; that is, each of those three properties holds of the object. The adjectives *rectangular* and *purple* here are what's known as **intersective** adjectives; they essentially just add their meanings on as additional properties of the object described by the noun. If it's true that Iris is a brown-eyed surgeon, it's true that she's brown-eyed and it's true that she's a surgeon: The set of things described by *brown-eyed surgeon* is the intersection of things described by *brown-eyed* and the things described by *surgeon.*
>
> But not all adjectives work this way (Kamp and Partee 1995). Consider first a word like *terrific*. If you're a *terrific dancer*, you're not necessarily both terrific and a dancer; rather, you're terrific at dancing. And if you're a *skilled baker,* you may be lousy at everything except baking; *skilled* and *baker* don't express distinct properties in the same way *rectangular, purple,* and *block* do. *Terrific* and *skilled* are called **subsective** adjectives. If it's true that Sally is a terrific dancer, it's true that she's a dancer, but not necessarily true that she's terrific, except insofar as *terrific* describes her dancing. Of all the things describable as dancers, Sally's in the subset of those that are terrific – at dancing.
>
> But there's a third class of adjectives that are neither intersective nor subsective, and that in turn brings us to *fake news*. The adjective *fake* in general doesn't behave like either of the above two classes of adjectives: A *fake diamond* isn't both fake and a diamond; it isn't a diamond at all. Similarly, a *former teacher* is neither former (whatever that would mean) nor a teacher. A *potential doctor* isn't a doctor yet. So *fake, former,* and *potential* are in a class of **nonsubsective** adjectives: If it's true that Zeke is a *former teacher*, it's not the case that he's both former and a teacher; and it's not the case that of everyone who's a teacher, he's among those who are former teachers. Instead, he's not a teacher at all.
>
> So – is *fake news* news? Is *fake* in the phrase *fake news* a subsective adjective, describing the subset of news that is fake news? Or is it a nonsubsective adjective, describing something that's not news at all? Or is it ambiguous

> between the two? Notice that such ambiguities are possible; a sentence like *Gilda is a beautiful skater* is ambiguous between subsectivity and intersectivity, since it can mean that Gilda's skating is beautiful or that Gilda is both beautiful and a skater.
>
> The question is: Is fake news (i.e., something untrue that's reported by the media) news that's fake (the intersective reading), or is it news that's fake as news (the subsective reading), or is it not news at all (the nonsubsective reading)? It matters, because, as linguist George Lakoff points out in a 2017 NPR interview (Kurtzleben 2017), if we interpret *fake news* as a type of news, that can influence the way we feel about news in general, making it less credible. And at the same time, the phrase *fake news* is increasingly being applied to real news, to undermine its credibility – as when, for example, very real and important scientific reports of climate change are dismissed as *fake news*.
>
> In short, beware of real reports of fake news, and fake reports of real news, and fake reports of fake news. And in all things, be a brilliant linguist – on both readings!

Notice also that hyponymy and entailment can give rise to **redundancy**, which is repetition of meaning:

(11) a ?My brother relative is tall.
       b ?John ran into the house moving.
       c ?Greta held a sign being held by her.

The phrase *brother relative* is redundant because *brother* is a hyponym of *relative*; so, since *brother* already contains all of the meaning of *relative*, the word *relative* adds nothing new. And for John to *run* into the house entails *moving*, so the word *moving* adds nothing new. And again, for Greta to hold a sign entails that it's being held by her – so again, *being held by her* adds nothing. All three of these sentences strike us as **anomalous**, which is to say, semantically odd – which is what the question mark at the beginning of each sentence indicates. Curiously, though, not every redundant sentence is anomalous:

(12) a Jake planted an elm tree.
       b Elaine repeated the story over again.
       c We're twins: My brother is the older one, and I'm the younger one.

Elm is a hyponym of *tree*, but (12a) seems fine. In (12b), *repeat, over,* and *again* all convey the sense of repetition, but most people wouldn't flinch on hearing it. And in (12c), the last two clauses mean exactly the same thing, but again the sentence is fine. In fact, language is full of redundancy, and that's actually helpful since we don't always catch every single syllable of what's said to us. What makes some redundancy seem odd and other redundancy seem fine is not entirely clear.

The flip side of redundancy is **contradiction**, which is an incompatibility of meaning. The sentences in (13) are contradictions:

(13) a Hazel failed the test she passed.
 b That mammal is a reptile.
 c My brother is older than his older sister.

You can see where the clash is in each of these (you can't both fail and pass a test, etc.). Recall also the logical contradiction above in (5), repeated here:

(14) Chairs exist, and all chairs have four legs, and no chairs have four legs.

This sentence is necessarily false because of its form; any proposition of the form *Xs exist, and all Xs are Y, and no Xs are Y* will necessarily be false. The sentences in (13a) and (13b) aren't logical contradictions; rather, the contradiction is each of these cases is due to the meanings of the words, not the form of the proposition. So, in (13a) there's an incompatibility between the meanings of *pass* and *fail*. In (13c), it's the meaning of the comparative suffix that causes the clash; if one thing is older than another, the other can't be the older of the two. So here the lexical semantics interact with the logic of comparison to result in contradiction.

Finally, just as **homonymy** can result in **lexical ambiguity**, as in (15a), homonyms in a sentence can result in **sentential ambiguity**, as in (15b):

(15) a bat (the animal vs. the baseball implement)
 b I saw a bat in the backyard.

But sentential ambiguity can also be caused by **structural ambiguity**, when two different structures give rise to two different meanings. So, to resurrect the examples from the beginning of the chapter:

(16) a Microsoft wants to update my hard drive and I find myself questioning seriously if I want to install something called "Malicious Software Removal Tool."
 b We love hurting people.
 c In response, one constituent in the audience exclaimed, "We're short congresspeople that take action!"

In (16a), *malicious software removal tool* could be structured with *malicious software* being a noun phrase (and the thing that's being removed), or with *software removal tool* being a noun phrase (and the thing that's malicious). In (16b), *hurting people* could be a noun phrase expressing whom we love, or it could be a verb phrase, expressing what we love to do. And in (16c), *short congresspeople that take action* could be a noun phrase expressing who we are, or *congresspeople that take action* could be a noun phrase expressing what we're short of. In all three cases, the two different meanings correspond to two different syntactic analyses. We'll examine the relationship between syntax and meaning in a lot more detail in Chapter 6.

BOX 3.3

"Hospitals named after sandwiches kill five"

Because of the need to be brief, newspaper headlines and the like often end up being subject to more than one interpretation, with amusing or puzzling results. These are known to linguists as 'crash blossoms', in honor of this one:

Violinist linked to JAL crash blossoms

The reader might be forgiven for thinking the violinist was linked to some strange new type of flower, but in fact the intended meaning was that a violinist whose father had died in a JAL (Japan Airlines) crash had gone on to blossom. Had the writer more space, they might have used a few more function words to disambiguate: 'A violinist who is linked to a JAL crash is blossoming'. But because newspaper headlines must be brief, those helpful function words tend to be left off, resulting in crash blossoms.

A marvelous 2010 *New York Times* article by linguist Ben Zimmer lists others that have appeared through history, including:

Giant Waves Down Queen Mary's Funnel
MacArthur Flies Back to Front
Eighth Army Push Bottles Up Germans
Squad Helps Dog Bite Victim
Red Tape Holds Up New Bridge
McDonald's Fries the Holy Grail for Potato Farmers

(Zimmer 2010)

The article includes plenty of other examples, and they're structurally and semantically fascinating. Quite often the confusion can be traced to words that can appear as more than one part of speech, such as *giant, waves,* and *down* in the first example: Is this a noun-verb-preposition string, in which case a giant is waving something down, or an adjective-noun-verb string, in which case giant waves have downed something? (I think we can all agree that the second reading was intended, but we wish it were the first.)

In this sense these headlines are like 'garden path' sentences, so called because they lead the reader 'down the garden path' of an incorrect parse, until incoherence results and they're forced to back up and try a different path, as in:

The horse raced past the barn fell.
Wood barns are built from grows in forests.

FIGURE 3.1 Dinosaur Comics, courtesy of Ryan North.

In case you can't figure these out: The first one means that a particular horse, which had been raced past the barn, fell. And the second means that the wood from which barns are built grows in forests.

And there's also this well-known gem:

Time flies like an arrow; fruit flies like a banana.

So what about those hospitals in the header above, from the 6/18/19 UK *Times*?

Hospitals named after sandwiches kill five

(Zimmer 2019)

I'd love to think this is a warning for us to stop naming our hospitals things like 'Ham and Cheese Medical Center' and 'Tuna Salad Memorial' – but the intended meaning is made clear from the initial sentence of the article: "All hospitals where patients have died from poisoning after eating sandwiches were identified yesterday."

Too bad; there's no end of jokes that could be made about the Mayo Clinic.

LOGICAL OPERATORS

So a proposition is a thing that can be either true or false, and a given proposition will be true in one set of possible worlds and false in another. And we've seen that we're going to need a metalanguage if we're going to get very far in talking about linguistic meaning without getting tangled up in the confusion between the language we're describing and the language we're using to describe it. This section will introduce the first bits of that metalanguage.

The metalanguage we'll be using is borrowed from the field of logic, and we're going to start with a handful of **logical operators**. These operators are 'functions' in that they perform a specific function on whatever inputs they're given and return an output. They're also called **truth-functional** operators, because what you put in and get out are truth-values.

Negation

Let's start with **negation**, the simplest of these operators. If you take a proposition – any proposition – and negate it, you'll flip its truth-value. For example:

(17) a Paper is made of metal.
      b Paper is not made of metal.
      c Paper is made of wood.
      d Paper is not made of wood.

Obviously, (17a) is false – and if you negate it, as in (17b), the result is true. Similarly, (17c) is true, and if you negate it, as in (17d), the result is false. And negation absolutely does not care what the proposition in question is; if the original proposition is true, the negation will be false, and vice versa. That's what makes it truth-functional; it only cares about the truth of the input and the output. Since the actual proposition doesn't matter a bit, we can replace it with a **variable**, which is just a place-holder. By convention, the letters $p, q, r\ldots$ are used as variables. So we can make a little table showing the effect that negation has on a proposition, as in Table 3.1.

This is called a **truth table**. Each row corresponds to a set of possible worlds, defined by the column (or columns) on the left. So in Table 3.1, the first line includes all the worlds in which some proposition p is true; that's what the T in the first column tells you. And what the F in the second column tells you is that in all of those worlds, $\neg p$ ('not p') is false – again, regardless of what p is. On the second line, we've got all the worlds in which p is false, and what the table tells us is that in all of those worlds, $\neg p$ is true. The reason we use the symbol $\neg$ rather than the word *not* is to remind ourselves that we're talking about logical operators here, not English words.

TABLE 3.1 Truth table for negation.

p	$\neg p$
T	F
F	T

Conjunction

Now let's try a slightly more complicated case. Suppose I connect two statements with the word **and**:

(18) a   Paper is made of wood.
     b   Guacamole is made with avocados.
     c   Paper is made of wood, and guacamole is made with avocados.

Logically speaking, if (18a) is true and (18b) is true, then (18c) is true. So in any world in which (18a) and (18b) are both true, (18c) is also true – and if either of the first two is false, then (18c) is also false. And this, again, has nothing to do with the actual content of the statements; it's a fact about the use of the word *and*. Now, I'll warn you in advance that in day-to-day English, we use *and* for some other purposes, which we'll talk about later – and that's precisely why a semantic metalanguage is useful. So to remind ourselves that here we're really only talking about **conjunction** as a **logical connective** (a logical operator that connects two propositions), we'll adopt another symbol for our metalanguage: We'll use '$\wedge$' for conjunction.

Table 3.2 shows the truth table for conjunction.

Notice that because we've got twice as many variables as we did for negation, we also need twice as many possible worlds to get all possible combinations of 'true' and 'false' for our propositions, and so we need twice as many rows to define these worlds. We've got four possible ways a world could be with respect to our two propositions: It could be the case that both of them are true (the first row in Table 3.2), it could be the case that p is true but q is false (row 2), it could be the case that p is false but q is true (row 3), or it could be the case that both of them are false (row 4). And this exhausts all of the possible worlds. It doesn't matter a bit what the two propositions are; every possible world will fit into one of those four categories.

And the table pretty well fits with our intuitions for the English word *and*; it certainly captures our intuitions with respect to (18) and our sense that anytime both of the conjoined propositions are true, the whole complex proposition *p and q* will be true, and that it'll be false otherwise. But it turns out that in natural language, that's not always the case:

(19)   I fell off my bike and broke my leg.

Anyone uttering (19) would be taken to mean that they broke their leg when they fell off their bike. But logically speaking – and semantically speaking – and according to the truth table in Table 3.2 – it doesn't matter whether the fall and the broken leg are related at all. If the

TABLE 3.2 Truth table for conjunction.

p	q	$p \wedge q$
T	T	T
T	F	F
F	T	F
F	F	F

TABLE 3.3 Truth table for disjunction.

p	q	p∨q
T	T	T
T	F	T
F	T	T
F	F	F

speaker fell off their bike on Tuesday and broke their leg in a car accident on Thursday, (19) is still true. We'll have a lot more to say about this below, but for now it's worth keeping in mind that there's a big difference between the logical meaning of these connectives and their natural-language use; it'll make some of the truth tables below a little easier to swallow.

Disjunction

An excellent example of this disconnect between logical meaning and natural-language use is provided by the truth table for **disjunction**, which corresponds roughly to English *or*, as seen in Table 3.3.

First, note the difference between the symbol we used for conjunction (∧) and the symbol for disjunction (∨). You'll get used to them soon, but in the meantime be careful to remember which is which.

What Table 3.3 means is that a disjunction (p∨q) is false only if both of its component propositions are false; if one or both of them is true, then the whole thing is true. Which makes sense for English *or* in lots of cases:

(20) Either my allergies are acting up or I'm getting a cold.

Now, suppose you're a doctor who can tell the difference between the symptoms of allergies and an incipient cold. If you decide the speaker's symptoms are due only to allergies, you'd say (20) is true – and likewise if you decide they're due only to an incipient cold. And if you decide the speaker has both allergies AND a cold? I'm guessing you'd still say that (20) is true. Certainly it would be weird for you to respond:

(21) That's false; I think you've got both.

On the other hand, we often behave as though *p or q* means that one or the other is true, but not both. So imagine you tell a friend:

(22) My family's going to Spain or Italy for vacation next year.

Your friend is likely to believe that you'll go to either Spain or Italy, but not both. But would (22) become false if you ended up going to both? Perhaps not. Let's take another example; suppose a parent tells a child:

(23) You will finish your peas or you won't get dessert!

If the child eats every last pea and still doesn't get dessert (meaning *p* and *q* are both true), they're likely to feel lied to, because they're relying on a reading of *p* or *q* in which if both are true, the whole thing is false. And the parent, even if they can pull out the truth table to support their claim that they didn't technically lie, is just being a jerk.

The reading of *or* represented by the truth table in Table 3.3 is what's called **inclusive 'or'**, and it's the reading generally assumed by logicians and semanticists. The reading on which the truth of both *p* and *q* renders *p*∨*q* false is called **exclusive 'or'**, and as we'll see in Chapter 4, this is not the semantic meaning of *or*, but instead is derived from pragmatic principles.

The conditional

Our next truth-functional connective is the **conditional** (sometimes called the **material conditional** or **material implication** or just **implication**), and it corresponds to the English *if… then* or just *if* (with *then* understood), as in (24):

(24)   If Bella is stung by a bee, she develops a rash.

What this means is that if *p* is true (i.e., if Bella is stung by a bee), *q* is necessarily also true (i.e., she develops a rash). But what if *p* isn't true? Well, that's where things get interesting. Take a look at the truth table in Table 3.4.

Again, we have here a difference between the logical meaning of the connective and the way speakers use the corresponding English expression. The first row behaves as we'd expect: In every world in which Bella gets stung and gets a rash, *p*→*q* is true. We call *p* the **antecedent**, and *q* the **consequent**. So we can say that here, in every world in which the antecedent is true, the consequent is true. And the second row makes sense too: In any world in which Bella is stung and doesn't get a rash, *p*→*q* is false; when the antecedent is true and the consequent is false, the whole thing is false.

The third and fourth rows, however, are really hard for a lot of people to wrap their heads around. In any world in which Bella isn't stung at all, (24) is true. And your immediate response is likely to be something like "Hold it! What if Bella isn't allergic to bees? What about a world in which, if Bella **had** been stung, she **wouldn't** have developed a rash?"

These are actually two slightly different questions, so let's take them one at a time. First, what if Bella isn't allergic to bees? Well, notice that (24) says nothing at all about Bella being allergic to bees, or even that the rash is a result of the bee sting; that's all stuff we infer. In a world in which Bella is stung by a bee and develops a rash as an allergic reaction to a peanut she had eaten immediately beforehand, (24) is still true. There are pragmatic reasons why it's an odd

TABLE 3.4 Truth table for the conditional.

p	*q*	*p*→*q*
T	T	T
T	F	F
F	T	T
F	F	T

thing to say (why are we talking about the bee sting at all, if it's irrelevant?), but logically, (24) is just as true in that world as (19) was in the case where falling off the bike had nothing to do with the broken leg. And if Bella isn't stung at all, then we have no basis for saying (24) is false. It seems odd, but in any world in which Bella isn't stung, *If Bella is stung by a bee she develops a rash* is said to be logically true; it's just that, well, she wasn't stung.

Likewise, if Bella has developed a rash, then we're in either row 1 or row 3, and in either case, $p \rightarrow q$ is true; regardless of whether she has in fact been stung, it's true that **if** she has been stung, she's developed a rash – because, sting or no sting, she's got the rash.

The second argument, "What about a world in which, if Bella **had** been stung, she **wouldn't** have had a rash?", appeals not to the third or fourth row of the truth table, but the second. Yes, in that case (24) is false, but you've performed a bait-and-switch, because we're now considering a possible world in which she has in fact been stung. In the realm of possible worlds, the notion that this isn't the world we're actually in has no force, so a world in which Bella had been stung is a second-row world.

And to help yourself feel a bit more comfortable with the fourth row, in which $p \rightarrow q$ is true even when both component propositions are false, imagine that you and a friend are disagreeing about sports, and you say something like:

(25) If that's a winning team, then I'm the Pope.

You're relying on the accuracy of that fourth row of the truth table: The whole thing is true (that's why you're saying it), but q is clearly false; you're not the Pope. (If the Pope is actually reading this, I apologize for the error.) That means our world must be a fourth-row world (there are no other options), which means that p must be false: That's not a winning team. The logic of the insult doesn't work unless the truth table is correct.

The biconditional

Okay, time for our last logical connective. This one is the **biconditional**, which corresponds roughly to the English *if and only if*:

(26) I'll go swimming if and only if you do.

You see the truth table in Table 3.5.

You can breathe a sigh of relief, because this one makes sense – which just means that it corresponds pretty well to the English *if and only if*. If both of the component propositions are

TABLE 3.5 Truth table for the biconditional.

p	q	$p \leftrightarrow q$
T	T	T
T	F	F
F	T	F
F	F	T

true, $p \leftrightarrow q$ is true, and if both of them are false, $p \leftrightarrow q$ is true. Similarly, if we both go swimming, (26) is true, and if neither of us does, it's true – but if I do and you don't, or if you do and I don't, it's false.

But again, keep in mind that while we feel better about truth tables that match our intuitions about natural language (as with the biconditional) than we do about those that don't (as with the conditional), that's just because we feel as though the way we use language ought to map onto these truth tables – in part because I've given a 'corresponding' English expression for each logical connective. But this assumes two things: First, that the meaning of the logical connective matches the semantics of the natural-language expression, and second, that the semantics of the natural-language expression matches its use in natural language. You already know that the second of these isn't true, because pragmatics also figures in; and, as it happens, pragmatics also plays a role in arguing that the first is actually correct. That is, as we'll see in Chapter 4, pragmatic theory can help explain how it is that these truth tables really do represent the semantic meaning of the corresponding English expressions, even though much of the time that's not how we use them.

PROPOSITIONAL LOGIC

So you may feel a little concerned at this point: It seems that we've spent a whole lot of pages and a whole lot of charts on, basically, the meanings of five English words and expressions, those that correspond to the logical connectives. (Yay! Only a million or so words to go!) But it turns out that we'll get a lot of mileage out of these expressions.

Analytic statements

First, they can help us to explain a class of statements that are **analytic** – that is, either necessarily true or necessarily false in every possible world, by virtue of their form. So consider (27):

(27) If Bea went to the party, Bea went to the party.

This can be represented as:

(28) $p \rightarrow p$

This means that in any world in which p is true, p is true, regardless of what p is. And that checks out: If Bea went to the party, Bea went to the party; and if all dogs are blue, all dogs are blue; and if Washington DC is in Zimbabwe, Washington DC is in Zimbabwe. Any sentence that can be represented as in (28) is true by virtue of its form; that is to say, it's a **tautology**. A statement that is necessarily false by virtue of its form is a **contradiction**:

(29) Bea went to the party, and Bea didn't go to the party.

This is represented as:

(30) $p \land \neg p$

TABLE 3.6 Truth table for a contradiction.

p	¬p	p∧¬p
T	F	F
F	T	F

TABLE 3.7 Truth table for conjunction.

p	q	p∧q
T	T	T
T	F	F
F	T	F
F	F	F

Again, you don't need to check what world we're in to see that this is false; any statement of this form is false in every possible world. In fact, you can check this with a truth table, as in Table 3.6.

The first column lists all the possible worlds: those in which p is true and those in which p is false. The second column just repeats what we've already seen in the truth table for negation: When p is true, ¬p is false, and vice versa. For the third column, we've just plugged the truth-values from the first two columns into the truth table for conjunction, repeated in Table 3.7.

The first line in Table 3.6 matches the second line in Table 3.7, where a world in which p is true and q is false is a world in which $p \wedge q$ is false. You just need to realize that ¬p in Table 3.6 is playing the role of q in Table 3.7. And the second line in Table 3.6 matches the third line in Table 3.7: A world in which p is false and q is true is a world in which $p \wedge q$ is false. So we plug those two 'false' conclusions into the third column of Table 3.6, and we discover that no matter what the world is like – whether p is true or false – it turns out that $p \wedge q$ is false; it's a contradiction! It can never be true in any world.

Synthetic statements

So tautologies and contradictions are both analytic, because their truth or falsity is determined entirely by their form, not by what world we're in. On the flip side, the truth of **synthetic** statements – which is all the rest of them – depends not on their form alone, but on what the world is like. Here's a synthetic statement:

(31) Bea went to the party and Alvin didn't go to the party.

Because *Bea went to the party* and *Alvin went to the party* represent different propositions, this would be represented in propositional logic as:

(32) $p \wedge \neg q$

And its truth table is shown in Table 3.8.

TABLE 3.8 Truth table for a synthetic statement.

p	q	¬q	p∧¬q
T	T	F	F
T	F	T	T
F	T	F	F
F	F	T	F

It will come as absolutely no surprise to see that, according to Table 3.8, p∧¬q is true only in a world in which p is true and q is false (line 2). But what that means is that the truth of p∧¬q can't be determined purely on the basis of its form; it will be true in some worlds and false in others, and so to figure out whether it's true or false in a given world you'll have to look at what that world is like.

In case you're underwhelmed by Table 3.8 and the conclusion that p∧¬q is true only in a world in which p is true and q is false (which, I'll admit, is pretty self-evident), notice that truth tables can you help you figure out the truth-conditions of some vastly less self-evident complex propositions. First, note that it matters how things are grouped, so we'll use parentheses for that purpose. This means that (33a) and (33b) have different truth-conditions, which is to say that they're true in different worlds, i.e., on different lines of the truth table:

(33) a   I love ice cream, and if there's ice cream in the freezer we're having a party.
     b   If I love ice cream and there ice cream in the freezer, we're having a party.

(34) a   p∧(q→r)
     b   (p∧q)→r

Here are the truth tables. First, the truth table for (34a), which you'll find in Table 3.9.

You'll notice that because we've added a third variable, we've had to double the length of the table again, basically considering each of our previous four world-sets and considering each of them in light of whether r is true or false, which doubles the number of ways in which our worlds can vary. Take a minute to satisfy yourself that these eight rows exhaust the set of ways a world can be with respect to the truth of p, q, and r (I'll wait here…). And now check my work in that fourth column, satisfying yourself that it correctly represents the truth of (q→r) in

TABLE 3.9 Truth table for (34a).

p	q	r	(q→r)	p∧(q→r)
T	T	T	T	T
T	T	F	F	F
T	F	T	T	T
T	F	F	T	T
F	T	T	T	F
F	T	F	F	F
F	F	T	T	F
F	F	F	T	F

TABLE 3.10 Truth table for (34b).

p	q	r	(p∧q)	(p∧q)→r
T	T	T	T	T
T	T	F	T	F
T	F	T	F	T
T	F	F	F	T
F	T	T	F	T
F	T	F	F	T
F	F	T	F	T
F	F	F	F	T

each of the eight possible worlds. And in light of those results, it should be straightforward to then use that column and the first column (*p*) to determine whether the final column – that is, *p*∧(*q*→*r*) – is true in each possible world.

Now consider the truth table for (34b), (*p*∧*q*)→*r*, shown in Table 3.10.

Run through the same process of double-checking each column that you used for Table 3.9 to satisfy yourself that Table 3.10 is correct. (This isn't just because I may have messed up, but rather because it'll help solidify in your mind how these things work.)

What you'll find is that the truth-values of *p*∧(*q*→*r*) and (*p*∧*q*)→*r* are the same in all worlds in which *p* is true, but they differ in all worlds in which *p* is false. In those worlds, *p*∧(*q*→*r*) is always false and (*p*∧*q*)→*r* is always true. Which means that in any world in which it's false that I love ice cream, the statement 'I love ice cream and if there's ice cream in the freezer we're having a party' is false (since I don't love ice cream). And in those same worlds in which it's false that I love ice cream, the statement 'if I love ice cream and there's ice cream in the freezer, we're having a party' is true (since in all those worlds, *p*∧*q* is false, which automatically makes the whole thing true). The upshot is that grouping matters.

If the complex proposition you're testing turns out to be a tautology, you'll end up with all Ts in the last column (showing that it's true in all possible worlds), and if it's a contradiction, you'll end up with all Fs (showing that it's false in all possible worlds). If that column ends up with a mix of Ts and Fs, it means the proposition is synthetic – that is, true in some worlds and false in others.

So back in Table 3.6, the table for (29) *Bea went to the party, and Bea didn't go to the party*, the table has only Fs in the final column, which makes sense since this is a contradiction. But you may feel a little less sure about (27) *If Bea went to the party, Bea went to the party*, which a quick truth table will verify is a tautology. The source of your uncertainty might be the fact that this statement can be used to mean things that can be either true or false, as in the exchange in (35):

(35) A Bea had absolutely no right to go to that party!
B Look, if Bea went to the party, Bea went to the party.

In (35), B's utterance might be intended to mean something like 'Bea's going to the party isn't a big deal' or 'Bea did have the right to go to the party' or 'there was no reason for Bea not to go to the party', and those things might in fact be false. But none of those is the **semantic** content of B's utterance; these are all **pragmatic** inferences based on what B has said, and we'll be talking about that sort of meaning in the next chapter. As far as semantics is concerned, B's utterance in (35) is tautological.

PREDICATE LOGIC

The tools of propositional logic are useful for understanding the semantics of the logical operators – and as we'll see in the next chapter, they're very useful for understanding, in turn, how actual speakers use these operators in natural language. But there's a lot more to language than connectives like *and* and *or*, and so far our tour of propositional logic has treated propositions as unitary objects: We can manipulate them and connect them and see how they relate to each other, but we still can't see inside of them to see how they're constructed.

That's where **predicate logic** comes in, and it will give us much more powerful tools for examining the meanings of propositions, and in turn of statements in natural language. (But keep in mind we're still in the world of semantics, so there may still be a gap between the meaning of a statement as shown using the tools of predicate logic and the pragmatic meaning of that same statement in a particular context.)

Predicates and constants

Let's start at the very beginning. What are the simplest sorts of things we might want to say using natural language? Here are a few possibilities:

(36) a Amy is tall.
 b Ben sings.
 c Carla is a doctor.

Each of the names represents some entity, and the rest of the statement says something about it. We say the statement **predicates** something of that entity, and the thing doing the predicating is called the **predicate**. (Fun fact: The last syllable of *predicate* as a verb and *predicate* as a noun are pronounced differently, just like *syndicate* as a verb vs. a noun.) In (36), we see that the predicates show up as an adjective in (a), a verb in (b), and a noun in (c), but no matter; they'll all be represented similarly:

(37) a TALL(a)
 b SING(b)
 c DOCTOR(c)

Since this isn't an advanced semantics textbook, I'm going to skip over some details, such as tense, so we'll be cheating by using the same predicate-logic representation for *Ben sang* that we use for *Ben sings*. But trust me; when you dig deeper into the field (after falling in love with it by reading this book), you'll see that there are notational tools for distinguishing them.

For now, what's worth noting is that in our predicate-logic notation for a proposition, the predicate comes first and is represented in all capital letters, and the entity comes after it, in parentheses, and is represented by a small letter. That small letter is a **constant**, which means that its meaning will remain constant throughout the formula:

(38) a LOVE(c,d)
 b LOVE(c,c)
 c LOVE(c,d) ∧ ANNOY(d,e)

So, (38a) might represent *Carla loves Dave*, (38b) *Carla loves herself*, and (38c) *Carla loves Dave and Dave annoys Edith*. But (38b) cannot represent *Carla loves Claudia*. So now you may be wondering how we'd represent *Carla loves Claudia*. But here's the thing: Although by notational convention we tend to use the first letter of a name as the constant for that person (and we conveniently avoid having two people whose names start with the same letter), it really doesn't matter at all. So (39) can also represent *Carla loves Dave*:

(39) LOVE(f,g)

And, for that matter, it can represent *Carla loves Claudia*. The important thing is that the constants remain constant – so if we're using *f* to represent *Carla* at one place in the formula, *f* will represent Carla throughout.

An **atomic proposition** consists of one predicate and its **arguments**, where the arguments are the participants – the entities represented inside the parentheses. A **one-place** predicate, like those in (37), takes one argument. A **two-place** predicate, like LOVE in (38), takes two arguments. You usually don't have sentences like *Frank loves*; you need Frank to be loving someone or something. And PUT is a **three-place** predicate; here's *Gerry put the ham in the icebox*:

(40) PUT(g,h,i)

You'll also notice in (38c) that you can combine those atomic propositions to get complex propositions, using our handy connectives:

(41) a MEET(j,k) ∧ EXCITED(j)   *Jackie met Ken and was excited.*
 b EAT(k,l) → SICK(k)   *If Ken eats liver, he'll be sick.*
 c (EAT(k,l) ∧ BAD(l)) → SICK(k) *If Ken eats bad liver, he'll be sick.*

You'll also notice that a single formula can represent more than one English sentence, since (41c) also represents *If Ken eats liver and the liver is bad, he'll be sick*. But the important thing is that every sentence represented by (41c) means, semantically, the same thing and is true in the same set of worlds (ignoring tense).

These formulas can get extremely complex:

(42) (SNEEZE(p)∧DISGUSTED(f))→(OFFER(f,p,t)∧TISSUE(t)∧USE(p,t))
 If Priscilla sneezes and Frieda is disgusted, then Frieda will offer Priscilla a tissue and Priscilla will use the tissue.

I don't know about you, but I love this; it's like knowing a secret code.

If you've got a formula that contains only a predicate and constants, it expresses a complete proposition – and because a proposition is, by definition, a thing that can be either true or false, that proposition will have truth-conditions; you'll be able to determine whether it's true in any given world.

Variables

So far all of our statements have featured constants, each of which represents a single nonvarying entity. But sometimes, you'll get a formula that contains a **variable**, which is exactly what it sounds like: Its meaning varies. So take (43):

(43)   SNEEZE(x)

We use x, y, and z as variables in our formulas. What (43) means is simply 'x sneezed'. Crucially, it does **not** mean 'someone sneezed'. That variable x is a placeholder, and until we do something about that, this formula represents an **open proposition** – a proposition that's missing one or more elements and can't be evaluated for truth until those elements are filled in. Because x is a variable, its meaning varies – so if, in our world, Priscilla sneezed but Seymour didn't, (43) is true when x stands for Priscilla and false when it stands for Seymour. And since our variable can stand for either one of them, (43) as it stands has no truth-conditions.

And that's why we can't say that it means 'someone sneezed' – because 'someone sneezed' **does** have truth-conditions: It's true in our world in which Priscilla has sneezed and Seymour hasn't. So (43) absolutely, positively does not mean 'someone sneezed'. It means 'x sneezed' – which is a totally different thing. SNEEZE(p) is a closed proposition with truth-conditions and a truth-value in a given world; SNEEZE(x) is an open proposition with no truth-conditions and no truth-value in any world.

Quantifiers

So now you're thinking that an open proposition seems like a pretty useless thing – but just wait! In Chapter 8, you'll find that open propositions play an important role in the structuring of a sentence. And in the meantime, we'll see that we can turn an open proposition into a **closed proposition** – a complete proposition with truth-conditions – in one of two ways: First, we can replace the variable with a constant:

(44)   a   SNEEZE(x)
       b   SNEEZE(p)

Okay, so that doesn't seem so impressive. The second way is to **bind** the variable with a **quantifier**. In (44a), the variable is said to be **unbound** or **free**; it could in principle stand for anything, which is why we can't say what the truth-conditions for (44a) are. To understand how binding works, let's meet two quantifiers:

(45)   a   ∃ the **existential** quantifier, meaning roughly 'there exists'
       b   ∀ the **universal** quantifier, meaning roughly 'for all'

This gives us two ways of binding the variable in (44a), which are shown in (46):

(46) a ∃x(SNEEZE(x))
     b ∀x(SNEEZE(x))

The formula in (46a) reads: 'There exists an x such that x sneezed.' And the one in (46b) reads: 'For all x, x sneezed. ' Intuitively, you can see that these have truth-conditions: The proposition in (46a) is true if **anyone** sneezed, and the one in (46b) is true if **everyone** sneezed.

Whereas (44a) has no truth-conditions because we don't know what x stands for, the propositions in (46) have truth-conditions because we're going to replace that x with every entity in the world, one after another, and see what happens. If **any** replacement value for x (such as, say, p) makes the proposition SNEEZE(x) true, (46a) is true. And if **every** replacement value for x renders the proposition SNEEZE(x) true, then (46b) is true. The value of 'x' is no longer free; it is **bound** by the quantifier, which controls its meaning.

Try it out for yourself: Look at the world you happen to be living in (the real world, that is), and decide whether these propositions, containing bound variables, are true or false:

(47) a ∃x(BIRD(x))
     b ∀x(BIRD(x))
     c ∃x(BIRD(x)) ∧ ∀x(BIRD(x))
     d ∃x(BIRD(x)) ∨ ∀x(BIRD(x))

Hopefully you decided that (47a) and (47d) are true, and (47b) and (47c) are false. There does exist a bird in this world (lots of them, in fact), so (47a) is true. But it's not the case that everything is a bird, so (47b) is false. In (47c), we've got 'there exists a bird and everything is a bird', which is false because the second half is false (it's not the case that everything's a bird). But (47d) is true because the disjunction requires only one of the two halves to be true; (47d) says 'either there exists a bird or everything's a bird', and since there exists a bird, the whole thing is true.

This whole system, by the way, is basically a notational variant of a system developed by our old friend Frege. What's worth noting here is that a quantified formula differs in an important way from something like SNEEZE(p), which straightforwardly breaks a proposition down into subject and predicate. In (46), those quantifiers aren't clear subjects or predicates – so there's not an obvious mapping in which the 'pieces' of propositional meaning map directly onto the 'pieces' of sentence meaning. The formula in (46a) stands for *Somebody sneezed* even though there isn't a single piece of the formula that represents *somebody*.

One other quick but important point: The existential quantifier expresses an **existential commitment**, but the universal quantifier does not:

(48) a ∃x(BIRD(x))
     b ∀x(BIRD(x))

That is, (48a) asserts that there **does** exist a bird, but (48b), surprisingly, doesn't. It only says that **if** there is an x, that x is a bird. But maybe you live in a world without any entities. Okay, that's unlikely, but it matters in a case like (49):

(49) ∀x(BIRD(x)→FLY(x))

This says that for all x (i.e., for everything in the world), if it's a bird, it flies. In our world, (49) is false; penguins are birds that don't fly. But there are also possible worlds without any birds in them. In such a world, (49) is true. (Remember our truth table for the conditional: If p is false, then $p{\to}q$ is always true, so if for every x it's false that x is a bird, then it's true for each of them that 'if x is a bird, then x flies'.) Similarly, in a world with no entities and therefore no birds, ∃x(BIRD(x)) is false but ∀x(BIRD(x)) is true. In short, (48b) and (49) don't require the existence of a bird in order to be true.

Ambiguity and scope

As I mentioned above, one of the great advantages of our metalanguage is that it's unambiguous, unlike natural language. So consider a very simple ambiguity:

(50) Everyone read a book.

This can mean one of two things: Either each person read some book (potentially a different book for each person), or there's a particular book that everyone read. So the sentence as it stands is ambiguous. But in our metalanguage, each of those two readings has a different representation:

(51) a ∀x∃y(BOOK(y)∧READ(x,y))
      b ∃y∀x(BOOK(y)∧READ(x,y))

Okay, let's unpack these. In (51a), we've got: For all x, there exists some y such that y is a book and x read y. Or, slightly more clearly, for every x, there is some book that they read.

Now compare that with (51b): There exists some y such that for all x, y is a book and x read y. Or, again more clearly, there is some book that everyone read. And notice that (51a) and (51b) only differ in the ordering of the '∀x' and the '∃y'.

Side note: I'm cheating by saying 'everyone', meaning I'm assuming everything is a person (which is impossible, since there exists at least one book). Strictly speaking, (51b) means that there's a book that every **entity** read, not that every **person** read. To limit our readers to people (to prevent, say, cupcakes from reading books, or books from reading each other), you'd need to replace (51) with these:

(52) a ∀x∃y((PERSON(x)∧BOOK(y))∧READ(x,y))
      b ∃y∀x((PERSON(x)∧BOOK(y))∧READ(x,y))

But for ease of discussion, let's stick with the shorter versions:

(53) a ∀x∃y(BOOK(y)∧READ(x,y))
      b ∃y∀x(BOOK(y)∧READ(x,y))

In (53a), for every person there's some book that they read – but not necessarily the same book. In (53b), there's some book that everyone read – the same book. And the only difference between the two is the order of '∀x' and '∃y'. We say that in (53a), the universal quantifier has **wide scope** (because it's on the outside) and the existential has **narrow scope** – and vice versa in (53b). And we say that in (53a), the existential is **inside the scope** of the universal, and vice versa for (53b). And finally, we say that in (53a), the universal **has scope over** the rest of the formula, whereas in (53b), the existential does.

As you can see, this scope difference corresponds to a difference in meaning: In (53a) everyone read a book, but not necessarily the same book; in (53b), there's a single book that everyone read.

Now for something harder. How many meanings can you think of for these two sentences?

(54) a Someone admires everyone.
     b Everyone admires someone.

Analogously to (53), you should be able to see two meanings in each of them. For (54a), there are the two meanings in (55):

(55) a There's a particular individual who admires everyone.
     b For every person, there's someone who admires them.

And for (54b), there are the two meanings in (56):

(56) a Every person has someone they admire.
     b There's someone everyone admires.

Having trouble seeing these different readings? Here are some contexts to help them along. For the readings of (54a) that you see in (55), consider these contexts:

(57) a Jane, you claim that there's no one on earth who admires everyone, but I disagree. I'm sure **someone** admires everyone.
     b Jane, you say there are people who are admired by nobody, but I disagree. I believe there's something admirable in everybody, so **someone** admires **everyone**.

And for the readings of (54b) that you see in (56), try these:

(58) a Jane, you claim there are people who don't admire anybody, but I disagree. I think everyone admires **someone**.
     b Hey, Jane – I was surprised to learn yesterday that Mother Teresa was universally beloved, which means that **everyone** admires someone, specifically Mother Teresa!

Okay, I won't keep you in suspense any longer; here are the formulas for these four meanings:

(59) a ∃x∀y(ADMIRE(x,y))
     b ∀y∃x(ADMIRE(x,y))
     c ∀y∃x(ADMIRE(y,x))
     d ∃x∀y(ADMIRE(y,x))

The formula in (59a) corresponds to the reading in (55a): There's an individual who admires everyone.

The formula in (59b) corresponds to the reading in (55b): Everyone has someone who admires them.

The formula in (59c) corresponds to the reading in (56a): Everyone has someone they admire.

And the formula in (59d) corresponds to the reading in (56b): There's an individual whom everyone admires.

Notice that the only difference between (59a) and (59b) is the ordering of those two quantifiers; and the only difference between (59b) and (59c) is the ordering of the variables after the predicate ADMIRE. In fact, if you take a minute to examine (59) carefully, you'll see that those four options represent every possible logical ordering of $\exists x$, $\forall y$, x, and y. And for each difference in the ordering of those elements, there's a difference in meaning. This is the goal of predicate logic: to be an unambiguous representation of meaning.

EXERCISES

Self-test:

1. The relation between *I ate a peach* and *I ate something* is one of
   a. paraphrase.
   b. contradiction.
   c. entailment.
   d. anomaly.
2. A truth table shows a proposition's truth-value
   a. in all possible worlds.
   b. in the worlds in which it occurs.
   c. when it is synthetic.
   d. when it is analytic.
3. When I say that a certain proposition is true in a given world, I am giving its
   a. truth-value.
   b. truth table.
   c. truth-conditions.
   d. truth function.
4. When we say that semantic disjunction is inclusive, we mean that
   a. if p is true and q is true, $p \vee q$ is true.
   b. if p is true and q is false, $p \vee q$ is true.
   c. if p is true and q is true, $p \vee q$ is false.
   d. if p is false and q is false, $p \vee q$ is false.
5. (This one is a lot easier than it looks!) In a world in which p and q are true and r is false, what's the truth value of the formula $r \rightarrow (((q \wedge r) \vee (p \vee q)) \vee \neg(p \wedge r)) \wedge (\neg q \wedge p)$?
   a. true.
   b. false.

c   neither true nor false.
d   impossible to determine.

6   Which of the following is a three-place predicate?
    a   eat.
    b   lend.
    c   sharpen.
    d   glow.

7   HAPPY(x) is best expressed in English as:
    a   someone is happy.
    b   everyone is happy.
    c   nobody is happy.
    d   x is happy.

8   Which of the following is the best English translation for the formula $\forall x \exists y((BOOK(y)) \land (SAD(x) \rightarrow READ(x,y)))$?
    a   'There is one book that all sad people read.'
    b   'For each person, there's a book they read when they're sad.'
    c   'All people are sad and read books'.
    d   'If there's a book and someone's sad, they read it'.

9   In the catchy formula $\forall x(SALTY(x) \rightarrow YUMMY(x))$, which of the following is true?
    a   SALTY(x) is within the scope of YUMMY(x).
    b   SALTY(x) is within the scope of the existential quantifier.
    c   YUMMY(x) is within the scope of the universal quantifier.
    d   YUMMY(x) is within the scope of the unbound variable.

10 Which of the following expresses an existential commitment?
    a   a universal quantifier.
    b   a free variable.
    c   an existential quantifier.
    d   a bound variable.

Comprehension questions:

I   Propositional logic: Answer questions 1-4 with respect to the following propositions:
    p = Nancy is nice.
    q = Mary likes mice.
    r = Sage is a spice.

    1   Which of the following propositions are tautologies?
        a   If Nancy is nice and Mary likes mice, then Nancy is nice or sage is a spice.
        b   If Mary likes mice, then sage is a spice.
        c   Nancy is nice.
        d. Sage is a spice if and only if sage is a spice.
    2   Which of the following propositions are contradictions?
        a $(p \land \neg p)$
        b $\neg q$

c $((p \lor q) \land (\neg p \land \neg q))$
d $((p \land \neg p) \lor \neg q)$

3 Consider the proposition $((p \lor r) \to \neg p)$.
   a How would you translate this proposition into English?
   b If p, q, and r are all true, is this proposition true or false?
   c Is it analytic or synthetic?
   d Rewrite the proposition, turning the conditional into a biconditional.

4 How would you translate the following into propositional logic notation?
   Either sage is a spice and Nancy is nice, or Mary likes mice and sage is not a spice.

II Predicate logic: Imagine a world that contains the following entities:
i=Imelda   h=Harold   k=Kevin   j=Jackie

And here are some true statements about this world:

Harold is an elegant goldfish.   *Kevin bothers Harold.*
Kevin is an athletic cat.   *Kevin bothers Imelda.*
Jackie is a cat.   *Harold fears Jackie.*
Imelda is a goldfish.   *Imelda is delicious.*

Assume no other properties are true of these entities. (Therefore, for example, you can assume that Jackie is not elegant.) Answer the following questions.

1 For each of the following: (i) give the English translation (as in, for example, 'everything's a goldfish', not as in 'for all x, x is a goldfish' – that is, have your translation be colloquial and free of variables), **AND** (ii) tell whether it's true or false.
   a $\exists x \exists y (FEARS(x,y))$
   b $DELICIOUS(i) \land BOTHERS(k,i)$
   c $\forall x (ELEGANT(x) \to GOLDFISH(x))$
   d $\exists x \forall y (CAT(y) \to BOTHERS(x,y))$

2 Translate each of the following into predicate logic notation, and tell whether it's true or false. (12 points – 3 points each)
   a Kevin bothers everyone, and Imelda is delicious.
   b There's an elegant goldfish that fears a cat.
   c If Jackie is a cat, then Imelda is a goldfish.
   d There's one individual who fears all cats, or Kevin is athletic.

III Scope: Answer each of the following questions.

1 Analyze the following conversation, describing each participant's interpretation of 'there is one true soul mate for every person' and giving the corresponding predicate-logic notation. (Use 'SOULMATE' for the predicate *is a true soul mate of*.)
   A: I believe there is one true soul mate for every person.
   B: He must be very busy.

(Scott Adams, 'Dilbert' comic strip)

2. Give an interpretation in English for each of the following:
   a. $\exists x \forall y (LOVE(x,y))$
   b. $\forall x \exists y (LOVE(x,y))$
   c. $\forall x \exists y (LOVE(x,y) \rightarrow HUG(x,y))$
   d. $\exists x \forall y (LOVE(x,y) \rightarrow HUG(x,y))$

   How do the worlds described by (2c) and (2d) differ?

Opinion questions:

1. What effect does adding the word *either* have on a sentence containing *or*? Consider examples like these:
   a. You're welcome to have cake or pie.
   b. You're welcome to have either cake or pie.
   In your opinion, is this effect truth-conditional? That is, does it change the truth-conditions of the sentence?
2. What are the advantages and disadvantages of using the metalanguage described in this chapter? Do you find it helpful, excessively cumbersome, or both? Are the advantages worth the trouble? (Note: The system goes way beyond what we've done here, and is used for a whole lot more types of analysis, so you might change your views with further study; but given what you've seen and used so far, what do you think?)
3. With a sufficiently worked out metalanguage, do you imagine we could describe a 'language of thought' that expresses all possible meanings, independent of any particular human language? (Researchers disagree on this!) Explain your reasoning.

Discussion questions:

1. What is the logical relationship between the following two sentences? How are they used in natural language?
   a. You'll finish your peas or you'll go to bed without dessert.
   b. If you don't finish your peas, you'll go to bed without dessert.
   If we represent *you finish your peas* as *p* and *you go to bed without dessert* as *q*, can a truth table help us? Consider the following:

   $(p \vee q) \leftrightarrow (\neg p \rightarrow q)$

   Do the truth table for this formula. How does the result bear on the discussion?
2. Consider the following two sentences:
   a. With your entrée, you may have soup or salad.
   Even on the reading where you may have only one of the two, both of the following are nonetheless true:
   b. With your entrée, you may have soup.

c   With your entrée, you may have salad.
   And yet the very stilted-sounding example in (d) below behaves quite differently:
   d   It's the case that you may have soup, or it's the case that you may have salad.
   Here, an exclusive-*or* reading excludes the possibility of both (e) and (f) being simultaneously true:
   e   It's the case that you may have soup.
   f   It's the case that you may have salad.
   In light of this, is $p \vee q$ a fair representation of (a)? How does (a) differ from (d)?
3. As mentioned in the discussion of example (35) above, a speaker can use a tautology to convey something that isn't tautological at all. Think of a couple more examples where someone might do this. Where do you think the intended, nontautological meaning comes from? How does the hearer know what's intended?

Data collection and analysis:

1. Choose a sentence from a novel, and give two entailments and two paraphrases of it. Now make minor changes in order to make it a) redundant, and b) contradictory.
2. Find three examples of scope ambiguity online, and for each, give two predicate-logic formulas to disambiguate the two readings. If you have trouble finding examples, keep in mind that you can think of, and then search for, examples that are similar in form to the ambiguous examples discussed in this chapter.
3. Find three naturally occurring examples of exclusive *or* and three naturally occurring examples of inclusive *or*.
4. In a 2018 interview with Chuck Todd, Rudy Giuliani said, *truth isn't truth*. Here's a snippet of the exchange:

   Giuliani: And when you tell me that, you know, he should testify because he's going to tell the truth and he shouldn't worry, well that's so silly because it's somebody's version of the truth. Not the truth ...
   Todd: Truth is truth. I don't mean to go like —
   Giuliani: No, it isn't truth. Truth isn't truth.

   (Phillips 2018)

   Obviously, *truth isn't truth* is semantically contradictory, and Giuliani took plenty of criticism for it. Look up the context of the exchange; what do you think Giuliani was trying to convey? Compare this exchange with the invented one in example (35). Are they similar or different? Was it fair for Giuliani to be criticized for saying that truth isn't truth? You might (or might not) find it helpful to compare this question with Discussion Question (2) above.

Answers to self-test:

1. c
2. a
3. a
4. a
5. a
6. b
7. d
8. b
9. c
10. c

CHAPTER 4

Pragmatics I: The Cooperative Principle

> **KEY CONCEPTS**
>
> - Cooperative Principle
> - maxims of Quantity, Quality, Relation, Manner
> - fulfill, flout, violate, opt out of (a maxim), maxim clash
> - implicate, implicature, conversational implicature
> - infer, inference
> - scalar implicature
> - tests for conversational implicature: cancellable/defeasible, calculable, nonconventional
> - conventional implicature
> - generalized/particularized conversational implicature
> - post-Gricean, neo-Gricean
> - explicature
> - impliciture
> - Q- and R-principles
> - Division of Pragmatic Labor
> - Q-, I-, and M-heuristics
> - Relevance theory: Cognitive and Communicative Principles of Relevance
> - what is said

We've already seen quite a few examples of cases where the meaning of logical connectives like '∧', '∨' and '→' don't seem to match the way the corresponding English connectives (*and*, *or*, and *if...then*) are used in natural conversation. We've see this in examples like these:

(1) a I fell off my bike and broke my leg. [= ch. 3, ex. 19]
  b You will finish your peas or you won't get dessert! [= ch. 3, ex. 23]
  c If you finish your peas, you can have dessert.

The logical meaning of *and* has nothing to do with ordering or causation; if *and* corresponds to ∧, then *p and q* is true just in case *p* is true and *q* is true. But if someone says (1a),

DOI: 10.4324/9781003351214-4

FIGURE 4.1 Courtesy of xkcd.com.

you're almost certainly going to understand them to mean two additional things: first, that the falling off the bike happened first, and second, that the fall caused the broken leg. And in (1b) we see our old friend exclusive *or*; if your mom says this to your kid brother, he's likely to assume that only one of the two clauses will hold – either he'll finish his peas or he won't get dessert – even though the logical meaning of *or* allows for both to be true. And finally, in (1c), we get what's called **conditional strengthening**: Even though $p \rightarrow q$ is true whenever p is false (so 1c is true if the kid doesn't finish his peas but still gets dessert), we're nonetheless likely to assume in (1c) that if he doesn't finish his peas he won't get dessert – which is usually the whole point of saying it. That is, in interpreting (1c), we strengthen the meaning from *if p then q* to *if and only if p, then q* – i.e., we strengthen it from the conditional $p \rightarrow q$ to the biconditional $p \leftrightarrow q$.

So: Do we care? Well, a philosopher named H. Paul Grice did. He set out to argue that the natural-language connectives do, in fact, have their logical meanings, but that when they're interpreted in context, there are a set of rules we naturally follow that 'fill out' these additional meanings. His **Cooperative Principle** was groundbreaking and opened up a whole new way of seeing how people are able to understand each other in conversation. In short, it gave us a whole new way of getting from the **semantic** meaning of a sentence to its **pragmatic** meaning when it's used in context.

REPRISE: SEMANTICS VS. PRAGMATICS

We've spent the past two chapters considering the semantic meanings of words and sentences – essentially, their literal, conventional, truth-conditional meaning (while acknowledging that those three things aren't necessarily identical; stay tuned for more on that issue). And you'll recall that the pragmatic meaning of an utterance goes beyond its strictly literal meaning to include the meaning that the speaker intended by using **that** sentence in **that** context. The tricky thing is, how on earth do you know what the speaker intended? It's easy enough (well, not really) in semantics: Since semantic meaning is conventional, it's at least shared. But pragmatic meaning can change from context to context. So I can say (2):

(2)   Lovely weather we're having.

And if it's a warm sunny day in June, you'll probably take me to be making a sincere comment about the beauty of the day, whereas if it's the middle of a February blizzard in Chicago, you'll probably take me to be sarcastically saying exactly the opposite. And of course this is perfectly obvious to you, but **why** is it obvious? What role does the semantic meaning play in helping us work out the pragmatic meaning, and how do we get from the semantic meaning to the pragmatic meaning? This is the problem Grice addressed in his Cooperative Principle. (And we'll see a bit later on that framing it as getting 'from the semantic meaning to the pragmatic meaning' turns out to not be quite accurate – but one thing at a time.)

THE COOPERATIVE PRINCIPLE

Grice's insight, in a nutshell, is that when we communicate, we try to be cooperative: We say things in a way that we think will make it easy for our listener to understand us. And the listener, in turn, gets to assume that we're doing exactly that. So the listener uses this assumption of cooperative behavior to help them get to the most 'cooperative' meaning in light of what the speaker said.

Here's the way Grice put it:

> **The Cooperative Principle:**
> **Make your conversational contribution such as is required, at the stage at which it occurs, by the accepted purpose or direction of the talk exchange in which you are engaged.**
>
> (Grice 1975)

Now, the first thing to point out is that even though this is stated as a command, Grice wasn't really telling anybody what to do. Remember that linguistic rules are descriptive, not prescriptive; so what he's doing here is **describing** how speakers behave. He doesn't have to tell us to be cooperative, because we're already doing that. He's just pointing it out.

The Cooperative Principle (CP) is a very wordy way of saying, essentially, 'in conversation, be cooperative': Make your contribution appropriate at this moment in this conversation.

Or, more accurately: In conversation, people **are** cooperative; they make appropriate contributions.

And this is something we generally do without thinking. Even when we think we're being supremely uncooperative – in a heated argument, say – we keep our utterances relevant and of appropriate length, and so on. So even if we're fighting with our spouse, we wouldn't respond to A's comment as B does here:

(3) A Dammit, you left the cap off the toothpaste tube again!
    B I really like apricots.

(Unless, of course, B's response is intended to convey 'I'm not going to engage in your topic', in which case it is totally relevant.) Instead, we're likely to respond with something contextually appropriate, like any of these responses:

(4) a Did not!
    b You're the one who left it off!
    c Who cares if the stupid toothpaste is capped?
    d Yeah, I prefer the cap off because it saves time unscrewing and rescrewing it.

These responses may display varying degrees of hostility, but they're all cooperative in the Gricean sense: They stick to the subject, they include the right level of detail, they're clear and concise, etc.

There are a very small number of contexts in which we do violate the CP, which we'll discuss below, but in general, we assume the folks we're talking with are trying to be cooperative. So in (3), A is likely to at least try to figure out the relevance of apricots to toothpaste before believing B is just spouting random nonsense.

As we'll see below, our assumption that we're both trying to be cooperative will give rise to **implicatures**, those elements of meaning above and beyond the semantics of the sentence. Terminologically, note that speakers **implicate** and hearers **infer** (and the word 'imply' has no part in pragmatics). We'll see plenty of examples below, as we work through the **maxims**, or subprinciples, of the CP. Grice listed a bunch of maxims and collected them together under four broad categories, but over time the four broad categories have themselves come to be known as the maxims of the CP, so we'll follow that practice.

The maxims

Here are the four maxims of the CP, along with their submaxims and the descriptions that Grice (1975) gave for them:

The maxim of Quantity

1   Make your contribution as informative as is required (for the current purposes of the exchange).
2   Do not make your contribution more informative than is required.

The maxim of Quality

Try to make your contribution one that is true.

1. Do not say what you believe to be false.
2. Do not say that for which you lack adequate evidence.

The maxim of Relation

Be relevant.

The maxim of Manner

Be perspicuous.

1. Avoid obscurity of expression.
2. Avoid ambiguity.
3. Be brief (avoid unnecessary prolixity).
4. Be orderly.

As you can see, taken together these are an effort to flesh out exactly what it means to be cooperative in a conversation: A cooperative speaker says enough but not too much, says only what's relevant, and so on. Speaker B in (3) has violated the maxim of Relation by saying something irrelevant.

We'll deal with each of the maxims in detail below, but first you should know that while you can **fulfill** the maxims (to use Grice's term), and may thereby create an implicature, there are also various ways in which you can fail to fulfill the maxims:

- You can quietly **violate** a maxim, in which case you may (perhaps intentionally) mislead your hearer.
- You can **flout** a maxim, by violating it so egregiously and blatantly that your hearer can't help but notice (and this is, in fact, what you intend); in this case an implicature will be generated.
- You can **opt out** altogether, by failing to cooperate and making it clear you're failing to cooperate.
- Or you may face a **clash** of maxims, requiring you to violate one maxim in order to fulfill another.

In the upcoming sections on the individual maxims, we'll see plenty of examples of fulfilling, violating, and flouting maxims, as well as examples of maxim clash. To opt out of the CP altogether is relatively rare but does happen. There's an argument to be made, for example, that pleading the Fifth Amendment in a U.S. court constitutes an assertion that you are opting out (by explicitly choosing not to answer the question(s) posed to you). Or you can opt out by simply walking out of the room rather than responding to a question, or by pretending you didn't hear it. Or consider a case like this one:

(5) A So has your friend Jim decided to take that other job and leave his current position?
    B I'm not at liberty to say.

In Grice's view, B here has opted out of the CP by letting A know that they will not be answering the question.

With that brief introduction to the maxims and their uses, we'll now take them one by one, with examples.

The maxim of Quantity

The maxim of Quantity has two parts:

1   Make your contribution as informative as is required (for the current purposes of the exchange).
2   Do not make your contribution more informative than is required.

These boil down to, basically, 'say enough, but don't say too much' – which means there's an interesting tension between them, which we'll discuss more later. For the moment, consider how fulfilling the maxim affects our interpretation of the second and last sentences in (6):

(6) What happened was the next thing to an explosion. Jagged pieces burst through the safety housing and ripped the forward part of the aircraft. The roto's momentum twisted the Stallion savagely around, and it dropped rapidly. Two of the men in the back, who had loosened their seatbelts, jerked out of their seats and rolled forward.
(Clancy 1984)

In the second sentence, we're told that *jagged pieces ... ripped the forward part of the aircraft*. Upon seeing this, a reader will generally infer that **only** the forward part was ripped, and not the rear. Similarly, in the last sentence we're told that *two of the men in the back ... jerked out of their seats and rolled forward*. Again, the reader will generally infer that only two did so, and not, say, three or four. Where do these inferences come from?

They are the result of **scalar implicatures**. There's an implicit scale in each case. In these cases, the scales run from 'less' to 'more': Part of an aircraft is less than the whole thing, and two of the men are fewer than three or four. If an entire aircraft is ripped by jagged pieces, it's also true that this has happened to the forward part, so the second sentence would be true even if the whole thing had gotten ripped up. But the maxim of Quantity tells us that a speaker should (and typically does) give as much information as required; so if the whole aircraft had been ripped by the jagged pieces, the speaker should have said so, and it would be uncooperative of them not to. That's why we can infer that if they only mentioned half the plane getting ripped up, that's the only half that did.

The situation is similar in the case of a number, as in the last sentence. If you tell me something happened to two people, that **licenses** me (roughly, gives me good reason) to infer that it didn't happen to four or six or 85 people. If someone tells you they have three children, you can safely infer they don't have a fourth one that they just chose not to mention.

But context can make a big difference:

(7) In Chicago, for example, you must be 21 to sell/serve alcohol…
(www2.illinois.gov/ilcc/about/Pages/FAQs-legal.aspx)

What's interesting here is that the reader will generally interpret this as meaning you must be **at least** 21 to serve alcohol, not that you must be exactly 21; the law obviously doesn't prohibit 22-year-olds from serving alcohol. (That would be a truly odd law.)

So why is it that a reader encountering *two* in (6) reads it as 'no more than two', while the reader encountering *21* in (7) doesn't read it as 'no more than 21'? It's the context, of course: By default, uttering an amount will induce a scalar implicature to the effect that no higher amount holds, for the reason given above: If it were true of more than two of the men, the writer shouldn't have said *two of the men*. But in (7) what's relevant is a minimum age, not a maximum age, because we know from general life experience that any law about who gets to drink, sell, serve, or otherwise handle alcohol will have to do with the minimum age they must attain, not the maximum or absolute age.

This example brings up an important point, which is that, as noted above, a speaker or writer may face a clash of maxims. The simplest case is where, say, Quantity clashes with Quality: Quantity says to say enough, and saying that 100 men came out of their seats is more informative than saying that two did – but if it's not true that 100 men did, Quantity runs up against Quality, and the writer is prevented by Quality from saying what they know to be false. In (7), there's a clash between Quantity and Relation, with Relation telling the writer to keep it relevant – and since the reader knows this, they can assume that the writer is talking about a minimum age (not the maximum age, and not the only permitted age), since that's what's relevant where alcohol is concerned. So the clash between Quantity and Relation helps the reader to get to the intended meaning, in that the reader needs to look at the context and determine how to weight the maxims to get at the most likely meaning.

So we've seen cases where the speaker fulfills the maxim of Quantity, and where they opt out of the maxims altogether, and where they deal with a maxim clash. The remaining two ways in which you can fail to fulfill a maxim are by violating it and by flouting it. A great example of a violation comes from a much-cited court case in which a certain Mr. Bronston was on trial for perjury. The claim was that he'd perjured himself by lying before the court in a previous trial. Here's the relevant dialog from that trial (Solan and Tiersma 2005:213):

(8) Q Do you have any bank accounts in Swiss banks, Mr. Bronston?
     A No, sir.
     Q Have you ever?
     A The company had an account there for about six months, in Zurich.

It turns out that Bronston had once had a very large Swiss bank account. So here he has clearly not said as much as is necessary; that is, he's violated the maxim of Quantity. And since his hearers will expect him to be fulfilling the maxim – saying as much as is necessary, hence mentioning any accounts he's had – his utterance implicates that he had no personal account in a Swiss bank. So he's implicating something false. On the other hand, he hasn't said anything that's semantically false; it's true that the company had any account in Zurich for about six months. The question is, did he lie? And that's a really interesting question, because it gets to the heart of what we consider 'truth' and what it means in court to tell 'the truth, the whole truth, and nothing but the truth'. Did Mr. Bronston tell the whole truth?

The initial court convicted him of perjury, but he appealed. The appeals court agreed with the lower court that he was guilty of perjury. But the U.S. Supreme Court disagreed and overturned the conviction, on the grounds that what he said was true. According to the Supreme Court, it was up to the lawyer to notice that Bronston hadn't really answered the question being asked, and to press him on it. In the broadest terms, what makes this case so interesting is that it addresses the place of pragmatic information in our courts: When Bronston implicates (but doesn't say!) that he didn't have a personal account in a Swiss bank, is he responsible for having purposefully misled the court (which he most certainly did)? Or should a witness be free to implicate as much false information as they want, so long as they don't say anything that's semantically false?

BOX 4.1

"I like beer"

In September of 2018, Brett Kavanaugh appeared before the Senate Judiciary Committee as a nominee for the Supreme Court, and had been accused of committing a sexual assault at a high school party after consuming alcohol. As part of those proceedings, this fascinating exchange took place:

Q: Did you consume alcohol during your high school years?

Kavanaugh: Yes, we drank beer, my friends and I, boys and girls. Yes, we drank beer. I liked beer. Still like beer. We drank beer. The drinking age, as I noted, was 18, so the seniors were legal; senior year in high school people were legal to drink. And yeah, we drank beer, and I said, sometimes, sometimes I probably had too many beers, and sometimes other people had too many beers. We drank beer. We liked beer.

What makes this fascinating is that Kavanaugh mentions beer no fewer than ten times during an exchange that lasts less than a minute – eight times stating either that he liked/drank beer then or that he still does, and the other two stating that either he or his friends sometimes had too many beers. And note that the question doesn't even mention beer specifically. (You can see video clips of this exchange by searching online for 'Brett Kavanaugh I like beer'.) By any measure, this is a violation of Quantity1; he's saying too much and saying it too often. What's going on?

> There was a great deal of commentary afterward on just this question, and there's no one right answer. Could it be that *We drank beer* was intended to invoke a scalar implicature to the effect that they drank only beer – that is, to steer the hearers away from thinking harder liquor was consumed? Was it to hammer home a point about how common a thing beer-drinking was, or (as some commentators suggested) to evoke a sense of being manly or 'one of the boys'? Was it intended to be read defiantly, essentially daring the hearer to disapprove of this enjoyment of beer? Or was it a variation on the classic *The lady doth protest too much* from Shakespeare's *Hamlet*, but with the twist of affirming, rather than protesting, too much? What do you think Kavanaugh is implicating with his many rapid-fire assertions of liking and drinking beer?
>
> One thing is clear: A nervous person trying very hard to say the right thing will be in danger of saying it far too many times and too enthusiastically, and will thereby betray the very thing they're trying **not** to betray – in this case, perhaps, just how much they like beer.

Finally, let's consider what a flouting of Quantity would be like. To adapt one of Grice's examples, suppose a student asks me for a letter of recommendation for graduate school, and I write something like this:

(9) Dear Admissions Committee:

My student Jane Doe has asked me for a letter of recommendation, and I'm happy to write one. Jane was a student in my Intro to Linguistics class. She came to class regularly, arrived promptly, and had excellent handwriting. She took all of the exams.

Sincerely, (etc.)

Do you suppose Jane will get into this graduate school? I doubt it. But why not? This letter is 100% positive; I've said nothing negative at all, and everything I've said is relevant. The problem is that I haven't said enough: There's all sorts of stuff a letter of recommendation ought to mention that I've left out, like whether Jane is smart, hard-working, a good writer, insightful, engaged, whether she actually passed those exams, and so on.

In light of what I've left out, my reader has two choices: They can either decide that I don't know what's needed for a good letter of recommendation, or they can decide that I **do** know what's needed, and I've gone to some trouble to avoid providing it. Since the first option is highly unlikely, it's the second that wins out: What I've done is to flout the maxim of Quantity by writing a letter that's so blatantly insufficient, falling so obviously short of what should be included, that I clearly expect the reader to notice. It's a tidy way of making my point clear (Jane's a terrible student) without stating it flat out. (Incidentally, this is why you should never simply ask your professor to write a letter of recommendation; instead, ask them if they'd feel comfortable writing a **strong** letter of recommendation.)

The maxim of Quality

Now that we've seen examples of fulfilling, flouting, and violating a maxim (as well as examples of maxim clash and opting out), we can move a bit more quickly through the remaining maxims.

The maxim of Quality says:

Try to make your contribution one that is true.

1   Do not say what you believe to be false.
2   Do not say that for which you lack adequate evidence.

Notice that Grice doesn't actually say, more straightforwardly, 'speak the truth' or 'don't say what isn't true' – for the simple reason that we don't always know what is and isn't true. I can't guarantee that what I say is true, but I can at least avoid saying what I believe is false, and what I don't really have any evidence for.

The implicature generated by fulfilling this maxim is not too exciting: By saying X, I implicate that I believe X is true, and therefore that it is indeed true. Fair enough. And to violate the maxim of Quality is to say something I believe is false – which is, usually, a lie.

But the interesting thing is that it may not always be a lie. Remember from Box 2.3 that Coleman and Kay (1981) did a terrific study showing that people treat the notion of a 'lie' as gradient, essentially as a fuzzy set in Prototype theory. In Coleman and Kay's account, you'll recall, a prototypical lie has three properties:

- It is false.
- The speaker believes it's false.
- In uttering it, the speaker intends to deceive the hearer.

And it's possible for an utterance to have zero, one, two, or all three of these properties. I can say something false that I believe is true, or something true that I believe is false. Or I can say something I think is false without intending to deceive the hearer (10a), or something I think is true while nonetheless intending to deceive the hearer:

(10)   a   I've eaten a ton of food today.
       b   Hmm… I just saw Jane with Herman.

In (10a), I've clearly said something false (I can't have eaten a literal ton of food), and I clearly know it's false, but I don't intend to mislead the hearer, since I know they'll know this is an exaggeration. Thus, this is a clear flouting of Quality; I've so clearly and egregiously violated the maxim that my hearer will know they're supposed to notice and draw an appropriate inference.

In (10b), I may indeed have seen Jane with Herman – in which case I've said something that's true and which I know is true. But I can still use it to try to mislead my hearer: So let's say I'm talking to Fred, and Jane is his wife, and for some nasty reason I want him to think she's being unfaithful. Depending on the context, I could well use (10b) to implicate that Jane is having an affair with Herman.

Now recall that Coleman and Kay found that the three properties of a lie aren't equally weighted. Instead, the most important factor is whether the speaker believes their statement is false, the second most important factor is whether the speaker intends to deceive the hearer, and the LEAST important factor is whether the statement was in fact false. So subjects in their experiment were far more likely to say an utterance was a lie if it was actually true but the speaker thought it was false than if it was false but the speaker thought it was true. That is to say, a purposeful violation of Quality tends to be judged as a lie – but not so much because it's false as because the speaker believes it's false.

We've seen a flouting of Quality in (10a), but it's worth noting that there's quite a range of ways in which you can flout Quality, including sarcasm, irony, and others:

(11) a Yeah, that Smith's a real genius.
   b Great weather again today.
   c If I do any more studying tonight, my brain will explode.
   d I'm parked behind the drugstore.
   e The White House issued a statement on climate change today.

If Smith has just said something profoundly stupid, I can use (11a) sarcastically to implicate that Smith is quite the opposite of a genius, and similarly in the middle of a brutal Chicago winter, I can use (11b) to implicate that the weather is the opposite of great. In (11c) let's hope nobody's brain will really explode. More subtly, in (11d) I'm not parked behind the drugstore at all, although my car presumably is. And in (11e), let's hope the White House itself hasn't developed the ability to speak, but rather that a spokesperson for the presidential administration issued the statement.

The notion of a Quality flouting is amusingly noted in this article ranking holiday songs:

(12) "(There's No Place Like Home) For the Holidays." I like that this is an entire song dedicated to selling you on the concept of going home for the holidays. This song both goes too hard and not hard enough. It suggests you will be "happy in a million ways" when you go home (this is just objectively incorrect, even if you do like your family) and then mentions the traffic. Pick one, song.

(Petri 2018)

Here the writer feigns an inability to see the obvious implicature behind the blatantly false *million ways*.

In a more serious vein, consider this example from Michael Cohen's written testimony to the House Oversight Committee:

(13) Mr. Trump did not directly tell me to lie to Congress. That's not how he operates. In conversations we had during the campaign, at the same time I was actively negotiating in Russia for him, he would look me in the eye and tell me there's no business in Russia and then go out and lie to the American people by saying the same thing. In his way, he was telling me to lie.

(AP, 2/27/19; token courtesy of Liz Coppock)

Here Cohen is saying that Trump would say something that he and Cohen both knew to be false – a flouting of Quality – and in that way, Trump would implicate that Cohen should repeat the falsehood to the American people. The interesting thing is that since the American people would not necessarily know it to be false, it would at that point (when Cohen repeated it) not be a flouting, but rather a violation, hence (by Cohen's own report) a lie. So what Trump said to Cohen was not quite a lie, but upon Cohen's repeating it to the American people, it definitely would be – another instance of the importance of context and mutual beliefs in communication.

The maxim of Relation

The maxim of Relation is super-quick and straightforward. It says simply:

> Be relevant.

What could be easier? But we'll see that this maxim gives rise to some very interesting implicatures, and indeed, as we'll see later, it serves as the basis for an influential later theory of pragmatics.

In general, when one utterance follows another, the maxim of Relation licenses us to infer that the two have something to do with each other:

(14) a I have a doctor's appointment today. I've been having sharp stomach pains.
 b Have you seen George today? I need this form signed.
 c Have you had lunch yet? I'm hungry.
 d I need to run to the store later. I'm out of milk.

These are all pretty straightforward: The speaker in (14a) implicates that the doctor's appointment is for the purpose of getting the stomach pains checked out, the speaker in (14b) implicates that they need George to sign the form, the speaker in (14c) implicates an invitation to have lunch together, and the speaker in (14d) implicates that they'll be buying milk at the store.

You can probably imagine situations in which this isn't the case – for example, in (14b), a situation in which the question about George and the need to have the form signed have nothing to do with each other. And you can make use of precisely that kind of misleading use of Relation by violating it in order to implicate something false. So consider a twist on the Jane/Herman example from (10b) above:

(15) A Why has Jane been looking so happy all of a sudden?
 B Well, I keep seeing her with Herman.

Now, it may be that Jane spends lots of time with Herman because they're co-workers, or volunteers for the same organization, or she's buying a car from him. But in the context here, B implicates that the relationship between Jane and Herman is causing her happiness, perhaps because they're in a romantic relationship. If B knows perfectly well that Jane is simply buying a car from Herman and has been coming around for test drives and to work out payments, etc., but B intends to implicate a romantic relationship without **technically** lying, their utterance in (15) is a violation of Relation that can serve that purpose. (But see the discussion above of *lie* as a gradient category, which greatly complicates the question of what is 'technically' a lie.)

In considering implicatures based on the maxim of Relation, note that the relevance in question needn't always be between two utterances; it can also be between an utterance and the context in which it occurs. Consider the following statement that is required by the FDA to appear on any table salt that doesn't contain iodide:

(16)   This salt does not supply iodide, a necessary nutrient.

This is only one utterance, so we're not considering the relationship between it and any other utterance, but rather the relationship between it and the context – specifically, its appearance on a container of salt. Now, on the face of it, you could argue that this is a weird statement; after all, there are plenty of other necessary nutrients that table salt doesn't supply: Protein, fat, vitamin C, vitamin A, and lots of others. And the package doesn't list any of those as being absent from the salt. So why specify iodide? The answer, of course, is that many table salts **do** contain iodide. (None, on the other hand, contain protein, etc.) So iodide is the only relevant nutrient in this context, the only one that a consumer might be wondering about. And if you didn't already know that many salts contain iodide, the statement in (16) in combination with the maxim of Relation would be enough to clue you in to this fact, and might even make you wonder whether this should affect your choice of salt.

So what would a flouting of Relation look like? Let's bring back our friend the Gricean letter of recommendation from (9) above, but this time instead of giving too little information (and thus flouting the maxim of Quantity) we'll give irrelevant information (and thus flout the maxim of Relation):

(17)   Dear Admissions Committee:

My student John Doe has asked me for a letter of recommendation for your graduate program in Linguistics, and I'm happy to write one. John was a student in my Intro to Linguistics class. He has excellent skills in soccer, art, and music, and he especially excels in the kitchen. He makes a jambalaya that can make you weep with joy. I admire him for his values, which have led him to volunteer for a wide range of charitable causes, from the local animal shelter to a campus beautification project. He has personally planted a lovely garden behind the Linguistics building, which brightens the day of everyone who sees it. In addition, he is one of the finest athletes on the soccer team, and scored the winning goal in the last game. In short, John has many artistic and culinary skills, and devotes large amounts of time to sports and volunteering. I hope this helps you decide whether John is right for your Linguistics program.
Sincerely, (etc.)

Okay, this is a significantly longer letter than the one I wrote for Jane in (9), and once again, everything I've said is positive – but once again, the applicant will be rejected. Why? Obviously, because nothing I've commented on – not his cooking, nor his gardening, nor his sports, nor his volunteerism – has anything to do with his ability to succeed in a graduate program in linguistics. I have flouted the maxim of Relation by giving only irrelevant information, and my reader will see it and draw the appropriate inference. Between the letter in (9) and this one, we can see is precisely why 'damning with faint praise' works so well.

BOX 4.2

What the meaning of the word *is* is

What's the meaning of the word *is*? Seems like an easy question, but in 1998 the attention of the country was focused on exactly this issue, when the President of the United States used this question and a tidy Gricean implicature to his advantage.

President Bill Clinton was under investigation for (among other things) having had an affair with Monica Lewinsky, which he denied. During a deposition, his lawyer, Robert Bennett, stated that "there is absolutely no sex of any kind" between Clinton and Lewinsky. Later, Clinton was challenged on this point, and was asked: "Whether or not Mr. Bennett knew of your relationship with Ms. Lewinsky, the statement that there was 'no sex of any kind in any manner, shape or form, with President Clinton', was an utterly false statement. Is that correct?" Clinton's response? "It depends upon what the meaning of the word *is* is." He then clarified: "If it means is, and never has been, that's one thing. If it means, there is none, that was a completely true statement."

Needless to say, that's technically true: The word *is* is present tense, and that's part of its meaning. So when Bennett said *There is absolutely no sex...*, he was saying something true; they had broken off their sexual relationship prior to that utterance. So Clinton here is showing that he's good with semantics. But he's even better with pragmatics: He knows darn well that Bennett was trying to convey something false – that is, that Clinton and Lewinsky not only weren't currently in a sexual relationship, but never had been. Since what's relevant in context is whether they had **ever** had a sexual relationship during Clinton's presidency, Bennett's response subtly violates the maxims of both Relation and Quantity1 by not saying what's relevant and by not saying enough.

At the very least, he's implicating (but not saying) that there was no sexual relationship at any point (i.e., that what he's saying is the most he can relevantly say); he's doubtless also hoping nobody will notice the difference or the fact that he's failed to be optimally relevant. And Clinton, playing innocent, backs him up: What he said was literally true. The truth came out, of course, as it generally does, but we see here an excellent example of the difference between semantics and pragmatics being used at the highest levels of government to influence the understanding of a nation.

The maxim of Manner

This one's a bit of a grab-bag:

Be perspicuous.

1. Avoid obscurity of expression.
2. Avoid ambiguity.
3. Be brief (avoid unnecessary prolixity).
4. Be orderly.

It's sometimes summarized as 'be brief, clear, and unambiguous'. The 'be brief' submaxim is similar to the second submaxim of Quantity, 'do not make your contribution more informative than is required' (and we'll talk more about that later). And many people have wondered whether the parenthetical in submaxim 3 is a little joke: *Prolixity* means excessive wordiness, so once you've said 'be brief', adding 'avoid unnecessary prolixity' is simply, well, unnecessary prolixity.

To see some Manner-based implicatures at work, let's consider the first submaxim, 'avoid obscurity of expression'. And returning to my unhelpful letters of recommendation, let's suppose that having written on behalf of Jane Doe and John Doe, I now write a letter for their sister Doris Doe, in which I say, among other things:

(18) Doris displays an interesting range of mental capabilities.

If what I want to say is that Doris is intelligent, or insightful, or clever, there are plenty of briefer and clearer ways to say it (such as *intelligent* or *insightful* or *clever*). By choosing the obscure expression that I've used, I convey, once again, that none of these quicker and clearer expressions would quite be appropriate. And presumably you're way ahead of me in noticing that (18) is also unnecessarily prolix.

These various floutings show an interesting way in which the Cooperative Principle works: The addressee wants to preserve, at all costs, their belief that the speaker or writer is trying to be cooperative. When it might seem that they haven't been cooperative in that they're apparently violating a maxim, as in (18), the addressee will go to some lengths to figure out a way in which they're nonetheless being cooperative. So when I write (18), I'm counting on my reader to not simply decide I'm being purposely unhelpful; they'll want to preserve the assumption of cooperativity. One way they can do that is to interpret (18) as a flouting intended to implicate my inability to say truthfully that Doris is intelligent, and that's how they get to the inference that I don't think she is.

Another reason to be purposefully obscure is to implicate that you don't want someone else to understand what's being said, as with (19) uttered in the presence of a toddler:

(19) Oh, please say we can have dinner somewhere other than M-C-D-O-N-A-L-D-S.

Here the last word is spelled out specifically in order to be obscure, and the flouting of Manner is likely to achieve its goal.

The second submaxim, 'avoid ambiguity', is often flouted for comic effect, as in the case of puns:

(20) The most remarkable object in a classroom is the whiteboard.

See, a whiteboard can be re-marked…. Okay, I'll spare you any more puns.
The third submaxim tells us to be brief, and we've already seen it at work in (18). Consider also (21):

(21) I travelled across country and joined the local train midway, expecting to find Sebastian already established; there he was, however, in the next carriage to mine, and when I asked him what he was doing, Mr. Samgrass replied with such glibness and at such length, telling me of mislaid luggage and of Cook's being shut over the holidays, that I was at once aware of some other explanation which was being withheld.

(Waugh 1945)

Here Samgrass is violating the maxim by not being brief at all, and in doing so, he accidentally betrays the fact that he's trying to hide the truth.

The fourth submaxim, 'be orderly', is the source of some of those pesky inferences associated with the word *and*. I say 'pesky' because, you'll recall, they were among the inferences that set Grice off on this whole search for the relationship between semantic and pragmatic meaning in the interpretation of the logical connectives. So at this point it's worth pausing to see where we've landed with respect to his efforts – which will also involve looking more closely at the maxims.

Revisiting Grice's problem

So recall the problem Grice was addressing in his landmark paper: The logical meanings of connectives like *and* and *or* don't always seem to match the meanings they have in natural-language settings. Suppose you encounter the following recipe instructions:

(22) a   Slide pizza onto stone or steel and bake until cheese is melted and crust underbelly is spotty brown, 6 to 12 minutes total.

(www.seriouseats.com/recipes/2013/05/vodka-pizza-recipe.html)

b   Sift together the flour and cocoa and, in a separate bowl, cream together the margarine and sugar.

(Karmel 2007)

c. There is a lot of oil in shredded coconut and it will burn quickly.

(www.tampabay.com/things-to-do/food/cooking/cookclub-recipe-no-36-baked-coconut-shrimp-with-curry-mango-sauce-w-video/2218514/)

In (22a), *Slide pizza onto stone or steel and bake* implicates an ordering: First slide the pizza onto the stone or steel, and then bake. In (22b), there's no such ordering; a set of ingredients must be sifted together in one bowl and another must be creamed together in another bowl, but it doesn't matter what order those two things happen in. And in (22c), rather than an ordering, what's implicated is causation: The oil in the shredded coconut will cause it to burn quickly.

The ordering in (22a) and the causation in (22c) go beyond the logical meaning of the conjunction, and the question facing Grice was whether the English connective *and* had a different meaning from the logical connective ∧. His conclusion was that the semantic meaning of English *and* does in fact correspond to ∧, in that *p*∧*q* is true whenever *p* is true and *q* is true – but that when you put that semantic meaning into a context and take into account the Cooperative Principle, additional meanings can be inferred. So in (22a), the fourth submaxim of Manner ('be orderly') leads to the inference that if an ordering is relevant, the elements should be presented in the appropriate order: First things first. (This is also why it drives me crazy to encounter a recipe that says something like *Mix the dry ingredients together, after sifting the flour*. By the time I see *after sifting the flour*, I've already mixed the unsifted flour into the other dry ingredients. This is also why you should always read a recipe all the way through before beginning.)

In (22b), there's no implicature of ordering, because the reader can see that ordering isn't relevant in this case; the two mixtures are being made in two separate bowls, so ordering doesn't matter. In (22c), Relation comes into play: Why did you just tell me about the oil content of coconut if it's not relevant to the burning that you're now warning me about?

Now, remember from Chapter 3 that the logical meaning of ∨ (corresponding to English *or*) is 'inclusive', which means that if both *p* and *q* are true, then *p*∨*q* is also true. But English *or* is frequently used in a way that seems to mean the opposite. So compare (23a) and (23b):

(23) a Camp, fish, swim or hike trails at the Big Birch Lakes Forest Recreation Area north of Melrose.

(http://files.dnr.state.mn.us/maps/state_parks/spk00136.pdf)

b I'm good with my clubs so I'm going to Hawaii or Vegas. Hawaii might be the safer bet so I can play more golf....

(www.thehackersparadise.com/forum/index.php?threads/5k-golf-vacation.8913044/)

In (23a) we see an example of 'inclusive *or*', which is to say the *or* that corresponds to the logical connective ∨. There's no suggestion that you can only choose one of the activities; in fact, you could choose to camp AND fish AND swim AND hike trails, and there's nothing about the *or* to suggest that this isn't allowed. But in (23b) we've got 'exclusive *or*': The writer clearly intends to go to either Hawaii or Vegas, but not both. That is, in this case of *p*∨*q*, either *p* holds or *q* holds, but they don't both hold. But that's not what the logical meaning of ∨ is, so what is it that's eliminating the 'both' possibility?

With the help of the Cooperative Principle, and specifically the maxim of Quantity, we can see this as a scalar implicature. The speaker in (23b) is in a position to know whether they'll be going to both Hawaii and Vegas, so if that were the case, according to Quantity, they should say as much as they truthfully can, so they should say *I'm going to Hawaii and Vegas*. Since they have chosen instead to say *I'm going to Hawaii or Vegas*, we can infer that they're not going to both, i.e., that *p* ('I'm going to Hawaii') and *q* ('I'm going to Vegas') are not both true. In essence, *Hawaii and Vegas* is more informative, so by choosing the less informative option, they're implicating that the more informative one doesn't hold.

Related reasoning gives us what's known as 'conditional strengthening', in which a conditional is interpreted as a biconditional:

(24) Look, if you clean your room, I'll put a sticker on your sticker chart.

(www.newyorker.com/humor/daily-shouts/please-please-clean-your-room)

Here, the child interprets $p \rightarrow q$ ('if p, then q') as the stronger $p \leftrightarrow q$ ('p if and only if q'). That is, *if you clean your room, I'll put a sticker on your chart* becomes *if and only if you clean your room, I'll put a sticker on your chart*. The conditional leaves it unspecified whether the kid gets a sticker if they don't clean their room, whereas the biconditional is clear: No clean room, no sticker. So where does the stronger reading come from?

Here it's a matter of Relation. Much as (22c) implicated causation by implicating that the oil in coconut was relevant to its tendency to burn, here the statement of *if you clean your room, I'll put a sticker on your chart* implicates via Relation that it's the room-cleaning that causes the sticker-granting; otherwise why mention the room-cleaning, if the kid's going to get the sticker anyway? So the implicature is: No clean room, no sticker. You get a sticker if – and only if – you clean your room.

In short, by proposing the Cooperative Principle, Grice has found a way to eat his cake and have it too: He can keep the logical meanings of the connectives, and he can keep their natural-language use by showing how the Cooperative Principle gets us from one to the other.

BOX 4.3

"I would like you to do us a favor though"

The first impeachment of President Donald Trump hinged to a large degree on this one sentence: *I would like you to do us a favor though*. Trump uttered the sentence during a July 25, 2019 phone call with President Volodymyr Zelensky of Ukraine that Trump considered 'perfect' and others considered, well, less than perfect. According to a White House memorandum (available at www.whitehouse.gov), this is the exchange in which that utterance occurred:

> Zelensky: I would also like to thank you for your great support in the area of defense. We are ready to continue to cooperate for the next steps specifically we are almost ready to buy more Javelins from the United States for defense purposes.
> Trump: I would like you to do us a favor though because our country has been through a lot and Ukraine knows a lot about it.

The two men have been talking about America's 'great support' of Ukraine in the area of defense, for which Zelensky is grateful. The favor in question turns out to be providing information that would be politically helpful to Trump. The question is, was this a *quid pro quo* – i.e., one thing in exchange for another? Which is to say, is Trump implicating here that the continued support in the area of defense depends on Zelensky's willingness to do this favor?

Since Trump has brought up the 'favor' in the context of defense support, the maxim of Relation would suggest that the favor is relevant to that support (and this reading is bolstered by the adverb *though*, which also suggests a connection).

If this isn't the case – that is, if Trump's bringing up the favor has nothing to do with defensive support – then it's a violation of Relation. Such changes of topic happen all the time, but they're frequently flagged with a change-of-topic discourse marker – anything from *So anyway* to an explicit *On another topic* in order to cancel the Relation-based implicature that what's being said now is relevant to what's been said before.

Cognitive scientist Steven Pinker argues in a *New York Times* opinion piece that the word *though* reinforces the implicature of relevance, because the word *though* "signals a violated expectation" (Pinker 2019). In essence, he argues, Trump is saying here that although the Javelin sale (benefitting both countries) may suggest that the two are now even, he wants something further. The *quid pro quo* aspect that was under discussion at the impeachment hearings was a matter of whether this further request was a precondition for further support.

The maxim of Relation would suggest that Trump's *I would like you to do us a favor though* is related to the immediately prior discussion of military aid, implicating a link between the two topics – but of course no such relationship is stated explicitly. Much as we saw above in the Bronston case, we're left to ask to what extent a person can be held responsible for what they have implicated but not explicitly stated. And as we see here, a great deal can hinge on the answer to that question.

Tests for conversational implicature

The implicatures we've been talking about thus far, licensed by the Cooperative Principle, are called **conversational implicatures (CIs)**. (In a little while we'll talk about another class of implicature.) Grice proposed a set of properties of conversational implicatures, which can in turn be used as tests for CI. The most helpful tests are these: A CI will be **calculable, cancellable**, and **nonconventional**.

First, a conversational implicature by its nature will be **calculable**, which just means that there's a rational way to get from the utterance, the CP, and the context to the implicature itself. Or, to put it another way, there's a path of reasoning from the context/utterance/CP triplet to the implicature. This does NOT mean that everybody hearing that utterance in that context will necessarily come to the same conclusion, but rather that it's a rational conclusion to come to. So recall our original, Quantity-flouting letter of recommendation:

(25) Dear Admissions Committee:
My student Jane Doe has asked me for a letter of recommendation, and I'm happy to write one. Jane was a student in my Intro to Linguistics class. She came to class regularly, arrived promptly, and had excellent handwriting. She took all of the exams. Sincerely, (etc.)

Why is it that the recipient will take this as a negative recommendation? Well, it seems obvious, but let's work through it anyway: At some level, the recipient realizes that I (as the writer) am trying to be cooperative. And they also realize that the point of a letter of recommendation is to give a certain amount of information, typically highly positive. So I must, as a cooperative person, intend to convey the expected information. And the maxim of Quantity tells me to be as informative as is required. Yet I've blatantly failed to do so. But the reader still clings to the belief that I'm trying to be cooperative; I'm trying to convey something about Jane's capabilities.

Since I've failed to be as informative as is required – that is, to say lots of highly positive things about Jane's intellect and academic abilities – the reader can only surmise that I am not in a position to do. And since I've flouted the maxim so blatantly, the reader will also surmise that I expected them to notice. Therefore, I must have wanted them to realize that I'm in no position to say lots of highly positive things about Jane's intellect and academic abilities. And since Jane was my student, if she HAD a strong intellect and academic abilities, I would have known it. Therefore, I must have wanted the reader to infer that Jane does not have these positive qualities.

The previous two paragraphs delineate the process of calculating the implicature. Now, it's quite likely that the reader won't have to explicitly work through each of these steps to reach the implicature; the test of calculability requires only that, in principle, they be able to. And that makes sense: If it's impossible to see a line of reasoning that would take a hearer (or reader) from an utterance to its intended meaning, there's no reason for a speaker to believe that their intended meaning will be understood.

The second – and to my mind, most reliable – test for CI is **cancellability**, also known as **defeasibility** – the idea being that a CI can be cancelled, or defeated. So let's take a standard scalar implicature:

(26)   I ate most of the brownies; in fact, I ate them all.

The first clause, *I ate most of the brownies*, would normally implicate 'I didn't eat them all'; this implicature is cancelled by the second clause, which specifies that I did, in fact, eat them all. There's nothing that feels contradictory about these two clauses, though. Now compare that with entailment:

(27)   a   #I ate most of the brownies, but I didn't eat anything.
       b   #I ate most of the brownies, but I didn't eat any of the brownies.

The first clause, *I ate most of the brownies*, entails both 'I ate something' and 'I ate some of the brownies' – but efforts to cancel those entailments are infelicitous. (The '#' mark indicates infelicity, i.e., pragmatic oddness.) An entailment can't be cancelled without contradiction, but it's a hallmark of conversational implicature that it can be cancelled without contradiction.

Relatedly, as Sadock (1978) points out, CIs can be **reinforced** without redundancy. So compare the examples in (28):

(28)   a   I ate most of the brownies, but I didn't eat them all.
       b   #I ate most of the brownies, and I ate something.
       c   #I ate most of the brownies, and I ate some of them.

Again, *I ate most of the brownies* implicates 'I didn't eat all of the brownies'; that implicature can be reinforced by being stated explicitly, as in (28a), and there's no sense of redundancy or infelicity. But the entailments 'I ate something' and 'I ate some of the brownies' can't be similarly reinforced, as in (28b) and (28c), without inducing a strong sense of redundancy and infelicity.

A third useful test is **nonconventionality**, which simply means that a CI is, by definition, not conventional. In some theories, conventionality is a defining feature of semantic meaning; in others, it's not (as we'll see below). But conversational implicature is by its very nature necessarily nonconventional. If, say, the exclusive reading were part of the conventional meaning of the word *or*, you wouldn't need the context and the CP (and calculability) to help you work it out (and Grice wouldn't have had anything to worry about to begin with). And likewise, if the exclusive reading were conventional, you wouldn't be able to cancel it without contradiction (as in *I'm going to have a muffin or a bagel, and possibly both*) or reinforce it without redundancy (as in *I'm going to have a muffin or a bagel, but not both*). Conventional meaning and conversational implicature are simply different beasts.

IMPLICATURE AND PRAGMATIC THEORY

Conventional implicature

The Cooperative Principle, as we've seen, combines with the context and the utterance to give hearers a method for deriving certain pragmatic meanings that they can reasonably assume the speaker to have intended, i.e., conversational implicatures. But Grice also proposed another class of implicatures, **conventional implicatures**. These meanings are conventional (hence the name), yet he considers them implicatures on the grounds that they're not part of the semantic (from his point of view, truth-conditional) meaning of the utterance.

Let's look at a few simple examples:

(29) a Will is a linguist, and he's smart.
 b Will is a linguist, so he's smart.
 c Will is a linguist, but he's smart.

We're familiar with the possibilities in (a): The maxim of Relation suggests that there's a reason these two properties of Will are being mentioned together; so, depending on the context, it might be possible to infer that being a linguist and being smart are correlated, or are both relevant to some other goal (maybe the speaker is listing Will's best attributes, or explaining how he got his tenure-track linguistics job, or whatever). But only the logical meaning of *and* – the truth of the two propositions being conjoined – is necessarily conveyed.

Now consider (29b). Here the truth of the two propositions is conveyed, but there's something more: (29b) tells the hearer that there's a sort of conditional connection between the two: Not only is it true that Will is a linguist and that he's smart, but the statement also seems to mean that if you're a linguist, you are smart. In short, *so* as it's used in (29b) seems to combine the meanings of conjunction and the conditional: Not only is it the case that $p \wedge q$, but also that $p \rightarrow q$. It's actually a bit looser than that, since *I've got money, so I'm going to the store* doesn't convey that if a person has money they go to the store, but rather that having money is a precondition for going to the store; in that use, the meaning conveyed is closer to $\neg p \rightarrow \neg q$. So the truth of p makes either possible or necessary the truth of q. We'll say, then, that *so* conveys not just logical conjunction, but also that accepting p provides a reason for accepting q. This is part of the conventional meaning of the word *so*. It doesn't depend on the context; it's the sort of thing you'd find in the dictionary definition. This is what we'll consider to be the **conventional implicature** in (29b). (Granted, there are other unrelated meanings of *so*, as in *I'm so bored* and *Because I said so!*, but it's easy to see that those are distinct.)

But these two bits of meaning – p and q both being true, and p being a reason for accepting q – have very different statuses. Suppose Will isn't smart at all; in that case, (29b) is false. The truth of the two conjuncts (the two things being conjoined) is necessary for the truth of the conjunction, just as we recall from our truth tables. But now suppose instead that Will is smart, but linguists are generally known to be dullards – just really, really dumb. Now (29b) is a peculiar thing to say, but is it false? Most people would say it isn't. At least, it's not nearly as clear that it's false as it was in the condition in which Will himself isn't smart. That is, while the meaning of the conjunction affects whether the sentence is true, the meaning of the conventional implicature doesn't – or to put it another way, conjunction is **truth-conditional** but conventional implicature is not.

For another example, look at (29c). Here, the word *but* again has two components to its meaning: One is just our old friend conjunction, and the other is a sense of contrast between being a linguist and being smart. Again, the first is truth-conditional, and the second is a conventional implicature and therefore isn't. So if you utter (29c) in a context where linguists are generally known to be geniuses, (30c) is a weird thing to say, but you probably wouldn't want to say it's false (assuming Will is in fact smart). To see this, consider (30):

(30)   A   Will is a linguist, but he's smart.
         B   That's not true!

B here might be denying that Will is a linguist or that Will is smart, but you'd never assume B is saying there's no contrast between being a linguist and being smart. You might, for instance, get the conversation in (31) but probably not the one in (32):

(31)   A   Will is a linguist, but he's smart.
         B   That's not true! He's dumb as a rock!

(32)   A   Will is a linguist, but he's smart.
         B   #That's not true! Linguists are very smart!

And again, the contrast associated with *but* is conventional; anywhere you encounter the word *but*, you'll encounter that implicature of contrast.

For one more piece of evidence that these are conventional, and not conversational, implicatures, let's pull our favorite test for conversational implicature out of our toolkit and try to cancel the implicates, to see once and for all whether they're conversational or conventional:

(33)   a   #Will is a linguist, so he's smart – but linguists aren't usually smart.
         b   #Will is a linguist, but he's smart – and linguists are usually smart.

These are pretty odd. At best, the hearer would want to respond with something like, *Then why did you use the word 'so'?* That's evidence that these are conventional implicatures and not conversational implicatures.

The Gricean world view

From a Gricean point of view, meaning breaks down as in Figure 4.2.

To start at the top: You may recall the difference between natural and nonnatural meaning from Chapter 1; natural meaning is automatic and nonintentional, as in *Those clouds mean rain* or *Those spots mean chickenpox*, whereas nonnatural meaning is arbitrary and intentional, as with a red octagon meaning 'stop', or the word *chair* meaning a piece of furniture you sit on. For Grice, language use counts as nonnatural meaning.

Within nonnatural meaning, we come to the distinction between what is said and what is implicated. For those who define semantics as truth-conditional meaning and pragmatics and non-truth-conditional meaning, the line between semantics and pragmatics falls between what is said and what is implicated. What is said is semantic, literal, truth-conditional meaning. What is implicated is everything else: pragmatic meaning.

Within what is implicated, we have two kinds of implicature: The first is conventional implicature, which we just talked about above; it shares with semantic meaning the property of being conventional, and with pragmatic meaning the property of being non-truth-conditional: The meaning of contrast that's associated with the word *but* doesn't affect the truth-conditions of a sentence, but it is conventionally associated with *but* and can't be cancelled.

And finally, within conversational implicature, Grice distinguishes between two types: **generalized** and **particularized**. The idea is that some implicatures, such as scalar implicatures, apply across a broad, definable class of utterances by default. For example, consider the class of scalar implicatures. Saying *most* implicates 'not all'; for example, *I ate most of the pizza* implicates 'I didn't eat all of the pizza', *I did most of my homework* implicates 'I didn't

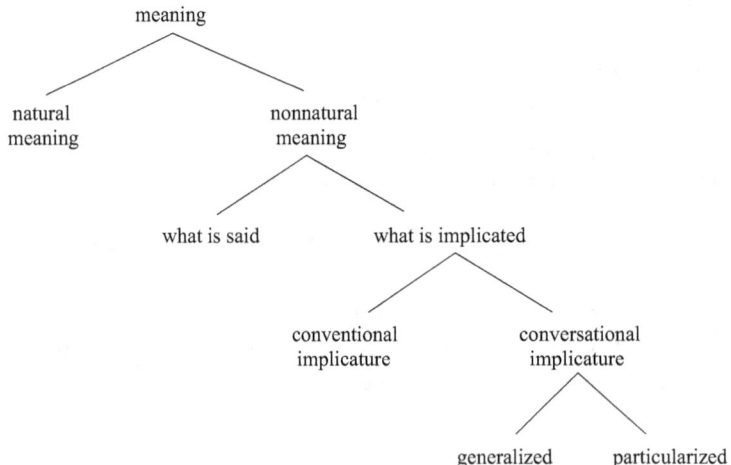

FIGURE 4.2 The Gricean world view.

do all of my homework', etc. As we've seen above, this can be cancelled (*I ate most, and in fact all, of the pizza*), but in general it holds. This is what Grice calls a **generalized conversational implicature;** it generalizes over an entire class of utterances. There may be cases in which it doesn't hold (so, as we've seen, *You must be 21 to enter* doesn't implicate 'you must not be over 21'), but it holds in general.

On the other hand, some implicatures seem to be specific to a single utterance in context, as in (34):

(34) A   Are you going to Cheryl's party tonight?
     B   I have to do my homework.

Here B implicates 'I can't go to Cheryl's party tonight'. But we wouldn't want to say that in general, utterances of *I have to do my homework* implicate 'I can't go to Cheryl's party tonight'; clearly that implicature is due to the particular context in which this specific utterance occurs. This is what Grice calls a **particularized conversational implicature**.

The distinction between generalized and particularized conversation implicature isn't sharp, however. For example, you could argue that there is indeed a generalized class of implicatures of which (34) is an instance, as schematized in (35):

(35) A   Are you going to X?
     B   I have to Y.
     implicature: 'I can't X'.

You can imagine a wide range of scenarios that would be covered by this schema: I can't go swimming because I have to mow the lawn, I can't help you wash your dog because I have to visit my aunt, I can't stir the soup because I have to chop this avocado, etc. So where the line should be drawn – or whether indeed a line should be drawn – between 'generalized' and 'particularized' conversational implicatures is an open question. (See also Hirschberg 1991 and Levinson 2000.)

PRAGMATICS AFTER GRICE

Since Grice, various researchers have suggested improvements, extensions, or modifications to his proposals. While each of these approaches and topics merits a good deal more space than I'm able to give them here, I will provide a brief summary of some of the most important of them, along with my urging that if you wish to do further research into pragmatics, you should definitely look them up and dig further into what these authors have to say.

Explicature

The Gricean view of meaning sketched in Figure 4.2 suggests that an utterance's meaning breaks down into what is said (literal semantic truth-conditional meaning) and what is implicated (pragmatic non-truth-conditional meaning). But consider cases like those in (36):

(36) a He finished.
   b They agreed then.

If I asked you, right now, whether (36a) is true or false, you'd be at a loss to answer (or you'd think I was crazy). You can't possibly decide whether it's true or false until you know who *he* refers to, and what it is that he did or didn't finish. That is to say, determining the truth-conditions of (36a) requires more information:

(37) John finished painting the chair.

That's better, although you'd also need to know which *John* I'm talking about (John F. Kennedy? John Quincy Adams? Your friend John who lives down the street?) and what chair I'm talking about. But with all of that filled in, we'd finally have a proposition whose truth-conditions could be determined:

(38) Your friend John who lives down the street finished painting the chair that's been sitting on his deck for a week.

This information is pragmatic, in the sense that deciding who *he* refers to requires consideration of the context (e.g., the fact that John F. Kennedy and John Quincy Adams don't happen to be alive at the moment, so they're out of the running). But these expansions don't seem to be implicatures; the implicatures we described above consider a proposition in its context and determine what is meant above and beyond that proposition. And remember that a proposition is by definition truth-evaluable; it is something that can be either true or false. In (36a), on the other hand, we don't have a proposition at all – nothing that is truth-evaluable – until we flesh it out with the necessary additional pragmatic information about who I mean and what he finished.

And the same thing holds for (36b): Who is meant by *they*? And what did they agree about? And when? Without this information, which can only be supplied by the context, we can't begin to assign the sentence any truth-conditions; we don't yet have a proposition. The fully-worked-out proposition including both the semantic meaning and the contextual information that's required to get us to a full proposition (but not the implicatures!) is called an **explicature** (Sperber and Wilson 1986; Carston 2002). So the explicature for (36a) might be something like (38), and the explicature for (36b) might be something like 'The 2020 U.S. Senate agreed at 4:45 p.m. on September 12, 2020 that they would discuss the national budget'.

For many researchers, this suggests that communication isn't a simple process of establishing the semantics of an utterance, feeding those semantics into the context, and coming out with the pragmatic meaning. Instead, they argue for something like an interleaving of semantics and pragmatics, in which we consider the context in order to work out a fully truth-evaluable proposition, and then consider that proposition in working out the implicatures and the full pragmatic meaning.

Impliciture

A very similar notion is that of **impliciture** (Bach 1994). Consider these examples:

(39) a I haven't eaten.
    b Frank is tall.

In each of these cases, there is a full, truth-evaluable proposition, but part of what's meant, and part of what's needed to evaluate the truth of what's meant, is implicit. So in (39a), what is strictly said is that I haven't eaten – but what is more likely meant is that I haven't eaten yet today – or more specifically, if it's uttered in the afternoon, that I haven't eaten lunch yet today, and if it's uttered in the evening, that I haven't eaten dinner yet today. Going only on the basis of what's explicitly stated in (39a), we'd have to say that the utterance is virtually never true, because anyone old enough to utter it must have eaten at some point in order to live long enough to acquire English. But what's implicit affects the truth-value of the statement.

What we see in (39b) is both similar and different: Here again there's something implicit, but now what's implicit is a contrast set. In order to determine whether it's true that Frank is tall, we need to implicitly ask 'compared to what?' So if Frank is a six-foot-tall jockey, Frank is tall; if Frank is a six-foot-tall professional basketball player, he is not. Again, unlike the case with explicature, we've got a complete proposition, yet there's still implicit material that contributes to our sense of its truth-conditions for a given context of utterance. Or as Bach puts it, in implicature you communicate something in addition to what you've said, whereas in impliciture you communicate something else that's close to what was said.

While explicature and impliciture aren't identical notions – and I've somewhat exaggerated the difference here for clarity – there's certainly overlap, and authors often use similar sorts of examples. But the two arise out of different theoretical frameworks, with explicature being closely related to Relevance theory, which we'll discuss below. The important point for both, however, is that they point to the need for inference and context to feed into even the semantic content of an utterance.

Neo-Gricean theory

One thing you may have noticed in the discussion of the CP is that a lot of those maxims and submaxims seem to overlap. For convenience, here they are again:

The maxim of Quantity

1   Make your contribution as informative as is required (for the current purposes of the exchange).
2   Do not make your contribution more informative than is required.

The maxim of Quality

Try to make your contribution one that is true.

1   Do not say what you believe to be false.
2   Do not say that for which you lack adequate evidence.

The maxim of Relation

Be relevant.

The maxim of Manner

Be perspicuous.

1   Avoid obscurity of expression.
2   Avoid ambiguity.
3   Be brief (avoid unnecessary prolixity).
4   Be orderly.

So consider the second submaxim of Quantity – "Do not make your contribution more informative than is required." This seems to overlap with Relation – "Be relevant" – because, after all, if you're saying more than is required, you're getting less relevant, and conversely, saying what isn't relevant is definitely giving more information than is required. (And we've all been stuck in those conversations.) And for that matter, if you're giving irrelevant information (violating Relation) and thereby being more informative than is required (violating Quantity2), I think we can all agree that you're also not being sufficiently brief (violating Manner3).

In fact, Horn (1984) argues that there's a tension between two forces in communication, one of which is 'speaker-based' in that it's in the speaker's interest to say as little as possible (and thus conserve effort) and one of which is 'hearer-based' in that it's in the hearer's interest for the speaker to say as much and be as explicit as possible (and thus spare the hearer the effort of having to infer what's meant). This tension is seen most clearly in Quantity1 and Quantity2, but incorporates Relation and Manner as well. (Quality is seen as a sort of uber-maxim without which the whole system crumbles.) Horn describes these two interacting forces in terms of his **Q-principle** and **R-principle**:

The Q-principle: Say as much as you can, given R.
The R-principle: Say no more than you must, given Q.

Roughly speaking, the Q-principle corresponds to Quantity1 and Manner1&2, while the R-principle corresponds to Relation, Quantity2, and Manner3&4. Note that the two principles refer to each other, nicely incorporating their interaction into their definitions.

This interaction, in turn, is negotiated with the help of what Horn calls the **Division of Pragmatic Labor**, which states that an unmarked utterance licenses an R-based inference to the unmarked case, whereas a marked utterance licenses a Q-based inference that the unmarked case doesn't hold, hence an inference to some marked situation. (Recall from Chapter 2 that an unmarked expression is the default, while a marked expression is unusual or nondefault in some sense.) To make this a little clearer, let's look at some examples:

(40)   a   Jason was able to fix the computer.
       b   I chipped a tooth yesterday.

(41) a Jason had the ability to fix the computer.
     b Leah caused the stinkbug to die.

The examples in (40) use unmarked expressions, and because the hearer assumes the speaker is saying no more than they must (the R-principle), the hearer is likely to make an R-inference to the unmarked case. In (40a), that means inferring that Jason was not only **able** to fix the computer, but in fact did so; and in (40b), it means inferring that the tooth I chipped was one of my own, not, say, the next-door neighbor's.

The examples in (41), on the other hand, use marked – longer and less common – expressions, and because the hearer assumes the speaker is saying as much as they can (the Q-principle), the hearer is likely to make a Q-inference to the effect that the unmarked case doesn't hold. In (41a), that means inferring that Jason didn't necessarily fix the computer, and in (41b), that means inferring that Leah didn't directly kill the stinkbug. (Perhaps she sealed it into a plastic zippered bag knowing it would eventually suffocate, rather than squash it and release its odor.)

Because the speakers in (41) are going out of their way to avoid a shorter, simpler way of speaking that would have induced an R-inference to the default case (*Jason was able to fix the computer* and *Leah killed the stinkbug*), the hearers are licensed to infer that the default case doesn't hold, or at least that the speaker doesn't want them to assume that it does.

Horn's Q/R theory is neo-Gricean in the sense that it preserves Grice's fundamental insight that interlocutors are negotiating the tension between potentially conflicting forces, and that this negotiation gives rise to implicatures. For Grice, the maxims act to limit each other; for example, the maxim that tells us to be as informative as possible (Quantity1) is limited by (among others) the maxim of Quality, which tells us not to say what we have no evidence for; it's this limit that gives rise to scalar implicatures (i.e., the implicature that the speaker couldn't have said more without violating Quality). Because of this interaction among the maxims, Quantity1 actually ends up effectively telling the speaker to say as much as possible without violating Quality (or, say, Quantity2, or Relation). Horn builds this tension (and hence, these mutual limits) into the wording of his Q and R principles.

Another system that is similarly neo-Gricean is that of Levinson (2000). Levinson offers three 'heuristics' for interpreting utterances:

The Q-heuristic: What isn't said, isn't.
The I-heuristic: What is simply described is stereotypically exemplified.
The M-heuristic: A marked message indicates a marked situation.

The Q-heuristic licenses scalar implicatures, in that whatever value on a scale a speaker chooses to affirm, the hearer can infer that no higher value applies: In short, if I say I ate *most* of the chocolate, I implicate that I didn't eat *all* of the chocolate, because what I haven't said (*all*) isn't the case. Levinson's I-heuristic licenses the same sorts of implicatures to a stereotypical situation that we saw above in (40): If I say *I chipped a tooth*, I've described the situation simply, and my hearer can infer that this simple description applies to the stereotypical situation, in which it's my own tooth that I've chipped, not someone else's.

The M-heuristic addresses examples such as those in (41), where instead of using a simple description, the speaker has gone out of their way to express something in a marked way, and this marked message indicates a marked situation. If I go out of my way to say *Leah caused the stinkbug to die*, it's most likely because I was not in a position to truthfully say *Leah killed the stinkbug*. For Horn, the implicature is that the speaker has said as much as they could (the Q-principle); and since *killed* is more informative than *caused to die*, their failure to say *killed* implicates that it doesn't hold (cf. McCawley 1978). For Levinson, the M-heuristic tells the hearer that the marked message (*caused to die*) indicates a marked situation, so the unmarked situation of killing the stinkbug doesn't hold.

Relevance theory

As we've seen, neo-Gricean theories depend on implicatures that arise from the tension between a set of (potentially or necessarily) opposing forces, but boil these forces down to a much smaller number than Grice's original set. The 'post-Gricean' account known as Relevance theory goes farther, boiling all of implicature down to a single principle of Relevance (Sperber and Wilson 1986). Relevance theory has its basis in a principle that is taken to be central to all of human cognition, not just communication; this is the **Cognitive Principle of Relevance**:

> **Cognitive Principle of Relevance:** Human cognition tends to be geared to the maximization of relevance. (Wilson and Sperber 2004)

And because cognition is geared to maximize relevance, the next principle follows naturally:

> **Communicative Principle of Relevance:** Every ostensive stimulus conveys a presumption of its own optimal relevance. (Wilson and Sperber 2004)

'Ostensive' means essentially defining something by example or by pointing to an example; all you really need to know for our purposes is that the set of things that count as an 'ostensive stimulus' would include linguistic utterances. So the Communicative Principle of Relevance means that anytime I say something, there's a presumption that what I've said is optimally relevant. In short, the first principle says humans automatically look for maximal relevance; the second principle says, therefore, that utterances come prepackaged with an assurance that this is the most relevant thing the speaker could have said. So the hearer, in turn, can safely assume that the message will be worth the trouble of interpreting.

For Sperber and Wilson, the tendency to maximize relevance renders the rest of the maxims unnecessary. Relevance is measured in terms of **positive cognitive effects** (changes in world view, beliefs, inferences, etc.) compared to processing costs. The interpretation that results in the greatest number of positive cognitive effects at the lowest cognitive cost is the one that's most relevant, and therefore the one to be preferred. So in this view, the tension that gives rise to implicatures isn't between potentially conflicting maxims or between the speaker's and the hearer's interests, but rather between cognitive cost and cognitive payoff. And the search for optimal relevance is a principle that's not unique to communication but rather is fundamental to human cognition.

It's worth noting that Grice himself made a similar point about his Cooperative Principle and its maxims: They're not specific only to communication, but apply to all cooperative interaction. If you ask me for a cup of milk, I won't empty the entire contents of the fridge onto your plate; I'll give you as much as required and no more. If we're fixing a bike together and I see that you need a wrench, I won't hand you a hammer. And if we're baking a cake together, I'll hand you the ingredients in the order in which you need them. In short, we try to be cooperative in general, in ways analogous to those that Grice detailed for communication. And Relevance theory retains that insight – but strips cooperative behavior down to a single goal of maximal relevance. Because the speaker wants the hearer to understand them, they'll be maximally relevant; and because the hearer knows that this is how the speaker will behave, they'll search for the maximally relevant interpretation. So let's consider again (40a) and (41a), here (42a) and (42b):

(42) a Jason was able to fix the computer.
      b Jason had the ability to fix the computer.

The question for the hearer is, what interpretation will give me the biggest bang for my cognitive buck? Which will give me the greatest number of positive cognitive effects? In (42a), making the simple interpretive jump to 'and he did so' adds a cognitive effect, a new bit of information, at little additional cost. In (42b), however, the speaker has gone out of their way to avoid licensing this inference; and this additional effort must itself have some relevance, some positive cognitive effect – in this case, the additional inference that Jason did not in fact do so.

Or consider again the Gricean letter of recommendation in (25), here (43):

(43)   Dear Admissions Committee:

      My student Jane Doe has asked me for a letter of recommendation, and I'm happy to write one. Jane was a student in my Intro to Linguistics class. She came to class regularly, arrived promptly, and had excellent handwriting. She took all of the exams.

      Sincerely, (etc.)

The reader is looking for the greatest number of positive cognitive effects. They can be assumed to know that a standard letter of recommendation is long, but this one isn't; and they can be assumed to know that a standard letter of recommendation includes very high praise; but this one doesn't. And finally, they can be assumed to know that a standard letter of recommendation mentions the student's intellect, work ethic, past work, etc. – none of which is addressed here. What cognitive effects can this lead to? In each case, the background information that such a letter is expected to provide X, yet this letter doesn't, gives rise to the cognitive effect that X doesn't apply. And because this inference is a positive cognitive effect, it increases the total relevance of the letter, so the reader can assume that this inference was intended by the writer.

Relevance theory and neo-Gricean theories are at odds in some ways, but all are efforts to streamline Grice's original maxims while retaining Grice's fundamental insight that meaning is a cooperative, rational, and inferential process by which information that isn't explicitly stated by the speaker is nonetheless inferred by the hearer on the basis of principles that the speaker and hearer share.

Boundary disputes

Among the issues on which Relevance theorists and neo-Griceans differ is the question of where precisely to draw the line between semantics and pragmatics. Recall the Gricean view of meaning, repeated here as Figure 4.3.

For Grice, the dividing line between semantics and pragmatics is drawn on the basis of a truth-conditional semantics. That is, all truth-conditional meaning is semantic in nature; this is the category of 'what is said'. Everything that is **said** is semantic, and everything that is **implicated** is pragmatic. For Grice, then, conventional implicatures like the contrast associated with the word *but* are pragmatic: Although they're conventional, they don't contribute to the truth-conditions of an utterance, so they're part of pragmatics. This is true for most neo-Griceans as well (though see Neale 1992 for an alternative view that groups conventional implicatures and 'what is said' into a single category of conventional meaning).

This line, however, doesn't match up with the difference between context-independent and context-dependent meaning; whereas the line between truth-conditional and non-truth-conditional meaning falls to the left of 'conventional implicature' in Figure 4.3, the line between conventional and nonconventional meaning falls to the right of it: The sense of contrast associated with the word *but* is conventional (i.e., context-independent), yet doesn't contribute to truth-conditions. So we can't say that truth-conditional meaning is the same as conventional, context-independent meaning. A truth-conditional semantics draws the line between semantics and pragmatics on the basis of truth-conditional meaning, but that leaves a little bit of conventional meaning on the 'pragmatics' side of the line.

There's also the question of how to deal with explicatures. As we saw above, contextual information may be needed in order to flesh out a full proposition:

(44) He put it there.

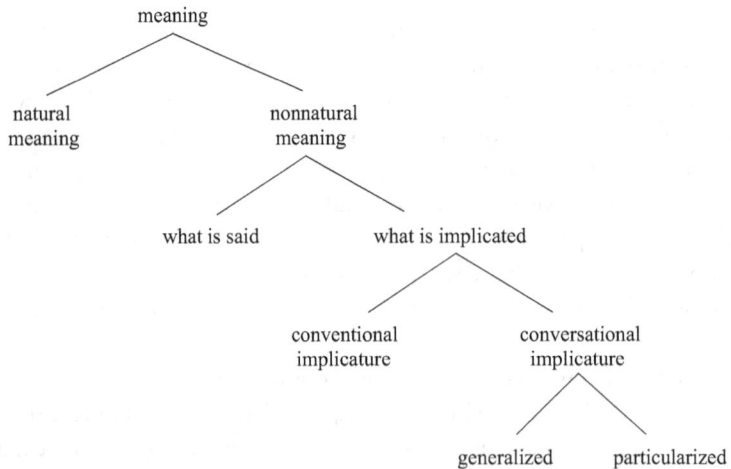

FIGURE 4.3 The Gricean world view.

As it stands, (44) can represent any number of propositions. In order to be able to evaluate the truth of (44) in a given scenario, we need to know what's meant by *he, it,* and *there*. At that point we've got a truth-evaluable proposition, but to get there we have to look at the context – which means that contextual meaning is affecting truth-conditional meaning. So we can't just say that truth-conditional meaning is the same as context-independent, conventional meaning. In short, you can draw the semantics/pragmatics line at truth-conditions or at context-independence, but you can't do both.

For neo-Griceans, maintaining the distinction between semantics and pragmatics as the distinction between truth-conditional and non-truth-conditional meaning (which, after all, was the driving force behind Grice's theory to begin with) means **not** drawing the semantics/pragmatics line between conventional and nonconventional meaning.

Relevance theorists in general disagree. For them, the distinction between semantics and pragmatics is the distinction between what is encoded and what is inferred. What is encoded is purely semantic, conventional meaning, and it may fall short of a full proposition. What is inferred includes both what is explicated and what is implicated. What is encoded and what is explicated combine to get us to a full truth-conditional meaning (i.e., the explicature), which includes both semantic and pragmatic information. The implicature, in contrast, is purely pragmatic.

To make this all a bit clearer, Figures 4.4 and 4.5 show the relevant distinctions between the neo-Gricean world view (Figure 4.4) and the Relevance theory world view (Figure 4.5).

Neo-Griceans allow contextual information to affect the truth-conditions of a sentence (as in, e.g., (44)), but retain a clean semantics/pragmatics distinction based on truth-conditions. Relevance theorists take the explicature/implicature distinction as central, and the distinction between truth-conditional and non-truth-conditional meaning does not align with the semantics/pragmatics distinction.

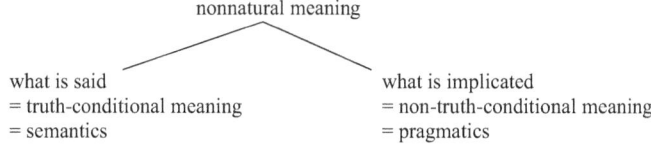

FIGURE 4.4 The Neo-Gricean world view.

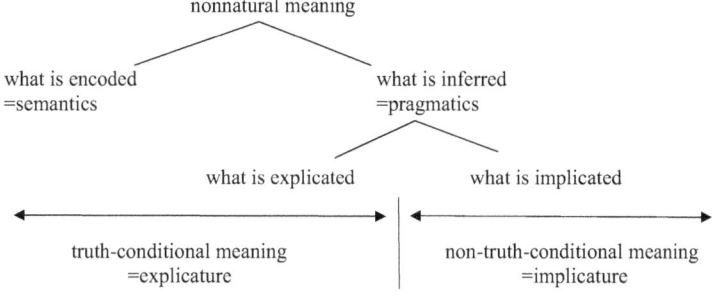

FIGURE 4.5 The Relevance theory world view.

It should also be noted that whereas neo-Gricean theory retains the distinction between generalized and particularized conversational implicature (omitted from the diagram in Figure 4.4 for clarity), Relevance theory does not recognize generalized conversational implicature as a category. Levinson 2000 criticizes Relevance theory for this omission, arguing that by ignoring generalizations among classes of inferences that behave alike, the theory assumes more cognitive effort than is actually needed. In short, a Relevance theorist would assume that the inference from *most* to 'not all' needs to be calculated anew every time the word *most* is encountered, whereas Levinson argues that this inference is made by default upon encountering the word *most*.

Over the years, various border skirmishes have been fought (on topics such as the correct analyses of explicatures and scalar implicatures), but in many ways the two sides have come closer to agreement as they've looked more closely at the data – and that is precisely how science should work.

EXERCISES

Self-test:

1. The main point of the Cooperative Principle is that
    a. speakers are polite.
    b. speakers are cooperative.
    c. speakers are succinct.
    d. speakers are honest.
2. The maxim of Quantity can be best summarized as
    a. Say enough, but not too much.
    b. Make your contribution relevant.
    c. Talk as much as you possibly can.
    d. Make your contribution orderly and unambiguous.
3. The maxim of Relation can be best summarized as
    a. Family groups talk alike.
    b. Make your contribution orderly and unambiguous.
    c. Say enough, but not too much.
    d. Be relevant.
4. If you disobey a maxim so obviously that you clearly intend your hearer to notice, you've
    a. flaunted the maxim.
    b. flouted the maxim.
    c. violated the maxim.
    d. reticulated the maxim.
5. Conversational implicatures are
    a. conventional, defeasible, and calculable.
    b. calculable, cancellable, and nonconventional.
    c. defeasible, Gricean, and conventional.
    d. generalized, semantic, and calculable.

6   Two major current approaches to implicature are based on the theories of
    a   conventional and conversational theorists.
    b   generalized and particularized conversational implicature.
    c   the neo-Griceans and the Relevance theorists.
    d   the generative semanticists and the Russellian presuppositionalists.
7   The Division of Pragmatic Labor negotiates the tension between
    a   neo-Griceans and Relevance theorists.
    b   the Q-principle and the R-principle.
    c   conventional and conversational implicature.
    d   saying what's true and saying what you have insufficient evidence for.
8   Which is most likely to be a flouting of the maxim of Quality?
    a   *I really admire you.*
    b   *I ate two brownies yesterday.*
    c   *My sister is the smartest person on earth.*
    d   *That dinner was excellent.*
9   The Communicative Principle of Relevance says, in essence, that
    a   if a speaker says something, you can assume they're being as relevant as they can.
    b   when a speaker says something irrelevant, they are trying to be optimally communicative.
    c   speakers are cooperative only when they're communicating.
    d   the relevance of an utterance interferes with its communicative potential.
10 Conventional implicatures are
    a   cancellable but context-dependent.
    b   context-dependent but truth-conditional.
    c   uncooperative but calculable.
    d   conventional but non-truth-conditional.

Comprehension questions:

1   In each of the following, tell which of Grice's maxims Kim's inference is most clearly based on:
    a   Alex said, "If I eat one more piece of cake, I'll explode." Kim inferred that Alex felt full.
    b   Alex said, "My dad has offered to pay half of my tuition." Kim inferred that Alex's dad won't pay the entire tuition bill.
    c   Alex said, "Chris broke up with Pat, and Pat moved out." Kim inferred that Pat moved out after the break-up.
    d   Alex said, "Can you tutor me in linguistics? I'll pay you $20." Kim inferred that the $20 would be payment for the tutoring.
2   The discussion of example (30c) above includes the following sentence, concerning two pieces of meaning:

    > Again, the first is truth-conditional and the second is a conventional implicature and therefore isn't.

Here, the word *therefore* itself carries a conventional implicature (independent of the one the sentence is about). What is it, and how can you argue for its status as a conventional implicature?

3 In saying *It depends upon what the meaning of the word is is*, Bill Clinton argued that the statement *There is absolutely no sex* [between Clinton and Lewinsky] meant there was not a sexual relationship at the point when the utterance was made. Now imagine Clinton and Lewinsky were still in a sexual relationship at that point, but weren't having sex at the precise moment of the utterance; could he have argued as convincingly that the present-tense *is* makes his statement true? How is Bach's notion of impliciture relevant to this question?

4 Explain how the everyday use of the English word *or* differs from the meaning of the corresponding logical operator, and why.

5 Is the metaphor *Jaime is an open book* (to mean Jaime is easy to understand) best handled truth-conditionally or as a flouting of a maxim – and if the latter, which maxim? Explain your reasoning.

Opinion questions:

1 Do the implicatures of ordering and causation that are frequently associated with *and* constitute generalized or particularized conversational implicatures? What factors do you need to consider in order to decide? And does the fact that the use of *and* sometimes implicates one but not the other (e.g., ordering but not causation) make a difference?

2 Has Grice succeeded in solving the problem of the truth-conditional meaning of the logical operators and their natural-language use? Explain your reasoning.

3 Recall example (15) above:

A: Why has Jane been looking so happy all of a sudden?
B: Well, I keep seeing her with Herman.

Suppose speaker B knows perfectly well that there's nothing going on between Jane and Herman, but wants to implicate that they're romantically involved, in order to mislead speaker A. Nonetheless, it's perfectly true that B keeps seeing Jane with Herman, because he's paying her to tutor him in calculus. Do you think speaker B has lied? What would Coleman and Kay say? (You can review their account of what constitutes a lie in the discussion of the maxim of Quantity above.)

4 Is the distinction between generalized and particularized conversational implicatures a useful one? Consider the Quality-based implicature from my saying *It's gonna snow later today* to your inference that I believe it's going to snow later today and that I have some evidence for saying so. Is this a particularized conversational implicature, since 'Betty Birner believes it's going to snow later today' is a pretty context-specific implicature? Or is it generalized, because it's part of a larger class of implicatures from utterance of p to the inference that the speaker believes (and has evidence for) p? Can a similar question be asked

about scalar implicatures? If you find the generalized/particularized distinction helpful, where would you draw the line between them?

Discussion questions:

1. Courtrooms provide some fascinating opportunities for pragmatic investigation. For example, there's an argument to be made that questioning a witness for the opposition is an inherently uncooperative situation. Do the maxims still apply? In example (8) above, Mr. Bronston is clearly being uncooperative. Is he violating a maxim or opting out? Where do you draw the line between the two? What would you as the judge have decided regarding whether he has committed perjury, and why?

2. In 2017, Jared Kushner was listed in *Time* magazine as one of the 100 most influential people of the year. Henry Kissinger was enlisted to write a brief piece about Kushner; normally such pieces are filled with praise. Kissinger wrote this:

   > Transitioning the presidency between parties is one of the most complex undertakings in American politics. The change triggers an upheaval in the intangible mechanisms by which Washington runs: an incoming President is likely to be less familiar with formal structures, and the greater that gap, the heavier the responsibility of those advisers who are asked to fill it.
   >
   > This space has been traversed for nearly four months by Jared Kushner, whom I first met about 18 months ago, when he introduced himself after a foreign policy lecture I had given. We have sporadically exchanged views since. As part of the Trump family, Jared is familiar with the intangibles of the President. As a graduate of Harvard and NYU, he has a broad education; as a businessman, a knowledge of administration. All this should help him make a success of his daunting role flying close to the sun.
   >
   > (Kissinger 2017)

   Analyze this as a case of a 'Gricean letter of recommendation', along the lines of (9) and (17) above. What maxim or maxims are involved, and are they being fulfilled, flouted, or violated? The last line makes reference to the myth of Icarus (if you're not familiar with it, look it up); what might one infer from its inclusion here? (See Blake 2017 for a nice analysis.)

3. Compare the case of Mr. Bronston with Bill Clinton's lawyer's utterance *There is absolutely no sex of any kind* between Clinton and Lewinsky. Bronston was cleared of guilt because he only implicated, but didn't explicitly state, that he never personally had a Swiss bank account; Clinton's lawyer implicates but doesn't say that Clinton and Lewinsky never had an affair. Are the two cases parallel? Are the two speakers equally innocent, or equally guilty, or is there a difference between the two cases that makes you think one should be held more responsible than the other?

Data collection and analysis:

1. Try to find a naturally occurring example for each cell of the following grid. For any cell you are unable to fill, explain why you think it's harder to find examples of that phenomenon than the others.

	Quantity	Quality	Relation	Manner
fulfilled				
violated				
flouted				

2. Create a small corpus of 10-15 utterances by public figures that someone else has labeled as untrue (e.g., you can find a bunch at politifact.com, or factcheck.org, or by checking the transcript of any presidential debate). Evaluate each statement in terms of the three criteria for a 'lie' proposed by Coleman and Kay above. That is, for each statement, as best you can, tell whether the statement was false, whether the speaker believed it to be false, and whether the speaker's intent was to mislead. Are any of these putative untruths based entirely on an implicature?

3. Collect a corpus of at least 50 naturally occurring utterances of the word *but*. This chapter described its conventional implicature as 'contrast', but that's pretty vague; based on your corpus, how well does that account for the data? Can you come up with a more specific description of the implicature? Are there any problematic cases in the corpus?

Answers to self-test:

1. b
2. a
3. d
4. b
5. b
6. c
7. b
8. c
9. a
10. d

CHAPTER 5

Pragmatics II: Speech acts

> **KEY CONCEPTS**
>
> - speech act
> - performative, constative
> - explicit vs. implicit performative
> - declarative, interrogative, imperative
> - direct vs. indirect speech act
> - felicity conditions
> - propositional content, preparatory, sincerity, and essential conditions
> - misfire, abuse
> - locutionary, illocutionary, perlocutionary force
> - politeness theory
> - face needs
> - positive/negative face
> - face-threatening act
> - honorific

So why do we open our mouths to speak, anyway? There's always some purpose we're trying to achieve in speaking – something we're trying to do. Every act of speaking is, well, an act. That doesn't sound too profound, but in this chapter we'll see that the wide variety of acts a person can perform in speaking can give us important insights into the nature of communication and the structure of discourse.

We will start with J.L. Austin's crucial insights into how to do things with words (from his crucially insightful book, *How To Do Things With Words*). As we'll see, there are utterances that can perform the acts they describe (such as *I hereby christen this ship the Titanic*) and others that perform other acts (such as saying *I'm sorry* to perform an apology). And as we've already seen, especially in the last chapter, there are utterances that can perform acts indirectly (such as *I'd like more water* as a way of indirectly requesting that somebody pass the water pitcher). The question, as always, is how we know what the speaker means by what they say – and it won't surprise you at all to learn that this question will be bound up in what we've learned about the Cooperative Principle and about speakers and hearers as collaborators in the construction of meaning.

SPEECH ACTS

Austin began his journey into the world of speech acts by noticing that certain utterances change the world in an interesting way: They **do** what they describe; they perform some act in the world. He called these **performatives**. But he quickly realized that really, every utterance does something in the world. It may not perform the act it describes, but utterances do all sorts of things: They describe, request, ask, warn, persuade, compliment, etc. In this way, his focus shifted from the traditional philosophical question of an utterance's truth or falsity to what the speaker uses it to do. This was the jumping-off point for his theory of speech acts. But before we get too far ahead of ourselves, let's start at the very beginning – with performatives.

Performatives

What do the following utterances have in common?

(1) a I take this man to be my lawful wedded husband.
    b I apologize for breaking your treasured bobble-head doll.
    c I promise to plant the petunias.
    d I warn you not to open that door.

First off, you'll notice that they're all in the first-person singular, which is to say they all have *I* as their subject. (Although it's also possible to get first-person plural cases, as with *We find the defendant not guilty*.) Second, they're all in the present tense. Third, and most importantly, they all describe what they're doing at the very moment that they're doing it – or, to flip that description, they all do what they're describing at the very moment that they're describing it. And it's the saying it that counts as doing it.

So the speaker uttering (1a) is not only taking some man to be their husband at the very same time that they're saying that they're doing so, but it's the saying so that does it; saying *I take this man to be my lawful wedded husband* is, itself, the taking of that man to be your lawful wedded husband. And the same holds for the other cases: Uttering (1b) is itself the act of apologizing, uttering (1c) is itself the act of promising, and (1d) is itself the act of warning. In each case, saying it counts as doing it.

And that's why it makes sense that these utterances are in the first-person singular. If you're performing an act by virtue of saying that you're performing it, you can only speak for yourself. The examples in (2) aren't performative:

(2) a My cousin takes this man to be their lawful wedded husband.
    b Chris apologizes for breaking your treasured bobble-head doll.
    c Stacey promises to plant the petunias.
    d Tracy warns you not to open that door.

None of these in itself counts as the act described: (2a) isn't an act of taking a man as husband, (2b) isn't an act of apology, (2c) isn't a promise, and (2d) isn't itself a warning but rather a report of a warning. Similarly, shifting the time reference of the utterances in (1) to be past or future robs them of their performative force:

(3) a I will take this man to be my lawful wedded husband.
    b I will apologize for breaking your treasured bobble-head doll.
    c I promised to plant the petunias.
    d I warned you not to open that door.

The first two cases simply report what will happen in the future, while the last two report what has happened in the past, but none of them perform the act they describe.

Because a performative enacts what it describes, adding the word *hereby* is a handy test for performativity:

(4) a ?I hereby will take this man to be my lawful wedded husband.
    b ?Jan hereby apologized for breaking your treasured bobble-head doll.
    c I hereby promise to plant the petunias.
    d I hereby warn you not to open that door.

The word *hereby* means 'by means of this' – so it doesn't make any sense in a statement describing what will be done in the future or has been done in the past, or is being done by someone else. That makes it useful for double-checking that what is being described is also being done right now, by the speaker, in using the utterance that describes it.

Constatives

In contrast to performatives such as those in (1), Austin observed that some statements simply express a state of affairs, as exemplified in (5):

(5) a The economy is improving.
    b Norma has finished painting her house.
    c Everyone reading this book is enjoying it immensely.

You could obviously come up with hundreds of your own examples (an infinite number, quite literally). Clearly none of these are performatives; uttering (5a) doesn't improve the economy, uttering (5b) doesn't get anyone's house painted, and uttering (5c), unfortunately, doesn't make it true that everyone reading this book is enjoying it.

Constatives have truth-conditions; clearly if the economy in some possible world is improving, (5a) is true in that world, whereas if it's not, (5a) is false. By contrast, consider a performative like *I warn you not to open that door*. Under what circumstances is it true? It's not technically a tautology, yet it seems that uttering it causes it to be true; that is, if I utter it, I've warned you.

But wait – that's not quite right either. Suppose I walk up to a random male stranger on a street corner and say *I take this man to be my lawful wedded husband*. Have I in fact taken him to be my lawful wedded husband? Setting aside the tangential issue of what my actual husband would think of this, not to mention the probable reaction of the stranger himself, I think we can all agree that I will not have succeeded in taking him to be my lawful wedded husband – which in turn makes the utterance false.

The crucial thing, as we'll see below, is that there are certain conditions that have to be satisfied in order for a performative to take effect (what we'll call **felicity conditions**), much as there are certain conditions that have to hold in order for a constative to be true. In order for a man to become my lawful wedded husband, he has to agree to it, and we need to be standing before someone authorized to perform weddings, and we in fact have to be in the middle of a wedding ceremony. It won't help if the random stranger decides he'd be happy to marry me, and if there's a clergyperson conveniently standing nearby; I can't simply declare then and there that I take him to be my husband and expect that this has made us a married couple.

Types of speech acts: first pass

So far we've got performatives, which enact what they describe, and constatives, which simply describe a state of affairs without enacting it. But there are also utterances that perform some act without technically being performative in form:

(6) a   Thanks.
    b   Be careful!
    c   Shut up!
    d   Please hand me that book.

Compare these with the corresponding utterances in (7):

(7) a   I thank you.
    b   I warn you, be careful!
    c   I command you to shut up!
    d   I request that you hand me that book.

The utterances in (6) aren't performatives in the sense that we've discussed them so far. They don't have the form of a performative (since they lack both a subject and a performative verb); and they don't quite as clearly perform the action they describe, since they don't quite describe an action. And they fail the *hereby* test: While I can perfectly well say *I hereby thank you*, it sounds perfectly ridiculous to say #*Hereby thanks*. I'll leave it to you to check that the remaining examples in (6) fail the *hereby* test, while the performatives in (7) pass it.

And yet, each of the statements in (6) does perform the same act as the corresponding performative in (7). The utterance in (6a) performs the act of thanking, (6b) the act of warning, (6c) the act of commanding, and (6d) the act of requesting. So although these aren't **explicit performatives**, they are **implicit performatives**.

An interesting comparison, in fact, can be made between the two utterances in (8):

(8) a   I apologize.
    b   I'm sorry.

In (8a) we've got an explicit performative, and it passes the *hereby* test, unlike (8b):

(9) a   I hereby apologize.
    b   #I'm hereby sorry.

And by uttering (8a), the speaker is indeed apologizing, whereas by uttering (8b) they're not being sorry. They may indeed be sorry, but they may not; in any case, (8a) itself constitutes an apology, but (8b) doesn't itself constitute being sorry. And yet it too constitutes an apology.

Thus, we've got **constatives**, which describe a state of affairs and can be true or false, and we've got **performatives**, which perform some action and can be felicitous or infelicitous. And performatives themselves can be either **explicit**, in the sense that they make explicit the act that's being performed, or **implicit** in that they perform some act without stating explicitly what act they're performing. And performatives, be they explicit or implicit, themselves can perform a wide variety of actions: stating, warning, promising, apologizing, commanding, thanking, requesting, and so on.

So it might seem that we, and Austin, have resolved all of our issues in terms of putting together a typology of speech acts. But (you'll be unsurprised to learn) it's not so simple. Austin then noted that constatives are performing an act as well; they're performing the act of stating something. That is, just as (10a) is an act of requesting the pencil, (10b) is an act of stating the color of the pencil:

(10)   a   Please hand me that pencil.
         b   The pencil is yellow.

So, Austin realized, every utterance performs some act; constatives are no exception. As a broad generalization, utterances that are **declarative** in form tend to function as statements; that is, they perform the act of stating something. Utterances that are **interrogative** in form tend to function as questions; they perform the act of asking something. And utterances that are **imperative** in form tend to function as requests or commands; they perform the act of requesting or commanding something, depending on how forcefully they're stated:

(11)   a   I have misplaced my porcupine.
         b   Have you seen my porcupine?
         c   Please buy me a new porcupine.
         d   Buy me a new porcupine!

Here, (11a) is a declarative in form and functions as a statement, (11b) is interrogative in form and functions as a question, and (11c) and (11d) are imperative in form and function as a request and a command, respectively. While the difference between a request and a command lies formally in the difference in force and intonation with which they're uttered and to some extent in their form (including the presence or absence of a softening *please* and, in writing, the presence or absence of an exclamation point), which one is chosen will also depend on the context and the relative status of the two individuals. An employee making a request of their supervisor would be wise to use the softer form and include the word *please;* a supervisor making a request of an employee might be wise to do so too, but also has the option of the stronger command, especially under deadline or other pressure. (For more on how relative status affects the form communication takes, see the section on Politeness theory later in this chapter.)

In short, then, we (with Austin) have arrived at a theory in which to speak is to act – and every act of speaking is a speech act. They all perform some action, whether an act of stating, asking, requesting, warning, promising, etc. Some utterances are explicitly performative – that is, performative in form as well as effect – and some are merely implicitly performative, but all utterances are ultimately 'performative' in that they perform some speech act.

INDIRECT SPEECH ACTS

Recall from Chapter 4 the following exchange between President Zelensky of Ukraine and U.S. President Donald Trump:

(12)   Zelensky: I would also like to thank you for your great support in the area of defense. We are ready to continue to cooperate for the next steps specifically we are almost ready to buy more Javelins from the United States for defense purposes.

Trump: I would like you to do us a favor though because our country has been through a lot and Ukraine knows a lot about it.

Trump's statement *I would like you to do us a favor though* is, strictly speaking, a constative. It has declarative form and expresses a state of affairs that can be either true or false: Either Trump would or would not like Zelensky to do a favor for him (and whoever else is included in the referent of *us*). But it's also perfectly clear that he's using this declarative form to make a request – in particular, to request that Zelensky do this favor.

As we saw in the previous section, declaratives in general tend to function as statements – but here, the declarative is functioning indirectly as a request. The request is indirect because it doesn't take the form of a request; that would be something like *Please do us a favor*. More generally, semantically declaratives tend to express statements, interrogatives tend to express questions, and imperatives tend to express requests or commands, but it's possible for any of these forms to serve any of these functions:

(13)   a   Bertha built a boat.   [declarative as statement]
       b   I'm curious whether Danny is dating a dentist.   [declarative as question]
       c   I'd appreciate it if you passed the potatoes.   [declarative as request]

(14)   a   Is Danny dating a dentist?   [interrogative as question]
       b   Did you hear that Bertha's building a boat?   [interrogative as statement]
       c   Could you pass the potatoes?   [interrogative as request]

(15)   a   Please pass the potatoes.   [imperative as request]
       b   Be advised that Bertha is building a boat.   [imperative as statement]
       c. Tell me whether Danny is dating a dentist.   [imperative as question]

In each set above, the (a) example is a direct speech act, in which the form matches the function with which it is conventionally associated, while the (b) and (c) examples are indirect speech acts, in which the function needs to be inferred. So for example, in (13b) there's nothing about the form of the utterance that explicitly tells you that I'm asking a question, but you can infer it on the grounds that in most contexts, if I'm telling you that I'm curious about something, it's likely that if you happen to know the answer, I'd like you to tell me; hence my expression of curiosity doubles as a question I'm asking of you.

And it's not just statements, questions, and requests that can be performed indirectly. Consider the following real-life example:

(16) Daniels said she was in a parking lot preparing to go into a fitness class, and was pulling her infant daughter's car seat and diaper bag out of her vehicle.

"And a guy walked up on me and said to me, 'Leave Trump alone. Forget the story,'" Daniels said. "And then he leaned around and looked at my daughter and said, 'That's a beautiful little girl. It'd be a shame if something happened to her mom.' And then he was gone."

(Bradner and Vazquez 2018)

In this rather chilling example, Daniels (Stormy Daniels, who had been sharing potentially damaging information about Donald Trump) takes the comment about her daughter as a threat, and with good reason; I think most of us would take it that same way. But notice that the threat is indirect: The stranger doesn't explicitly use the form of a threat (something like *If you don't forget the story, something bad will happen to you*). Instead, he makes a declarative statement which in itself is simply true: It would indeed be a shame if something happened to the little girl's mom (i.e. Daniels). But in context, the threat is virtually as clear as if he'd uttered it.

In short, we've expanded our taxonomy of speech acts. We've got performatives, which can be explicit or implicit. And within the category of implicit performatives, we've got direct speech acts and indirect speech acts:

(17) Taxonomy of speech acts
- Explicit performatives perform the act they describe:
  I promise to pickle the peaches.
- Implicit performatives:
  - Direct speech acts perform an act that corresponds to their form:
    Has Harriet held the hamster?
  - Indirect speech acts do neither: *Could you carry the coconuts?*

And a given intention can often be phrased in any one of these three ways. In (18), for example, the speaker's intention is to get the addressee to carry the coconuts:

(18) a. I command you to carry the coconuts! [explicit performative]
     b. Carry the coconuts! [direct speech act]
     c. It would be cool if you could carry the coconuts. [indirect speech act]

Not surprisingly, which form a speaker chooses depends on all sorts of things, including the interlocutors' relationship, the context, and conventions concerning what makes for a felicitous speech act. Not every speech act is felicitous, after all, as we saw when we considered taking a stranger as our lawful wedded spouse above. So now let's take a closer look at what makes for a felicitous speech act.

FIGURE 5.1 Courtesy of xkcd.com.

Felicity conditions

We've seen that there are certain conditions that have to be met in order for a given speech act to be felicitous. These (surprise!) are called its **felicity conditions**. What conditions have to hold in order for me to felicitously take someone to be my lawful wedded husband? Well, first off, I have to be single – not currently married. And the same has to hold for my target husband-to-be. The other person needs to be male; if it's a female, she'd be my wife, and if nonbinary, they'd be my spouse. There needs to be someone present who is legally entitled to wed us. We both need to actually intend to become married. And we need to be currently participating in a wedding ceremony, and one which is intended by all parties to be a wedding ceremony.

Now, I'll admit I'm no lawyer, so I don't know for sure what the conditions are for a legal wedding. In *The Bad Beginning*, the first book in Lemony Snicket's children's book series entitled 'A Series of Unfortunate Events', our sinister fiend arranges for a drama group to put on a play that includes a wedding in which he plays the groom and an actual judge plays the judge. After the wedding scene, he declares that by law, because he and the girl playing the bride have said the right words in the presence of a judge, they are now in fact legally married and he is the inheritor of the bride's fortune. It's a cute premise, but (I'm pretty certain) it wouldn't hold water in real life, because a crucial aspect of a wedding is that the participants actually intend it to be a wedding. What that means, interestingly, is that some felicity conditions have to do with saying the right thing in the right context, but others have to do with the speaker's intentions and sincerity.

Let's take another example, one where the situation is flipped: Here everyone has the right intentions, but they say the wrong thing.

On Inauguration Day in 2009, Chief Justice John Roberts goofed in administering the oath of office to Barack Obama. Here's what he should have said, with Obama repeating after him, phrase by phrase:

(19) I, Barack Hussein Obama, do solemnly swear that I will faithfully execute the Office of President of the United States, and will to the best of my ability preserve, protect, and defend the Constitution of the United States.

Instead, here's what Roberts said:

(20) I, Barack Hussein Obama, do solemnly swear that I will execute the Office of President to the United States faithfully....

There are two differences here: The word *faithfully* has been moved to the end of the clause, and the word *of* has been replaced with the word *to*. If you watch a video of the event (easily found online), you'll see that Obama pauses, recognizes the error, and smiles at Roberts, who then tries to back up and get it right; then Obama goes ahead and utters it with *faithfully* at the end (and it's hard to hear, but it appears he does correctly say *of* rather than *to*). Because of the bobble, just to be safe, they later re-did the oath in private.

So what are the felicity conditions on taking the oath of office of President of the U.S.? Again, I'm no legal scholar, but I'm guessing that these might be included:

(21) a. The individual has been elected President of the U.S.
b. The individual has agreed to be President of the U.S.
c. The participants are the Chief Justice of the Supreme Court and the elected individual.
d. The elected individual utters the Oath of Office.
e. The elected individual intends to do what the oath says.

But you'll notice that this last one is a bit different from the others. If one of the other conditions doesn't hold – for example, if the individual hasn't in fact been elected President, or declines to utter the oath – then they will not have been sworn in, and they won't be President. The swearing-in, in effect, won't 'take'. But if (21e) doesn't hold – if, say, the elected individual satisfies all the other requirements but has no intention of executing the Office of President faithfully or defending the Constitution – then (unfortunately) the swearing-in nonetheless takes effect and the person does become President.

We see here a distinction between a **misfire**, in which failure to satisfy a felicity condition prevents the speech act from taking effect, and an **abuse**, in which it takes effect, but insincerely. Suppose you say *I bet you ten bucks the Cubs will win today*. If the Cubs in fact aren't playing today, then the attempted speech act will misfire and there's no bet. If, however, you simply have no intention of paying off on the bet if the Cubs lose, then it's still a bet, but an insincere one – an abuse. Here's Austin's list of felicity conditions on a speech act:

- (A.1) There must exist an accepted conventional procedure having a certain conventional effect, that procedure to include the uttering of certain words by certain persons in certain circumstances, and further,
- (A.2) the particular persons and circumstances in a given case must be appropriate for the invocation of the particular procedure invoked.
- (B.1) The procedure must be executed by all participants both correctly and

- (B.2) completely.
- (C.1) Where, as often, the procedure is designed for use by persons having certain thoughts or feelings, or for the inauguration of certain consequential conduct on the part of any participant, then a person participating in and so invoking the procedure must in fact have those thoughts or feelings, and the participants must intend so to conduct themselves, and further
- (C.2) must actually so conduct themselves subsequently.

Failure to meet one of the A or B conditions can result in a misfire; failure of one of the C conditions constitutes an abuse.

Similarly, Searle (1969) distinguishes among a number of categories of felicity conditions: The **propositional content condition** requires that the utterance be semantically appropriate to the act; for example, you can't normally take someone as your spouse by saying *I christen this man Fred Flintstone*. **Preparatory conditions** are those that have to hold in advance for the act in question to be felicitous; so, for example, preparatory conditions on a request include the speaker wanting the request to be fulfilled (or at least purportedly wanting it to be fulfilled), the hearer being in a position to fulfill it, and so on. The **sincerity condition** is simply the requirement that the speaker be sincere in their intentions; for example, if you are vowing to preserve, protect, and defend the Constitution of the U.S., the sincerity condition requires you to actually intend to do so (and if you don't intend to do so, it'll be an abuse). Finally, the **essential condition** is the essence of the act; for example, the essential condition on a promise is that it obligates the speaker to do what they've promised.

BOX 5.1

What can you 'hereby' order?

The 'hereby' test for performatives works because the meaning of *hereby* is essentially 'by means of this here action/utterance', where *this* is the utterance in progress. (Compare with *thereby*, which means essentially 'by means of that there action/utterance', as in *He thereby lost the game*.) If I say *I hereby cancel class*, it means that 'by means of this very utterance, I am cancelling class'. If, for one reason or another, the utterance can't do what it says it's doing, it's not performative and the word *hereby* doesn't work. You can't say, for example:

(a) #I hereby love ice cream.

Saying you love ice cream isn't in itself the act of loving ice cream. And similarly, if you're not the professor in the class, you can say *I hereby cancel class* all you want, but class won't be cancelled.

In August 2019, in griping about U.S. trade with China, President Trump tweeted:

(b) Our great American companies are hereby ordered to immediately start looking for an alternative to China, including bringing our companies HOME and making your products in the USA.

Trump took a good deal of mockery in the press for this, on the grounds that he can't 'hereby' order whatever he wants; in particular, being President doesn't grant a person the authority to tell private companies where or how to conduct their business.

To a linguist, of course, the interesting question here (well, okay, there are lots of interesting questions here, but the **linguistically** interesting question) is whether the use of *hereby* is felicitous – which is to say, is Trump's tweet a performative (i.e., an explicit performative)? If I say *I hereby order X* when I have no actual authority to bring X about, have I in fact ordered it? Have I satisfied the felicity conditions on the order? And if not, is (b) an abuse or a misfire?

It doesn't quite seem like an abuse, because Trump is sincere; he really does intend to order American companies to seek alternatives to China. But he doesn't have the authority to effect this result – so in a way, it's very similar to my walking up to a stranger and announcing that I take him as my lawful wedded husband. It's doesn't matter how sincere I am; the wedding won't 'take'.

So even though it seems that Trump in (b) has in fact ordered American companies to seek alternatives to China, in a very real sense it doesn't count as an order at all, because he lacks the authority to do so. No matter how sincere he is in producing this would-be order, it's not properly an order at all, and although companies can decide to follow his wishes or not, they needn't do so because of the tweet in (b). As quite a few commentators immediately pointed out, the order is infelicitous (though I can assure you that almost no commentators used that word). And just as with my declaration that I'm taking some poor befuddled stranger as my lawful wedded husband, it doesn't matter how sincere Trump is; the order won't 'take'.

Felicity conditions, speech acts, and the Cooperative Principle

These last two examples – *I take this man…* and Obama's Oath of Office – have to do with felicity conditions for explicit performatives. But other speech acts are subject to felicity conditions as well. So consider apologies:

(22) a   I'm sorry.
     b   I apologize.

Although (22a) is the default form of an apology in English, so it's easy to think of it as an explicit performative, it's actually an implicit performative: You are not sorry by virtue of having uttered (22a). The actual explicit performative is (22b): By saying it, you apologize. But both of the two are subject to the same felicity conditions, some of which are given in (23):

(23) a   The speaker must have harmed the hearer or done something the hearer dislikes.
      b   The speaker must regret having done so.
      c   The speaker must intend the utterance to count as an apology.

Similarly, consider the indirect requests in (24):

(24) a   Can you pass the salt?
      b   Would you mind passing the salt?
      c   Is the salt over there?
      d   I need the salt.
      e. I'd like the salt.

As Searle (1975) notes, one very common way to perform an indirect speech act is to either ask whether one of the felicity conditions holds or to state that it does. So in (24a-c), the speaker asks whether various felicity conditions on a request for salt have been met, such as:

(25) a   The speaker is able to satisfy the request.
      b   The speaker is willing to satisfy the request.
      c   The speaker has the necessary means to satisfy the request.

The speaker doesn't automatically know whether these conditions hold, so it makes sense to ask. For the utterances in (24d-e) above, the speaker does know that the conditions hold, so it makes sense to say that they do:

(26) a   The speaker needs the request to be satisfied.
      b   The speaker would like the request to be satisfied.

Any of the utterances in (24) would be more polite in most contexts than a bald *Pass the salt*. By simply asking whether the felicity conditions on salt-passing have been met, or stating that they in fact have been, the speaker isn't fully responsible for having made the request but instead leaves an opening for the hearer to fail to satisfy it by noting that some felicity condition doesn't, in fact, hold:

(27) a   Sorry, I can't reach it.
      b   Sorry, I don't want you having that much sodium.
      c   There's no salt over here.
      d   Have you tasted the food? It's already insanely salty.
      e   Very funny. I happen to know you despise salt.

So how does the hearer get from one of the utterances in (24) to an understanding that the speaker is making an indirect request? Once again, the Cooperative Principle comes to the rescue – in this case, the interaction of the maxim of Relation and the maxim of Quantity (or, in Horn's (1984) terms, the interaction of the Q and R principles). So take (24a), *Can you pass the salt?* Recall also from our discussion of tests for implicature that implicatures must be calculable. So here's a calculation that could get a hearer from (24a) to the indirect request:

(28) a The speaker has asked whether I can pass the salt.
 b I assume the speaker's utterances are relevant.
 c I also assume the speaker is saying no more than is necessary.
 d Therefore, the query as to my ability to pass the salt is necessary and relevant.
 e Therefore, this query serves some function that's relevant in this context.
 f The context is that we are all eating dinner together.
 g Many people like to put salt on their dinner.
 h The speaker might be one such person.
 i This desire would make my salt-passing abilities relevant.
 j This desire would therefore make the query relevant.
 k Therefore, I conclude that the speaker desires the salt.
 l I have the means and ability to pass the salt.
 m Therefore, the speaker desires me to do so.
 n The speaker's desire for me to pass the salt is therefore the reason for the query.
 o The speaker knows that I can figure all this out.
 p Therefore, the speaker wants me to infer that they hope I will pass the salt.
 q Therefore, the speaker intends this query to count as an indirect request that I pass the salt.

Whew! Do I think the hearer goes through this series of internal argumentation every time they hear someone say *Can you…* No, of course not. The phrase is used often enough that that's not necessary (it's what Grice would call a generalized conversational implicature) – but for it to be an implicature, such a path of reasoning must in principle exist. And as always, it's cancellable:

(29) Can you pass the salt – that is, later on if I need it? I'm fine for now, but I want to make sure there'll be some available.

And there are contexts, of course, in which the path of reasoning in (28) doesn't hold; for example, if we're staging a play and working out who's going to do what and when, the director might ask me *Can you pass the salt?* without intending that I do so just then. In that case, the line of reasoning in (28) breaks at (28f): There's no meal, hence nothing to actually put salt on.

In summary, speech acts in general are subject to the satisfaction of felicity conditions on their performance, and indirect speech acts can often be performed by asserting or questioning the satisfaction of a felicity condition, with the Cooperative Principle playing a crucial role in establishing the inference to the speech act intended by the speaker.

BOX 5.2

It's hard for me to say I'm sorry

In the wake of Bill Clinton's affair with Monica Lewinksy being discovered, the next logical step was for him to apologize to the American people. This turned out to be tricky, however. First, let's check the felicity conditions on his apology, using Searle's (1969) categories:

- **propositional content condition:** Does what he says have the semantic meaning of an apology?
- **preparatory conditions:** Did he do something that harmed the people he's apologizing to?
- **sincerity condition:** Is he in fact sorry?
- **essential condition:** Does this utterance count as an apology?

Now, let's look at a bunch of his attempted apologies over several months:

a. I did have a relationship with Miss Lewinsky that was not appropriate. In fact, it was wrong. I misled people, including even my wife. I deeply regret that. (8/17/98)
b. I made a big mistake. It is indefensible, and I am sorry. (9/4/98)
c. I ask you for your understanding, for your forgiveness on this journey we're on. (9/9/98)
d. I hope that you and others I have injured will forgive me for the mistakes I've made, but the most important thing is you must not let it deter you from meeting your responsibilities as citizens. (9/9/98)
e. I agree with those who have said that in my first statement after I testified I was not contrite enough. I don't think there is a fancy way to say that I have sinned. (9/11/98)
f. What I want the American people to know, what I want the Congress to know, is that I am profoundly sorry for all that I have done wrong in words and deeds. (12/11/98)

(www.perfectapology.com/clinton-apology-quotes.html (citing the *Atlanta-Journal Constitution*), 12/21/09)

The reason he had to keep going back and trying again is that the American people weren't accepting the early apologies (nor, for some of them, the later ones). As he himself notes in (e), he wasn't contrite enough in (a). It's not clear that the propositional content condition has been met; that is, regretting something isn't quite the same as apologizing for it. It might count as an implicit apology, but in this case what America wanted was an explicit apology. In (b) he gets the propositional content right – he utters the crucial words *I'm sorry* – but this still doesn't convince the public that he's sufficiently sincere. And throughout the evolution of his apologies, the biggest issue was people's uncertainty that the sincerity condition has been met – that is, that he's truly sorry. That's what he's really getting at when he says he wasn't contrite enough.

In (c) and (d) the apologies are even more implicit – *I ask for your understanding* and *I hope that you will forgive me… for the mistakes I've made* – and again, they don't do the trick. Not until (f), uttered four months after the initial effort in (a), do we get an apology that checks all the boxes: It's the right form (*I am profoundly sorry*), hence satisfies the propositional content condition. It satisfies the preparatory conditions: It specifies the offended parties, and notes that he's apologizing for what he's *done wrong in words and deeds*, rather than 'mistakes' he's made. (Interestingly, part of the issue is the question of whether the preparatory conditions have been met: The American public was divided as to whether his offense was an offense against the American public, without which no apology is needed.) It satisfies the sincerity condition in that it's good and grovelly (*profoundly sorry for all that I have done wrong in words and deeds*) – sufficiently so that America is (mostly) willing to believe that he's sincere. And finally, it satisfies the essential condition: It counts as an apology, which was of course the central issue all along.

Types of speech acts: second pass

Above, we saw that all utterances are speech acts; some are explicit performatives, in that they explicitly name the act they're performing, and others are implicit, in that they perform an act without naming it explicitly. And implicit performatives can be further broken down into direct and indirect speech acts, where direct speech acts perform the function conventionally associated with their form and indirect speech acts perform a function not conventionally associated with their form. (In principle, explicit performatives can be broken down into direct and indirect varieties as well, but it's a less useful distinction there, distinguishing between the direct 'I tell you he's a crook' and the indirect 'I tell you I'd like to know the time'. The latter type don't seem very common.)

Now I'll introduce one last three-way distinction. Unlike the direct/indirect and explicit/implicit distinctions, this one doesn't distinguish among different utterances, but rather among different acts simultaneously performed by a single utterance.

Consider the example in (30), from James Comey's testimony before the Senate Intelligence Committee in June 2017:

(30) In his prepared testimony, Comey recalled that, at that Oval Office meeting, the president said: "I hope you can see your way clear to letting this go, to letting Flynn go. He is a good guy. I hope you can let this go."

"I took it as a direction," Comey told the Senate hearing Thursday. "I mean, this is a president of the United States with me alone saying, 'I hope this.' I took it as, this is what he wants me to do. I didn't obey that, but that's the way I took it."

(Pramuk and Schoen 2017)

At the time of the conversation Comey is reporting here, he was Director of the FBI, hence a subordinate of President Trump. The interesting thing is that there are several aspects to the meaning of Trump's statement *I hope you can let this go*:

(31) a I hope you can let this go. [what Trump stated]
     b I am/am not convinced to let this go. [possible effects on Comey]
     c I direct you to let this go. [how Comey believes Trump intended it]
     d ??? [how Trump actually intended it]

In (31a), we've got what's called the **locutionary force**, which is simply the conventional meaning of what has been said. The locutionary force of Trump's statement is that he hopes that Comey will be able to let the Flynn matter go.

In (31b), we have what's called the **perlocutionary force**, which is the effect of the utterance on the hearer: Comey either will or won't be convinced to 'let this go'. This is also sometimes called the **perlocutionary effect** since it's the effect on the hearer. In the creepy example in (16) of a stranger saying to Stormy Daniels, *That's a beautiful little girl. It'd be a shame if something happened to her mom*, the perlocutionary effect is Daniels feeling threatened.

In (31c), we have what Comey believes to be the **illocutionary force**, which is to say the force that the speaker intended the utterance to have – the speech act they intended to be performing. Comey took the statement as a direction; he believed that Trump was directing him to let the matter go. And (31d) is the actual illocutionary force. If Trump actually meant to be directing Comey to let the Flynn matter go, then this was an indirect speech act, an indirect request or command (depending on his intent), and that's the illocutionary force. The reason I put question marks there in (31d) is that only Trump knows for sure what his illocutionary intent was. To see this, consider (32):

(32) …one of the first to spring to the President's defense was his son Donald Trump, Jr., who took to Twitter and parsed the reported encounter in his own fashion. "I hear 'I hope nothing happens but you have to do your job,'" he wrote, describing the President's words as "very far from any kind of coercion or influence and certainly not obstruction!"

(Lane 2017)

Here Trump Jr. tells us that he believes the illocutionary force was simply that of a declarative: Trump Sr. was expressing a hope.

In Trump Jr.'s account, since Trump Sr. was president, he of course wouldn't have wanted to obstruct the law, hence he must have intended *I hope you can let this go* as 'I hope the law permits you to let this go' rather than 'I direct you to let this go'. In Comey's account, since Trump Sr. was his boss, his saying *I hope you can do X* can be interpreted as 'I direct you to do X'.

Since Comey and Trump Jr. interpret the utterance differently, we cannot say for certain what the actual illocutionary intent was; only Trump Sr. is in a position to know that. And as always, the gap between the illocutionary force and the perlocutionary force is bridged by the inferences of the hearer, made with the help of the conventional meaning of the utterance, the context in which it is uttered, and the Cooperative Principle.

BOX 5.3

"You made me an offer that I accepted"

A truly wonderful case of battling speech acts occurred in April 2019 between Treasury Secretary Steven Mnuchin, who was testifying before the House Financial Services Committee, and Maxine Waters, chair of the committee. At issue are how long the current session will run and whether Mnuchin will need to return for further questioning. Mnuchin, eager to end matters, has said he has an appointment with a foreign dignitary that he doesn't want to be late for. At that point, the exchange below occurs:

(a) Waters: If you wish to leave, you may.
Mnuchin: Can you clarify that for me?
Waters: Yes. If you wish to leave, you may.
Mnuchin: OK, so we're dismissed. Is that correct?
Waters: If you wish to leave, you may leave.
Mnuchin: I don't understand what you're saying.
Waters: You're wasting your time. Remember? You have a foreign dignitary in your office.
[…]
Mnuchin: If you'd wish to keep me here so that I don't have my important meeting, and continue to grill me, then we can do that. I will cancel my meeting and I will not be back here. I will be very clear. If that's the way you'd like to have this relationship.
Waters: Thank you. The gentlemen, the secretary, has agreed to stay to hear all of the rest of the members. Please cancel your meeting and respect our time. Who is next on the list?
Mnuchin: OK, so just let's be clear to the press. I am canceling my foreign meeting. You're instructing me to stay here and I should cancel.
Waters: No, you just made me an offer.
Mnuchin: No, I didn't make you an offer.
Waters: You made me an offer that I accepted.
Mnuchin: I did not make you an offer. Just let's be clear. You're instructing me. You're ordering me to stay here.
Waters: No, I'm not ordering you; I'm responding. I said you may leave any time you want. And you said "OK. If that's what you want to do, I'll cancel my appointment and I'll stay here." So I'm responding to your request.

This is so wonderful I can hardly control myself. Waters tells Mnuchin *If you wish to leave, you may*. Thereafter, the battle is on: She wants to frame that statement as granting permission (her illocutionary force), whereas he wants it to be considered a dismissal. But she's having none of it; if they're going to adjourn, she wants it to be due to his unwillingness to remain. By saying *If you wish to leave, you may*, she frames it as his choice; by responding with *If you'd wish to keep me here…and continue to grill me, then we can do that*, he reframes it as her choice. With *The gentleman…has agreed to stay*, she reframes his clearly antagonistic comment as 'agreement', and now he's the one who's having none of it.

At that point, it becomes a speech-act free-for-all, with the following assertions (boiled down):

(b) W: The secretary has agreed to stay.
 M: No, you're instructing me to stay.
 W: No, you made an offer.
 M: I did not make an offer.
 W: You made an offer that I accepted.
 M: I did not make an offer. You instructed me to stay. You ordered me to stay.
 W: I'm not ordering; I'm responding.

The exchange includes arguments over at least eight different types of speech act: granting permission, dismissing, agreeing, instructing, offering, accepting, ordering, and responding. For extra fun, watch the exchange online (it's easy to find if you search for 'Mnuchin Waters') and watch for the moment shortly after this when Mnuchin, still trying to get Waters to perform an official adjournment, says *Please dismiss everybody; I believe you're supposed to take the gravel and bang it* – while miming the banging of a gavel (which he delightfully mispronounces as *gravel*). I think it's fair to say that rarely do you find such an explicit discussion of speech acts in the halls of Congress.

POLITENESS THEORY

Grice never intended his theory to cover all of the factors that contribute to the interpretation of an utterance in context. We've seen how his Cooperative Principle contributes to a hearer's interpretation of a speech act – that is, how it contributes both to that act's perlocutionary force and therefore (since the speaker knows what inferential paths a hearer is likely to take) also to its illocutionary force. But Grice (1975) notes that "There are, of course, all sorts of other maxims (aesthetic, social, or moral in character), such as 'Be polite', that are also normally observed by participants in talk exchanges, and these may also generate nonconventional implicatures."

The most well-fleshed-out account of such 'other maxims' is Politeness theory. I include it here because it has to do with (among other things) the relative status of the speaker and hearer; and as we've seen above, the form that a speech act will take, and the way in which it is interpreted, depend in large part on such statuses. Recall the exchange between Trump and Comey discussed above. As Comey makes clear, the status of Trump as President affected his interpretation of Trump's utterance:

(33) "I took it as a direction," Comey told the Senate hearing Thursday. "I mean, this is a president of the United States with me alone saying, 'I hope this'.

What is clear is that if, say, the roles were reversed, the utterance *I hope you can let this go* would not have been taken as a directive; it's specifically because Trump is Comey's superior that his stated 'hope' is interpreted as a directive.

Likewise, you can immediately infer which of the following statements are likely to be directed from a child to their parent, and which from parent to child:

(34) a   Stop that!
     b   May I have some?
     c   Is it okay if I go outside?
     d   Yes, you may.

Children ask permission (34b-c), parents grant permission (34d), and parents issue commands (34a). Similarly, forms of address differ depending on who is addressing whom. I refer to my physicians using the honorific *Dr.* followed by their last name, while they refer to me as *Betty*. It's interesting to note that American professional interactions have become increasingly informal over the years; a half-century to a century ago, a doctor would have called me *Mrs. Birner* or (a few decades later) *Ms. Birner*. My undergraduate students call me *Prof. Birner*, while I urge my graduate students to simply call me *Betty* – though many of my colleagues prefer that all of their students use *Prof.* or *Dr.* in referring to them. And I have noticed over the years that graduate students from some Asian countries have difficulty calling me by my first name, since this is forbidden in their culture; they sometimes compromise with *Dr. Betty* or *Prof. Betty*.

Clearly there are differences from culture to culture and from language to language in how we address each other, and what one person can felicitously say to another, and which speech acts can felicitously be performed in what circumstances and by what people. **Politeness theory** (Brown and Levinson 1978; Goffman 1955; Lakoff 1973, inter alia) addresses the background concerns that give rise to these differences. According to Politeness theory, each person has a set of conflicting needs that are always in tension, and part of what we do with language is to negotiate this tension. (This is of course reminiscent of Gricean and Neo-Gricean theory, as you'll recall from Chapter 4.) These are our **face needs**, and they have to do with the self-image that we project (and protect) in interaction.

Each person has a **positive face**, which is their desire for closeness, inclusion, solidarity, being liked, intimacy, etc. And each person also has a **negative face**, which is their desire for autonomy, privacy, respect, etc. And even though they are on opposite ends of a spectrum, they are both important. When we interact with each other, we do more than just exchange information and perform the myriad of speech acts discussed above; we also maintain our relationship. And that's a balancing act between respecting each other's negative face and respecting their positive face. Failure on either front can constitute a **face-threatening act**.

So let's take an example. There are a whole bunch of ways to request a pen:

(35) a   I hereby request a pen.
 b   Please hand me a pen.
 c   Gimme a pen.
 d   Dammit, I need a pen!
 e   Pen!
 f   May I have a pen?
 g   If you please, could I possibly have a pen?
 h   Be a dear and hand me a pen.
 i   If it isn't too much bother, would you mind terribly handing me a pen?
 j   My love, hand me a pen, darling.

First off, you can see that the list includes an explicit performative, some direct speech acts, and some indirect speech acts. And they're of wildly varying levels of formality and intimacy. Almost nobody would ever use (35a), except if you wanted to request a pen from a bitter enemy with whom you're generally not on speaking terms. The tone is so formal that it would threaten the listener's positive face in virtually any situation. On the other hand, (35j) is so intimate that unless you're in a very close romantic relationship with the listener, it would constitute a serious threat to the listener's negative face. If I addressed (35a) to my husband, he'd probably worry that I was furious with him, whereas if I addressed (35j) to one of my students, they'd be well advised to drop the class and notify the department chair.

But it can get tricky. Suppose that your high school chemistry teacher, Sally Smith, is a longtime family friend. When you were a child, you called her *Ms. Smith* because you were speaking as a child to an adult. When you were in high school, you called her *Ms. Smith* because you were speaking as a student to a teacher. How long after graduation do you continue to call her *Ms. Smith*? How many family dinners, how many years of adulthood, need to pass before you can safely move to calling her *Sally*? And suppose that shortly after you've made that shift, she completes her Ph.D. and gets a job teaching in the very same university department where you're getting your college degree – NOW what?

And if you're a native English speaker, feel thankful that you don't need to deal with the complex systems of address that are found in some other languages. To take one of the more straightforward examples, some languages have two second-person singular pronouns. In French, the informal or familiar word for 'you' (singular) is *tu*; the formal or polite form is *vous*. In German, the same contrast is marked by *du* (familiar) and *Sie* (polite). So for a German speaker, there are two ways to tell an individual that they are right about some matter:

(36) a   Du hast recht.
 b   Sie haben recht.

Literally, these both translate as 'you have right'. But the first one would be used when speaking to a child, a close friend or family member, a student (if the speaker is their teacher), an employee or subordinate, etc. The second would be used by a child speaking to a parent, a student speaker to a teacher, or an employee or subordinate speaking to a superior, or anyone who's talking to a stranger or someone they know only in a relatively distant or professional context.

But it doesn't take much imagination to see that it can get tricky again. The same sorts of scenarios (like the Sally Smith scenario above) that can make the choice between first and last names complicated can also make the choice between *du* and *Sie*, or between *tu* and *vous*, complicated for German or French speakers. And the lines aren't drawn at the same spot: An English speaker being introduced to a new colleague is likely to call them by their first name, but a German speaker might use *Sie* for such a person until they become more friendly. Precisely when in the developing friendship the shift is appropriate can be, again, tricky. I have a good friend who is the Mother Abbess at an abbey in Germany. Despite the fact that they live together, pray together, work together, and take all their meals together, the sisters in the abbey use *Sie* in speaking to each other. When I visited, I was stumped as to how to refer to my friend; do I use *du* based on our 30-year friendship? *Sie* because that's the custom in the abbey? Or, again, *Sie* in acknowledgment of her status as head of the abbey? Answer: *du*. (I gave up and asked her.)

Terms like *Mr., Prof., Ma'am, Sir, Sie, vous, Dr., Your Highness*, and so on are called **honorifics**. As noted above, English is pretty simple in its system of honorifics, but many other languages have much more extensive systems. Japanese, for example, has a very extensive system: You might add *-san* to someone's name if they're of roughly equal status to you, or as a default if you're not sure (somewhat like *Mr.* and *Ms.* in English); but to show respect to someone of higher status, you might instead add *-sama*, while for someone younger or of lower status you might add *-chan* (particularly to indicate endearment or cuteness, as with babies), or you might add *-kun* (especially for younger men). There are other options for indicating degrees of affection or endearment, seniority (e.g., in business), respect for teachers, unfamiliarity with the addressee, and so on.

Again, honorifics are a matter of face: Referring to my friend the German abbess as *Sie* would respect her negative face, but referring to her as *du* respects her positive face and our long friendship. If I co-teach a course with a longtime friend, the situation is similar: Do I refer to her in class as *Prof. Smith,* respecting her negative face, or as *Sally,* respecting her positive face? I'm certainly not going to use, say, a childhood nickname or an endearment like *Sweetheart*; either of those would threaten her negative face (i.e., her need for distance and respect in the classroom context). But I'm also not going to call her *Ma'am*; that would threaten her positive face (i.e., her need for solidarity and acknowledgment of our relationship).

In short, when dealing with strangers or my superiors, I need to avoid choosing a term of reference, or even a way of requesting a pen, that rudely suggests we are close or that we're social equals; when dealing with children or friends, I need to avoid choosing expressions that will rudely suggest that we're **not** close, or that the child is a social equal. And I not infrequently have to gently point out to new college students that it's inappropriate for them to call me *Betty* – if only to spare them the wrath of the next professor they try to greet by their first name. In this way, every utterance involves taking into account the relationship between speaker and hearer, and adjusting the utterance accordingly. Face needs can be extremely complicated to negotiate, and yet we do so every time we interact.

EXERCISES

Self-test:

1. Which of the following is an explicit performative?
    a. I hate taking quizzes.
    b. May I please skip this quiz?
    c. I hereby declare my hatred of quizzes.
    d. Please take this quiz away.
2. Which of the following is a constative?
    a. I sure love taking quizzes!
    b. I request another quiz!
    c. I hereby declare my love of quizzes!
    d. I thank you for this delightful quiz!
3. Illocutionary force is to perlocutionary force as
    a. the baking of a pie is to the tasting of it.
    b. the chewing of a pie is to the recipe for it.
    c. the crust of a pie is to its filling.
    d. the third digit of pi is to the rest of the digits.
4. A felicity condition on a speech act is
    a. whether it is direct or indirect.
    b. its effect on the hearer.
    c. the constativity of its performativity.
    d. a condition that's necessary for its felicity.
5. Which of the following is not one of Searle's categories of felicity conditions?
    a. the sincerity condition.
    b. the essential condition.
    c. the imperative condition.
    d. the preparatory conditions.
6. If you apologize for something but you're not really sorry you did it, you've committed
    a. an abuse.
    b. a misfire.
    c. an indirect speech act.
    d. a crime against speech acts.
7. Which of the following is most likely to be an indirect speech act?
    a. Can you tie my shoes for me?
    b. I think this quiz is pretty easy.
    c. Who won the 2016 World Series?
    d. Get over here right now!
8. Which of the following is an interrogative?
    a. Which of the following is an interrogative?
    b. One of the following is an interrogative.
    c. Find the interrogative!
    d. What fun it is to search for interrogatives!

9 Which of the following is most likely to be a face-threatening act?
   a What time is it?
   b I'm out of potato chips.
   c No, you can't come.
   d I'm thinking of getting a nose job.
10 Your negative face includes
   a your desire to be included.
   b your desire to be loved.
   c your desire to be left alone.
   d your desire to be a cosmetic surgeon.

Comprehension questions:

1 *I'm sorry* is the standard form for an apology, but it's not explicitly performative. In fact, it's an indirect speech act in that its form is that of a declarative. So it can also be used as a constative statement, to simply describe your state of mind. Invent two examples where it's used as an apology, two where it's used as a statement, and two where it's left purposely ambiguous. When might such an ambiguity come in handy?
2 Explain why an explicit performative generally needs to be in the first-person singular present tense, and why the *hereby* test works.
3 As mentioned in the discussion of Politeness theory above, Grice (1975) notes that "There are, of course, all sorts of other maxims (aesthetic, social, or moral in character), such as 'Be polite', that are also normally observed by participants in talk exchanges, and these may also general nonconventional implicatures." We've seen how indirect speech acts are related to, and make use of, the Cooperative Principle. How is Politeness theory related to the CP, and in what ways might their interaction lead to implicatures?

Opinion questions:

1 If your housemate said *I'll bring home a pizza for dinner* and failed to show up at dinnertime with a pizza, would you say they'd broken a promise? If you accused them, saying *But you promised to bring home a pizza!*, would they be within their rights to say *No, I didn't*? Explain your reasoning.
2 In May 2020, in the midst of the COVID-19 pandemic, President Trump stated that he had been taking hydroxychloroquine, a potentially lethal chemical that had not been shown to have any beneficial effects on COVID-19. The next day his doctor released the following statement:
   (a) As has been previously reported, two weeks ago one of the President's support staff tested positive for COVID-19. The President is in very good health and has remained symptom-free. He receives regular COVID-19 testing, all negative to date.

   After numerous discussions he and I had regarding the evidence for and against the use of hydroxychloroquine, we concluded the potential benefit from treatment outweighed the relative risks.

> In consultation with our inter-agency partners and subject matter experts around the country, I continue to monitor the myriad studies investigating potential COVID-19 therapies, and I anticipate employing the same shared medical decision making based on the evidence at hand in the future.
>
> (Conley 2020)

As various commentators noted, this statement doesn't explicitly say either that the doctor had prescribed hydroxychloroquine or that Trump had taken it. In your opinion, are these two things implicated by this statement? Describe, in your opinion, the illocutionary force of the middle paragraph, and its likely perlocutionary effect on members of the two major political parties.

3. Consider the following text from a book by humorist Mike Royko:
   (a) I apologize to Mrs. Manor and all others whose sensitivities were offended by my reference to sauerkraut on hot dogs. Put anything you want on a hot dog. It is your right as an American.

   (Royko 1999)

   Clearly this apology is intended sarcastically. With that in mind, would you consider this an explicit performative, an implicit performative, or neither? Is it a direct speech act, an indirect speech act, or something else? Is this a felicitous apology, a misfire, or an abuse?

4. *I'm sorry you feel that way*: This statement often enrages the hearer. Why? Is it an apology? Which of the felicity conditions of an apology are satisfied, and which aren't?

Discussion questions:

1. When a head juror announces *We find the defendant to be not guilty*, is that a performative utterance? Why or why not? How about when a parent says *Jimmy apologizes for picking your tulips, don't you, Jimmy?* and little Jimmy ruefully responds *Yes*? How about when someone authorized to speak on behalf of a committee chair says *The committee chair declares these proceedings to be closed*?
2. Are (19) and (20) truth-conditionally equivalent? What if nobody had noticed the error? Would Obama still have been President? Suppose someone had noticed the error six months later; would it, or should it, have made a difference?
3. Are there any speech acts for which there are no felicity conditions?
4. In July 2009, the U.S. Senate approved a resolution apologizing for the enslavement and segregation of African-Americans. The statement read, in part:
   (a) The Congress… apologizes to African-Americans on behalf of the people of the United States, for the wrongs committed against them and their ancestors who suffered under slavery and Jim Crow laws.

   Such apologies issued by an institution on behalf of a group of people are not unusual. What are the felicity conditions on such an apology? Do they differ from the felicity conditions on a personal apology? Or would you say that (a) is not a felicitous apology at all?

5   Are there some people with whom you are more likely to use indirect speech acts and others with whom you are more likely to use direct speech acts? More generally, what relationships (if any) lend themselves to more indirect speech acts, and what relationships lend themselves to direct ones? Why? How does Politeness theory help explain this?

Data collection and analysis:

1   Using Google's Ngram Viewer, compare *I apologize* and *I'm sorry* between 1800 and 2008. Do you find anything surprising about the results – and do you have any thoughts on why *I'm sorry* has taken the path it has?
2   Again using the Ngram Viewer, compare *I promise you, I threaten you,* and *I warn you*. How do you explain the results for *I threaten you* relative to the other two?
3   Type *Can you tell me* into the Google search engine and see what it lists as the top suggested completions (note: suggested completions for the phrase, not actual hits). Ignoring the song titles, how many of them look like indirect speech acts? Does it strike you as surprising that people would expect a machine to understand an indirect speech act? Why or why not?
4   Select a novel with a good deal of dialog. (You can find a lifetime's supply of online novels for free at www.gutenberg.org.) In the novel, try to find five explicit performatives, five direct speech acts, and five indirect speech acts. List the examples you find, and comment on any difficulties you encounter.

Answers to self-test:

1   c
2   a
3   a
4   d
5   c
6   a
7   a
8   a
9   c
10 c

CHAPTER 6

Language structure

KEY CONCEPTS

- innateness
- language universals
- Critical Period Hypothesis
- poverty of the stimulus
- grammar, Universal Grammar
- rule-governed nature of language
- phoneme, allophone
- minimal pair
- complementary distribution
- morpheme, allomorph
- parts of speech
- constituent
- structure dependency
- phrase structure tree
- recursion
- head, complement, adjunct
- X-bar schema

Language differs from other forms of communication in that it conveys meaning through structure. Birdsong can convey meaning, a dog's howl can convey meaning, and a bee's dance can convey meaning – but none of them is a language; none of them has a structure made up of individual units that can be manipulated in a rule-governed way to affect meaning. Human language is structured at the level of the sound, the word, and the sentence (as well as the discourse, which we'll cover in a later chapter). Three things that make human language unique among communicative systems are that 1) the pieces are discrete, 2) reordering or replacing them changes meaning, and 3) they are organized hierarchically. So take a sentence like:

(1) That pup is a poodle.

If you change, say, each *p* here to a *d*, you get *That dud is a doodle*, which means something completely different. And if you then swap the second word with the last, you get *That doodle is a dud*, which means yet something else altogether. And because we know *that pup* is a noun phrase, it can be replaced with another noun phrase, to say (for example) *My pet is a poodle*, or it can be replaced with a pronoun like *it* to make *It is a poodle*. We'll talk about all of this in more detail below, but the point I want to make here is that if we want to talk about meaning in human language, we have to talk about structure.

THE CHOMSKYAN REVOLUTION

If you hang around a group of kindergartners, you'll find they do an impressive job of talking. They can use language to give you information, ask questions, make requests, complain, compliment, promise, apologize – pretty much everything we talked about in the last chapter in our discussion of speech acts. If I, as an adult who's (don't ask) years old, moved to China or Russia or India or Tanzania and lived there for five years, I wouldn't end up anywhere near as fluent in the local language as those kindergartners are in theirs. In fact, those kids already know their native language better **implicitly** than any linguist on earth can describe it **explicitly**. And they acquired it without books and study and drills and conjugation charts and language labs and everything that undergraduate students find frustrating about a language class. So how do they do it?

B. F. Skinner in his 1957 book *Verbal Behavior* argued for a **behaviorist** approach: According to Skinner, a child was born as a 'blank slate' and learned through a process of positive and negative reinforcement. So a child acquired a language similarly, by having their utterances subject to positive and negative reinforcement by other speakers. Sounds reasonable, right? Well, enter Chomsky.

If there's one name in linguistics that you knew before opening this book, it would almost certainly be the name Noam Chomsky, by far the best-known linguist currently living. His critique of Skinner essentially dealt a death blow to behaviorist approaches to language. Chomsky's claim, which was shocking at the time and rocked the world of linguistics, was that the child was born with a great deal of linguistic knowledge already built in – that is, that much of our linguistic knowledge is **innate**. Languages do differ in many ways, but they differ within a set of limits defined by this innate knowledge. Chomsky called this innate knowledge **Universal Grammar** – the universal set of principles that determine what is and is not a possible human language. This was the basis of the Chomskyan Revolution – the claim that revolutionized linguistics.

It may surprise you, but there are in fact a whole lot of properties that every one of the roughly 7,000 currently existing human languages have in common. These are called **language universals** – properties that are true of every human language. For example, all languages make use of lexical categories (noun, verb, etc.) and a hierarchy of phrases (e.g., in English a noun phrase like *the couch* can be part of a prepositional phrase like *on the couch*, which in turn can be part of a verb phrase like *sit on the couch*, etc.).

To take another example of a language universal, languages with 'agreement' all have similar constraints on what can or can't agree with what; so, consider English subject/verb agreement:

(2) a The dogs sit on the couch.
    b The dog sits on the couch.

That 's' on *sits* in (2b) is an agreement marker; it's there when the subject (here, *the dog*) is in the third-person singular, and the verb is present tense. This sort of agreement is pretty common in language. But notice that if you embed one sentence inside another, you can't get agreement between the 'outside' subject and the embedded verb:

(3) a My friends told me that the dogs sit on the couch.
    b *My friend told me that the dogs sits on the couch.

That is, the embedded verb *sit* cares about whether *the dog(s)* is singular or plural, but it doesn't care whether *my friend(s)* is singular or plural; making *my friend* singular doesn't mean you get that singular ending for *sits*. The funny thing is, this is true of ALL human languages; to the best of my knowledge, there's not a single one in which an embedded verb agrees with the outside subject. And there are lots and lots of other such generalizations – facts that are true not only of every human language, but presumably true of every **possible** human language. These are part of Universal Grammar, part of our genetic endowment.

Want more evidence? Of course you do. First, any child who is exposed to human language acquires it – pretty much effortlessly. (The exception is in the case of pathology or injury.) You don't need to teach a child to talk, and in fact trying to do so is pointless. You don't teach your child to talk any more than you teach them to walk. You can have great fun letting them hang on to your fingers and take faltering steps, but ultimately if you completely ignore their efforts they'll still end up walking. No adult is unable to walk because their parents forgot to teach them – and no adult is unable to talk because their parents forgot to teach them. It comes naturally.

And it comes early. There seems to be a **critical period** for the acquisition of language. (This is the **Critical Period Hypothesis**.) If I take a three-year-old and we move to France together, in a year or two that kid will be a fluent speaker of French, and I'll still be mangling my efforts to order a meal in a restaurant. Honestly, we do kids a terrible disservice when we wait until high school or college to start teaching them a foreign language; it almost seems intentionally cruel to wait through all those years when they could acquire a new language effortlessly, and then once the critical period has passed – around the end of puberty – announce to them that now that it's finally going to be extremely difficult, we're going to require them to learn a foreign language!

Another bit of evidence: the **poverty of the stimulus**. This just means that what children hear (the 'stimulus') is often a pretty poor example of the language they're acquiring, and they have no way of distinguishing what's actually a good example of the grammar of their language and what's a bad example. So consider (4):

(4) a Hey, Hon – Where's my – oh dangit, where'd she put – hey, have you seen my – dammit, there it is – never mind, got it!
    b Hey, Honey, I can't find my wallet; do you know where it is? Oh, never mind; I found it!

Now, we can all agree that (4b) would be a more useful piece of data for a child trying to piece together the grammar of English; but I suspect they're a lot more likely to hear utterances like (4a), at least a great deal of the time. Yet despite such poor input, they're able to put together a grammar that enables them to produce a limitless set of extremely complex sentences.

So there's good reason to believe that a child's innate capacity to acquire language is part of their genetic endowment, much like the bird's capacity to acquire its song. It's their implicit knowledge of what is and isn't possible in human language, and as we'll see below, these boundaries greatly simplify the job of acquiring a language. And as the child grows, they develop native-speaker **competence** in their native language.

This competence is implicit – no five-year-old is going to explain to you the rules for forming a noun phrase – but it guides their language production nonetheless, and it's essentially flawless. Sure, our **performance** may be full of what can be considered 'errors' in that they don't match up with the implicit grammar of our language (as in (4a)), but when I say your grammar is essentially flawless, I mean that each person's grammar is very slightly different (your accent isn't identical to mine, and neither is your vocabulary, and quite likely not even all your grammar rules), and it makes no sense to say that one person's implicit, internal grammar is 'right' and another person's is 'wrong'. It would be like telling a bird they're off-key, or telling a daisy it's got too many petals. You wanna split your infinitives, end sentences with a preposition, or sprinkle your sentences with double negatives? No linguist is going to tell you you're wrong; they'll just assume that this is part of the grammar of your particular dialect. Suppose a linguist hears someone utter (5):

(5)   Ain't nobody gonna go to no party.

The linguist won't ever tell you this is ungrammatical, because it isn't: It's generated by the grammar of the speaker's dialect, and that grammar is governed by a set of rules, just like every dialect of every language. Telling the speaker in (5) that their language use is wrong, ungrammatical, sloppy, or bad is just a way of privileging the speakers of one dialect over another. It may be an effective means of social control and oppression, but it's not a valid scientific conclusion, it's not kind, and it's not good linguistics.

SOUND STRUCTURE

At the beginning of the chapter, I said that two of the things that make human language distinctive among communicative systems are that the pieces are discrete, and that reordering or replacing them changes meaning. Let's see how this works with sounds.

(6)   a   pat
      b   cat

The way we know that *pat* and *cat* are different words with different meanings lies entirely in the difference between the sound /p/ and the sound /k/. Now first, notice that we're talking here about **sounds**, not spelling, and that's what the slashes indicate – so /p/ indicates the first sound in the word *pat*, and /k/ indicates the first sound in the word *cat*. (There's an entire

International Phonetic Alphabet that gives symbols for the full range of sounds of the world's languages; to check it out, go to www.internationalphoneticalphabet.org and click on 'IPA Symbols Chart Complete'. It's great fun.)

The crucial thing to note is the relationship between sounds and meaning: If you change one sound in a word to be a different sound of the language, it changes the meaning. Change /p/ to /k/ and you've changed the word. This isn't the case in other communicative systems; a dog can't pull out one specific bit of its howl and replace it with another and change the meaning of the howl.

Now, it's not the case that you can change just anything about a sound to turn it into another sound. So consider these two words:

(7) a pot
    b spot

If you place your open hand an inch or two in front of your mouth and pronounce these two words in a natural way (it might help to pronounce them in the context of a sentence), you will probably feel a little puff of air after the /p/ in *pot* but not after the /p/ in *spot*. But ordinarily we perceive both of these sounds as 'the same'; they're both /p/. That little puff of air is called **aspiration**, and if you replace the aspirated /p/ in *pot* with an unaspiration /p/ like the one in *spot*, you'll still have the word *pot*; it'll just be pronounced a little oddly. The same holds for pronouncing *spot* with an aspirated /p/; it's still the same word, but pronounced oddly. You may in fact find it quite hard to do in both cases, because the rules of English tell you whether or not to produce that little puff of air for a /p/ that appears in a given position, and it's hard to violate those rules.

Interestingly, every language has a different set of sounds that can change one word into another; these are called **phonemes**. In English, /p/ and /k/ are different phonemes, but aspirated and unaspirated /p/ aren't; they're two different forms of a single phoneme. Different forms of a single phoneme are called **allophones** of that phoneme. So aspirated [pʰ] and unaspirated [p] are two different allophones of the phoneme /p/.

If you're wondering whether two sounds are different phonemes in a given language, see if swapping one for the other can change one word into another, as with *pat* and *cat* in (6). A pair of words like these prove that the two sounds in question are different phonemes in that language; the pair of words is called a **minimal pair**, because it's a pair of words that differ minimally (in only one phoneme).

It may seem like I'm making a mountain out of a molehill, since you may feel that it's obvious that /p/ and /k/ are different phonemes. But now consider the following three sounds, where the square brackets indicate that we're dealing directly with sounds rather than phonemes (reserving slashes to represent phonemes), and the raised 'h' indicates aspiration:

(8) a [pʰ]
    b [p]
    c [b]

As we've seen, the difference between (8a) and (8b) is the aspiration. And technically, the difference between (8b) and (8c) is **voicing**, which is to say whether the vocal folds in your larynx are vibrating. To feel voicing, put your hand on the front of your throat and make the /s/ sound; then make the /z/ sound. You should feel a buzz with the /z/ that's absent with the /s/; that's the voicing, the vibration of the vocal folds. Similarly, though it's a bit harder to detect, if you make a [p] sound **without adding a vowel sound** to it, you won't feel the buzz, but with [b] you will.

In English, [pʰ] and [p] are allophones of the same phoneme, but [b] is a different phoneme, as seen in the minimal pair *pat* and *bat*. Because English speakers perceive [b] as a distinct sound, it changes the word being uttered. And because they perceive [pʰ] and [p] as a single sound, they won't perceive *spot* pronounced with a [p] and *spot* pronounced with a [pʰ] as being different words with different meanings, which makes sense if they don't perceive [p] and [pʰ] as different sounds.

In Korean and Thai, however, the sounds group differently. In Korean, [p] and [b] are allophones of the same phoneme, but [pʰ] counts as a different phoneme. So in Korean [pʰul] means 'grass', but [pul] means 'fire'; the difference between [pʰ] and [p] can change a word because they count as different phonemes. And in Thai, [pʰ], [p], and [b] represent three different phonemes. So again [pʰ] and [p] can distinguish between words in a way that they can't in English: For example, in Thai [pʰaa] means 'split', but [paa] means 'forest'. Because of the difference it can make in word meaning, we say that aspiration is **phonemic** in Thai and Korean but not in English.

On the flip side, in English the sounds [l] and [r] represent two different phonemes (which we'd represent as /l/ and /r/, with the slashes representing phonemes as opposed to just sounds); for this reason we can get a minimal pair like *lap* and *rap*. But in Japanese they represent the same sound, and so in Japanese there's no such minimal pair. This is the source of the stereotype of native Japanese speakers having trouble with [l] and [r], but it's an unkind stereotype; keep in mind that a native English speaker would have exactly the same kind of problem with Korean [pʰ], [p], and [b].

And the problem, in a nutshell, is that not only do allophones of a single phoneme count as a single sound, but there are rules for which allophone gets used in which context. Recall I said above that you'd probably have a hard time pronouncing the /p/ in *pot* without aspiration, because the rules of English require aspiration for a /p/ that appears in this position. In fact, the rule is broader than that: It applies to every voiceless 'stop' in English, where a **stop** is a sound that completely stops the flow of air momentarily and then releases it again. The voiceless stops in English are /p/, /t/, and /k/, and all of these sounds are subject to the same rule that requires them to be aspirated before a stressed vowel. This is evidence of the **rule-governed** nature of language, which we'll see all through this chapter; we have implicit rules we follow without even knowing we're following them, like the rule for aspiration.

Because there's a rule that tells English speakers when to aspirate a voiceless stop and when not to, you'll never get a case where you've got a choice. For every phonetic environment, every position in every word, the rule determines whether you get the aspirated or the unaspirated version. We say that the aspirated and unaspirated versions are in **complementary distribution**. And this is our clue that they count as the same sound, the same phoneme. Because they're in complementary distribution – because [p] and [pʰ] can't appear in the same environment – there can never be two words that differ only in whether they have [p] or [pʰ] in a certain position. So you can never get a minimal pair.

Now if you try to learn Korean, it's going to be very hard to learn the rules that govern when the /p/ phoneme is pronounced as a [p] and when it's pronounced as a [b], because that's not something your native language has trained you for. It'll be equally tough to remember which words contain the /p/ phoneme and which contain the /pʰ/ phoneme. And the hardest of all will be to train yourself **not** to follow the English rules that tell you when to aspirate a [p] sound, because you've been following those rules all your life without being aware of it – but if you follow those rules when speaking Korean, half the time you'll be saying the wrong Korean word. And that's also why it's sometimes hard for a native Japanese speaker to **not** follow the rules of Japanese for pronouncing [l] and [r] in various contexts – rules they've been following all their life without thinking about it.

WORD STRUCTURE

Morphemes

Although swapping out one phoneme for another can make a difference in a word's meaning, a phoneme itself has no meaning; the /k/ in *cat* doesn't contribute any part of its meaning. It's true that there are words made up of only one phoneme (such as English *I*), but that phoneme doesn't carry its meaning to other words that contain it (such as *hide*).

The smallest linguistic unit that actually carries its own meaning or function is called a **morpheme**. Some words are made up of a single morpheme:

(9) a cat
      b jump
      c banana
      d consider
      e while
      f and
      g catastrophe

None of these words can be broken down into smaller meaningful bits. The meaning of the word *cat*, for example, isn't present in *catastrophe*, despite the spelling. Nor is the meaning of the word *fee* in there, despite the last syllable of *catastrophe* being pronounced like *fee*. A morpheme is a sound/meaning combination, and that sound/meaning combination isn't present in *catastrophe*. So it's clear that *catastrophe*, despite being four syllables, is only one morpheme.

Other words are made up of more than one morpheme:

(10) a happiness   happy   –ness
       b undeniable   un–   deny   –able
       c recapitulation re–   capitulate –tion

Don't worry about the fact that the letter *y* in *happy* changes to an *i* in *happiness* or that the *te* in *capitulate* merges with the *ti* in *–tion*; these are spelling details that we don't need to worry about. (The rule affecting the sound /t/ in *capitulate* when adding *–tion* is more interesting, but again not important here.) We use the hyphen to indicate a **bound** morpheme, which is one that has to be attached to another morpheme, like *–ness*; you can't use *–ness* as a word by itself. Words that can appear on their own, like *happy*, are called **free** morphemes.

Allomorphs

Just as a phoneme may have variants, a morpheme may have variants – and just as the variants of a phoneme are called **allophones**, the variants of a morpheme are called **allomorphs**. So consider the examples in (11):

(11) a a dog
     b a sandwich
     c a firetruck
     d an ostrich
     e an elephant
     f an ambulance

You're way ahead of me on this one: You know that before a consonant, you get *a*, and before a vowel, you get *an*. The two are really variants of a single morpheme: They're allomorphs, with a rule that tells you which allomorph to use in what contexts, just as there was a rule to tell you which allophone to use in what contexts. The technical way to say this is that allophones and allomorphs are **conditioned by their environment**. Here's a slightly more complicated example:

(12) a cats
     b dogs
     c ducks
     d turtles
     e swans
     f giraffes

Although in terms of spelling (which, remember, we don't care about here) the plural ending on all of these looks like *–s*, it has two different pronunciations in these words – two different allomorphs. Remember how some sounds are voiced (made with vibrating vocal folds) and others are voiceless (made with the vocal folds not vibrating)? See if you can tell which of the plural endings in (12) are pronounced as voiceless (and therefore sound like [s]) and which are pronounced as voiced (and therefore sound like [z]).

You'll probably find that you pronounce the final sound in *cats, ducks*, and *giraffes* with the voiceless allomorph (i.e., as [s]), and the final sound in *dogs, turtles*, and *swans* with the voiced allomorph (i.e., as [z]). And the rule you're following, though this is less obvious, is that you choose the allomorph that matches the voicing of the consonant it follows: [t], [k], and [f] are voiceless, so they take the voiceless allomorph of the plural ending, and [g], [l], and [n] are voiced, so they take the voiced allomorph of the plural ending.

There are plenty of other allomorphs of the plural ending we haven't talked about – think about words like *bushes, men, children*, and *sheep* – but the two important points here are simply

152 LANGUAGE STRUCTURE

FIGURE 6.1 Courtesy of xkcd.com.

that morphemes have variants (just like phonemes), and that your choice of which variant to use is rule-governed (again, just like phonemes).

Words: a review

So now that you've got a handle on what a morpheme is, we'll tackle something considerably more complicated – **words**. You may think you know what a word is, but recall from Chapter 2 that it's not all that obvious. For one thing, a meaning that can be expressed as a single word in one language may take several words in another:

(13) a Atawapenda
     b He will like them.

Both of these mean the same thing, but the Swahili version in (13a) takes only one word, and the English version in (13b) takes four.

We say that a **word** is the smallest **free** form in a language – the smallest unit that can meaningfully stand alone. Recall from above that a free morpheme is one that can stand alone, which means that a free morpheme is a word. A word, in turn, may be a free morpheme, or it may be made up of several (or many) morphemes, as with *houses, unfathomable*, and *antidisestablishmentarianism*.

Don't be fooled into thinking that a word is a string of letters with a space on either side. Remember, that's just spelling; the language itself is primarily spoken, not written, and plenty of languages don't have a writing system at all. (And children acquire language naturally, whereas a writing system is a secondary encoding of language that needs to be explicitly taught.) There are no spaces in spoken language. If you look at a spectrogram of spoken language, it's continuous. There are no silences that separate the words.

More importantly, the spaces will lead you astray. A word acts as an **island**: It can stand alone (as discussed above), its parts can't be rearranged (*dogs* can't become **sdog*), and it can't be broken up by other morphemes (*cute dogs* is okay, but not **dogcutes*). Now, here's the perhaps surprising thing: A compound word is considered a single word, because it too acts as an island – regardless of whether there's a space in it or not:

(14) a You're going to need to make up yesterday's test.
     b You're going to need to make yesterday's test up.
     c I like to wear bright makeup.
     d *I like to wear makebrightup.

(15) a My uncle lives in a white house.
     b My uncle lives in a white two-story house.
     c The President lives in the White House.
     d The President lives in the *White two-story House.

In (14a) and (14b), *make up* is two words, as you can see from the fact that the two parts can be separated in (14b). In (14c) and (14d), *makeup* is a single word, and as expected, it can't be broken up (as in (14d)). And again unsurprisingly, *white house* in (15a) is two words, and in (15b) we can separate those two words with *two-story*. But in (15c) an (15d), *White House*, despite the space between its two parts, is a single word, as evidenced by the fact that you can't separate those parts as in (15d).

Another piece of evidence is stress: In the case of two words, each of those words gets its own stress, but in the case of a compound word, one part of the word — usually the first syllable if it's a two-syllable word — will get primary stress. So in (14a-b), the words *make* and *up* are each stressed, and likewise for *white* and *house* in (15a-b). But in the compounds *makeup* and *White House* in (14c-d) and (15c-d), the first syllable is stressed and the second is unstressed: *MAKEup, WHITE House*.

Parts of speech

As we all know, words fall into 'parts of speech' — categories like noun, verb, adjective, and preposition. And maybe back in what used to be called 'grammar school' you were taught helpful little rules like these:

(16) a A noun is a person, place, or thing.
     b A verb is an action word.
     c An adjective describes a noun.
     d An adverb modifies a verb or adjective.

I'm going to argue against every one of these, because I'm feeling grumpy. And also because they're wrong.

Let's start at the beginning. I know a lot of you are already thinking you can fix the first one; somewhere along the way teachers realized that there are a huge number of nouns that can't possibly be considered a person, place, or thing: nouns like *love, sincerity, indignation, concept,* and *reason*. So more recently, (16a) has been amended to:

(17) A noun is a person, place, thing, or idea.

Fixed? Well, no. For one thing, what does it mean to say *sincerity* is an 'idea'? In what sense is *sincerity* more of an idea than *sincere*? As far as I can tell, *sincere* and *sincerity* differ only in one attribute, and that's that one is an adjective and one is a noun. To say that *sincerity* is an 'idea' and *sincere* isn't an idea is just another way of saying *sincerity* is a noun and *sincere* isn't.

Okay, so what about (16b)? Isn't a verb an action word? Well, not always. What about the verbs in these sentences?

(18) a This book has *grown* dull.
 b The water in the pond has *stagnated*.
 c The peach *rotted*.
 d Roberta *owns* two cars.
 e Sarah *heard* an owl in the distance.
 f Phineas *resembles* his sister.
 g Your knowledge of physics really *impresses* me.
 h Cora *felt* tired.

I can't see any sense in which the italicized verbs describe actions. It's hard to imagine anything less active than stagnation or resemblance – and please note that *stagnation* and *resemblance* are the noun forms of *stagnate* and *resemble*. If *stagnate* is an action, so is *stagnation*.

Moving right along, it's equally unclear how an adjective describes a noun in any way that a verb doesn't. If I talk about *a stagnant pond*, I'll agree that *stagnant* describes the pond. But if I say *the pond is stagnating*, I think *stagnating* has described the pond as well. Again, as far as I can see, the only difference between *stagnant* and *stagnate* is that one is an adjective and one is a verb. And finally, in (16d), if anyone can explain to me what *modify* means in this usage, or how it differs from describing, I'd be very grateful.

But that's not to say that meaning is irrelevant. Some types of meaning really do lend themselves more easily to certain parts of speech. If you want to refer to an object such as a tree or an elbow, that will often call for a noun. And if you want to talk about some particularly active thing someone did, a verb is probably going to come in handy. But it's also worth noting that different languages might assign different parts of speech to a given meaning. As we'll see in Chapter 9, the Hopi language uses verbs for meanings like 'lightning', 'wave', 'noise', 'meteor', and 'spark', whereas English uses nouns.

So if a word's part of speech isn't determined entirely by its meaning, what else is there?

BOX 6.1

Hooray for *they*!

Each year the American Dialect Society selects a word (or phrase) as its Word of the Year (WOTY). It's frequently a newly coined word, or a familiar word with a new use, as with its 2013 WOTY, *because* (as in 'because science!'). In 2015 the winner was *they*. This might seem a bit puzzling; hasn't the word *they* been around pretty much forever?

The interesting thing about *they* is that its use is changing, and not in the way you might think. For many years, prescriptivists fought against the use of *they* in singular gender-neutral contexts, as in:

(a) If anyone knows the answer, they should write it down.

Back in the Dark Ages when I was going to school, we were taught that this was incorrect because *they* is plural; instead, we were told that (b) is the 'correct' way to phrase it:

(b) If anyone knows the answer, he should write it down.

We were assured that *he* here is generic, referring to any gender. But in the wake of studies showing that sentences like (b) do in fact bring a male to mind, it was recognized that treating maleness as the default was less than fair; and now it's commonly accepted for *they* to serve a gender-neutral role as in (a).

But this isn't what earned it its WOTY status in 2015. Regardless of how prescriptivists might have felt about it, *they* has been serving this function for hundreds of years, under the pens of some of our most respected English-language writers. This has been shown beautifully by linguist Mark Liberman on the Language Log blog (https://languagelog.ldc.upenn.edu/nll/?p=24504), where he gives dozens of examples ranging from Chaucer to Eliot and beyond, including these:

(c) And whoso fyndeth hym out of swich blame,
    They wol come up.
    (Chaucer, "The Pardoner's Prologue")

(d) There's not a man I meet but doth salute me
    As if I were their well-acquainted friend.
    (Shakespeare, Comedy of Errors, act IV scene 3)

(e) Every fool can do as they're bid.
    (Jonathan Swift, *Polite Conversation*)

(f) ...something suggested to me, "Everybody has their own burden to bear."
    (Charlotte Brontë, *Henry Hastings*)

(g) The fact is, I never loved any one well enough to put myself into a noose for them.
    (George Eliot, *Middlemarch*)

So *they* has been singular as well as plural for a very long time. (And this is no cause for sorrow; we've managed with *you* as both singular and plural for quite some time now.) But until recently, it was used in the singular only for cases of unknown or nonspecific individuals, as in the above examples. What's new and WOTY-worthy about *they* in its recent usage is, as the ADS press release put it, "its emerging use as a pronoun to refer to a known person, often as a conscious choice by a person rejecting the traditional gender binary of *he* and *she*" (www.americandialect.org/2015-word-of-the-year-is-singular-they). So this allows both the clearly female use in (h) and the nonbinary use for a specific individual in (i):

(h) Of course, no expecting mother has to worry about scientists disrupting the REM sleep of their developing fetus.

(Walker 2018)

(i) They wore a gray V-neck T-shirt and jeans. With an ankle crossed over the other knee, they picked at the rubber rim of one of their sneakers….

(Bergner 2019)

So join the crowd adopting gender-neutral *they* for specific individuals! It not only solves the age-old problem that it's been quietly solving for centuries (as in (c)-(g)), but it also makes it easy to talk about the full range of people of all gender identities in a kind and uncomplicated way. And if there are still a few prescriptivists out there who aren't crazy about this new use? As with all linguistic innovations, they'll adjust… or not… but the language will manage just fine.

Structure and function

A word's part of speech has to do with how it relates to other words in the sentence. The way you know something is a noun is that it acts like a noun in a sentence. To put it bluntly, a noun is a word that can fit in a frame like this:

(19) That _____ is very impressive.

Words like *dog* and *house* fit here, but so do words like *love, sincerity,* and *indignation*. And a verb is a word that can fit in a frame like one of these:

(20) a They will probably _____ tomorrow.
      b Otherwise, they will _____ each other.

Active words like *run* and *sing* fit in (20a), but so do words like *stagnate* and *rot*. And words like *hug* and *tickle* fit in (20b), but so do words like *hear* and *resemble*.

So a noun isn't a person, place, or thing; it's a word that fills a 'noun' slot in a sentence. And a verb isn't an action word; it's a word that fills a 'verb' slot in a sentence. And so on.

There's no single definitive sentence that provides a frame for all nouns or all verbs; as you see in (20), for example, we need different frames for transitive and intransitive verbs – that is, for verbs that take a direct object (transitive) and those that don't (intransitive). (We know both types are verbs in part because so many verbs can appear in either frame – *I ate* vs. *I ate rice* – and partly because all verbs take tense: *hug/hugged/resemble/resembled*.) We'll talk more about these differences later in the chapter. But part of your implicit linguistic competence as an English speaker is knowing the difference between where you can put verbs and where you can put nouns (etc.), and part of knowing a word is knowing whether it can act as a verb or a noun (or both, as with *run* in *I ran yesterday* vs. *I went for a run yesterday*).

So part of knowing a word is knowing its meaning, and part is knowing its function – and the same holds for bound morphemes. Part of knowing the morpheme *–ness* is knowing that it turns an adjective into a noun:

(21) happy + –ness = happiness

Not every morpheme changes the part of speech of the **stem** it's attached to. So take the word *unhappy*:

(22) un– + happy = unhappy

Adding *un-* to the stem *happy*, which is an adjective, doesn't change its part of speech; *unhappy* is still an adjective.

Here's another bit of evidence that our knowledge of morphemes involves not just meaning but also function. Consider these three words:

(23) a happier
     b singer
     c winter

What is the status of *–er* in each of these words? You'll immediately realize that *winter* in (23c) is a single morpheme; it just happens to end in *–er*, but *–er* isn't a separate morpheme, so it doesn't have its own meaning and doesn't serve a distinct function in this word.

In (23a) and (23b), though, each of these *–er* endings has its own meaning and serves a function, but they're different in the two cases. In (23a), *–er* means 'more' and attaches to an adjective stem (*happy*) to result in another adjective. In (23b), *–er* means 'one who does X' and attaches to a verb stem (*sing*) to result in a noun. Because these two instances of *–er* have different meanings and serve different functions (by virtue of attaching to different parts of speech and resulting in different parts of speech), we know they are two different morphemes that just happen to have the same form. They're homonyms, like *light* (meaning 'illumination') and *light* (meaning 'not heavy').

Representing word structure

The most important thing to realize about word structure is that it's not 'flat', but hierarchical. Consider the three proposed structures for the word *undesirable* in Figures 6.2, 6.3, and 6.4.

Diagrams like these are called **word structure trees**. (When we do syntax, we'll get **phrase structure trees**.) The structure in Figure 6.2 is a flat structure: It suggests that the word *undesirable* is made up of three morphemes of equal status strung together. The structure in Figure 6.3 suggests that the word has a hierarchical structure, with *un-* first joining to *desire* to make *undesire*, and *–able* attaching to that, to result in our final word *undesirable*. And the structure in Figure 6.4 suggests that the word has a hierarchical structure in which *–able* first attaches to *desire* to get *desirable*, and *un-* then attaches to that to give us *undesirable*.

Your intuitions are probably already telling you that Figure 6.4 is the correct structure, because you realize that what *undesirable* means is 'not desirable', and the morpheme *un-* here means 'not'. That's an argument for this structure based on meaning, but there's also an argument based on function: The morpheme *un-* that means 'not' can only attach to an adjective (*unhappy, unstable*), not to a verb like *desire* as in Figure 6.3. *Undesire* just isn't a combination that

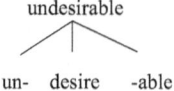

FIGURE 6.2 *undesirable*, option 1.

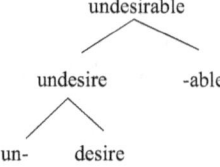

FIGURE 6.3 *undesirable*, option 2.

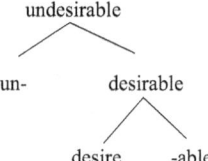

FIGURE 6.4 *undesirable*, option 3.

means anything; you can't say *I undesire another piece of cake* to mean you do not desire another piece of cake. So the structure in (24b) is, in a word, undesirable.

Instead, Figure 6.4 is the clear winner, in that it shows in graphic form what an English speaker knows about the structure and meaning of the word *undesirable*. And corresponding to this structure and meaning are a set of **rules** that guide us – the rules that tell us that *un-* is a morpheme meaning 'not' and attaches to an adjective, and that *–able* is a morpheme that means 'capable of being, or likely to be, X'd' and attaches to a verb (which corresponds to the 'X').

Now, there is a distinct, homonymous morpheme *un-* that does in fact attach to verbs, as in *untie*; the way you know it's a distinct morpheme from the *un-* in (24) is that it has a different meaning ('to reverse a process') as well as a distinct function (attaching to a verb to create another verb). So now we have two different *un-* morphemes: One attaches to adjectives and means 'not', and one attaches to verbs and means 'reverse a process'. This gives rise to the possibility of structurally ambiguous words, as we see in (24):

(24) This sweater is unbuttonable.

This sentence can mean either that the sweater in question cannot be buttoned (perhaps because it has no buttons), or that it can be unbuttoned (in which case it does have buttons). Clearly these two meanings describe two very different sweaters. And accordingly, there are two different structures corresponding to these two meanings, as seen in Figure 6.5 and Figure 6.6.

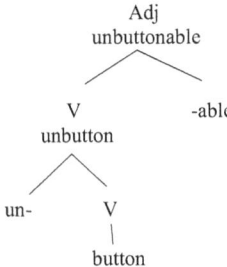

FIGURE 6.5 *unbuttonable*, option 1.

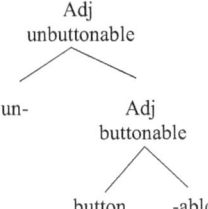

FIGURE 6.6 *unbuttonable*, option 2.

Can you tell which structure matches which meaning? The answer is that Figure 6.5 means 'able to be unbuttoned', whereas Figure 6.6 means 'not buttonable'. Notice that *unbutton* is a unit within Figure 6.5, while *buttonable* isn't; on the other hand, *buttonable* is a unit within Figure 6.6, while *unbutton* isn't. These units are called **constituents**, and they are extremely important within linguistics. As we've already seen, **constituent structure** is an important aspect of word meaning; in 26, different structures correspond to different meanings. Linguists talk about the **structure dependency** of language, by which we mean that the meaning of a word or sentence depends on its structure. This will become even more important when we talk about syntax.

Other ways of building words

The kind of word-building we saw in the last section is called **derivation**, which we discussed in Chapter 2 as well; we derive new words by building them up out of smaller pieces in a hierarchical fashion. And functional morphemes like plural or past-tense endings are added via a process of **inflection**, which can usually be included in our word structure tree, for example to turn *song* into *songs* or *jump* into *jumped* or *unbutton* into *unbuttoned*. Derivational affixes typically change the meaning of a word in a substantial way – as with *play/replay* and *sing/singable* – whereas inflectional affixes typically have to do with grammatical notions like tense, gender, and agreement. These inflectional categories often result in paradigms of, for example, verb suffixes that depend on the tense of the sentence and the person and number of the noun, as you see here for German:

spielen 'to play'

person	present-tense form
first-person singular	*spiele*
second-person singular	*spielst*
third-person singular	*spielt*
first-person plural	*spielen*
second-person plural	*spielt*
third-person plural	*spielen*

And more columns could be added for additional tenses.

But not every polymorphemic word (i.e., not every word made up of more than one morpheme) can easily have its structure shown in tree form: A word like *men* is two morphemes – *man* and 'plural' – but those two morphemes don't break up into two tidy pieces. Similarly for certain irregular plurals like *sheep* and *stimuli*, or irregular past-tense words like *had* or *went*.

And other languages have many other morphological processes that we don't have in English – far too many to deal with here. In particular, many other languages have vastly more complicated inflectional systems than English does.

For just one example, consider Classical Hebrew, as illustrated in Figure 6.7.

Keeping in mind that Hebrew script reads from right to left, look at the top line, where you'll see three letters. The first one – the one on the right – corresponds to the English /m/ sound, the middle one to the English /l/ sound, and the leftmost one to the English /k/ sound. As you see in the left-hand column, each of the words in the list incorporates these letters, along with other letters and diacritics. The central column gives a rough idea of how each word is pronounced, and the right-hand column gives its English equivalent. The diacritics – the little dots and lines below and next to the letters – tell you what vowel sound goes along with each consonant, which accounts for the pronunciation difference between, say, 'malak' (line 1), 'moleyk' (line 3), and 'melek' (line 4).

The fascinating thing about Hebrew is that these additional sounds and vowel changes correspond to changes in meaning in a rule-governed way. So adding those two /a/ sounds (pronounced roughly 'ah'), as you see in the first line, doesn't just turn /mlk/ into third-person past tense; it does the same thing for other verbs throughout Hebrew: For example, /zkr/ is the root for 'remember', and /zakar/ is 'he remembered'. The language largely consists of three-sound roots, which are then altered in rule-governed ways to result in new but related

מ ל ך

מָלַךְ	malak	'he reigned'
יִמְלֹךְ	yimlok	'he reigns'
מֹלֵךְ	moleyk	'reigning, reigning one'
מֶלֶךְ	melek	'king'
מְלָכִים	mlakim	'kings'
מַלְכָּה	malkah	'queen'
מַלְכוּת	malkut	'royalty, reign'
מַמְלָכָה	mamlakah	'kingdom'

[adapted from C.L. Seow, *A Grammar for Biblical Hebrew*, Nashville: Abingdon, 1995, p. 24]

FIGURE 6.7 Classical Hebrew morphology (adapted from Seow 1995, p. 24).

meanings. It's a consistent, patterned, rule-governed system – but very different from what we're used to with English.

Returning to English, we should pause to note that we also have plenty of ways of creating new words. Recall from Chapter 2 some of the creative ways in which English gets new words and morphemes:

- coinage – just making them up: *nerd, nylon, quark*
- onomatopoeia – imitating their sound: *chirp, crash, fizz*
- clipping – shortening an existing word: *burger, gym, bike*
- acronyms – using the first letters of a phrase: *snafu, scuba, NASA*
- blends – combining two or more words: *brunch, smog, Brexit*
- backformation – misanalyzing an existing word: *edit* (from *editor*), *pea* (from *pease*), *apron* (an *apron* from misanalyzed *a napron*)
- eponym – using someone's name: *Levi's, sandwich* (from the Earl of Sandwich), *watt*
- borrowing – taking words from another language: *gesundheit, sushi, fiancee*
- conversion – changing a word's part of speech: *butter* (from noun *butter* to verb *to butter*), *process* (from noun to verb), *run* (from verb to noun)

In short, there are lots of sources of new words. But inflection and derivation are unique in that they allow us to build larger words from existing parts (morphemes), and thus show the structure of the resulting words and, most importantly, the rule-governed nature of morphology. As we'll see in the next section, rules and structure are absolutely central to our knowledge of language and how linguistic meanings are expressed and understood.

SENTENCE STRUCTURE

Ambiguity and constituency

We saw with the word *unbuttonable* that having two different structures renders a word **ambiguous**. There are actually two kinds of ambiguity: Lexical ambiguity is when two words are homonymous, as we saw with *light* ('not heavy') and *light* ('illumination'). Structural ambiguity is when a word or sentence has two distinct structures and hence two distinct meanings, as with *unbuttonable*. In English, this is a lot more common in sentences than in words. Consider the examples in (25), a couple of which you saw back in Chapter 3:

(25) a   Microsoft wants to update my hard drive and I find myself questioning seriously if I want to install something called "Malicious Software Removal Tool."
(Maleckar 2019)

b   We love hurting people.
(church sign image posted on Facebook, July 2019)

c   In April 2016, their conversation wound up on a stage at a conference on consciousness in Tucson, Arizona, where the two met for the first time....
(Pollan 2019)

d For our unrepresented staff and faculty, the university will need to defer a decision on providing an increment in FY21 until the September board meeting. For those in bargaining groups, conversations are currently underway....

(email from university president to employees, June 2019)

e I have been watching her shop.

(Harris 2000)

The example in (25a) comes from a humor piece; obviously what's meant is a software tool that removes malicious software: a [malicious software] removal tool. But the humorist claims to be taking it as possibly a software removal tool that's malicious: a malicious [software removal tool]. As with *unbuttonable* above, we've got two different constituent structures here.

In (25b), *We love hurting people* can mean either 'we love to hurt people' or 'we love people who are hurting', depending on whether *hurting* is a verb and *people* is its direct object (i.e. people are who we hurt) or *hurting* is an adjective and *hurting people* is the direct object of *love* (i.e. hurting people are who we love).

FIGURE 6.8 Courtesy of sadanduseless.com.

In (25a-b), the ambiguity is intentional, for the sake of humor. In (25c-d), it's unintentional and possibly harder to spot. In (25c), *a conference on consciousness in Tucson, Arizona* could be (as intended) a conference on consciousness that's held in Tucson, Arizona: a [conference on consciousness] in Tucson, Arizona. Or it could be a rather curious conference that takes as its topic the issue of consciousness in Tuscon: a conference on [consciousness in Tucson, Arizona].

In (25d), *our unrepresented staff and faculty* could be (as intended) our staff and faculty who are unrepresented: our unrepresented [staff and faculty]. Or it could be our unrepresented staff and all our faculty: our [unrepresented staff] and faculty. As the next sentence makes clear, it's the former meaning that's intended: The deferral applies to anyone (staff or faculty) who's not represented by a bargaining group.

Finally, in (25e), either I'm watching her as she shops, or what I'm watching is [her shop] – i.e., the shop she owns. (It's the latter reading that's intended.)

In each case, each constituent structure corresponds to a different meaning. In (25b), there's a difference in the part of speech assigned to *hurting* (akin to a linguistics ambiguity classic – *Flying planes can be dangerous*), but in the others, it's purely a matter of constituency, which is to say which words form 'blocks', or **phrases**. I've shown the constituency differences using brackets; in the discussion above each set of brackets indicates a constituent. But there's a clearer way to show constituency using the same method I used above for word structure, which is to use tree diagrams. In the case of phrases and sentences, we call these **phrase structure trees**.

BOX 6.2

Language invention

All of the structures we've talked about in this chapter develop naturally in natural languages – languages that have evolved over generations, with earlier versions slowly changing into newer versions, dialects breaking off and slowly developing into distinct languages, and so on. This is what happened with Latin, for example: Although it's often called a 'dead' language, it never really died; it lives on in its descendant languages like Spanish, French, and Italian, just as Old English lives on as Modern English.

Alongside natural languages, however, we have the increasingly popular hobby of inventing new languages, often for fictional planets or populations. Consider Tolkien: He wasn't just a great novelist; he was a great philologist, where a 'philologist' is someone who studies words and language structures and their history (basically the precursor to today's linguists). His fictional world has not only a stunning array of different creatures and cultures, but also an even more stunning array of well-developed languages. One of his great joys in writing his books was the creation of these languages – and he was well-placed to do so, having so thoroughly studied the properties of human languages.

Today it is not unusual for a novelist or screenwriter to invent a language for their characters, but this is actually fairly new. Perhaps the most influential early work in this vein was linguist Mark Okrand's creation of Klingon for the Star Trek universe (and the corresponding publication of his 1992 *Klingon Dictionary*). A number of websites now offer instant Klingon translations (search for "Klingon translator") for your interstellar travel needs.

Nonetheless, language invention itself isn't new at all; for centuries people have tried to develop languages that would either (in the creator's view) improve on natural language, or provide a universal language that everyone on earth could use to communicate. The most famous of the latter group is Esperanto, developed by Ludwik Zamenhof in 1887. He envisioned it as a second language for all the peoples of the world, in order to provide a universal communicative system and foster world peace. Unfortunately, it turned out to be rather difficult to convince everyone in the world to learn a language you've invented, and Esperanto hasn't taken the place on the world stage that Zamenhof hoped for. Nonetheless, it has attracted a surprisingly large following, with tens of thousands (and possibly millions) of speakers and reportedly more than a thousand native speakers.

Want to try your hand at creating a language? Here are some of the things you'll want to consider:

- Who speaks this language? How and where do they live? What do they eat and wear, and what tools do they use? In short, what will they need words for?
- Phonetics: What is their sound system like? Human languages vary widely in the sounds they do and don't include. For example, the two English "th" sounds (as in *think* and *that*) are pretty rare in the world's languages. What sounds will you want your language to include? Consider both the set of consonants and the set of vowels you'll use.
- Phonology: In English, whether the plural ending is pronounced as [s] or [z] depends on what sound comes before it (compare the final sound in *cats* and *dogs*). Every human language has similar rules affecting how its sounds are produced. What rules will affect the way sounds in your invented language are produced?
- Morphology: In English, prefixes and suffixes can be added to root words (as in *unhappy* and *indescribable*), and compounds can be created from smaller words (as in *toothpick* and *sleepwalk*). What will the rules be for forming words in your language? Will it have extremely long words stringing together lots of morphemes, or will it, like English, mostly be made up of words with no more than a few morphemes?
- Syntax: The basic word order in English is subject-verb-object (as in *The girl ate the spaghetti*) and its phrases put the head before the complement (as in *ate the spaghetti*, *into the basement*, and *head of the phrase*), but these things differ in different languages. What will be the basic word order of your

language? Will its phrases be consistent in where they place the head with respect to the complements? How will it form questions and commands?
- Orthography: Does your language have a writing system? If so, does it use an alphabet, a syllabary (one symbol per syllable), or a set of logograms (one symbol per idea or word) – or some other system, or a combination?

Clearly, creating a language will teach you a lot about your own language – but just as important, it can be great fun. Try it – and enjoy!

Representing sentence structure

One of the primary questions of linguistics theory – maybe the biggest question of all – is how a child almost effortlessly acquires a system as complex as human language in a very short period of time. While they're still struggling to tie their shoes, learn the alphabet, and balance their peas on a fork, children pick up amazingly subtle details of their native language without even thinking about it. To take just one of an infinite number of examples, consider (26):

(26) a When did Jan say she would do her work?
     b When did Jan say how she would do her work?

Even small children recognize that (26a) is ambiguous: The speaker might be wondering when Jan said something, or they might be wondering when Jan is planning to do something. In (26b), the ambiguity goes away: Now the only possibility is that the speaker is wondering when Jan said something. You know this, but you'd probably be at a loss to explain how you know it, except that it has something to do with the addition of *how* in (26b).

How on earth do kids pick up linguistic subtleties like that? As you know from earlier in the chapter, Chomsky argues that there's an innate Universal Grammar. We're going to look very briefly at the sorts of information this UG contains. But to do that, we need to look in more detail at how to represent sentence structure.

Using brackets, as I did above to distinguish, say, a malicious [software removal tool] from a [malicious software] removal tool, is fine for highlighting a single constituent like *malicious software*, but if you want to show all the details of structure for a sentence, it can get ugly, with brackets inside of brackets inside of brackets inside of brackets…. So instead, we use trees of the sort we used above for morphology – but as you'll see, phrase structure trees for a complete sentence are a lot more complicated.

Let's start with a simple sentence:

(27) People surprise me.

What part of speech is *people*? Yup, it's a noun. And not only that; it's also a complete *noun phrase*. How do we know? Well, recall that in order to know what part of speech something is, you just check where it goes in a sentence: A noun goes in a noun slot, which is to say it can replace nouns in other sentences:

(28) a <u>Unicorns</u> surprise me.
     b <u>Hazelnuts</u> surprise me.
     c <u>Books</u> surprise me.

Likewise, a noun phrase is something that goes in a noun phrase slot:

(29) a <u>Unicorns with wings</u> surprise me.
     b <u>Purple hazelnuts</u> surprise me.
     c <u>Books about unicorns eating hazelnuts</u> surprise me.

Since *unicorns* can fit in the same slot as *unicorns with wings*, it counts as a full-fledged noun phrase – which is handy, because it means we don't need two different rules for what can serve as the subject of a sentence, one for noun phrases and one for bare nouns. A noun all by itself can serve as a noun phrase (NP), a verb all by itself can serve as a verb phrase (VP), a preposition all by itself can serve as a prepositional phrase (PP), and so on:

(30) a Unicorns <u>eat hazelnuts</u>. [VP]
     b Unicorns <u>eat</u>. [VP]
     c Unicorns fly <u>around mountains</u>. [PP]
     d Unicorns fly <u>around.</u> [PP]

Okay, so our first phrase structure rule will need to say that a noun phrase can be made up of a noun. We show this with an arrow:

NP →N

So *mountains* is both a noun and an NP. We show this with the super-simple tree in Figure 6.9.

How about *around mountains*? That's a prepositional phrase containing a preposition and a noun phrase:

PP →P NP

The tree is shown in Figure 6.10.

But just as an NP can be made up of only an N, a PP can be made up of only a P, as we saw in (30d); unicorns can just *fly around*. Since *around* and *around mountains* have the same syntactic distribution (i.e., they turn up in the same places), they're the same kind of phrase, a PP. So let's make the NP in our PP rule optional by putting parentheses around it:

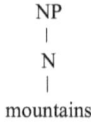

FIGURE 6.9 *mountains.*

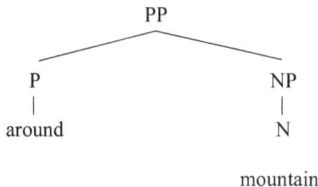

FIGURE 6.10 *around mountains.*

PP →P (NP)

But now consider this perfectly good sentence:

(31) Unicorns eat hazelnuts from California.

You can tell *hazelnuts from California* is a single phrase, because if you passivize the sentence, the whole phrase moves to the front and becomes the subject:

(32) Hazelnuts from California are what unicorns eat.

So what kind of phrase is *hazelnuts from California*? It's an NP. And what is *from California*? A PP. And of course *hazelnuts* is still a noun. So we need an expanded rule for what can be included in an NP:

NP →N PP

But of course unicorns can eat just *hazelnuts*, so that PP is optional:

NP →N (PP)

I'd like to pause here and note something wonderful, which is that with just two rules we've now made it possible to create phrases that are (in principle) infinitely long:

NP →N (PP)
PP →P (NP)

(33) lots of authors of books on management of conferences of societies of researchers into origins of species of whale

The tree is shown in Figure 6.11.
You might argue that this is a very silly phrase, but it's at least imaginable in context:

(34) A Who was at that super-esoteric meeting of the Sealife Conference Management Association?
     B Oh, the usual: lots of authors of books on management of conferences of societies of researchers into origins of species of whale.

168 LANGUAGE STRUCTURE

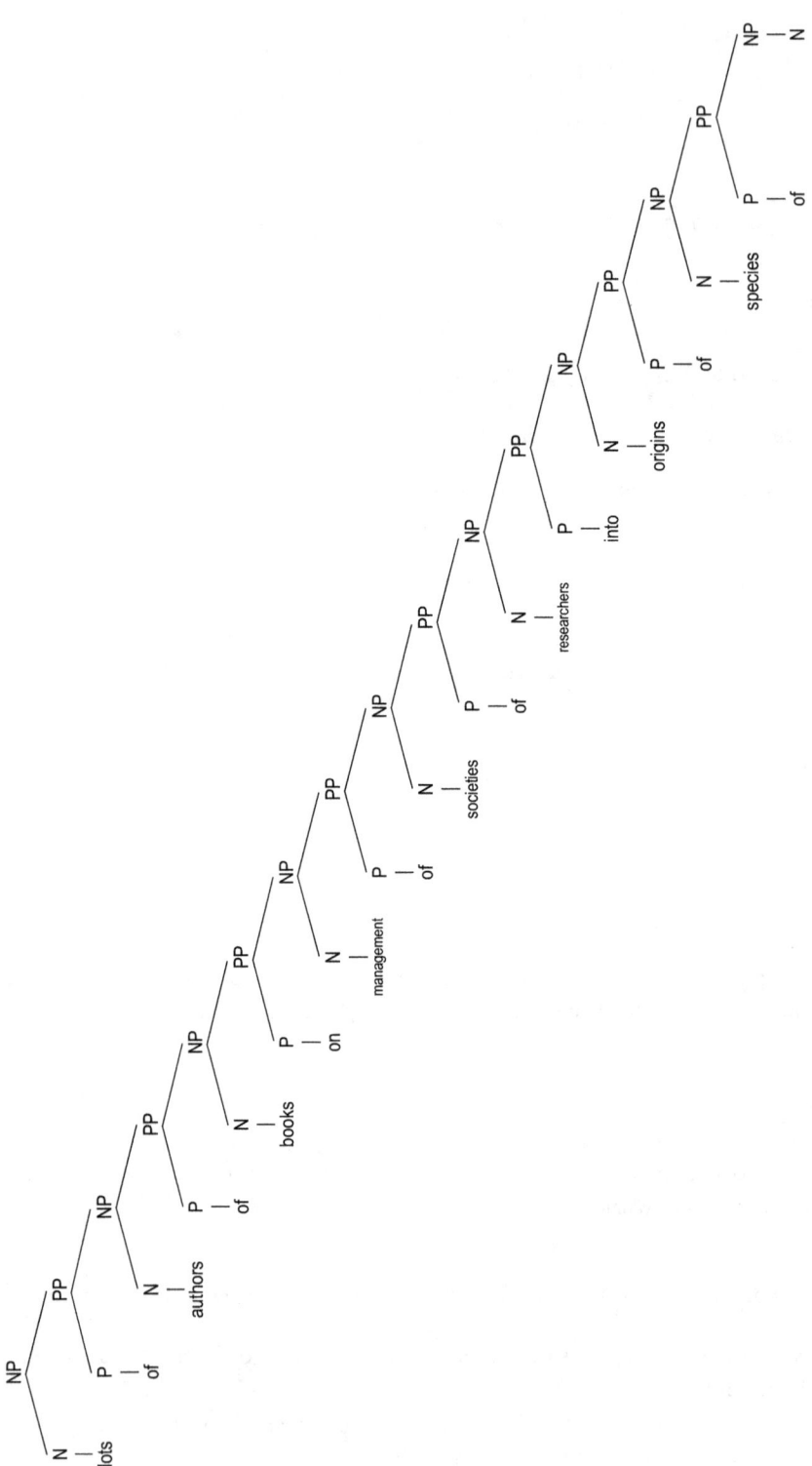

FIGURE 6.11 *lots of authors of books on management of societies of researchers into origins of species of whale.*

And every single branching node in that tree is an instance of one of these two rules:

NP →N (PP)
PP →P (NP)

And lest you doubt that these are all NPs and PPs, you can try our handy distributional test and see that, for example, the NPs all fit in the NP slot in a sentence like (27) above:

(27) People surprise me.

(35) a Lots of authors of books on management of conferences of societies of researchers into origins of species of whale surprise me.
      b Authors of books on management of conferences of societies of researchers into origins of species of whale surprise me.
      c Books on management of conferences of societies of researchers into origins of species of whale surprise me.
      d Management of conferences of societies of researchers into origins of species of whale surprises me.

…and so on, right down to *Whales surprise me*, with only the agreement marker on *surprise* changing depending on whether the subject (which is everything but *surprise(s) me*) is singular or plural.

The great takeaway here is that as long as we've got two rules that refer back to each other in the circular way that these two do, we've got **recursion**, and where we've got recursion, we've got infinity – or at least infinity in theory. (In practice, I can't utter an infinitely long sentence, because eventually I'll die – and I doubt any of my loved ones would take up the effort to continue the sentence afterward.)

So at this point we've got two parts of speech and two rules, and we can already create phrases of any length, and (hence) an infinite number of different phrases – which in turn means that we can create phrases nobody has ever uttered before in the history of the world, and our hearer can understand them (such as (33) above). And a side effect of all that is that children do not, and cannot, learn their native language by memorizing all of its grammatical sentences (since there are an infinite number of them); instead, they learn the **rules** governing the language, and by mastering a very small number of rules become able to construct an enormous (infinite) variety of sentences.

Expanding our grammar

Now, suppose our phrase is instead:

(36) the authors of books on management of conferences of societies of researchers into origins of species of whale

We already know what *authors of books on management…* etc. is; it's a noun phrase. What's *the*? You may have been taught either that it's an article or that it's a determiner; we'll use the word **determiner**. Articles like *a* and *the* are one category of determiner; another category is demonstratives like *this* and *these*:

(37)   these authors of books on management of conferences of societies of researchers into origins of species of whale

Now, recall that so far, we've got rules saying that a noun phrase is made up of an obligatory noun plus an optional prepositional phrase, and a prepositional phrase is made up of an obligatory preposition plus an optional noun phrase. We see in (36) and (37) another kind of phrase, one that's made up of a determiner plus a noun phrase – and again, the NP is optional:

(38)   a   I love these authors of books on management of conferences of societies of researchers into origins of species of whale.
      b   I love these.

So what we've got here, on analogy with our previous rules, is a determiner phrase, made up of an obligatory determiner and an optional NP:

DP → D (NP)

The obligatory element in each of these rules is called the **head**; for example, the D is the head of the DP. And the optional phrase is called the **complement**.

And we may as well keep going; what are these?

(39)   a   applauded these authors of books on management of conferences of societies of researchers into origins of species of whale
      b   ate some artichokes
      c   swept the floor

In each case we've got a verb (*love, ate, swept*) plus a DP. And you won't be surprised to learn that the DP is optional:

(40)   a   I applauded these authors of books on management of conferences of societies of researchers into origins of species of whale.
      b   I applauded.
      c   I ate some artichokes.
      d   I ate.
      e   I swept the floor.
      f   I swept.

So here we've got a verb phrase, containing an optional DP:

VP → V (DP)

And finally, we get adjective phrases that behave similarly, both with and without following PPs:

(41) a Jane was happy (about the dinner).
    b Phyllis felt sorry (for Harry).
    c The dessert was rich (in chocolate).

So we can add this rule:

AP → A (PP)

So far, then, we have the following rules:

DP → D (NP)
NP → N (PP)
PP → P (NP)
VP → V (DP)
AP → A (PP)

In each case we've got a phrase made up of an obligatory head plus an optional phrasal complement.

But there's a fly in the ointment: Although the complements shown here in parentheses are typical, each of these phrases allows for other complements as well:

(42) a *The poor* need our help.   DP → D (AP)
    b The streets were full of *potholes deep and wide*.   NP → N (AP)
    c The plane went *through the clouds*.   PP → P (DP)
    d The plane went *up through the clouds*. PP → P (PP)
    e I'm so *happy to help*.   AP → A (VP)
    f I *love candy*.   VP → V (NP)
    g Fiona *went into the garage*.   VP → V (PP)
    h George *grew tired*.   VP → V (AP)

So really, what we ought to say is that each of these rules says that the phrase consists of an obligatory head and an optional phrase of any category:

DP → D (_P)
NP → N (_P)
PP → P (_P)
VP → V (_P)
AP → A (_P)

And at this point, it has become clear that these are all really the same rule, varying only in terms of what phrase category we're dealing with. So we can greatly simplify things by replacing the head category and the complement category with **variables**:

XP → X (YP)

A variable can stand for any category, but a given variable must stand for the same category throughout the entire rule. So what this rule means is that a particular kind of phrase (XP) is made up of a head of the same category (X) plus an optional complement of any category (Y). This one rule captures exactly the same thing that we previously were using five rules to say.

This is half of Chomsky's famous **X-bar schema**, which itself consists of just two rules and accounts for a vast amount of linguistic structure. There are three important points to make about this rule, in Chomsky's theory:

1. It is part of every human being's genetic endowment – except that whether the complement is on the right or the left side of the head is unspecified and will vary from language to language.
2. Once a child encounters their native language and discovers whether their language is **head-first** (like English) or **head-final** (like Japanese), this one rule plus some vocabulary enables them to produce a phenomenal number of very complex structures (as in (35) above).
3. Most importantly, this helps to explain how it is that something as complex as human language can be acquired so quickly and apparently effortlessly by toddlers.

And to prove how quick and easy it is to develop linguistic structures based on a single, quickly learned rule, let me show you how easy YOU will find it to draw the trees for these structures now that you know the rule.

You'll notice that so far we only have rules for phrases, not a complete sentence. It turns out that a sentence is just another kind of phrase that behaves pretty much like the phrases above, following the XP rule – but with some additional details about things like tense. So allow me to leapfrog over those complications by adding one 'cheater' rule for a sentence:

S →(XP) VP

The XP here is the subject of the sentence, and it's usually an NP or DP, but it doesn't have to be:

(43) a Under the bed is a good place to hide, isn't it?   [PP subject]
        (Plumley, L. *Chances Are*)
     b To read is a great pleasure.   [VP subject]
     c Afraid is the worst way to feel.   [AP subject]

So how do we show the structure of a sentence? We'll start with our cheater rule, as shown in Figure 6.12.

And then we'll draw the rest of the tree just as we did for (35) above, starting with replacing that XP with whatever kind of phrase serves as the subject. Not sure how much of the sentence to include in that subject? There are two easy ways to be sure: First, find the main verb in the sentence; everything before that is the subject. Second, try turning the whole thing into a question using a *wh*-word like *who* or *what*:

(44) a The problem with our plan is the issue of funding.
     b Main verb = *is*; so the subject = *the problem with our plan*
     c *What is the problem with our plan?* [subject = *the problem with our plan*]

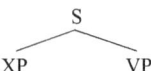

FIGURE 6.12 S →XP VP.

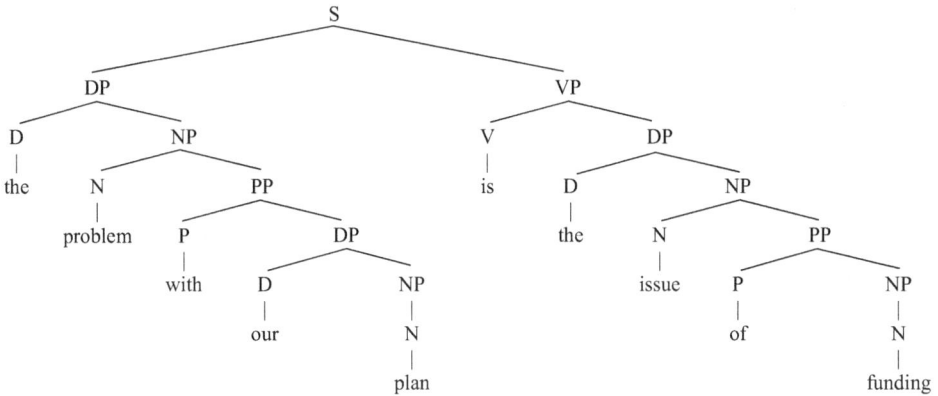

FIGURE 6.13 *the problem with our plan is the issue of funding.*

So once we're clear that *the problem with our plan* is the subject and *is* is the verb, it's easy enough to fill in the structure of the subject, the verb, and the rest of the verb phrase. The tree for the sentence in (44a) is given in Figure 6.13.

BOX 6.3

Different dialects, different rules

By now you know that language is rule-governed, and also that linguists are descriptivists, not prescriptivists: We study the rules of language as it is actually used, not as someone thinks it should be used. So where does that leave a sentence like (a)?

(a) She going to the store.

In Standard English, this sentence would be rendered as in (b):

(b) She's going to the store.

That little *'s* is of course a shortened form of the word *is*, which is itself a form of the word *be*. *Be* and its various forms (*is, are, was, were*) are called **copulas,** for the connecting role they play in the sentence (yep, just like the word *copulate,* which denotes a rather different sort of connecting). The thing is, other than marking number and tense agreement with other parts of the sentence, they don't really contribute anything to the sentence's meaning. In fact, lots of languages allow the copula to be omitted altogether, just like it is in (a). And obviously the meaning of (a) is no less clear than the meaning of (b).

In Standard English, the copula is required unless some other verb fills the main verb slot, such as in (c):

(c) She considered going to the store.

But in certain nonstandard dialects – particularly in what's called African American Vernacular English (AAVE), Black English, or Ebonics – the copula can be omitted under certain circumstances; this is called a **zero copula.** If you're a prescriptivist, you might be quick to decry (a) as ungrammatical – but it's very easy to show that it is indeed grammatical. Consider the paradigms in (d)-(f):

(d) She is going to the store.
She's going to the store. [contraction]
She going to the store. [zero copula]

(e) That's the way life is nowadays.
*That's the way life's nowadays. [contraction]
*That's the way life nowadays. [zero copula]

(f) I asked whether she's going to the store, and she is.
*I asked whether she's going to the store, and she's. [contraction]
*I asked whether she's going to the store, and she. [zero copula]

The thing to notice here is that the rules in AAVE for using the zero copula are precisely parallel to those in Standard English for using a contraction. Among other things, the rules forbid contraction – and likewise zero copula – if the copula would receive emphatic stress (as in (e)) or would be the last word in its clause (as in (f)). (See Pullum 2018: 72-3 for a fuller statement of the rules.) Clearly we cannot claim that *She going to the store* is 'ungrammatical' if we acknowledge that *She's going to the store* is grammatical, since they're obeying almost exactly the same grammar rule. The truth, of course, is that both are grammatical, just in different dialects.

So why does this matter? It matters because we have a long history of telling children that the way they talk is ungrammatical, sloppy, lazy, bad, or stupid. Which of course tells them that THEY are bad, lazy, stupid, etc.... and worse yet, that pretty much everyone they know and love is bad, lazy, stupid, etc., since they all share the same dialect. Which is a problem for a number of reasons:

- First, because as I've just shown, it's just plain false. Every single dialect of every single language is equally systematic, rule-governed, complex, and useful for communication. There is absolutely no such thing as a bad dialect.

- Second, because it's cruel. Making children feel terrible about themselves is bad, period. (Certainly much worse than being a speaker of a zero-copula dialect.)
- Third, because it's racist. Recall that the zero copula is a feature of AAVE, which is largely (but not exclusively) spoken by some (but not all) Black people in America. AAVE is a rich dialect with a great many rules that I could have chosen to focus on, all of which are exactly as systematic as the one featured here (and exactly as systematic as the corresponding rules of Standard English).

Standard English, like every standard dialect, is the language of prestige and power, and it's also the primary means for communicating across dialects in English. Because it serves this cross-dialect communicative function, it's handy to have – but because it's the language of prestige and power, it's also dangerous. It's well known among linguists that speakers' judgments of nonstandard dialects generally reflect their social judgments of the speakers of those dialects – since, of course, no dialect has inherently greater value. The prestige dialect has its status purely for historical reasons, not because it's a better way to talk. We like to believe it's a better way to talk, because that allows us to use language as a proxy for human value, and – to be quite blunt – to make sure the people currently in power stay in power.

In short, let's not throw out Standard English; it serves a useful function. But more importantly, while we're teaching Standard English to schoolchildren, let's also teach them that the way they talk at home and on the playground is also good and serves a useful function. Because honestly, it's the truth, and it's kind, and it's just. And those strike me as three pretty good reasons.

Structural ambiguity

Now recall our ambiguous sentences, and the fact that the ambiguity in a sentence like (25c), repeated here as (45), depends on how the sentence is parsed – that is, how it's broken down into its constituents:

(45) In April 2016, their conversation wound up on a stage at a conference on consciousness in Tucson, Arizona, where the two met for the first time....

The phrase *a conference on consciousness in Tucson, Arizona* is ambiguous between the following two phrase structures:

(46) a   a conference on [consciousness in Tucson, Arizona]
      b   [a conference on consciousness] in Tucson, Arizona

One thing to notice is a difference between *on consciousness* and *in Tucson, Arizona*. There is a tight relationship between *conference* and *on consciousness* that doesn't exist between *conference* and *in Tucson, Arizona*. That is, only a relatively small number of nouns denote things that can be *on consciousness* – you have conferences on consciousness or books on consciousness, but you don't usually have dogs on consciousness or couches on consciousness or rice on consciousness or trees on consciousness. And seen from the other side, to be a conference is in its essence to be a conference **on** something, whereas to be a conference isn't in its essence to be a conference somewhere. Or, to put it yet another way, just about **anything** can be in Tucson, Arizona – dogs, couches, rice, trees – but not just anything can be on consciousness.

What all of this means is that *on consciousness* is a **complement** of *conference* – a phrase it 'selects' as a preferred object, whereas *in Tucson, Arizona* is an **adjunct** of *conference* – a phrase that adds some addition information but isn't any more tightly connected to the meaning of the head of the phrase (i.e., *conference* as the head noun of the whole NP *conference on consciousness in Tucson, Arizona*) than it would be to any other potential head noun.

Notice also that a head might take one or maybe two complements: The noun *put*, for example, takes an NP and a PP:

(47) Sally puts yogurt on her granola.

Here, *yogurt* is an NP and *on her granola* is a PP.

But while a head takes a very small number of objects (usually zero or one), you can string together adjuncts like holiday lights:

(48) Barry polished his car yesterday in his driveway under a big tree for seven hours out of boredom while eating apricots.

Here, *his car* is the complement (i.e., the object) of *polished*: the verb *polish* is transitive and takes a direct object, and *his car* is that object. It's the thing being polished. To polish is, in its essence, to polish **something**. But the rest of the phrases in (48) are utterly optional:

(49) a yesterday
      b in his driveway
      c under a big tree
      d for seven hours
      e out of boredom
      f while eating apricots

All of these phrases add detail to the polishing of the car, but they're adjuncts; they have no close semantic relationship to the event of polishing. Barry might have done virtually anything yesterday in his driveway under a big tree for seven hours out of boredom while eating apricots.

So we don't want these phrases in the complement spot that we've established as the sister of the noun in an NP. We need to add a slot, and we need it to be recursive so we can add as many adjuncts as we want. Chomsky calls this the 'X-bar' slot, and we'll use the notation X' to represent it.

The complement will generally be closer to the head than the adjunct will, except in the case of very long complements (which prefer to appear at the end of the sentence):

(50) a   I read a book on the couch.
     b   *I read on the couch a book.
     c   I read on the couch a book that my mother had been recommending to me for years.

And you of course have already noticed that (50a) is ambiguous between whether the reading happened on the couch – *I read a book [on the couch]* – or whether the book was on the couch – *I read [a book on the couch]*. So with all our new tools in hand, we can represent this difference with the trees in Figure 6.14 and Figure 6.15.

Notice that in Figure 6.14 *read a book* is a constituent, and *on the couch* is a sister to this phrase, showing where the reading happened, whereas in Figure 6.15 *a book on the couch* is a constituent, showing what was read. And these two constituent structures map nicely onto the two meanings of this sentence.

So what's the point?

Let's just take stock for a moment. We've seen that language is hugely complicated and full of ambiguities, yet children seem to master it quickly and effortlessly at an age when much simpler tasks are beyond their abilities. How do they do it?

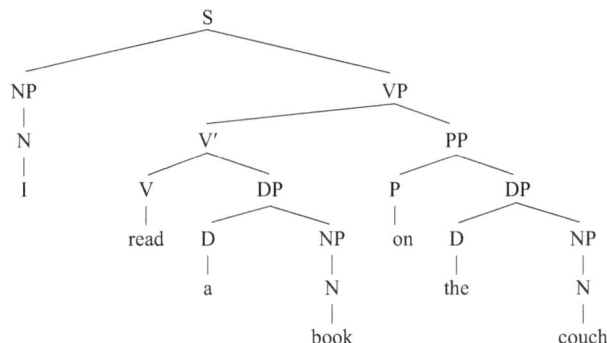

FIGURE 6.14 *I read a book on the couch*, option 1.

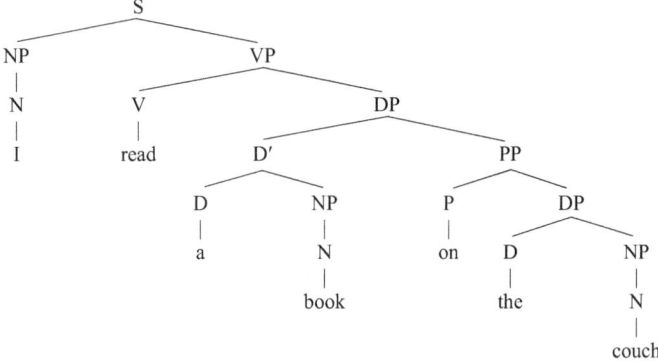

FIGURE 6.15 *I read a book on the couch*, option 2.

Now look at what you mastered in a relatively few pages. You can draw structures for phenomenally complicated phrases and sentences; just look back at (35)! How did **you** do it? For Chomsky, the answer to both is the same: There's a template that recurs over and over in language, with some very small differences in the template between one language and another. He posits a **Universal Grammar** that is part of our genetic inheritance and includes rules like XP →X (YP) that apply to phrase after phrase within a given language. Just understanding that in English a phrase is made up of a head plus an optional complement phrase allowed you to suddenly understand the structures of a vast range of English phrases; and so it is with a child, who is born implicitly knowing this rule and only needing to determine whether their native language puts the head before or after the complement. Once they settle that little detail, they know a huge amount about the structure of the phrases in their language, and much of their language-acquisition task from then on will focus on things like learning the words of their language. And of course one of the things they'll learn along with each new word is what sorts of complements (if any) it takes. Our XP →X (YP) rule isn't the only rule of language – not by a long shot – but seeing what this one rule makes possible should give you a sense of how acquiring such a complex system is possible so quickly and effortlessly for the mind of the language-acquiring child.

EXERCISES

Self-test:

1. When linguists say language is 'rule-governed', they mean that
    a. prescriptive rules apply to the syntax of all languages.
    b. it makes use of the rules of classical Latin grammar.
    c. every native speaker's competence includes a set of grammar rules.
    d. our parents have taught us what sentences are and are not grammatical.
2. A language universal is
    a. a property that is true of one or more human languages.
    b. a property that is true of no human languages.
    c. a property that is true of every communicative system.
    d. a property that is true of every human language.
3. According to Chomsky, Universal Grammar
    a. explains how a child can acquire language effortlessly.
    b. provides the child with the words of his or her language.
    c. is made up of both competence and performance.
    d. results in all languages having the same ordering of elements.
4. The 'poverty of the stimulus' refers to the notion that
    a. our competence does not perfectly reflect language universals.
    b. Universal Grammar does not provide the child with the words of his or her language.
    c. general properties of cognition are insufficient to explain language acquisition.
    d. what a language learner hears is flawed.

5   The Critical Period Hypothesis states that
   a   writing systems that include punctuation tend to survive longer historically.
   b   it is much easier for a child to acquire a language before puberty.
   c   the vocal tract became capable of speech when our ancestors began to walk upright.
   d   animals' inability to use punctuation prevents them from developing a writing system.
6   A feature is phonemic in a language if
   a   changing it changes the word being uttered.
   b   it is made in the front of the vocal tract.
   c   it prevents morphemes from combining.
   d   it appears within the left branch of a phrase structure tree.
7   An allomorph is
   a   a variant of a phoneme.
   b   a variant of a morpheme.
   c   a type of inflection.
   d   a type of derivation.
8   A **word** can be identified by the fact that it
   a   has spaces before and after it.
   b   is composed of morphemes.
   c   is subject to allophonic constraints.
   d   acts as an island.
9   A sentence is structurally ambiguous if it
   a   exhibits recursion.
   b   has two or more distinct structures.
   c   has a constituent structure.
   d   is structure-dependent.
10   Which of the following makes it possible for a sentence to be infinitely long?
   a   recursion
   b   phonemics
   c   structural ambiguity
   d   variables

Comprehension questions:

1   Imagine a Greek-speaking adult man is moving to America with his infant daughter. What would you predict about their relative ability to acquire English, and why? What well-known linguistic hypothesis addresses this issue?
2   Consider the following words in Persian, and answer the questions that follow. Note that [æ] represents the vowel sound in the word *cat*, and [ʃ] represents the sound at the beginning of the word *shoe*. (Data are taken from Mahootian 1997.)

   a   [bil]   'shovel'   h   [pa]   'foot'
   b   [boz]   'goat'   i   [pær]   'feather'
   c   [berenj]   'rice'   j   [sæbz]   'green'
   d   [buq]   'horn'   k   [peste]   'pistachio'
   e   [moz]   'banana'   l   [æbr]   'cloud'

f [ba] 'with' m [ʃepe] 'louse'
g [ʃepur] 'horn' n [barik] 'narrow'

   (i) Are [b] and [p] allophones of the same phoneme or different phonemes? Give evidence for your answer.
   (ii) Are [b] and [m] allophones of the same phoneme or different phonemes? Give evidence for your answer.
   (iii) Note that [b] and [m] are produced identically except for nasalization (in which the velum is lowered so air can escape through the nose). The same is true of [d] and [n], where [n] is nasalized but [d] is not. In light of this information, is nasalization phonemic in Persian? How do you know?
   (iv) Would you expect Persian to contain minimal pairs differing only in whether they contain [d] or [n]? Why or why not?

3 Lewis Carroll's poem 'Jabberwocky' begins:

'Twas brillig and the slithy toves
    Did gyre and gimble in the wabe;
All mimsy were the borogoves,
    And the mome raths outgrabe.

For each of the following invented words, determine whether it is a noun, a verb, or an adjective, and tell how you know: *brillig, slithy, toves, gyre, gimble, wabe, mimsy, borogoves, mome, raths, outgrabe.*

4 Draw a word structure tree for each of the following words: *unmentionable, directors, redirection.* Draw two trees to show the ambiguity of the word *unpacked.*

5 Draw a phrase structure tree for each of the following sentences. Treat 'fruit flies' in (b) as a single word, and assume that (a) is about a property of time, whereas (b) is about a property of fruit flies.
   a *Time flies like an arrow.*
   b *Fruit flies like a banana.*

Opinion questions:

1 In our discussion of morphology, we saw an example of Hebrew, a language in which words are constructed very differently from how they're constructed in English. It would be difficult or impossible to use a word structure tree to represent the structure of a Hebrew word. Does this suggest that these trees are not the best approach to English word structure and that we should search for a more universal approach to word structure? Or should we take different approaches to different language structures? Does the existence of English words like *children, mice,* and *feet* influence your view?

2 Draw a tree for the following sentence: *Sentences about the habits of fruit flies belong in books about biology.* (Again, treat *fruit flies* as a single word.) Should the PPs headed with *about* be considered complements or adjuncts? Explain your reasoning.

3 We saw in ex. (33), and in its structure in Figure 6.11, that repeatedly embedding complements can result in indefinitely long phrases. We also hinted at the fact that a string of adjuncts can have a similar result, as in (48) above and (a) below:

a   *The woman in the beautiful long flowing striped yellow dress has a Ph.D.*
    Do you think long strings of adjuncts like the one here have an embedded structure like that in Figure 6.11? Why or why not?

Discussion questions:

1   You are teaching English overseas, and your students are having some pronunciation problems: They can't distinguish between the vowels in *pane* and *pen*, and they also can't distinguish between aspirated and unaspirated /p/. Which of these two problems would you as a linguist consider more serious, and why?
2   We used the commonality of structure among phrase types as evidence for Chomsky's Universal Grammar. Explain in your own words how this combines with the evidence at the beginning of the chapter to support Chomsky. Are you convinced? (Not everybody is.) Can you think of other evidence that might argue against Chomsky's account?
3   One of the fundamental concepts in linguistic theory is that of **types** and **tokens**. A type is a general category, whereas a token is a specific instance of that category. If you look carefully, you can see this distinction throughout linguistic structure. Explain how you see it in allophones, allomorphs, and the X-bar schema. Can you find it anywhere else in language?

Data collection and analysis:

1   Present **three** minimal pairs for each of the following pairs of sounds to prove that they are distinct phonemes in English:
    a   [t] and [d]
    b   [s] and [ʃ] (as in *shoe*)
    c   [r] and [l]
    d   [o] (as in *show*) and [u] (as in *due*)
2   Collect a real-life use of each of the following word-formation processes **other** than the words given as examples in the chapter. Give the citation showing where the use appeared. (If you don't happen to know any other examples in the category, you can look up lists of examples online and then search for a real-life use.) Note that I'm not asking for the actual formation of a word or its first use, but simply an example of the use of a word that was formed by the process.
    a   coinage
    b   onomatopoeia
    c   clipping
    d   acronym
    e   blend
    f   backformation
    g   eponym
    h   borrowing
    i   conversion
3   Find a published sentence that's at least six words long that you can draw a complete tree for, given the tools from this chapter. Draw the tree and give the source of the sentence. Was it hard to find a suitable sentence? Why or why not?

Answers to self-test:

1 c
2 d
3 a
4 d
5 b
6 a
7 b
8 d
9 b
10 a

CHAPTER 7

Interfaces I: Semantics, pragmatics, and philosophy

> **KEY CONCEPTS**
>
> - reference, referent
> - psychic continuity
> - deixis: personal, spatial, temporal, discourse
> - anaphora, cataphora, indexical
> - pro-form
> - definite vs. indefinite NP
> - familiarity
> - identifiability
> - presupposition
> - trigger
> - factive
> - cleft
> - change-of-state verb
> - iterative
> - common ground
> - accommodation

We've already seen that there are a lot of interactions among the fields of semantics, pragmatics, and philosophy. Many of the primary figures in pragmatics have been philosophers, and the truth tables from philosophical logic provide one of the bases for truth-conditional semantics. Both philosophical logic in general and truth-conditional semantics in particular provided the initial impetus for Grice's development of the Cooperative Principle. Different researchers draw the boundary between semantics and pragmatics differently. In a way, all of this makes sense, because all three fields (truth-conditional semantics, pragmatics, and formal philosophy) address closely related questions of meaning (and we've already seen how many meanings the word *meaning* has, reflecting the wide range of aspects of 'meaning').

In this chapter we'll start by refreshing your memory on the semantics/pragmatics boundary disputes, and on the issues of reference that we talked about way back in Chapter 1, where we covered the views of a range of philosophers on issues of reference. From there we'll move on to discuss reference in more depth, asking what exactly we're referring to when we use a referring expression. Then we'll move on to some of the most fascinating questions in the area of reference, such as the meaning of the definite article (what's the difference in meaning between *a mouse* and *the mouse*?) and the relationship between presupposition and truth (e.g., is *The King of France is bald* true or false if there isn't a King of France to begin with?). As always, we'll have more questions than answers.

Let's start with that memory-refresher on basic issues in reference and the semantics/pragmatics boundary.

REFERENCE AND THE SEMANTICS/PRAGMATICS BOUNDARY

Recall from Chapters 1 and 4 that different researchers, and different schools of thought, take different perspectives on what counts as semantics and what counts as pragmatics. One major quarrel you'll remember from Chapter 4 is whether the boundary should be drawn on the basis of truth-conditions (with semantics being about truth-conditional meaning and pragmatics being about non-truth-conditional meaning) or on the basis of conventional vs. inferential meaning (with semantics addressing what is conventionally encoded and pragmatics addressing what must be inferred). And it gets stickier yet, since our philosophers back in Chapter 1 were already arguing over what does and doesn't affect the truth-conditions of an utterance. So you'll have fond memories of our friend the nonexistent King of France from sentences like (1):

(1) The King of France is bald.

Given that there's currently no King of France, is (1) true, false, or none of the above? If one of the issues at the semantics/pragmatics boundary is the question of what status truth-conditions hold, that means that such a sentence teeters at the boundary between semantics and pragmatics.

A sentence like (1) **presupposes** the existence of a King of France, and as we've seen, when this presupposition is false, it leaves curious problems in its wake regarding the status of the sentence as a whole. But let's assume for a moment (incorrectly) that the presupposition is true. What status does the proposition 'there is a King of France' hold in the interpretation of (1)? Or, to make things slightly easier, let's take a sentence in which the presupposition is (at the moment) true:

(2) The President of the U.S. is bald.

If I utter (2), my meaning includes, in some sense, that the U.S. has a president. But in what sense? Is that part of the semantics of (2), part of its pragmatics, or neither? This question will reverberate throughout this chapter, especially in its later sections as we consider what the word *the* contributes to the meaning of a noun phrase (spoiler: it's frustratingly hard to say for certain) and how it also contributes to what is presupposed in uttering a sentence.

At the moment it may seem a bit academic, without much in the way of practical applicability, but just stop for a moment to think about the Second Amendment to the U.S. Constitution:

(3) A well regulated Militia, being necessary to the security of a free State, the right of the people to keep and bear Arms, shall not be infringed.

The right of the people – uh-oh; suddenly the interpretation of that little word *the* seems pretty important. Does it presuppose that such a right exists – and if so, what does that mean for what the amendment is saying? And what about that first clause about the necessity of a well-regulated Militia? It seems to presuppose the necessity of a militia, and the right to keep and bear arms seems predicated on that necessity – but if no such militia is in fact necessary (i.e., if the presupposition is false), what does that do to the meaning of the whole?

The above examples show how important reference, definiteness, and presupposition are to the meaning of an utterance. Consider also the oath made in courtrooms, to tell the truth, the whole truth, and nothing but the truth. It would seem to be pretty important to be able to tease apart what counts as part of 'truth' and what counts as something else, and to decide which aspects of meaning in fact matter in court. Recall, example (8) from Chapter 4, repeated here as (4):

(4) Q Do you have any bank accounts in Swiss banks, Mr. Bronston?
    A No, sir.
    Q Have you ever?
    A The company had an account there for about six months, in Zurich.

By finding that Bronston had not perjured himself by implicating (but not stating) that he himself hadn't had such an account, the Supreme Court was essentially finding that pragmatic meaning isn't part of 'the truth, the whole truth, and nothing but the truth', which is to say that truth-conditional semantics is the standard in court. (But see Solan and Tiersma 2005 for a brilliant argument that our criminal justice system isn't at all consistent on this topic.)

All of this hinges in part on the question of reference: What is it that we refer to when we use a referring expression? And that's where we'll turn next.

What do we refer to when we refer?

I talked above about 'referring expressions' – but what exactly are they? One might say they're expressions that refer, but of course expressions just sit there; they don't do any referring. So we could say a little more pedantically that they're expressions that people use in order to refer. In order to refer to what, though? And that's where it gets interesting.

Let's just say that what is referred to is a **referent**. Obviously this doesn't make any headway on the question, but it does give us a handy term to use for whatever it is we're referring to. And the obvious place to locate referents is in the world; after all, if I say *My husband has a beard*, I intend to say that something has a beard, and that something – the referent – is a particular object in the actual world. But then recall this example from Chapter 1:

(5) **Constabulary Notes from All Over**
From the Winchester (Mass.) Star.
Police responded to Winchester Place for a report of a suspicious person. Police spoke to a resident of the building who said a bald man dressed in maroon was standing outside her door and appeared to be waiting for the elevator. She said the man had been standing in one spot for nearly 20 minutes. The woman said she saw the man through a peephole. When police brought the woman into the hall she was embarrassed to find the man in question was her neighbor's Christmas wreath.

Do we say here that in saying *the man*, the woman was referring to a wreath? If so, do we want to say that by saying the man was bald, she was actually asserting that the wreath was bald? Or was she actually predicating baldness of some man in her discourse model, who doesn't actually exist in the real world?

Recall from Chapter 1 that there are two schools of thought on this question: Referentialists believe that the referent is a real-world entity; after all, the woman didn't intend to posit baldness of something in her head. Mentalists (aka cognitivists), on the other hand, argue that the referent is a mental entity – a discourse entity – since we can refer to things incorrectly, we can refer to things that don't exist, and in fact we can refer to nonexistent things without ever realizing they're nonexistent. For a group of people to have a rousing discussion about God does not require that there actually be a God, or even for the group to believe there is; a group of atheists can discuss God at length. All they need is the shared concept – or not even that. In actual fact, all they need is the **belief** that there's a shared concept (since after all, the neighbor's discourse-entity wreath will differ in innumerable details from the woman's discourse-entity man).

Now suppose the woman in (5) never called the police, but a month later – after all the holiday decorations have been removed – she mentions to her neighbor the man she saw standing outside their door, and the neighbor responds, *I'm so glad he didn't steal our wreath!* Now who's referring to what? Does the neighbor's word *he* refer to the nonexistent man, to the discourse-model man, to the wreath, or to all three? If we're going to take a referentialist perspective, what is the real-world referent of an expression? Is it whatever the phrase semantically picks out in the world (in which case *the man* can't very well refer to a wreath), or is it whatever the speaker believes it picks out in the world?

Moreover, recall that Heraclitus said you can never step in the same river twice. It'll be a different river, composed of different water droplets, traveling in slightly different patterns. In what sense can it possibly be said to be the same river?

Noam Chomsky's answer is that it's the same in the sense of having **psychic continuity** for individual minds. Chomsky, in short, is a cognitivist. He notes that "the Charles River would remain the very same river under quite extreme changes, and would not be a river at all under very slight changes" (http://bostonreview.net/chomsky-what-we-know). You could divert it, or you could even change the direction of its flow, as they did with the Chicago River (truly!), but it remained the Chicago River. But if you retained the path of the Charles River but hardened it (I dunno, pour in some concrete?) and started driving on it, it's no longer a river but rather a highway. Chomsky's point is that there's no one entity with a set of fixed properties that we think of as the Charles River, but rather a mental entity with a set of fixed attributes in our mental model of it, and that is what determines the referent of *the Charles River*.

DEIXIS AND ANAPHORA

Recall that one of the points of interaction between semantics and pragmatics concerns the interpretation of pronouns. We can't know the truth-conditions for *He's in the kitchen* without first knowing who *he* is, since the truth-conditions for the sentence will be quite different if *he* refers to Tom than if it refers to Ted. So, as we saw above, the notion of explicature was brought in to mediate the problem: The explicature is what you get when you add in just enough contextual information to result in a truth-evaluable proposition. But just how to resolve the reference (which is to say, figure out what the pronoun was intended to refer to) is a quintessentially pragmatic problem, since it involves context, inference, and beliefs about your interlocutors' intent, all of which are the top concerns of pragmatics. So perhaps the semantic meaning of an utterance isn't quite as separate from pragmatics as has sometimes been assumed; pragmatics runs through every aspect of communication.

Pronouns are expressions that are inherently contextual in their interpretation, by which I mean that to know who or what *he* (or any other pronoun) is meant to refer to, you've got to know at least something about who uttered it and/or in what context. But pronouns aren't the only expressions that have this property, and the prior discourse isn't the only place to find the answer to these questions. In what follows we'll distinguish between **deixis** (roughly, direct reference to something in the context) and **anaphora** (roughly, coreference with another expression in the discourse). We'll start by talking about the whole class of **indexicals**.

Indexicals

Certain expressions in a discourse are 'indexed' to the context; these are called **indexicals**. To see what I mean by 'indexed to the context', consider (6):

(6) a You missed an excellent speech.
　　b The President made some good points.
　　c The Vice President said she agreed.

In (6a), the word *you* cannot be interpreted unless you know who the addressee is. The addressee might be an individual, or a group, or even the intended audience for a newspaper article, TV show, or book; but unless you know who this addressee (or group of addressees) is, you can't fully interpret the utterance. In this way the interpretation of the word *you* is indexed to the addressee.

You might be a little more puzzled looking for the indexical element in (6b), but it's right there: It's the past tense. Again, unless you know when (6b) was uttered, it's not entirely clear what time span is indicated by the past tense. It's not just 'sometime in the past'; rather, it's sometime that counts as being in the past from the perspective of the utterer of (6b). If this sentence appears in a novel set in the distant future, then the past tense will cover a stretch of time that still lies in our future, and the time reference for the President's speech will similarly lie in our (fictionalized) future. So the past tense here is indexed to the time of utterance. (But see below for other possibilities.)

Finally, in (6c), the word *she* is our old friend the pronoun, and here it's quite clear that its interpretation depends on the prior discourse. If this sentence were to appear in a newspaper, and you found a torn portion of the newspaper's page that included *she agreed* but lacked the first half of the sentence, you obviously wouldn't know who *she* referred to.

So all three examples in (6) involve indexicals. The *you* in (6a) is a deictic; the case of tense, as in (6b), is related to the temporal deictics we'll talk about shortly; and cases of anaphora, as in (6c), will be discussed below.

All of these indexicals depend on context for their interpretation. In the case of deictics, the expression directly 'points to' or picks out some element of the context and refers to it; in the case of anaphora, the expression shares a referent with some other, more descriptive expression in the discourse, and so to interpret the expression one must look to that other expression. And in the case of tense (and, similarly, aspect), there are inflectional or functional cues (e.g., a past-tense suffix or the modal *will*) to indicate the temporal relationship between the time of speaking and the time being described.

Deixis

First, a quick terminological clarification: The term **deixis** means the phenomenon, whereas the term **deictic** is either a noun meaning an instance of deixis (as in 'three deictics') or an adjective describing something as deictic (as in 'a deictic pronoun'). Deictics are words whose sense – whose literal semantic meaning – necessarily makes reference to the discourse context. Suppose you're writing a dictionary definition for the word *you*; it would be impossible to do without mentioning the discourse (or conversation, or text, etc.) in which the word *you* picks out the addressee, or at least that *you* picks out an addressee (which in turn assumes a discourse). In this way it's different from the word *cat*, which can – and should – be defined without reference to any discourse whatsoever.

Now suppose you've found someone's cell phone lying on the sidewalk. You pick it up, and notice that a text has just come in:

(7) Hey, should I come by when I'm on my way, or do you want to stop by here and we can head over there together?

The deictic expressions here are (at the very least) *I, come, I'm, my, you, here, we,* and *there*. The phrases *on my way* and *together* also have deictic aspects, in that there's a missing argument in the first case (on my way where?) and the interpretation of *together* in the second depends on who *I* and *you* are. Without knowing whose phone it is, who sent the text, where they're planning to go, and so on, it will be impossible to determine what precisely is meant.

To make sense of this, we'll now briefly talk about four types of discourse: Personal, spatial, temporal, and discourse deixis.

Personal deixis

Personal deixis points to some entity in the discourse context. *I* and *you* are obvious cases, because they necessarily look to the discourse context for their referents, but words like *she* and *they* can also be used to pick out something particularly salient in the context. You might, for example, notice someone arriving at a party in a garish outfit and say *Look what she's wearing*, with *she* referring directly to that salient person. The plural pronouns *you* and *we* are interesting cases, because each of them can refer either to more than one participant in the discourse, or to a single participant in the discourse plus some number of additional participants outside of the discourse, or to a combination of the two:

(8) a Hey, you two! I really like your matching outfits.
    b Joe, I admire your month-long family trips, but how do you stand being together that long?
    c I heard that your committee will be attending next week's protest. Will you be bringing signs?

In (8a), we can imagine a scenario in which the speaker is using the word *your* to refer to two people who are being jointly addressed. In (8b), the speaker could be using the word *your* to refer to the addressee and *you* to refer to that addressee plus additional family members who aren't present. And in (8c), *you* could plausibly be used to refer to a mixed group of committee members, some of whom are present and being addressed and some of whom aren't.

The pronoun *we* is similar, but has the additional property that it can either include or exclude the addressee:

(9) a Grab your coat, George; we need to leave.
    b Thanks for the lovely dinner, you guys, but we need to leave.
    c Thanks for the lovely dinner, you guys; we need to get together more often!
    d Thanks for the lovely dinner, but once I find George, we'll need to leave.
    e Get the kids, George; we need to leave.
    f Our families get along so well; we really should get together more often!

So in English, *we* can pick out any of the following (where S is the speaker, A is the addressee, P is someone else present, and NP is someone else not present):

- S and A, but not P
  [as in (a), where *we* = S and George, the addressee]
- S and P, but not A
  [as in (b), where *we* = S and George, who's present but not addressed]
- S and A and P
  [as in (c), where *we* = S, the hosts being addressed, and George, present but not addressed]
- S and NP, but not A
  [as in (d), where *we* = S and George, not present]
- S and A and NP
  [as in (e), where *we* = S; George, who's present; and the kids, who aren't]
- S, A, P, and NP
  [as in (f), where *we* = S; the hosts being addressed; George, who's present; and the kids, who aren't]

You could argue that this is ridiculous and *we* just means 'the speaker and someone else', regardless of who that someone else might be; but it's worth noting all of these possibilities for two reasons: First, this range is unique to *we*; you can't, for example, use plural *you* to refer to the speaker and the hearer, but you can use *we* for this. Second, languages actually differ in how they divide up the second-person plural options into pronouns. Chechen, for example, has different pronouns for 'you, I, and possibly others' and 'others and I, but not you'; that is, it has one second-person plural pronoun for groupings that include the addressee (**inclusive** 'we') and another for groupings that don't (**exclusive** 'we').

Spatial deixis

Spatial deixis has to do with location in space, so it includes words like *here, there, this, that, these, those, come*, and *go*. You've probably already noticed that these frequently come in pairs, with one member of the pair denoting something nearby and the other denoting something farther away. The terms that pick out something close to the speaker are called **proximal** deictics, and those that pick out something far from the speaker are called **distal** deictics. So *here* is proximal, while *there* is distal; *this* is proximal, while *that* is distal, and so on. But there are several interesting things to note about this distinction. First, there's a fuzziness to where the boundary between 'proximal' and 'distal' is drawn. Consider (10), with the phrases of interest italicized:

(10) "See *this* piece *here*? It screws on and turns down *here*. You couldn't get out of *that* yourself."

(Steinbeck 1952)

Pay special attention to the italicized deictics. The speaker is showing a raccoon trap to the hearer. The interesting thing is, if you assume the speaker is holding the trap or sitting right next to it and pointing to the parts in question, it's just as easy to imagine him saying:

(11) "See *that* piece *there*? It screws on and turns down *there*. You couldn't get out of *this* yourself."

And you could imagine him saying it in exactly the same proximity to the trap. And proximity can be relative: If there's a book one foot from me and another book three feet from me, it's easy for me to imagine saying:

(12) I'll look at this book now, and at that one later.

Here the natural interpretation would be to assume that *this book* is the one closer to me and *that book* is the one that's farther away. Now assume the books are four feet and 12 feet away from me. In this case, uttering (12) gives us a similar interpretation, again with the closer book counting as *this book* and the farther one counting as *that book*. But that means that what counts as *that book* in the first case (three feet away) is closer than the one that counts as *this book* in the second case (four feet away). Everything's relative.

Even more interesting is the fact that what the deictic is relative **to** can vary. This is what's known as the **deictic center**. In cases like (10)-(12), the deictic center is the speaker at the time of utterance. Likewise, if I say *Come here*, I generally mean 'come to where I am right now, as I'm saying this'. But not always. Suppose the trap in (10) is in a barn 100 yards away; the speaker could say *Come here* as he walks toward the barn. In that case he means 'come to the place where I'm headed'. It's fine if the hearer walks to the speaker and joins him for the walk to the barn, but it's also fine if the hearer walks straight to the barn and joins the speaker there. Or consider (13):

(13) In the kitchen a light was already on, and Charles Wallace was sitting at the table drinking milk and eating bread and jam....

"Why didn't you *come* up to the attic?" Meg asked her brother, speaking as though he were at least her own age.

(L'Engle 1962)

Here the speaker and hearer are both in the kitchen, but they're talking about a previous event in which the speaker, Meg, had been in the attic. In this case *come* doesn't mean 'come to where I am now' or even 'come to the place where I'm headed', but 'come to the place where I was previously, at the time we're talking about'.

While English distinguishes between proximal and distal locations, many other languages make a three-way distinction between what's close to the speaker, what's close to the hearer, and what's distant from both; and there are languages with even more complicated systems with different words depending on whether the object is visible, out of view, just now became out of view, etc.

Temporal deixis

Temporal deixis is deixis denoting time, and you could probably fill in examples yourself: *now, then, yesterday, last month, three years ago*.... And again we have a proximal/distal distinction, with *now* being proximal (i.e., close to the time of speaking) and *then* being distal (farther from the time of speaking). And again the deictic center can vary. Consider the italicized phrase in (14):

(14) The wind booms down the curved length of the trailer and under its roaring passage he can hear the scratching of fine gravel and sand. It could be bad on the highway with the horse trailer. He has to be packed and away from the place *that morning*.

(Proulx 2005)

Here, the author is the deictic center; *that morning* means a morning other than the one belonging to the day on which the author is writing. To see this, compare it with the variant in (15):

(15) The wind booms down the curved length of the trailer and under its roaring passage he can hear the scratching of fine gravel and sand. It could be bad on the highway with the horse trailer. He has to be packed and away from the place *this morning*.

This version is equally acceptable, but a subtle change has occurred, in that *this morning* here picks out the morning of the events being narrated. Here the deictic center is the character denoted by *he*, whose point of view is represented in this passage. For him, the morning is the same one he is living (so to speak), so it is *this morning*. In this case, the time reference isn't indexed to the time of utterance, but rather the time of a particular character's point of view.

Discourse deixis

Finally, discourse deixis makes reference to a stretch of the discourse itself: an expression, a sentence, or a larger stretch. It's to be distinguished from anaphora, which doesn't refer to a piece of the discourse but rather co-refers with some earlier piece of the discourse. So consider the italicized *that* in (16):

(16) Perhaps we could argue, as Roy Scranton does in his *New York Times* essay "Raising My Child in a Doomed World," that "we [were] not free to choose how we live[d] any more than we [were] free to break the laws of physics." The ability to save ourselves, and save them, was not in our hands. But *that* would be a lie.

(Foer 2019)

Here, *that* refers to the argument in the previous two sentences – that we weren't free to choose, that the ability to save ourselves was not in our hands. Compare this with the anaphoric use of *that* in (17):

(17) Foer wrote a book about climate change a couple of years ago, and *that* convinced me to be a vegetarian.

Here we have a different situation; *that* doesn't refer to the phrase *a book about climate change*, but rather to the book about climate change itself. That is, the phrase *a book about climate change* and the word *that* both refer to the same object, which is external to the discourse (regardless of whether you take the referent to be a real-world object or a discourse-model object). In (16), however, *that* refers back to a stretch of the discourse itself, and that stretch of discourse doesn't co-refer with *that* to something outside the discourse.

Anaphora

In our discussion of deixis, we've said a lot about anaphora, so hopefully you're already pretty clear on what it is: the use of an expression that co-refers with, and takes its reference from, some earlier expression. The simplest case is a pronoun:

(18) My dining-room table is broken. *It* needs to be fixed.

Here, *it* shares with deictics the property of needing some help from the context for its reference; the hearer can't tell from the pronoun alone what it refers to. But in the case of anaphora, instead of finding its referent in the extralinguistic context as you would with a deictic, you instead find something else in the discourse context (the **antecedent**) that refers to the same thing, and that referent for the antecedent is the referent for the pronoun as well. (Here's a case where the explanation takes something simple and straightforward and makes it seem confusing and complicated.) There are three interesting issues to address with respect to anaphora: first, the question of reference resolution; second, the related phenomenon of cataphora; and third, the range of phrase types it permits.

Reference resolution

Anaphora is a deeply contextual – hence deeply pragmatic – phenomenon. Recall from Chapter 4 that it posed a problem for a clean division between semantics and pragmatics. We can't possibly know whether the second sentence in (18) is true until we know what the referent of *it* is, and we can't possibly know that without looking at the context – in this case, the previous sentence. So you might be inclined to allow multiple sentences to contribute to the semantics at a time, declare the problem solved, and call it a day. Unfortunately – and yes, you're way ahead of me on this – it's not that easy. Consider the headline in (19):

(19) Russia has been mounting a disinformation campaign for years to frame Ukraine for its 2016 election meddling, American intelligence officials told senators.

(Weiland 2019)

Here, the referent of *its* is not clear from the syntax and semantics alone; the headline would be equally grammatical if *its 2016 election meddling* referred to meddling by Russia or to meddling by Ukraine. Only our understanding of the word *frame* and who frames whom tells us that it would be impossible for Russia to frame Ukraine for something Ukraine in fact did; therefore, it must be the case that Russia is framing Ukraine for something that Russia itself did. So to determine the reference for *its*, we have to resort to reasoning based on other factors in the sentence and in our world knowledge.

Or, to streamline it further:

(20) Mary took a photo of her house, and then Sally took a photo of her house, too.

This is ambiguous: The second instance of *her house* can be interpreted as referring to either Mary's house (what Ross (1967) called 'strict identity') or Sally's house (what Ross called 'sloppy identity'). That is, either Mary and Sally each took a photo of Mary's house or Mary and Sally each took a photo of her own house. There is nothing in the syntax or semantics of (20) that can tell you which is correct; you'll have to infer it from the context, or sometimes from the intonation:

(21) Mary took a photo of her house, and then Sally took a photo of HER house, too.

Here the stress on *her* is what's called 'contrastive stress', and it cues the listener that there's a contrast between the two referents of *her* – hence that Sally is taking a photo of her own house.

Similarly, consider Lakoff's well-known example in (22):

(22) a John called Bill a Republican and then he insulted him.
     b John called Bill a Republican and then HE insulted HIM.

(Lakoff 1971)

In (22a), the most likely reading is one in which John called Bill a Republican, and then John insulted Bill. In (22b), the contrastive stress on *he* and *him* in the second clause again serves as a cue that the referents have changed – in this case, swapping places so that it is now Bill who is calling John a Republican. And as an interesting side effect, the word *insulted* is de-stressed, suggesting a lack of contrast between calling someone a Republican and insulting them, which leaves us with an interpretation in which not only have the participants switched roles, but to call someone a Republican is an insult.

Note that even when there is nothing in the syntax, semantics, or intonation to give the hearer or reader a clue as to the referent, there may be entirely pragmatic factors that will make it clear that the most recent available antecedent is in fact the wrong one and must be essentially 'jumped over':

(23) Reader, I married him. A quiet wedding we had: he and I, the parson and clerk, were alone present. When *we* got back from church, I went into the kitchen of the manor-house, where Mary was cooking the dinner....

(Brontë 1847)

Take a look at second instance of the word *we*, which I've italicized here. The most recent set of individuals that this might refer back to is *he and I, the parson and clerk*. But it's clear in context that the narrator and her new husband have gone back to the manor-house, and that the parson and clerk haven't come along. In essence, the referential chain goes from the *I* and *him* of the first sentence to the *we* of the second (referring to that same pair), jumps over *he and I, the parson and clerk*, and is returned to as the antecedent of that second *we*.

Finally, notice that reference resolution can cause you to go back and re-interpret the earlier discourse:

(24) My husband and I have decided we don't want to have children. We will be telling them tonight at dinner.

(online meme; example courtesy of Gregory Ward)

The humor in this example is, of course, that it's not until the reader reaches the word *them* and realizes that it needs a referent do they re-interpret the first sentence as referring to specific already-existing children. Compare this with (25):

(25) *My husband and I have decided we don't want to have children. We don't like them.*

Here, *children* in the first sentence and *them* in the second are both likely to be interpreted as referring to children in general. It's the reference to telling them in (24) that requires an entity that can be told something at dinner (which eliminates the 'children in general' reading), causing the reinterpretation and the humor.

Cataphora

As we've seen, anaphoric pronouns get their reference from some expression that occurs earlier in the discourse. But it's also possible for a pronoun to gets its reference from an expression that occurs **later** in the discourse, as in (26):

(26) If you don't have it, download the Zoom app in advance of event.
(email, North Shore Center for the Performing Arts)

Here, *it* is coreferential with *the Zoom app*. But the Zoom app hasn't yet been mentioned when the reader encounters the word *it*. In such cases, the reader must essentially recognize that there's no available referent yet and hold the word *it* in memory while awaiting the referent. Fortunately, it usually comes along pretty quickly, as it does here.

Anaphora and phrase types

When we were in grade school, most of us were taught that a pronoun takes the place of a noun, but this isn't true at all. Consider (27):

(27) My wonderful next-door neighbor gave me a blueberry pie. She baked it herself.

What does the pronoun *she* stand for here? It's not standing in for the word *neighbor*, since you can't replace *neighbor* with *she* in the first sentence, nor can you replace *she* with *neighbor* in the second:

(28) a ★My wonderful next-door she gave me a blueberry pie.
     b ★Neighbor baked it herself.

Instead, what results in grammaticality is swapping the pronoun with the entire NP:

(29) a She gave me a blueberry pie.
     b My wonderful next-door neighbor baked it herself.

Sure, these two sentences don't combine to make a felicitous discourse due to the unresolved pronoun in (29a), but their grammaticality shows that what a pronoun stands in for isn't a noun at all, but actually an entire noun phrase.

Moreover, noun phrases aren't the only category of phrase that can take a 'stand-in' in this way. Consider the examples in (30):

(30) a I put the laundry in the dryer, but now it's not there.
     b Jane is super-smart, as is Fred.
     c I've never studied a second language, but I'd love to do so.
     d I've never studied a second language, but I'd love to try it.

Each of these sentences contains what linguists call a **pro-form**, analogously to pronouns. So in (30a) the word *there* is a pro-form – essentially a pro-PP – that stands in for a prepositional phrase and is coreferential with the PP *in the dryer* in the previous clause, just as *she* in (27) is a pronoun that stands in for a noun phrase and is coreferential with the NP *my wonderful next-door neighbor* in the previous sentence. In (30b), *as* is a pro-form that stands in for the adjective phrase *super-smart*, and in (30c) and (30d), *so* and *it* stand in for the verb phrase *study(ing) a second language*. In short, even though pronouns get all the attention, language actually gives us a wide range of tools to save our having to repeat information that has already appeared.

DEFINITENESS

You know how I keep raising an issue and then telling you it hasn't been resolved? Nowhere will this be more true than with definiteness. (Side note: The word *this* in that last sentence is a discourse deictic – and so is the word *that* in the first clause of this one – and the phrase *this one* just a few words ago.)

BOX 7.1

Here's something being discussed by the linguists

Take a look at these two sentences, and see if you feel a difference:

(a) Academics are interested in definiteness.
(b) The academics are interested in definiteness.

If you're like most people, you'll feel a bit of distance in (b), as though 'the academics' is a group that the speaker is purposely standing apart from – in a sense saying 'they are interested in this, but I'm not one of them'. In (a), in contrast, it's unclear whether the speaker is being included in the group of academics – whether the sentence is intended to convey that 'they' are interested in definiteness or that 'we' are.

A recent study by Eric Acton (2019) shows that using *the* with a plural reference to a group of people "tends to depict that group as a monolith separate from the speaker". Using a corpus of U.S. House of Representatives proceedings, Acton examined more than 50,000 instances of the use of the words *Democrats* and *Republicans*. Interestingly, members of each party were significantly more likely to use *the* when talking about the opposing party than when talking about their own party: That is, Democrats were more likely to refer to *the Republicans* than to *the Democrats,* whereas Republicans were more likely to refer to *the Democrats* than to *the Republicans*. Speakers were using the word *the* to distance themselves from the group being talked about.

So if you thought the header above seemed a bit weird, you're right: I'm clearly a linguist, so my use of *the linguists* for a group I consider myself to be a part of is odd (especially in a linguistics book); it would be better without the *the*. But if for some reason I were describing an issue of particle physics here in my linguistics book, it would be fine to use the header *Here's something being discussed by the physicists*; it wouldn't have that same oddness. (A physicist I'm not.) The intuitions are subtle, as is often the case in linguistics – and that makes it all the more fascinating that so many people share them. As Acton puts it, "the English definite article is most assuredly not a word to be trifled with."

Definiteness is one of the hardest aspects of English to grasp for those who are learning English as a second language in a classroom, because no native speaker – not even among linguists – seems able to provide a simple rule to explain when you use a definite as opposed to an indefinite noun phrase. In this section, we'll focus on the definite article *the* and its indefinite colleague *a(n)*. We will consider various possibilities for determining when we use one and when we use the other. And, spoiler alert, we will find no one rule that covers all situations. For adult English-language learners, it's frustrating, especially for those whose native language doesn't have markers of definiteness and/or indefiniteness. For small children acquiring English naturally as a second language, of course, it's no problem whatsoever; they just acquire the rule(s) for definiteness in the same way that native English speakers do – whatever that rule, or those rules, may be.

Definiteness as uniqueness

Remember from back in Chapter 1 that Russell (1905) analyzed the meaning of (31) as (32):

(31) The King of France is bald.
(32) a   There is a King of France,
      b   there is only one King of France, and
      c   he is bald.

To put this in predicate logic terms (which you'll recall from Chapter 3), the semantic meaning of (31) for Russell is expressed in (33), where 'K' stands for 'King of France' and 'B' stands for 'bald':

(33) $\exists x((K(x) \wedge \forall y (K(y) \rightarrow y=x)) \wedge B(x))$

To take this piece by piece:

- $\exists x$ means 'there is some x such that'
- $K(x)$ means 'x is a King of France'
- $\wedge$ means 'and'
- $\forall y$ means 'for all y'
- $K(y) \rightarrow y=x$ means 'if y is a King of France, then y is x'
- $\wedge B(x))$ means 'and x is bald'

So if you put it all together, you get:

- There is some x such that x is a King of France,
- and for all y, if y is a King of France, then y is x,
- and x is bald.

Which in turn gives you (32) above: There is a King of France, and there's only one, and he is bald.

The interesting thing here is that under this analysis, if any one of these three conjuncts is false, then the whole sentence is false. Obviously if there's a King of France and he's not bald, then *The King of France is bald* is false. But on this account, it's equally false if there's no King of France (i.e., if the first conjunct is false) or if there are several Kings of France (i.e., if the second conjunct is false). The three conjuncts are equally asserted semantically by the sentence *The King of France is bald*.

But that seems counterintuitive. Worse yet, if there's no King of France, it could be (and has been) argued that both of the following sentences must be false:

(34) a The King of France is bald.
     b The King of France is not bald.

That is, if part of the meaning of any sentence whose subject is 'the King of France' is 'there exists a King of France', then both of these sentences require the existence of a King of France in order to be true, and they're false otherwise. And since there's no King of France at the moment, Russell would have to say that both of these sentences are currently false. And that seems contradictory.

Strawson (1950) gets around this problem by arguing that if there's no King of France, *The King of France is bald* isn't false, but it's not true either. For Strawson, if there's no King of France, that sentence is neither true nor false; instead, it has no truth-value at all. This solves the problem, sort of – but at the cost of abandoning the two-valued system of truth-values we've been assuming so far. That is, we've now got three options for a given proposition: It can be true, it can be false, or it can be truth-valueless. So we're left at a crossroads: Do we want to retain our **bivalent** (i.e., two-valued) system of truth-values and reject Strawson's solution, or do we want to accept Strawson's account and rebuild our system of truth with more than two values? We'll return to these questions when we discuss presupposition later in the chapter.

In the meantime, it's worth noting that there are two major camps of theories about definiteness. The first is based on **uniqueness** – that is, the idea that felicitous use of the definite requires that the expression pick out some unique entity. So suppose I utter (35):

(35) The dog is running loose in the neighborhood.

The use of the definite in *the dog*, on this account, indicates that I'm talking about an individual uniquely described by the phrase *the dog*. Now, it's immediately obvious that there are lots of dogs in the world, so it can't be the case that *the dog* is meant to pick out the one unique thing in the world that's described by that phrase; instead, perhaps, it picks out the one **uniquely identifiable** thing in our shared discourse model. (Different theories differ on the details.) In that case, if Sally utters (35) to Pat, it will pick out some dog that is unique to their shared discourse model – such as the one they jointly own. It would obviously be bizarre to use (35) to refer to an unknown dog that Sally has just seen running around the neighborhood. In that case, she'd use (36):

(36) A dog is running loose in the neighborhood.

This brings to mind some nonunique dog. You can imagine a Gricean or neo-Gricean account to explain why: Fido being *the dog* (that they share knowledge of) entails Fido being *a dog*, but not vice versa; so *the dog* constitutes a higher value on a Horn scale than *a dog*, and therefore if *the dog* applies, I should use that expression. Using *a dog* implicates (via scalar implicature) that I could not have felicitously said *the dog*, so it implicates that the dog in question isn't the interlocutors' shared pet. This account explains both why (35) suggests a uniquely identifiable dog and (36) suggests some other dog.

You see this scalar implicature at work in Donald Trump's utterance during his notorious photo op in front of a church in 2020

(37) Reporter: Is that your Bible?
Trump: It's *a* Bible.

He stresses the word *a* to help ensure that the implicature goes through – the implicature being that it's not a Bible that could felicitously be referred to as his Bible, hence it's not his.

Unfortunately, accounts based in uniqueness do not account for all of the data. Consider (38):

(38) "I don't mean to be rude, but *I* think it is ridiculous to have ears on the sides of one's head. It certainly *looks* ridiculous. You ought to take a peek in the mirror some day and see for yourself."

(Dahl 1961)

Here the suggestion isn't that there's a specific, identifiable mirror that James should check to see how ridiculous his ears look; and the semantics of *the mirror* certainly don't denote a single identifiable entity. Nonetheless, the definite is felicitous. Similar examples are common:

(39) a I need to use the bathroom.
b Take the elevator to the fifth floor.
c Please pass the milk.
d Answer the phone.
e Open the window.

Here, there's no suggestion that there's a uniquely identifiable bathroom, elevator, container of milk, phone, or window that is being referred to; any bathroom, etc. will do. Indeed, it's frequently the case that there are multiple bathrooms, elevators, etc., present.

Definiteness as familiarity

So perhaps the second camp of theories of definiteness is better. Here the basic claim is that definiteness marks **familiarity** (i.e., that the speaker believes the hearer is familiar with the intended referent). Certainly that seems to be the case in some instances. So recall (35) and (36), repeated here:

(40) a The dog is running loose in the neighborhood.
b A dog is running loose in the neighborhood.

Taking a familiarity-based approach, we could say that (40a) suggests that the dog in question is familiar to the hearer, whereas the dog in (40b) is not familiar, hence the default inference in (40a) that it's the dog belonging to the interlocutors (or some other especially familiar or salient dog). But this doesn't quite work either:

(41) a The oldest person on earth is 116.
 b You need to read the new book about pragmatics and brain structure.
 c I love the woman who lives next door.

None of these assumes that the hearer is familiar with the referent. In (41a), the NP *the oldest person on earth* defines a unique referent, but not one the hearer is assumed to be familiar with. In (41b), *the new book about pragmatics and brain structure* presumably denotes a unique book, but again, not one that the hearer is assumed to be familiar with. And finally, in (41c), *the woman who lives next door* may be unique – but then again, she may not, since any given person may have more than one female next-door neighbor – but in any case, the felicity of the definite doesn't require that the hearer be familiar with the referent.

At this point, you might decide that maybe there's a set of two constraints here – that the felicitous use of the definite requires **either** that the referent be unique or that it be familiar. But (yep, you know where this is heading) that doesn't work either. Consider the italicized NPs in (42):

(42) a I've just been admitted to *the hospital*.
 b I need to see if *the library* has that book.
 c My kids love hanging out at *the beach*.
 d I'll be home after I stop at *the store* for bread.
 e I was really impressed by *the food* in Spain.
 f Oh no – I've spilled tomato sauce all over *the rug*!

In each case, you can easily imagine felicitous uses in which the referent isn't unique and the hearer isn't expected to be familiar with it. In (42a), if I call my brother (who lives 2,000 miles away) and tell him that I've just been admitted to the hospital, he won't complain about the use of the definite on the grounds that there are several hospitals nearby and he doesn't know which one I'm talking about (at least, I **hope** that wouldn't be his first reaction). What (42a) really conveys is a paraphrase of 'I've been hospitalized'; the particular hospital needn't be known or familiar.

The situation is similar for *the library*, *the beach*, and *the store*; what's conveyed in each case is library-going, beach-going, and store-going, but there's no sense that the particular location in each case is known, identifiable, or even relevant. These are what have been termed 'weak definites', and there's reason to believe that they don't evoke an actual referent in the same sense that other definite NPs do; consider the examples in (43):

(43) a Now my sister and brother are both in the hospital!
 b Mae spent the day at the beach, and so did Sheila.
 c Dave is at the library, and Carla is too.

In (43a), the two siblings needn't be in the same hospital for the utterance to be felicitous, and likewise for the other two examples. Interestingly, though, they do suggest that the people in question are there for the prototypical activity. So in (43a) the siblings are assumed to be patients, not plumbers working on the pipes – and if they in fact are plumbers working on the pipes, *the hospital* takes the usual definite meaning of being one specific, known hospital that they're both in. And again, this is true for the other cases as well.

In (42e), the food in question obviously doesn't include all of the food in Spain, even though if I say *I ate the brownies in the kitchen* it does suggest that I ate all of the brownies in the kitchen. And you and I can both say *I loved the food in Spain* even if we didn't have any of the same food at all – say, if I focused entirely on tapas and you had nothing but paella, and even if each of us had one or two dishes that we actually didn't like. So here again we have a definite that marks information that is neither familiar (you needn't know what food I'm referring to) nor unique; instead, it seems to indicate some generic sense of 'food in Spain'. And finally, in (42f), the rug in question again needn't be known to the hearer nor uniquely identifiable; instead, it conveys that rug-spillage occurred.

And lest we decide that there are simply some semantic categories that are arbitrarily definite, we'd still need to deal with intriguing groups like these:

(44) To get to Sacramento…
    a I'm going to take the train.
    b I'm going to take the bus.
    c #I'm going to take the plane.
    d #I'm going to take the cab.

(45) a I'm going to the hospital.
    b I'm going to the store.
    c I'm going to school.
    d I'm going to church.
    e I'm going to a restaurant.
    f I'm going to a party.

It would be hard to come up with a rule that explains why we take *the train* and *the bus* but not *the plane* or *the cab*; instead, we take *a plane* or *a cab* (unless there is a single mutually known plane or cab that goes to Sacramento, a caveat that is not needed for *the train* or *the bus*). And of course it remains a mystery (to me, at least) why we go to *the hospital* and *the store* but also *school* and *church* (with no article whatsoever) and *a restaurant* or *a party* (never *the restaurant* or *the party* unless the particular restaurant or bar in question is known to the hearer). And of course some of these are regional; while in the U.S. a broken leg might land me *in the hospital*, in the UK I'd instead end up *in hospital*.

Finally, there are cases where the referent is flat-out brand-new and still okay as a definite:

(46) Sorry I'm late. I had to walk the dog.

Here I could be speaking to someone I've never met before, who has no idea that I have a dog; but they'll happily infer that I do, and the conversation will be none the worse for it. Fine, you say; this is a case of a uniquely identifiable dog, right? But then consider this:

(47) Sorry I'm late. #I had to eat the sandwich.

This is distinctly bizarre with no prior knowledge of a sandwich. Why? Well, far be it from me to provide answers when I can simply provide more questions – but it's deeply related to the question of presupposition, to which we now turn.

PRESUPPOSITION

As we've seen over and over, pragmatics is crucially dependent on interlocutors' beliefs about each other's mental worlds: in particular, what they can expect each other either to already know about or to be able to infer given the context of the conversation. Nowhere is this more true than with presupposition. In fact, **presupposed** information can be loosely defined as information that the speaker is treating as shared between speaker and hearer; and when such an assumption about shared information is encoded linguistically, it's called a **presupposition**. Why 'loosely defined'? Because, as it turns out, researchers disagree about how to define presupposition. Much as with Supreme Court Justice Potter Stewart's famous comment about obscenity, however, we know it when we see it (well, mostly). So let's start with some examples, and then we'll see what they have in common.

(48) a   I have to pick up my daughter.
        [presupposes that I have a daughter]
   b   I've given up drinking.
        [presupposes that I used to drink]
   c   What I sent you was my latest book.
        [presupposes that I sent you something]
   d   I want to go back to Spain.
        [presupposes that I've been to Spain previously]

In each of these cases, the utterance treats the bracketed information as being shared information. And certainly each of them would be bizarre if we mutually knew that the bracketed information weren't true: If in (48a) you knew that I had no daughter, this utterance would bring the conversation to a standstill until we dealt with the 'hold it – what daughter?' issue. But the strength of the presupposition differs: If you have no beliefs about whether or not I have a daughter, you're likely to let (48a) go by without comment, whereas if you have no beliefs about my having sent you anything, (48c) is likely to seem quite odd. And if this strikes you as being very similar to what we saw with definiteness, you're on the right track.

Testing for presupposition

First, although I said above 'we know it when we see it', that's obviously unsatisfactory. We need a way of distinguishing presupposition from other phenomena, and the obvious other phenomenon we need to distinguish it from is entailment. Recall that A entails B if in any possible world, if A is true B is necessarily also true. So the sentences in (49) entail the sentences in brackets:

(49) a John ate a sandwich.
         [entails 'John ate something']
      b Sally has a dog and a cat.
         [entails 'Sally has a dog']
      c Clyde took two trips this year.
         [entails 'Clyde took a trip this year']

It seems clear enough that if John ate a sandwich, he necessarily ate something, and so on. And a helpful check on this intuition is to try negating the entailment to see whether it is indeed an entailment: So let's negate 'John ate something', giving us 'John didn't eat something'. If that's true, then it can't be true that John ate a sandwich. That is, if the entailment is false, the sentence that entails it must also be false. So in (49b), if we negate the entailment – giving us 'Sally doesn't have a dog' – then the entailing sentence must also be false: If Sally doesn't have a dog, Sally doesn't have a dog and a cat. And likewise in (49c): If Clyde didn't take a trip this year, Clyde didn't take two trips this year.

Remember, that's a test for entailment. What we want now is a test for presupposition. The standard test for presupposition is **constancy under negation**. What that means is that we negate the sentence and see whether the presupposition survives. So let's try negating the presuppositions above in (48):

(50) a I don't have to pick up my daughter.
         [still presupposes that I have a daughter]
      b I haven't given up drinking.
         [still presupposes that I used to drink]
      c What I sent you wasn't my latest book.
         [still presupposes that I sent you something]
      d I don't want to go back to Spain.
         [still presupposes that I've been to Spain previously]

In each case, the presupposition survives the negation: *I don't have to pick up my daughter* presupposes that I have a daughter, *I haven't given up drinking* presupposes that I used to drink (while asserting, essentially, that I still do), and so on. (Questioning works the same way: *Have you given up drinking?* presupposes that you used to drink.)

So now let's imagine that we want to know whether some proposition is a presupposition or an entailment of a given sentence, going back to our old friend the King of France:

(51) The King of France is bald.
      ['there is a King of France']

Let's say we want to know whether the bracketed proposition is a presupposition or an entailment of *The King of France is bald*. We try our presupposition test:

(52) The King of France is not bald.

This clearly passes the test for presupposition: We still seem to be presupposing that there's a King of France. Now we'll try the entailment test:

(53)   There is no King of France.

Now what? If there's no King of France, is the sentence *The King of France is bald* false? This should all sound hauntingly familiar, since we dealt with it in Chapter 1. The question is, what happens to the truth-value of a sentence if it presupposes something false? And as you can see, this is closely related to the question of whether a sentence entails its presuppositions. These questions will require a quick review of our philosophers' views from Chapter 1, which in turn will lead us into a consideration of whether presupposition is a semantic or a pragmatic phenomenon. But before we wade out into those murky waters, let's take a moment to look at some **triggers** for presupposition.

Presupposition triggers

A presupposition trigger, you will not be shocked to learn, is an expression that triggers a presupposition. Or to put it another way, if a presupposition is a linguistically encoded assumption about what information is shared between interlocutors, presupposition triggers are those linguistic encodings. For one example, consider Frege's statement:

> If anything is asserted there is always an obvious presupposition that the simple or compound proper names used have a reference. If one therefore asserts 'Kepler died in misery', there is a presupposition that the name 'Kepler' designates something.
>
> (Frege 1892)

So we can say that a proper name is a presupposition trigger; to use a proper name is to presuppose that it designates something. There are lots of other presupposition triggers; a selection is given in (54), with examples:

(54)   a   Definite NPs:
             The King of France is bald.
             My sister saw a raccoon.
             The dog needs to go out.
        b   Change-of-state verbs:
             The steak thawed slowly.
             Kay woke up.
             Sylvia has recovered from COVID-19.
        c   Factive verbs:
             I regret that I didn't call. Jenny didn't realize that it was cold out.
             Caleb recognizes that the world is round.
        d   Cleft constructions:
             What Steve wanted was a new refrigerator.
             It was the cold air that really bothered me.

Chocolate is what keeps me awake at night.
   e   Iteratives:
       Donald violated his parole again. Halley's comet is due to return in 2061. I'm rewriting this story.

Proper names are a subset of definite NPs, and we see others in (54a), which presuppose the existence of the King of France, my sister, and the dog, respectively. Change-of-state verbs presuppose the prior state before the change – here, that the steak was previously frozen, that Kay was previously asleep, and that Sylvia previously had COVID-19. Factive verbs like *regret, realize,* and *recognize* presuppose their sentential complement – so in these examples, they presuppose that I didn't call, that it was cold out, and that the world is round, respectively. Incidentally, you can use factive verbs in your writing to cue the reader to how you feel about the complement. So compare these options:

(55)   a   In her book, Smith observes that...
       b   In her book, Smith recognizes that...
       c   In her book, Smith acknowledges that...
       d   In her book, Smith claims that...
       e   In her book, Smith insists that...

In (55a-c), the factive verbs *observes, recognizes,* and *acknowledges* cue the reader that the writer wants Smith's claim to be taken as accepted fact. On the flip side, (55c-d) avoid the factive and thereby suggest that the reader shouldn't necessarily take Smith's claim as fact. (To see the difference, compare *Smith doesn't recognize that...* with *Smith doesn't claim that...*, where the first negation clearly preserves the presupposition while the second is clearly neutral.)

Cleft constructions come in a range of subtypes, exemplified in (54d), and we'll talk about these types in more detail in Chapter 8. But they're called clefts because they 'cleave' or split a proposition into two parts, a focus and a presupposition. In (54d), *What Steve wanted was a new refrigerator* essentially splits the proposition 'Steve wanted a new refrigerator' into the presupposition 'Steve wanted X' and the focus 'a new refrigerator' (which fills in the X – i.e., what Steve wanted). That's what's known as a *wh*-cleft, due to the word *what*, which uses one of a group of question-introducing words that generally begin with *wh* in English: *who, what, when, where, why*. Not all of these can be used for *wh*-clefts in all dialects; for example, *Who's next is Steve* is terrible for me, but presumably it's fine for all of those retail workers who say things like *I can help who's next*, which for me is impossible. *It was the cold air that really bothered me* is an example of an *it*-cleft (for obvious reasons), splitting the proposition into the presupposition 'X bothered me' and the focus 'the cold air'. And *Chocolate is what keeps me awake at night* is a reverse *wh*-cleft, with a structure like a regular *wh*-cleft but swapping the position of the presupposition ('something keeps me awake at night') and the focus ('chocolate'). And again, to check the status of the presupposition, simply negate the sentence: In *Chocolate isn't what keeps me awake at night*, there's still something that keeps me awake at night; the presupposition survives.

Finally, the iteratives in (54e) describe repetition: something returns, repeats, or reoccurs, presupposing that there was an earlier occurrence. So *Donald violated his parole again* presupposes that he violated it before, *Halley's comet is due to return in 2061* presupposes that it has come around before, and *I'm rewriting this story* presupposes that I've written it previously. And needless to say, negation preserves the presupposition: *I'm not rewriting this story* still presupposes the prior writing of the story.

Theories of presupposition

In Chapter 1 we took a whirlwind tour of (some) philosophers of language, and we saw that there was considerable disagreement about the status of a sentence containing an expression whose referent doesn't exist – our friend the King of France being Exhibit A. Recall that for Frege, the referent of a sentence is either the True or the False; and because the reference of a sentence is built up from the reference of its parts, if one of those parts doesn't actually have a referent, then neither does the sentence – meaning it ends up being neither true nor false.

Russell, as we've seen, disagrees; for him, 'there is a King of France' is one of the entailments of *The King of France is bald*. So for Russell if there's no referent for that definite NP, it renders the entire sentence false, just as the falsity of any other entailment renders a sentence false: If it's false that 'I ate', then the sentence *I ate a potato* (which entails 'I ate') must also be false.

Strawson sides with Frege, saying that a given use of the sentence *The King of France is bald* has no truth-value in the absence of a King of France, and argues that there's a distinction to be made between what such a sentence **presupposes** (that there's a King of France) and what it **asserts** (that he's bald). For Strawson, the satisfaction of the presupposition is required for the sentence to count as either true or false; if there's no such king, then whether he's bald or not just isn't an issue, and the question of whether the sentence is true or false doesn't arise. Notice that with Strawson, pragmatic factors are starting to come into the picture; he speaks not of the truth-value of a sentence but rather the truth-value of some particular use of that sentence (recall, after all, that France did once have a king), and of what is or isn't an issue in a particular utterance (which again, isn't a semantic question).

So we seem to have three choices with respect to presupposition:

- It's a semantic phenomenon, and the presupposition is entailed, a la Russell. If the presupposition is false, the whole sentence is false.
- It's a semantic phenomenon, and a false presupposition leaves the sentence without a truth-value. We need to change our semantic theory, which is currently bivalent, to allow for a third possibility (i.e., that a sentence might be neither true nor false).
- It's a pragmatic phenomenon, having to do with what is appropriate, at issue, or being asserted in a given context.

There's a lot to be said for that third option. First of all, we've already seen the problems resulting from the first two options. Second, a pragmatic view of presupposition lets us keep our handy bivalent semantics. Third, it makes intuitive sense: If there's no King of France, why are we discussing whether or not he has hair?

But there's plenty of other evidence that presupposition is actually pragmatic. For one thing, presuppositions aren't all equally strong. Consider (56):

(56) a The King of France is bald.
   b My father met the King of France yesterday.
   c My father wants to meet the King of France.
   d My father wishes he could meet the King of France.
   e My father is the King of France.
   f There is a King of France.

We've talked about (56a) enough; it clearly presupposes (56f) and gives rise to all the usual queasiness about whether it's true or false. Curiously, though, (56b) seems much more clearly false. (56c) could actually be true, if your father is confused about the state of France's government. And (56d) could be true even with a knowledgeable father who wishes France's government were otherwise. In (56e) we have another case of a clearly false sentence (in today's world), but it certainly doesn't seem to presuppose (56f) as strongly as, say, (56a) and (56b) do. And in (56c-d) we have what are known as **opaque contexts**, in which the father's beliefs concerning the king make a difference. Consider (57):

(57) a My father wants to meet Joe Biden.
   b My father wants to meet the President of the U.S.

Here, it's possible for (a) to be true while (b) is false (at the time of this writing), if my father is hideously underinformed about who is president. (And under similar conditions, it's possible for (a) to be false while (b) is true.) Which means that it's possible for my father to want to meet the King of France even if there is no such person.

So presupposition varies in strength, and it depends on beliefs and on context (since again, whether France has a king depends on where in human history we happen to be standing). These are all hallmarks of pragmatic phenomena. And presuppositions can sometimes be cancelled or suspended:

(58) a The King of France isn't bald; there is no King of France!
   b The King of France lives in Paris, if he exists.

In (58a), the presupposition of the king's existence is cancelled via what Horn 1989 calls 'metalinguistic negation'; in (58b) it's suspended. And whereas (59a) seems to presuppose that Gina finished her soup, (59b) obviously doesn't:

(59) a Gina sighed before she finished her soup.
   b Gina died before she finished her soup.

So there are plenty of good reasons to consider presupposition to be a pragmatic rather than a semantic phenomenon. That still leaves us with the question of how it should be defined, and no end of ink has been spilled debating whether to consider presuppositions to be that information which is taken for granted, nonasserted, uncontroversial, common ground, 'given' information, or mutual knowledge. But what all of these analyses have in common is that they all involve speaker intent, and specifically, the speaker's beliefs about the hearer's knowledge store and the speaker's intent to encode something involving that knowledge store. What all of these analyses also have in common is that they can't account for all so-called presupposed information:

(60) a It was at this moment that the courtroom lights flickered in the storm, flickered again, and went out.

(Guterson 1994)

b It had been the judge's bailiff, Ed Soames, who'd answered the door when Art Moran knocked at five after five on the evening of the sixteenth and asked to see Lew Fielding.

(Guterson 1994)

c It was on the bus ride between Talequa and Epiphany that Berkeley Sims left her seat, walked to the front of the bus, picked up the microphone that was used for announcements, and began to sing.

(Konigsburg 2004)

Prince (1978) dubbed cases like these **informative-presupposition *it*-clefts**, on the grounds that, unlike other *it*-clefts, these introduce brand-new information in their presuppositions. Their structure is the same as any other *it*-cleft: 'it was X that/who Y...'. But in each case the 'presupposed' information not only isn't already known to the hearer but in fact is a crucial part of the new information that the sentence is being used to convey. In (60a), the whole point is to tell the reader something new, which is that the lights flickered and went out. Likewise, in (b) the point of the sentence is to convey that Soames answered the door, and in (c) the point is to convey that Sims left her seat, went to the front of the bus, and began to sing. In each case what is actually new information is being presented by means of a construction whose purpose is more generally to convey mutually known information.

And it's not just this one construction that can perform such a feat. We began our discussion of presupposition with the following examples ((48a–d), repeated here as (61a–d)):

(61) a I have to pick up my daughter.
       [presupposes that I have a daughter]
     b I've given up drinking.
       [presupposes that I used to drink]
     c What I sent you was my latest book.
       [presupposes that I sent you something]
     d I want to go back to Spain.
       [presupposes that I've been to Spain previously]

Here, three of the four can be used felicitously even when the information in the presupposition is new to the hearer. I can use (61a) whether or not my hearer knows that I have a daughter, I can use (61b) whether or not my hearer knows that I used to drink, and I can use (61d) whether or not my hearer knows that I've ever been to Spain. Only (61c) seems odd if the presupposition is false; it's odd to say *What I sent you was my latest book* if you have no knowledge that I've sent you something.

The interesting difference, in fact, between the cases in (60) and those in (61) are that the construction in (60) is being used precisely to convey the 'presupposed' information (which is what makes it a really interesting construction), but in (61) that's not the point of the utterance at all. In (61a) my purpose isn't to tell you that I have a daughter; that's just a side effect, as it were, of telling you that I have to pick her up. I'm treating the daughter as though she's already known, even though I know she isn't, because I know that you'll cooperatively add her to your knowledge store and the conversation won't miss a beat. In essence, you figure 'she's presupposed a daughter; I guess she has a daughter'. You have, as Lewis 1979 put it, **accommodated** my presupposition.

Accommodation

Lewis's basic idea is that language is like a baseball game, with each utterance constituting, essentially, a play. And our discourse model is the scoreboard. As we converse, we keep the conversational 'score' – essentially, where things stand conversationally: what's known to me, what do I think is known to my hearer, what entities have been discussed, what properties we mutually believe those entities to have, and so on. Without such a conversational scoreboard, I might walk into a classroom and begin my lecture by saying:

(62) She didn't do so.

At this point, everyone else in the room would be deeply confused, having no idea who *she* represents and what it is that the referent didn't do. What prevents me from doing this is my understanding that the conversational score at this point doesn't include those two bits of information.

According to Lewis, the conversational score at any given point will include the currently shared presuppositions. And these current presuppositions depend entirely on what the prior presuppositions were and what's happened to update them. This is much like the score in baseball, which depends on what the prior score was and what's happened since then to update it. Each play has the potential to update the baseball score, and each utterance has the potential to update the conversational score.

So far, so good. By uttering (63), I can update the conversational score to add a new individual and the fact that she's my daughter:

(63) I have a daughter.

And now our future conversational moves can presuppose this daughter:

(64) My daughter has a dog.

Here, my daughter is presupposed, and the dog is added, along with the relationship between the two. But then comes the wrinkle; I can also simply presuppose a daughter without first adding her to the model; if you and I are chatting about pets, I can utter (64) whether or not you're aware that I have a daughter, and you will gamely (so to speak) update the conversational scoreboard by adding my daughter. As Lewis puts it, "Conversational score [tends] to evolve in such a way as … to make whatever occurs count as correct play." So by acting **as though** my daughter were mutual knowledge, I in fact **cause** her to become mutual knowledge. By treating my daughter the same way I'd treat any other presupposed information, I cue you to take her to be presupposed. This won't work in a baseball game; you can't add points to the scoreboard by acting **as though** you'd hit a home run. But it works in conversation.

This is what Lewis calls **accommodation**. The hearer accommodates the speaker's use of the phrase *my daughter*, thinking more or less along these lines: 'The speaker has presupposed the existence of a daughter. I didn't know she had a daughter, but it's certainly plausible that she does, and since she's presupposing that she does and I assume she's being cooperative, I'm going to give her the benefit of the doubt and add the daughter to my discourse model'. Well, okay, the hearer actually doesn't think all of those things consciously, but that's in effect the line of reasoning that justifies accommodation in general.

BOX 7.2

Messing with people's memories

We've seen that people will readily accommodate presupposed information that they didn't previously know: If I say *I need to feed my cat*, you'll add the fact that I have a cat to your discourse model without questioning it. If, on the other hand, I say *I need to feed a cat*, there's no presupposition trigger, and consequently no presupposition that I have a cat.

So our tendency to accommodate presupposed information gives speakers a way to add information to a hearer's view of reality with having to explicitly assert it, which would put it 'on the table', as it were, for questions of truth and falsity:

(a)   A: I have a cat.
       B: That's not true!
(b)   A: I need to feed my cat.
       B: That's not true!

In (a), B's response is taken to negate the assertion, so it means 'you don't have a cat'. And in (b), it also negates the assertion, so it means 'you don't need to feed your cat'. What it doesn't mean, without some further explanation, is 'you don't have a cat'. Instead, A's presupposition quietly adds a cat to the discourse model without making it quite as readily open to question.

That probably seems fine, and we obviously do this all the time – but what about contexts where it really matters whether that presupposed material is actually true? Can a speaker cause a change in the hearer's beliefs by quietly presupposing what isn't true? Well, obviously yes: If I say *I need to feed my cat* when I have no cat at all, I'll cause you to believe what isn't true, but to little effect; after all, who cares whether I have a cat? But now consider advertising. An ad that says a medicine will help with 'your allergy symptoms' presupposes that you have allergy symptoms. Could it cause someone who doesn't have them to assume they do? Or in a restaurant, can

> a server sell more desserts by asking *What would you like for dessert?* (presupposing that you would like something for dessert) than by asking *Would you like something for dessert?*
>
> Or, more importantly, consider the courtroom: A lawyer can ask a witness directly whether something happened, but they can also simply presuppose that it happened and ask the witness about it. Can presupposition affect someone's memory of their own experience?
>
> There's research to suggest that it can. Loftus and Zanni (1975) showed subjects a film of an auto accident and then asked half of them questions like (c), and half of them questions like (d):
>
> (c) Did you see a broken headlight?
> (d) Did you see the broken headlight?
>
> As you've probably already guessed, the subjects who were asked (d) were much more likely to report seeing a broken headlight than those asked (c) – despite there having been no broken headlight in the video.
>
> Loftus and Zanni note that (c) asks essentially two questions – 'was there a broken headlight?' and 'did you see it?' – whereas (d) essentially says 'there was a broken headlight; did you see it?', which is much more likely to elicit a 'yes' response. They note, "Different forms of questions can be consciously used to elicit desired answers from a witness, and also to create a desired influence upon the jury." Although there are rules against using such 'leading questions', they also observe that "the definition of leading is a long way from being precise." And did you notice how my use of the words *note* and *observe* in these last two sentences presupposes that I believe Loftus and Zanni, and thereby suggests that you should too? Did you assume that they're correct in a way that maybe you wouldn't have if I'd used the word *claim*?
>
> If you're heading to law school, it's handy to know some linguistics – not because you can use it to insidiously affect what people believe they saw (you're a good person and would never do that), but to be able to recognize when someone else is doing it. Presupposition matters!

That all might sound great, but (as always) there's a hitch – two hitches, actually. First, there's a hitch in the theory. If what's presupposed equals what's in the common ground – but we can presuppose stuff that's not in the common ground by accommodating it – and there are no limits to what can be accommodated – then the whole thing starts to sound pretty vacuous. If there's nothing that can't be presupposed (because it can always be accommodated), then what's the point of saying these things are 'presupposed' at all?

Fortunately, hitch #1 is rescued by hitch #2, which is that it's not actually the case that everything can always be accommodated:

(65) a Hi, class! Sorry I'm late; I had to feed the dog.
     b Hi, class! Sorry I'm late; #I had to eat the sandwich.

In (65a), the class will happily accommodate a previously unknown dog. In (65b), they're much less likely to accommodate a previously unknown sandwich, and infelicity results. And recall (61c) above, where *What I sent you was my latest book* was seen to be infelicitous if the presupposition ('I sent you something') isn't in the common ground; accommodation won't save the cleft. And we can multiply the examples:

(66) Hi, class! Sorry I'm late; I had to…
  a call my daughter.
  b #chop my pickles.
  c take out the garbage.
  d #put away the onions.
  e finish my grading.
  f #finish my cooking.
  g finish my book.
  h #finish the book.

You can see that it's not a matter of *my* vs. *the* (exx. a-d), except when it is (exx. g-h). It's likely to involve how plausible the presupposed item or activity is (exx. a-b), except when it doesn't (exx. e-f, g-h). And if you're thinking this is closely related to the question of when a definite NP is felicitous in general, you're absolutely right. There are almost certainly a number of interrelated factors at play – and as always with pragmatics, the one at the top of the list is the speaker's beliefs about the hearer's beliefs, and vice versa – what each of them believes is and isn't shared, and is and isn't at issue, and is and isn't new to the discourse.

EXERCISES

Self-test:

1 'Psychic continuity', according to Chomsky, explains
  a presupposition.
  b the sameness of a referent over time.
  c the difference between anaphora and deixis.
  d the relationship between familiarity and definiteness.
2 Deictics are one type of
  a uniqueness.
  b presupposition.
  c accommodation.
  d indexical.

3 The word *afterward* is an instance of
  a a definite NP.
  b temporal deixis.
  c psychic continuity.
  d implicature.
4 Cataphora could be described as
  a forward-looking anaphora.
  b plural indefiniteness.
  c null anaphoric reference.
  d phrase-level anaphora.
5 A bivalent system of truth is one that
  a only allows propositions to be either true or false.
  b requires truth-conditions and truth-values to match.
  c denies that presuppositions have a truth-value.
  d denies that presuppositions affect the truth of a sentence.
6 One theory of definiteness argues that the definite article *the* marks
  a anaphoric reference.
  b cataphoric reference.
  c psychic continuity.
  d familiarity.
7 A pronoun could best be described as
  a a word that takes the place of a noun.
  b a word that takes the place of a noun phrase.
  c a word that points forward to a verb phrase.
  d a word type that doesn't really exist.
8 If, as Russell argues, a sentence entails its presupposition, then
  a the falsity of the sentence entails the falsity of the presupposition.
  b both of them must be true.
  c the falsity of the presupposition entails the falsity of the sentence.
  d both of them must be false.
9 The fact that a presupposition can sometimes be cancelled or suspended could be used to argue that
  a sentences entail their presuppositions.
  b presupposition is a semantic phenomenon.
  c presuppositions entail the sentences they appear in.
  d presupposition is a pragmatic phenomenon.
10 If I say *The tulip bed in my front yard is blooming*, but you didn't previously know I had a tulip bed in my front yard, you'll probably
  a wait before adding it to the discourse model.
  b accommodate it.
  c consider it a case of anaphoric reference.
  d wonder why I didn't use an indefinite NP.

Comprehension questions:

1. It could be argued that just as there is backward-looking anaphora and forward-looking cataphora, there is a similar distinction to be made in discourse deixis. Create three examples each of backward-looking and forward-looking discourse deixis.
2. In your own words, describe the relationship between definiteness and presupposition.
3. How is a conversation like a baseball game, according to Lewis? How is it unlike a baseball game?

Opinion questions:

1. Not everyone recognizes discourse deixis as a category of deixis. Do you think it should be included, or do you think it's just a variety of anaphora? Explain your reasoning.
2. Of the two primary approaches to explaining definiteness – familiarity and uniqueness – which do you think comes closer to explaining the use of the definite article, or explains a greater range of the cases? Explain your reasoning.
3. We've seen that 'informative-presupposition *it*-clefts' take the form of a presupposition-marking construction, but the information marked as presupposed is in fact new. Why might a speaker use such a construction? What function might it serve? Give an example of a case in which you might choose it over a noncleft and explain why. (Such questions will be a major focus of the next chapter.)

Discussion questions:

1. Imagine you're teaching English to speakers of another language that doesn't have markers for definiteness. How would you go about teaching them when to use the word *the*? What tips would you give them for choosing between a definite and an indefinite?
2. The word *the* isn't the only marker of definiteness, although it's the one we've focused on. To what extent do our discussions of when to use *the* also apply to other definite NPs, such as possessives and demonstratives?
3. Considering as wide a range of examples as possible, discuss what sorts of examples do and don't allow for accommodation, and correspondingly, what factors seem to be involved. Obviously you're not expected to come up with a theory of accommodation that covers all examples, but try to agree, as a group, on a reasonably broad account, and then discuss the examples it doesn't cover and where the problem seems to be.
4. In Eric Acton's paper (discussed in Box 7.1), he gives the following example from Bernie Sanders's presidential campaign website:
   (i) Paid for by Bernie 2016 (not **the billionaires**). (Acton 2019, ex. 4, boldface his)
   What does the definite NP seem to be doing here? How would the meaning of this example be subtly changed without it? (Acton's paper is available online at www.linguisticsociety.org/sites/default/files/03_95.1Acton_0.pdf, if you'd like to see his neo-Gricean approach to the difference in meaning.)
5. As we'll see in detail in the next chapter, some information can be inferred in context without having to be mentioned explicitly. For example, if I mention an individual, *their*

face is inferrable after that (since you can infer that a person has a face). But what about *their shoes* or *their hat*? Most people can be assumed to be wearing shoes; a hat, less so. What about *their cleats* or *their helmet*? (Probably inferrable in the context of a football game, but not in the context of encountering someone on the street.) Discuss where – or how – you might draw the line between what is inferrable and what is accommodated, or whether a line needs to be drawn at all.

Data collection and analysis:

1. Open a novel to a random page, and find the first dozen presuppositions. Describe what type of trigger each has. Be careful not to focus on definites to the exclusion of other types – clefts, change-of-state verbs, and so forth. Skip over some definites if you have to in order to get to a wider variety of trigger types.
2. Using the same novel as in question 1, look at the first 25 uses of the word *the* that you encounter (either at the beginning of the novel, or if it's one you're familiar with, starting at a random point). To what extent do the theories discussed in this chapter successfully account for each of them? Where do you run into trouble, and why?
3. Re-do questions #1 and #2, first using a nonfiction book you own, and then using a Google search. How do your results differ in the three cases, if at all?
4. Using instances from conversations you participate in or overhear, collect 10 examples of accommodation. Keep in mind that a presupposition needn't have been explicitly mentioned in the prior discourse to count as shared (and thus not count as accommodation). For example, we all share, and can therefore presuppose, *the sun* and *the U.S.*; and as noted above in discussion question #5, certain things can be inferred without necessarily needing to be accommodated (e.g., given mention of an individual, their face counts as inferrable).
5. Choose a conversation you're a participant in and casually use a presupposition that you think the other participants will be unwilling to accommodate. (I recommend you do this with good friends or family members, in a very low-stakes conversation, and explain yourself immediately afterward.) Describe the other participants' reaction, if any, and why you think they react (or fail to react) as they do.

Answers to self-test:

1. b
2. d
3. b
4. a
5. a
6. d
7. b
8. c
9. d
10. b

CHAPTER 8

Interfaces II: Structure and meaning

> **KEY CONCEPTS:**
>
> - semantic roles
> - agent, patient, theme
> - argument structure alternations
> - information structure
> - canonical vs. noncanonical word order
> - information status
> - given vs. new information
> - discourse-status, hearer-status
> - inferential relations
> - preposing
> - postposing
> - existential, presentational
> - argument reversal
> - inversion, passivization, long passive
> - bridging, elaborating inferences
> - open proposition
> - clefts: *wh*-cleft, *it*-cleft
> - construction, alloform
> - type, token

You've known since forever that these two sentences mean the same thing:

(1) a Sam threw the stick.
    b The stick was thrown by Sam.

But have you ever stopped to wonder why English gives you two ways of saying the exact same thing? In general, language tries to avoid duplication: We don't say *typer because we've already got the word *typist*. Sure, we've got synonyms, but many people believe there's always some difference: *hide* and *conceal* might mean the same thing in lots of contexts, but I can *run*

DOI: 10.4324/9781003351214-8

behind the couch and hide, whereas I can't *run behind the couch and conceal. And while *car* and *automobile* mean the same thing, they're at different registers; if I told my husband *I'm going to put some gas in the automobile* he'd think I'd lost my mind. And again, while *pop* and *soda* refer to the same stuff, the terms are used in different parts of the country.

In short, where language allows duplication, there's usually a good reason. Yet it seems like at the level of syntax, it allows all sorts of duplication:

(2) a A pie sat on the counter.
    b On the counter sat a pie.
    c There sat a pie on the counter.
    d What sat on the counter was a pie.
    e It was a pie that sat on the counter.
    f On the counter a pie sat.
    g On the counter there sat a pie.

Believe me, I could go on for a long time with this exercise. But linguistic options develop for a reason. What are the reasons for these apparent duplications? That's the topic of this chapter. It all has to do with the interaction between structure and meaning.

SEMANTIC ROLES

You may recall from Chapter 3 that a proposition is made up of a predicate and its arguments. So in a sentence like *Sally saw a snake*, the predicate is *saw* and the arguments are *Sally* and *a snake*. A two-place predicate like *saw* has two arguments – in this case, the one doing the seeing and the one being seen. There are also one-place predicates like *slept* (so a sentence like *Sammy slept* has only one argument, i.e., one participant), and three-place predicates like *give* (as in *Gregory will give a grapefruit to Gary*, where the arguments are *Gregory, a grapefruit,* and *Gary*). If you use the wrong number of arguments with a given predicate, you'll get ungrammaticality, as in *Gregory slept a grapefruit to Gary*.

One of the handy things about syntax is that it helps us to identify what arguments are playing what roles. So consider these sentences:

(3) a Harry hugged a hermit.
    b A hermit hugged Harry.

The syntactic relationships between a subject and a verb, and between a verb and a direct object, tells us who's doing what. And it's not just a matter of linear order:

(4) a Harry hugged a hermit.
    b Harry was hugged by a hermit.

Here, *Harry* and *a hermit* are in the same order in both sentences, but who's doing what has been flipped in (4b). The passive is a syntactic structure in which the argument appearing before the verb plays the role that's played by the post-verbal argument in the active (i.e., nonpassive) sentence. What this means is that (3b) and (4b) mean the exact same thing:

(5) a A hermit hugged Harry.
    b Harry was hugged by a hermit.

That is, they have the same truth-conditions – and so they represent the same proposition, despite being different sentences with different word orders.

We say that *Harry* and *a hermit* play the same **semantic roles** in (5a) and (5b). In both cases, *a hermit* is what we call the **agent**; it's the argument that's actively, purposely doing the thing described by the verb. And *Harry* is the **patient** or **theme**, which is the entity that's undergoing whatever action is described by the verb. (Incidentally, these roles are called semantic roles, thematic roles, and theta-roles by different authors working in different frameworks.)

Different authors identify different sets of semantic roles (sometimes using different terms), but you'll most frequently run across these:

- agent: the entity actively performing the action
- patient/theme: the entity being affected by or standing in the state described by the verb
- instrument: an entity being used to perform the action
- source: the starting point of the action
- goal: the end point of the action
- location: the location of the action or situation
- experiencer: the entity experiencing the action or situation

Sometimes you'll find **patient** listed as an entity undergoing the action and being affected by it and **theme** as an entity undergoing the action without being affected by it. In that system, *the paint* in (6a) is a theme, whereas in (6b) it's a patient.

(6) a The paint was red.
    b The paint was removed.

In other cases both are called themes. In yet other cases you'll see 'theme' defined as an entity undergoing movement or change of location. We'll use the two terms pretty much interchangeably.

But you already can see the problem here, which is that there's a lot of slipperiness between the various roles, which is why different authors use different sets. If Rachel falls and accidentally rolls down a hill, what's her semantic roll in (7)?

(7) Rachel rolled down the hill.

Is she the theme, the patient, or the experiencer?

On the other hand, these roles can capture some pretty interesting meaning differences. For example, (7) is actually ambiguous between two slightly different meanings. If Rachel is playing in the snow and lies down and rolls down the hill on purpose, that can be described by (7) as well, but the role Rachel plays in the action is different; now she's an agent.

In some languages, agents and themes are treated differently; an agent appears in subject position, but a theme appears as the direct object of the verb. And that kind of makes sense, since on one reading of (7) Rachel makes sense as the subject, but on the other reading, where she's a theme, rolling is happening to her, just as it is in the sentence *Mary rolled Rachel down the hill*, where she's a direct object. So it makes perfectly good sense that there's a whole set of languages (called 'ergative' languages) in which the theme behaves like a direct object all the time, and only agents get to be subjects. In English (and other so-called 'accusative' languages), agents and themes can both appear in subject position, which means that some themes show up as direct objects (when there's an agent showing up as subject) and others show up as subjects (when they're the only argument of an intransitive verb).

Argument-structure alternations

At this point the interaction between syntax and thematic roles in English gets really interesting. Consider these sentences:

(8)   a   Barney broke the bowl with a baseball bat.
       b   A baseball bat broke the bowl.
       c   The bowl broke.

(9)   a   Mary melted the melon with the match.
       b   The match melted the melon.
       c   The melon melted.

Two things are immediately apparent: first, that the same scenario can be described by each of the sentences in (8), and similarly in (9); and second, that there's a pattern here. Most verbs don't work this way: *Sara saw the sundae with her spectacles* doesn't give rise to **Her spectacles saw the sundae* or **The sundae saw*; and even *Barney hit the bowl with a baseball bat* doesn't give rise to **The bowl hit*. So not all verbs work this way, but there's a subset that do; try, for example, *Bill opened the door with a key*. (See Fillmore 1970 for more detail.)

Notice also that the semantic roles of the participants don't change at all; in (9), *the melon* is the theme throughout, and *the match* is the instrument. One thing that's handy about semantic roles is that regularities in various arguments' roles can be described even when their syntactic roles change. In (9), *the match* is an object of a preposition in (a) but a subject in (b), and its semantic role stays the same.

The interesting thing is that different sets of verbs allow different alternations, a phenomenon documented at length in Levin 1993. So consider what Levin calls the class of 'spray/load' verbs:

(10)   a   Walter sprayed water on the wall.
        b   Walter sprayed the wall with water.

(11)   a   Wendy loaded wheat onto the wagon.
        b   Wendy loaded the wagon with wheat.

(12)   a   Pete packed pepper into the pipe.
        b   Pete packed the pipe with pepper.

An interesting property of this group is that they show a systematic but subtle difference in meaning depending on which syntactic framework they appear in: In each case, the (a) variant can be used when just a little water is sprayed, a little wheat is loaded, etc. – that is, when the wall, wagon, and pipe (i.e., the semantic 'goals') haven't been completely covered or filled. But in the (b) variants, there's a holistic effect; the reading you get is one in which the wall is covered with water (10b), the wagon is filled with wheat (11b), and the pipe is fully packed with pepper (12b). It would be very odd to use these for a situation where the wall (wagon, pipe…) isn't completely affected. The other, nonholistic reading is called the 'partitive' reading, because it allows for only part of the goal to be affected.

Other verbs in this class include *dust* (as in to dust a cake with powdered sugar – i.e., to add rather than remove dust), *heap, shower, spatter,* and *stuff*, among many others. You can test for yourself to see the holistic effect disappearing and appearing depending on the syntactic frame.

A similar holistic/partitive distinction is seen in 'butter' verbs:

(13) a Jane buttered the toast.
     b Jane put butter on the toast.

(14) a John salted the spaghetti.
     b John put salt on the spaghetti.

Again, you see the effect of the syntactic frame: In (13a), we get a sense that the toast has been completely covered with butter, whereas (13b) could describe a situation in which a small dab of butter has been applied to the toast – and similarly for (14).

Levin provides dozens of verbs that participate in each of these alternations – and she provides dozens of other verb classes that participate in other such alternations (with again many, many verbs listed for each). This shows an interesting interaction between syntax and semantics: As always, there are rules that we're following even when we don't realize we're following them. And while it's clear that the syntactic positions of subject and object help us to interpret the semantic differences between, say, *Mel saw Mary* and *Mary saw Mel*, there are a myriad of other syntactic differences that we may never have consciously thought about but which still affect the way we structure our messages and the way they're understood. Here we've seen how this plays out at the level of lexical semantics; next, we'll see it at work with respect to our assumptions about what our interlocutors do and don't know.

INFORMATION STRUCTURE

Recall the wide array of syntactic options in (2) above, repeated here:

(15) a A pie sat on the counter.
     b On the counter sat a pie.
     c There sat a pie on the counter.
     d What sat on the counter was a pie.
     e It was a pie that sat on the counter.
     f On the counter a pie sat.
     g On the counter there sat a pie.

These options seem different from the argument-structure alternations described above. There, the options were based on semantically coherent verb classes that gave rise to limited alternations. What we see here, instead, is a variety of constructions whose distribution doesn't depend as much on the verb. Virtually any intransitive verb that takes a locative PP complement will allow the options in (15); you could replace *sat* with *stood, lay, appeared*, or *emerged*, for example. And unlike the argument-structure alternations above, the felicity of these options depends on the discourse context in which they appear. For example, while the default or **canonical** word order in (15a) above is felicitous in most contexts, that's not true of the **noncanonical** word orders in (15b-g). For example, the felicity of (15b) depends on the prior discourse:

(16) a In the diner I saw a long blue counter. *On the counter sat a pie.*
      b In the diner I saw a large blueberry pie. #*On a counter sat the pie.*
      c In the diner I saw a large blueberry pie. #*On the counter sat a pie.*

Each of these examples ends in an **inversion** (shown in italics), which essentially switches the order of the NP and PP from their canonical positions in (15a). What's interesting is that in (16a) the inversion is felicitous, but in (16b) and (16c) it is not. As we'll see below, the difference has to do with the **information status** of the two 'inverted' phrases – that is, whether the speaker believes the information is known or salient for the hearer. In (16a), the counter has already been mentioned, but the pie hasn't; in (16b) and (16c) the pie has been mentioned, but the counter hasn't. Inversion, as we'll see, is infelicitous when the initial phrase is 'newer' than the final phrase. Roughly put, the construction prefers a known-before-new ordering to a new-before-known ordering. And the fact that (16b) and (16c) are both infelicitous shows that this is a fact about information status, not about definiteness.

Speakers use a wide range of **noncanonical-word-order (NWO)** constructions in order to arrange their sentences for the ease of the addressee, including such strategies as placing known, or **given**, information before new information. This is what's known as the **Given-New Contract** (Halliday 1967; Halliday and Hasan 1976). Consider (17):

(17) On a hill above the valley there was a wood.
      In the wood there was a huge tree.
      Under the tree there was a hole.
      In the hole lived Mr Fox and Mrs Fox and their four Small Foxes.
                                                    (Dahl 1970; valley previously mentioned)

Later on we'll discuss the specific constructions we see here, but the thing to notice now is the Given-New Contract at work, with each sentence placing the known information before the new bit, making the new bit now known, so that it can appear at the beginning of the next sentence. First, Dahl introduces the wood; then the wood can appear at the beginning of the next sentence, which introduces a tree, which can now appear at the beginning of the next sentence, and so on. What a speaker does in ordering their sentences in this way is known as **information packaging**. We'll see this packaging at work in a number of constructions below, starting with **preposing**.

Preposing

Among the noncanonical (but grammatical!) word orders of English is **preposing**, in which a complement of the verb gets moved ahead of the subject. So returning to our counter and pie:

(18) a A pie sat on the counter.
 b On the counter a pie sat.

In (18a) we have our old friend canonical word order (CWO). In (18b) the PP *on the counter* is preposed from its CWO position to a noncanonical position in front of the subject *a pie*. And notice that this is different from the inversion *on the counter sat a pie* since *a pie* remains in its CWO position in front of the verb.

Okay, so why does English give us the option of preposing? As shown in Ward 1988 and Birner and Ward 1998, preposed phrases must be **discourse-old** (Prince 1992). Discourse-old information is information that's already been evoked in the current discourse, whereas **hearer-old** information is information the speaker believes the hearer knows about (even if it hasn't been evoked in the current discourse). Discourse-old information includes **inferrable** information (Birner 1994, 1996), which is information that stands in an **inferential relation** to something in the prior discourse.

Preposed information needs to be discourse-old, which means it has either been explicitly mentioned in the prior discourse or it must stand in some sort of inferential relation to something in the prior discourse than renders it inferrable. For example:

(19) a As the balloon kept descending, I tried to calculate how fast we'd need to jump out of the basket and run for our lives. I figured the ballooner could handle himself, and if not, well, I was still grabbing Jai first. I loved her. *Him, I'd just met.*
(Pausch and Zaslow 2008)
 b Food companies had time to change their products, and *change they did*.
(Kummer 2019)
 c "You see, fellers," he had said, "as soon as my little girl told me that she simply *had* to have one of those Golden Tickets, I went out into the town and started buying up all the Wonka candy bars I could lay my hands on. *Thousands of them*, I must have bought."
(Dahl 1964)
 d "I like to mix the colors and also to mix glass and porcelain and the metal parts from Morris's old clocks."
"I saved all the old parts," Morris said. "*Worn-out gears, I saved*, and balance wheels. Sometimes there were chimes."
(Konigsburg 2004)

In (19a), *him* is preposed; the CWO variant would be *I'd just met him*. And the preposing is felicitous because the referent of *him* has already been evoked; it's the ballooner mentioned earlier. Similarly, the preposed *change* in (19b) picks up on the word *change* from the previous clause. In (19c), the preposed *thousands of them* refers to the previously mentioned Wonka candy bars. So far, so good. But what about (19d)? The worn-out gears haven't been specifically mentioned in the prior discourse. But the metal parts from the clocks have been – and the worn-out gears are a subset of these parts. That's what's meant by inferrable information – not that the reader would have necessarily jumped from 'clock parts' to 'worn-out gears', but rather that there's a relationship between the two (generally, as here, a set-based relation) so that when the gears show up, the reader isn't surprised; the relationship is clear and allows the gears to count as discourse-old.

BOX 8.1

Pragmatic borrowing

You already know that people who speak a second language often have an 'accent' in that language. Everyone has an accent, of course; I have a Chicago accent that's obvious to anyone from any other area of the country. And when I visit Germany, I speak German with an American accent (and also a Chicago accent, but I doubt most Germans are aware of that fact). The notion of speaking a second language with an accent simply means that you're applying the phonological rules of your first language to your second. The fronted vowels that sound perfectly normal here in the greater Chicagoland area are noticed as an accent elsewhere.

You're also aware of words that are borrowed from one language into another: Just as a speaker might import the phonology of a first language into a second one, they import lexical items too. And if those lexical items are useful enough that they become widely used by speakers of that second language, they become part of the language – 'borrowings' from one language into another. English is well-known for its wide range of borrowings, including such words as *gesundheit, café, macho, blitz, karate, sari, jodhpurs,* and plenty of food words like *catsup, pasta, pizza, tempura, soy, tagine, sauerkraut,* and *hamburger.*

What's less well-known is that pragmatic features can be borrowed, too. Ross (1967), Hankamer (1971), and Prince (1988), among others, have noted that for English speakers with a Yiddish-language background (i.e., those whose native language is Yiddish or who come from a community of speakers that grew out of a Yiddish-speaking community), the rules for preposing are slightly different from those for other English speakers.

Recall that a preposed phrase needs to be discourse-old. Additionally, much like clefts, preposings generally require a salient open proposition (basically, a presupposition; see p. 232). The interesting thing is that in the Yiddish-influenced dialect, the rules are slightly different. For these speakers, the preposed phrase can be new, and it's enough for the OP to be 'generally known' or 'plausible' (as Prince 1988 puts it) – that is, it just can't add new or surprising information:

(a) My son is picky about cars. Toyotas he loves; Fords, not so much.
(b) My son is driving me crazy. A new car he wants!
(c) My son is driving me crazy. #A car he stole!

(adapted from Prince 1988)

In (a), the usual requirements are satisfied: preposed discourse-old phrase (Toyotas stand in a set relation with the previously mentioned cars), and the OP is present (the son has X opinion of Y car). In (b), these conditions aren't satisfied; the preposed phrase *a new car* isn't discourse-old, and there's no salient OP of the form 'X wants Y' or the like – but it is the case that people generally want things, so the OP counts as generally known. So while (b) wouldn't be produced by most English speakers, it's fine for a Yiddish-dialect speaker. Other speakers, on hearing it, might think it shows a Yiddish accent. And (c), in which the OP 'X stole Y' doesn't count as generally known (most people don't steal cars!), the utterance is infelicitous even for Yiddish-dialect speakers.

You can see what's happening here: The Yiddish speakers have 'borrowed' one of their constructions into English. But the really interesting thing is **why** it's happening. As Prince (1988) argues, what's actually being borrowed isn't the structure itself, since English already has that; it's the discourse function. The logic runs like this: A Yiddish speaker learns English, and in the process notes that there's an English construction that preposes a phrase – just like in Yiddish! Great! What the speaker will never notice is that the constraints on the use of a preposing in English are tighter than the constraints on preposing in Yiddish. Since every English preposing satisfies the constraints on Yiddish preposing (the preposed phrase can be either old or new, and the OP doesn't have to be salient, but it can be), every English preposing sounds like a perfectly good English translation of a perfectly good Yiddish preposing.

And what about those Yiddish preposings that **don't** translate into a perfectly good English preposing, because they don't satisfy the constraints on English preposing? Well, our Yiddish speaker will never hear those coming from the mouth of a (non-Yiddish-dialect) English speaker, but people tend not to notice what they don't hear. It would be a surprisingly astute speaker who would think, "Huh! I never seem to hear English speakers using this construction with a discourse-new preposed phrase or a less-than-salient open proposition!" (Such a speaker should get to work on a linguistics Ph.D. pronto!) So Yiddish-dialect speakers will see that the English version of the construction appears to satisfy the same constraints as the Yiddish version, and they'll use it with those constraints, and the next thing you know, they're producing utterances like (b) above. For this reason, the construction in (b) is known as 'Yiddish-Movement', a subtype of English preposing that's specific to this dialect. That's why, for many of us, (b) has a Yiddish feel to it. And who knows, its use may spread – just like the use of those lexical borrowings listed above – and it may end up in Standard English as a pragmatic borrowing from Yiddish!

Postposing

Whereas preposing takes a phrase that normally appears after the verb and places it before the verb, postposing does the opposite: It takes the subject from its usual position before the verb and instead places it after the verb. But because English requires a subject, something's got to fill that spot, so a semantically empty *there* is pressed into service:

(20) a "Look at the picture," he said. I did as told. "See where the center comes?" I nodded. Then he said, "On the plain glazed surface of this old glass shade, *there will appear the succulent heart of the rose.*"

(Konigsburg 2004)

b Sure enough, the image zooms in. Just like using a smartphone. *There are a couple of sunspots on the left side of the image.*

(Weir 2021)

c "I want you to examine them and find out what you can."
"Yeah, you mentioned that earlier," I said. "But I have to believe *there are more qualified people to do this than just me.*"

(Weir 2021)

In each case, what would normally be the subject (*the succulent heart of the rose, a couple of sunspots on the left side of the image*, and *more qualified people to do this*) appears after the verb, and a semantically empty *there* shows up in subject position.

In the first two examples, you could argue that *there* is locative: that the heart of the rose will appear in the designated place, and that the sunspots are right there, on the left side. But if that were the case, *there* would receive some stress, as you can tell by trying to read them with that meaning. And of course in (20c) this doesn't work at all, as you can see first by trying to stress *there*, and secondly by trying to put *there* in what would then be its canonical position: *More qualified people are there* makes sense only if there's a salient place where these people are being said to be, and that's of course not what (20c) means at all. Instead, this use of *there* is what's called **dummy *there***. When you argue, say, that *there is a God*, you're making the claim that God exists, not that God is in a particular place.

Recall the Given-New Contract, which says that speakers of English typically place 'given' (or known) information before 'new' information in a sentence. We've seen this at work in preposing, and it's also at work in postposing. But whereas preposing is consistently sensitive to discourse-status – that is, the preposed information is required to be discourse-old – postposing generally requires the postposed information to be new:

(21) a There are two different types of postposing.
b There exist two different types of postposing.

Postposings whose main verb is *be*, like (21a), are called **existentials**, and postposings which have an intransitive verb, like (21b), are called **presentationals**. Transitive verbs, on the other hand, don't allow postposing, as shown in (22):

(22) a The girl threw the ball.
b *There threw the ball the girl.

The reason we care about the difference between existentials and presentationals is that they are subject to slightly different constraints. As we'd expect in light of the Given-New Contract, both types of postposing require the postposed information to be new, but the types of newness required are different. Existentials require the postposed phrase to represent hearer-new information, but presentationals only require it to represent discourse-new information (Birner and Ward, 1998). In the vast majority of cases, the phrase satisfies both requirements, as in (21), where the two types of postposing are new both to the discourse and (presumably) to the reader. But consider (23):

(23) a   The Vice President stepped up to the lectern. *Behind her there stood the President.*
   b   The Vice President stepped up to the lectern. #*Behind her there was the President.*

The intuitions here are subtle, but for most people (23a) is noticeably better than (23b). In each case the President can be considered discourse-new but hearer-old; that is, the President hasn't been mentioned in the prior discourse, but the reader can be expected to know that we have a President. So (23a) is felicitous because it satisfies the presentational's requirement for postposed discourse-new information, while (23b) is infelicitous because it doesn't satisfy the existential's requirement for postposed hearer-new information.

Another interesting difference between the two is that in many cases the nonpostposed version of an existential is unacceptable:

(24) a   Behind her the President stood.
   b   #Behind her the President was.

Whether you consider (24b) to be ungrammatical or simply infelicitous depends on whether you could ever consider such a structure to be okay; for most people, (25) is fine:

(25)   She didn't think the President was behind her, but behind her he was.

This suggests that (24b) is infelicitous rather than ungrammatical – that is, that the unacceptability is contextual (hence pragmatic) rather than syntactic. This also is relevant to the issue of why I've given the examples in (23)-(25) with a preposed PP (*behind her*). Replacing the italicized sentence in (23a) with *There stood behind her the President* is shaky, and *There stood the President behind her* is shakier yet. All three are grammatical, but in keeping with the Given-New Contract, the closer the discourse-old and highly salient *her* is to the front of the sentence – and the closer the discourse-new *President* is to the end – the better the sentence sounds.

BOX 8.2

There's the silliest claim going around

For years, there was the belief that a definite NP couldn't appear after the copula (the *be*-word) in an existential. There was, for example, the fact that sentences like (a) seem fine while sentences like (b) seem bad:

(a) On the table there was a book.
(b) #On the table there was the book.

Now, I'm not talking about the reading on which *there* means 'in that place', as in *On the table over there was the book.* I mean our old friend the existential, as in *In the world there are more than seven billion people.* The claim that definite NPs couldn't appear after the copula in such a sentence was called the Definiteness Effect, and linguists dutifully set about researching why such a constraint should exist.

Except that it doesn't. As you can see above, the heading and the first two sentences of this box all use definite NPs in precisely that position in an existential, and they're all pretty much fine. And once linguists studied large corpora of naturally occurring data, they found plenty of examples that violated the Definiteness Effect. So why did it seem like there was such an effect to begin with?

Well, to be fair, there are indeed lots and lots of contexts in which a definite NP is in fact bad in this position when an indefinite NP is fine (as in (a) and (b) above). It's actually a little tricky at first to come up with examples in which they're good, but after you get the hang of it it's really easy. The reason 'getting the hang of it' is involved is because the same types of examples keep turning up over and over (as shown in Ward and Birner 1995). So, consider these two examples:

(c) There's the silliest claim going around.
(d) There was the usual gang at the restaurant.

In (c), *the silliest claim* is a superlative, and only one claim can truly be the silliest; so even if it's just superlative due to exaggeration, *the silliest claim* still semantically picks out a single 'silliest' claim. That's why it's definite: There's no such thing as 'a' silliest claim. A phrase that fully and uniquely describes a single thing can earn a 'the', whether it's *the silliest claim, the tallest student in the class,* or *the claim that Ernie is the tallest student in the class* (since, after all, there's only one such claim). But in each case, the phrase can be used in an existential if it's hearer-new – and there's no reason why a phrase can't uniquely describe something that's new to the hearer. Because it's uniquely described, it's definite; because it's hearer-new, it's okay in an existential. So examples like (c) represent a large class of cases in which the Definiteness Effect can be violated.

What about (d)? Here *the usual gang* describes a known type (in this case, a known gang of people), but not precisely the same token of that type (because the members of the gang that show up at any given time will differ). So the known type justifies the use of the definite, while the hearer-new token – today's particular gang – justifies its appearance in an existential. Again, this sort of example represents a larger group of such examples (*the usual gang, the standard explanation, the normal bunch of people, the expected excuse,* etc.). There are a handful of other classes of examples, but in each case the definite is allowed because it describes something that's unique or familiar in some sense, while its position in an existential is allowed because that unique or familiar thing is nonetheless hearer-new. Most hearer-new information isn't unique or (especially) familiar, but there are still a few areas of overlap, and that's what makes these examples possible.

Linguists, like any other scientist, can be wrong in their initial conclusions based on their initial observations – and that's why it's important to keep studying, and especially to keep looking at actual language in its natural context, rather than relying on your own intuitions about whether something is possible.

Argument reversal

We've seen that preposing a phrase requires it to represent given information, and postposing a phrase requires it to represent new information. But we also find constructions in which it seems as though two phrases have essentially switched places:

(26) a   No portrait survives, but she seems to have inspired more than the usual ardor. […] *Pursuing her were several self-righteously pious and overenthusiastic suitors….*

(Fraser 2021)

   b   Soon there were a dozen cars lined up. *Inside them were people important to us* – Julie from the Agate, and Lydia, and Ann Fandeen; Marcus came, and Lily Pea arrived with Galen.

(Enger 2018)

(27) a   Omri shivered and changed the subject.
"As for our brothers coming," he said, "all I want of my brothers is to keep that rat in its cage." *The rat had been caught by Omri after a long, patient wait with cheese and a fishing net,* and Omri had threatened Gillon with the worst fate imaginable if he let it get away again.

(Banks 1980)

   b   Bre-X Minerals Ltd., under orders from the Indonesian Government, is in talks to sell 75 percent of its estimated $4.44 billion gold deposit on the island of Borneo to the Barrick Gold Corporation. […] Bre-X said *it was told by the Government to sell the stake in the Busang gold deposit by Dec. 4 and to enter a joint venture with Barrick.*

(Bloomberg News 1996)

The examples in (26) are **inversions**, in which the subject, which is canonically preverbal, instead gets positioned after the verb, while some other canonically postverbal argument of the verb is positioned before the verb – basically, a swap. (You'll recall inversion from (16) above.) So for the inversion in (26a), the CWO variant is *Several self-righteously pious and overenthusiastic suitors were pursuing her;* and for (26b) the CWO variant is *People important to us were inside them.*

And of course you'll recognize the examples in (27) as **passives**, with the subject moved after the verb into a phrase headed by the word *by*, and the direct object showing up in subject position. The CWO for (27a) is *Omri had caught the rat...*, and the CWO for (27b) is *The Government told it to sell the stake....* And these passives are specifically **long passives;** that is, they've got a *by*-phrase that represents what would, in CWO, be the subject – typically an agent (here, *Omri* in (a) and *the Government* in (b)). You can also have passives without this phrase:

(28)   a   The rat had been caught after a long, patient wait....
       b   Bre-X said it was told to sell the stake....

These obviously don't count as 'argument reversal', since they don't have the second argument, so we won't have anything further to say about them here – except to note that leaving off the agent can be especially handy when you want to avoid blame, as with *Hey, Mom – the vase has been broken!*

You might expect argument reversals to require the preposed phrase to be given AND the postposed phrase to be new, resulting in a given-new ordering, but the truth is more subtle than that. You do get that ordering in cases like (26a), where the preposed *her* is discourse-old and the postposed *suitors* are discourse-new. But you also get cases where the two phrases have the same status, as with (26b), where both phrases are discourse-old (but the preposed *them* represents the much more salient cars), or (27a) and (27b), where again the preposed *rat* and *it* are more recently mentioned (and therefore more salient) than the postposed *Omri* and *the Government*, but all of them count as discourse-old.

It turns out that the only combination that's infelicitous is discourse-new information in preposed position with discourse-old information in postposed position, as we saw in (16b) above:

(29)   In the diner I saw a large blueberry pie. #*On a counter sat the pie.*

So the two can have the same status, or the postposed phrase can be newer, but the preposed phrase can't be the newer of the two (Birner 1994, 1996). Which in turn means that either the preposed phrase must be discourse-old **or** the postposed phrase must be discourse-new, or both, but if neither holds, the reversal will be infelicitous. We'll return to this point shortly.

Inference

Prince (1981, 1992) uses the term **inferrable** to describe information that hasn't been explicitly evoked in the prior discourse, but which can be inferred from it. (And yes, she uses two *r*'s in 'inferrable', so most linguists using her framework follow suit.) For something to count as inferrable doesn't mean it's necessarily present; just that it stands in some 'inferential relation' (Birner 2006) to what has come before. Frequently that relation will be a set relation;

so the two might be members of the same set (e.g., *baseball* could make *football* inferrable), or one might be a subtype of the other (e.g., *baseball* could make *game* inferrable), or perhaps one is used in the performance of the other (e.g., *baseball* could make *bat* inferrable). So recall example (19d):

(30) "I like to mix the colors and also to mix glass and porcelain and the metal parts from Morris's old clocks."
"I saved all the old parts," Morris said. "*Worn-out gears, I saved*, and balance wheels. Sometimes there were chimes."

Here, the worn-out gears haven't been previously mentioned, but they're a subset of the metal parts from the old clocks. This is what's called a **bridging inference** (Clark 1977; Haviland and Clark 1974), because even though the mention of metal clock parts might not immediately bring to mind worn-out gears, once the reader encounters the worn-out gears they'll immediately realize that these are some of the previously mentioned metal parts, and they'll draw an inference that creates a cognitive bridge (metaphorically speaking) back to the mention of the parts. So consider the examples in (31):

(31) a St. Cloud's, Maine – the town – had been a logging camp for most of the nineteenth century. The camp, and – gradually – the town, set up shop in the river valley, where the land was flat, which made *the first roads* easier to build and *the heavy equipment* easier to transport. *The first building* was a saw mill.
(Irving 1985)
b I order my cookbooks by country, and then within that I try to keep them together by author. I'm not so successful at that, but that's what I try to do. For other books, I organize them by subject, so I have all my education books together, all my books about gardening together, all my art books together. *But the ones that I love the most I stack horizontally*, because I'm grabbing them so much.
(Waters 2021)

In (31a), given the establishment of a logging camp and a town, you can infer that there will be roads and buildings, and therefore that some will be the first roads and the first building, and likewise that heavy equipment will be needed for the logging camp – hence the definite NPs *the first roads, the heavy equipment*, and *the first building*. As the reader encounters each of these phrases, they can easily build an inferential bridge to the previously mentioned camp and town: *The first roads* are the first roads built for the logging camp, and so on.

In (31b), *the ones that I love the most* is not only definite but also preposed, indicating that it counts as discourse-old in the context. What 'ones' are being referred to? It's a very straightforward inference, but an inference nonetheless: These are the most-loved of the books she has been discussing.

Notice that while bridging inferrables (inferrable information based on a bridging inference) count as discourse-old, they are hearer-new. This initially seems odd, since presumably anything that's been evoked in the prior discourse should be known to the hearer if the hearer's been paying any attention. (Prince 1992 makes exactly this argument.) But recall that not everything that's discourse-old has actually been previously evoked; discourse-old information has

either been previously evoked **or** stands in an inferential relationship with something that has been. In the latter case, it may well be unknown to the hearer until it's mentioned, at which point the bridging inference is made. In that case, the inferrable is discourse-old but hearer-new. So in (31a) the first roads are new to the hearer, i.e. hearer-new; but they count as discourse-old because the reader can build an inferential bridge between the previously mentioned town and the roads that will exist within it (Birner 2006).

Okay, so bridging inferrables are discourse-old/hearer-new. There are other inferences that don't require this backward-looking bridge-building; these are called **elaborative** or **elaborating** inferences. Consider the following examples, taken from Birner 2006:

(32) a In one of the drawers there was a bundle of old letters, a dozen or more, tied together with a bit of rotten string. They were addressed Thomas Willingdon, Jr. Esq. at the Cordova Theological Seminary, in an emotional, flowery handwriting ornamented with Spencerian curlicues which began in a neat correct flourish and ended in a splatter of ink. *Across the face of the top letter was written in The Old Man's handwriting, "not to be forgotten."*

(Bromfield 1933)

b The house was particularly spacious. Set well back from the road, it was almost surrounded by wide lawns on which, each side of the house, grew a huge palm tree. *Beyond the right-hand palm could be seen a clothes line.*

(Upfield 1950)

c She got married recently and *at the wedding was the mother, the stepmother and Debbie.*

(conversation, 6/29/89)

In these cases, you don't need to wait for the mention of the inferrable to look back and figure out what it's connected to. To have a bundle of old letters pretty much entails that there will be a top letter (which will in turn have a face); thus, *the face of the top letter* is an elaborating inferrable. Likewise, if you've got a palm tree on each side of a house, there is necessarily a right-hand palm, and if someone gets married, you can infer that there's a wedding, before the wedding has been mentioned. These inferrables, then, count as hearer-old, since by the time they're mentioned they've already been in some sense implicitly inferred (though not necessarily consciously).

And as we would expect, bridging inferrables (discourse-old/hearer-new) can generally be postposed in existentials (which, recall, require hearer-new information), but elaborating inferrables (discourse-old/hearer-old) cannot, as we see in the bridging inferrable in (33a) and the elaborating inferrable in (33b):

(33) a I order my cookbooks by country, and then within that I try to keep them together by author. [...] *On the lower shelf there are the ones that I love the most.*

b The house was particularly spacious. Set well back from the road, it was almost surrounded by wide lawns on which, each side of the house, grew a huge palm tree. #*Behind a clothes line there was the right-hand palm.*

So far, the Given-New Contract is holding up pretty well.

Open propositions

Prince 1992 actually distinguishes among three types of givenness: Information can be discourse-old, hearer-old, or presupposed. We've talked quite a bit at this point about discourse- and hearer-status (which is to say, whether some bit of information is discourse-old or discourse-new, and hearer-old or hearer-new) and how they satisfy the Given-New Contract. Presupposition has of course been discussed in an earlier chapter. Now we'll see how noncanonical word order can take serve to mark information as presupposed. Consider the examples in (34), both taken from the same article:

(34) a Demagogues sometimes rant about irresponsible birthrates in developing-world countries, but the truth is the spike in global population has not been caused by some worldwide surge in fertility. In fact, people are having fewer babies per capita than ever. *What changed over the past two centuries, first in the industrialized world, then globally, is that people stopped dying – particularly young people.*

(Johnson 2021)

b Perhaps some rogue technology – nuclear weapons, bioterror attacks – will kill enough people to reverse the great escape. *Or perhaps it will be the environmental impact of 10 billion people living in industrial societies that will send us backward.*

(Johnson 2021)

In (34a), the italicized sentence presupposes that something changed over the past two centuries; and indeed this is reasonable for the author to presuppose, given the prior mention of a spike in global population. In (34b), the italicized sentence presupposes that something will send us backward; and again, this is reasonable for the author to presuppose, given the prior mention of a reversal.

These sentences exemplify the two main types of **clefts**. You'll recall clefts from Chapter 7, where we talked about their role as presupposition triggers. Clefts are constructions that express a proposition by 'cleaving' it into a presupposed portion and a **focus**, where the presupposition is, as always, information that is treated as shared, and the focus is information that's being treated as new and as the main point of the utterance. So in (34a-b), the italicized sentences break down as follows:

(35) a Presupposition: X changed over the past two centuries
Focus: people stopped dying
b Presupposition: X will send us backward
Focus: the environmental impact of 10 billion people living in industrial societies

The X in each case stands for a missing element in the proposition, which renders the proposition 'open' or incomplete; such propositions are called **open propositions (OPs)**. The OP is presupposed, but it needs the X to be filled in before it can be a complete proposition. The focus fills in the X. In essence, the OP in (34a) is a presupposition that something changed; what changed is that people stopped dying. Likewise, the OP in (34b) is that something will send us backward; what will do that is the environmental impact of 10 billion people living in industrial societies. The type of cleft in (34a) is called a **wh-cleft**, because it features the sort of question word that typically begins with *wh* (here, *what*), serving as a placeholder (corresponding to the 'X' in the OP). The type of cleft in (34b) is called an ***it*-cleft**, because it uses the word *it* in a similar way. (Sometimes the *it*-cleft is simply called a **cleft**, and the *wh*-cleft is called a **pseudocleft**.)

The type of presupposition here is very similar to the notion of the **Question Under Discussion (QUD)** developed in Roberts 2012 in taking a certain set of information as being saliently at issue – what we're talking about – while some other piece of information is what we're saying about it (the new part). But they're not exactly the same notion, since a presupposition isn't always a QUD; I can say *I need to walk the dog*, presupposing the existence of the dog but without the existence of the dog being a question under discussion.

Given that the OP represents presupposed information, clefts tend to be infelicitous if the OP isn't presupposed:

(36) a Demagogues sometimes rant about the cost of health care. #*What changed over the past two centuries is that people stopped dying.*
   b Nuclear weapons and bioterror attacks are likely to increase in the future. #*Or perhaps it will be the environmental impact of 10 billion people living in industrial societies that will send us backward.*

In (36a), by taking out the mention of birthrates and a spike in population, we've removed the notion that something has changed, and in (36b) by taking out the mention of a reversal, we've removed the notion that something will send us backward; and in each case, the cleft becomes worse.

You might also recall from Chapter 7 the one type of cleft that doesn't require the presupposition to be salient, which is what Prince (1978) calls **informative-presupposition** *it*-clefts. Recall these examples repeated from (59) in Chapter 7:

(37) a It was at this moment that the courtroom lights flickered in the storm, flickered again, and went out.

(Guterson 1994)

   b It had been the judge's bailiff, Ed Soames, who'd answered the door when Art Moran knocked at five after five on the evening of the sixteenth and asked to see Lew Fielding.

(Guterson 1994)

   c It was on the bus ride between Talequa and Epiphany that Berkeley Sims left her seat, walked to the front of the bus, picked up the microphone that was used for announcements, and began to sing.

(Konigsburg 2004)

What makes such examples interesting is that where an *it*-cleft typically places presupposed information, this type of *it*-cleft actually places the information that constitutes the point of the utterance. The information following the word *that* is still technically the 'presupposition' in the sense that the construction treats it as though it were presupposed, but in fact the information is completely new and informative. In this way, it's rather like accommodation; the hearer/reader encounters it, recognizes the form of a presupposition being used to present new information, and goes right ahead and takes it into the discourse model.

BOX 8.3

Mutual knowledge and writing

In nearly every class I teach on information structure, some student will point out that they've been taught to avoid using passives and the phrase *there is* in their writing. They tell me that they will get lower grades from their other professors for using these constructions. They're supposed to use more 'active' verbs than *is*, they're told – although it seems that poor old *is* only really gets them in trouble in this one construction – and I honestly don't know what the complaint against passives is.

Okay, I do know that so-called 'agentless passives' omit the agent – but that, of course, is the whole point. Just as no kid wants to say *I spilled the milk* when they could say *The milk got spilled* (using what's called a *get*-passive), no researcher wants to write an entire article saying things like *The difference in food affected the rats' performance* and *The difference in food also affected the mice* when they could simply establish that they were changing the food and then spend the rest of the paragraph saying things like *The rats' performance was affected* and *The mice were also affected*. And for descriptions of what they themselves have done, students are in a double bind, since they're also (inexplicably) told to avoid using the first person. So they can't say:

(a) We doubled the rodents' food. [the dreaded first person]
And they also can't say:
(b) The rodents' food was doubled. [the dreaded passive]
So they're stuck with something weird like:
(c) The researcher doubled the rodents' food.

This might not seem so bad, but to my ears (and eyes), by the time you've hit the seventh or eighth mention of this researcher in a paper that's written by that very same researcher, it starts to feel a bit tortured. As you know by now, the use of an existential or a passive serves a valid discourse function, and fluent speakers of English use them 'correctly' for these functions just as automatically as they put the determiner before the noun in a phrase like *the mice*. We choose our word order in large part because we're taking into account our assumptions about our addressee's knowledge.

And of course, it's not only word order that takes this into account, as we've seen since our first mention of the Cooperative Principle back in Chapter 4 (and before that, even). Prince (1981) gives a beautiful illustration of how we adapt our message to our beliefs about what our addressee does and doesn't know. In a footnote, she presents in full the recipe for roast suckling pig from Rombauer and Becker (1931), *The Joy of Cooking*, which runs to 201 words, by my count, including details like:

> *It takes 2½ quarts of dressing to stuff a pig of this size*
> and
> *Reduce the heat to 325° and roast until tender, allowing 30 minutes to the pound*
> and
> *Remove the foil from the ears and tail before serving.*
>
> In contrast, Prince offers the recipe for roast suckling pig from *Le Répertoire de la cuisine*, a text for professional French chefs. Although the recipe itself is of course in French, Prince helpfully translates it to English. Here's the recipe in its entirety:
>
> *English Suckling Pig: Stuff with English stuffing. Roast.*
>
> Left to their own devices, it turns out that writers are actually pretty good at crafting their message to suit their audience.

Constructions

The above discussion of noncanonical word orders and their functions gives rise to the question of what constitutes a **construction**. Typically, passivization is considered one construction, inversion another, preposing another, and so on. But a closer look suggests an alternative view, proposed in Birner (2018).

First, recall that inversions and long passives have a lot in common:

- They're both noncanonical orderings.
- They both reverse the order of the CWO subject and a complement of the verb.
- They're both constrained by the discourse-status of these two phrases.
- They both allow discourse-old information before discourse-new, discourse-old before discourse-old, and discourse-new before discourse-new.
- They both disallow discourse-new information before discourse-old.

So it seems they're doing the same thing in terms of discourse-status. In fact, the one big difference between them is their syntactic distribution: Inversions appear in sentences that have an intransitive verb or a **copula** (i.e., a form of *be*), but never when the sentence is transitive:

(38)   a   On the table sat a book.   [intransitive]
        b   On the table was a book.   [copula]
        c   *A book read John.   [transitive]

Meanwhile, passives appear in transitive sentences, but not in intransitive or copular sentences:

(39) a A book was read by John. [transitive]
    b *On the table was sat by a book. [intransitive]
    c *On the table was been by a book. [copula]

It's true that you can get *This bed was slept in by George Washington*, with only the NP *this bed* preposed, but note that here you can't get the corresponding inversion:

(40) a George Washington slept in this bed. [CWO]
    b This bed was slept in by George Washington. [passive]
    c *This bed slept in George Washington. [inversion]

(And in all of these cases, the asterisk means it's ungrammatical as an instance of the construction in question; obviously *This bed slept in George Washington* is a perfectly grammatical CWO sentence if you actually for some reason want to describe a bed sleeping in a person rather than a person sleeping in a bed.)

The fact that inversion and passivization are in complementary distribution – that they never appear in the same syntactic context – is the smoking gun here. Remember from Chapter 6 that if two sounds are in complementary distribution, that's solid evidence that they're actually allophones of the same sound. In the same way, the fact that inversion and passivization are in complementary distribution suggests that they are similarly two versions of the same construction – that is, **alloforms** of a single construction. And that makes sense, since allowing inversions of transitives would introduce all sorts of ambiguity into the language: It would be hard to tell whether *Alex admired Kim* was a CWO sentence describing Alex's state of mind or an inversion describing Kim's. With passivization, there's no such problem; in *Kim was admired by Alex* it's clear who's admiring whom.

But once we've allowed alloforms of a construction, more intriguing possibilities emerge. In Birner (2018), inversion and passivization are argued to also be alloforms of both preposing and postposing, occurring in different contexts – in the same way that the consonant sound in the middle of *latter* and *ladder* (which are pronounced identically in casual contexts) will be an allophone of /t/ in the first case and of /d/ in the second.

Consider the evidence: Right now we've got this really weird constraint on inversion: It allows every possible ordering of information except for new-before-old (i.e., new/new, old/old, and old/new). How could a child acquire such a constraint? Rather than noticing one information-structure ordering that occurs repeatedly, they'd have to notice the one that **doesn't** ever occur, or the **three** that do, neither of which is easy.

Alternatively, if every instance of inversion is an alloform of either preposing or postposing, you'll automatically get this exact set of possible orderings: You'll have old/old, because those are preposings and satisfy the constraint on preposing (the preposed phrase is old), and you'll have new/new, because those are postposings and satisfy that constraint (the postposed phrase is new), and you'll of course have old/new, because those could be either, since they satisfy both constraints. But you'll never get new/old, since that would satisfy neither constraint – the preposed phrase isn't old, and the postposed phrase isn't new. And of course all of this holds true for passives as well. So by taking this view, not only do you not need to posit an unnecessarily complicated constraint for English inversion and passivization, you don't need to posit any constraint at all. Their behavior follows automatically from the constraints we already have for preposing and postposing.

This means that there's a single preposing construction in English that has three alloforms – regular old preposing, plus inversion and passivization – and which one shows up depends on various factors including whether the sentence is transitive, intransitive, or copular. And similarly for postposing, although that one gets a little more complicated because there are two types of postposing (remember existentials vs. presentationals?) that are subject to two different constraints; it turns out that it's presentationals that stand in an alloform relationship with inversion and passivization, since all three of them care about discourse-status rather than hearer-status.

In short, it appears that constructions are defined in terms of a combination of their structure and function. (This, by the way, meshes nicely with the theoretical framework known as **Construction Grammar**, which defines a construction as a form-function pairing. See Fillmore et al. 1988; Goldberg 1995; Kay 1997, inter alia.) This means that syntactic constructions behave a whole lot like units at other levels of the grammar – phonology, which has phonemes and allophones; morphology, which has morphemes and allomorphs, and now syntax, which has constructions with their own alloforms. This brings us to the distinction between **types** and **tokens**.

The type/token distinction

Are you sitting on a chair right now? I am. Are you sitting on a piece of furniture? I'm doing that too. So which is it – am I sitting on a chair or a piece of furniture? Okay, that's just a dumb question, because obviously I'm doing both. Furniture is a **type** of thing, and individual chairs are **tokens** of it – and so are tables and couches and desks and so on. But at the same time, 'chair' itself is a type, and each individual chair in the world is a token of that type. Recall the taxonomy in Figure 8.1, from Chapter 2.

Suppose you have a little toy poodle named Pierre. (I did, as a child.) Pierre is a token of the type 'toy poodle', as well as a token of the types 'poodle' and 'dog' and 'animal'. The world of is full of 'isa' relationships, which are type/token relationships.

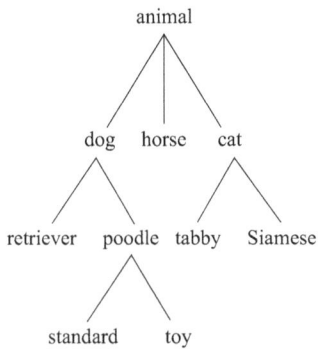

FIGURE 8.1 Taxonomy (repeated from Chapter 2).

Linguistics is full of them, too; these are the 'allo-' relations we've seen repeatedly throughout this book. An allophone is a token of a phoneme, which in turn is the type. So if I pronounce the 'p' in *pot* as [pʰ], with a little puff of aspiration (just as any other native English speaker would likely pronounce it), that is a token of the type /p/ – which in turn is the phoneme, the type of which the allophone is a token. In a sense, nobody ever pronounces the phoneme itself; the phoneme is a cognitive category. Anytime you try to pronounce it, what you're really producing is one of its allophones – a token of the type (and, for that matter, a token of that particular allophone). It's the same sense in which you don't just sit on 'furniture' as a category; you're always sitting on some token of furniture – a particular chair or table or couch or desk.

Similarly, we see the difference between types and tokens at the level of morphology, in which allomorphs are tokens of morphemes, and at the level of syntax, in which particular word orders are tokens of syntactic constructions. This is a particularly cool, or at least useful, property of the human mind: It is in our nature to categorize things. (And we're far from the only creatures that do this; any animal that couldn't categorize plants and other animals into at least the categories 'food' and 'nonfood' would have a problem.) The ability to categorize, in turn, is a prerequisite for language: We can't label something as, say, a *chair* unless we can conceptualize 'chair' as a category. In the next chapter we'll take a closer look at both the human brain and its use of categorization in understanding and labeling the world.

EXERCISES

Self-test:

1. A theme is
   a. the entity actively undertaking an action.
   b. the entity in some state or undergoing some action.
   c. the entity being used to perform an action.
   d. the starting point of an action.
2. An argument-structure alternation is
   a. a set of word-order patterns shared by a group of verbs.
   b. different explanations for a syntactic structure.
   c. the relationship of meaning between a word and the sentence it appears in.
   d. the relationship between two alloforms.
3. The Given-New Contract tells us to
   a. consider all argument-structure alternations before we choose one.
   b. put relatively known information before relatively unknown information.
   c. package information with new information in initial position.
   d. give only new information.
4. Preposed information in English is required to be
   a. hearer-old.
   b. hearer-new.
   c. discourse-old.
   d. discourse-new.

5   Existentials and presentationals are two types of
    a   verb alternations.
    b   givenness.
    c   preposing.
    d   postposing.
6   An informative-presupposition *it*-cleft
    a   is a kind of existential.
    b   doesn't require known information in the presupposition.
    c   is a kind of presentational.
    d   requires its preposed NP to represent discourse-old information.
7   Two kinds of argument reversal are
    a   preposing and inversion.
    b   alloforms and constructions.
    c   existentials and presentationals.
    d   long passives and inversion.
8   An open proposition is
    a   a proposition in which some element is unspecified.
    b   a proposition that is expressed noncanonically.
    c   a proposition that satisfies the Given-New Contract.
    d   a proposition that constitutes an alloform.
9   Inferrable information that requires the hearer to build an inference back to previously evoked information is called
    a   an elaborating inferrable.
    b   a bridging inferrable.
    c   a containing inferrable.
    d   a given inferrable.
10 Because inversion and passivization serve the same discourse function in different syntactic contexts, we can infer that they are
    a   two different types of clefts.
    b   unrelated constructions.
    c   informative-presupposition constructions.
    d   alloforms of a single construction.

Comprehension questions:

1   For each of the sentences below, describe a scenario in which the subject is an agent and one in which the subject is a theme:
    a   Ruth smelled a rose.
    b   Danny tore his sleeve.
    c   Dora sat on the bench.
2   Write a paragraph in which you violate the constraints on a preposing, a postposing, a passivization, and an inversion. That is, you should use each of these sentence types, but in such a way that they're infelicitous because their information-structure constraints aren't satisfied. Needless to say, your paragraph should sound perfectly terrible.

3   For each of the following, describe an open proposition that must be salient in the context for the sentence to be felicitous:
    a   What Craig ate was a pizza.
    b   It was yesterday that Sara wrote the story.
    c   Chocolate I love.
4   Consider the following sentences:
    a   I need to pick up the supplies for tomorrow's party. I plan to get ice cream first.
    b   I need to pick up the supplies for tomorrow's party. Ice cream I plan to get first.
    In (a), the second sentence is ambiguous: Either I'm planning to get some ice cream before picking up the party supplies, or ice cream is part of the party supplies I'm getting. This ambiguity disappears in (b). Keeping in mind the constraint on preposed information, explain why. That is, state which meaning (b) has, why it has the meaning it does, and why the other reading that (a) has isn't an option in (b).
5   There are two semantically identical ways of describing a transfer of possession:
    a   Phil gave a piano to Janice.
    b   Phil gave Janice a piano.
    Would you consider this an argument-structure alternation or two alloforms of a single construction, or neither? Give your reasoning.

Opinion questions:

1   It's noted above that "Sometimes you'll find **patient** listed as an entity undergoing the action and being affected by it; in that case **theme** is taken to be an entity undergoing the action without being affected by it." Does this seem like a useful distinction to make? Why or why not?
2   Would you consider the two kinds of clefts discussed here (*wh*-clefts and *it*-clefts) to constitute alloforms of a single construction? Why or why not?
3   Obviously the account of passives here only applies to those that end in a *by*-phrase. Do you think short passives (those without such a phrase) serve an information-packaging function as well? Imagine some felicitous and infelicitous uses of such passives and see whether you think such categories as discourse-status, hearer-status, and open propositions affect their felicity.

Discussion questions:

1   Sentences like those in (a)-(c) below (called 'extrapositions') are noncanonical, but Miller (2001) argues that an information-structure constraint is imposed on the canonical variant ((d)-(f)) rather than the noncanonical variant:
    a   It surprises me that Yuko plays the cello.
    b   It's crazy that they're building a store on the corner.
    c   It horrified Harry that Hilda helped Hannah.
    d   That Yuko plays the cello surprises me.

e That they're building a store on the corner is crazy.
f That Hilda helped Hannah horrified Harry.

Discuss the following questions:

i Why are (d)-(f) considered the canonical variants?
ii What do you think the constraint on the canonical form might be?
iii Is there any constraint on the canonical variant?
iv Does it pose a problem for the account of information structure for there to be a construction whose constraint is on the canonical rather than the noncanonical variant?

2. Why might a language have the sorts of information-packaging constraints we've seen here? More specifically, why might it be preferable to have given information precede new information in a sentence? What, if anything, does it suggest about human cognition, language processing, or the construction of discourse models?

3. In what ways are allophones, allomorphs, and syntactic alloforms alike, and in what ways do they differ? Do you think the similarities indicate something deep about the human language faculty (or about Universal Grammar), or is it no more than the fact that reality is full of cases of types and tokens?

Data collection and analysis:

1. Collect 10-15 preposings and/or inversions. Keeping in mind that discourse-old information includes both information that has been previously evoked and that which stands in some inferential relation to something that has been evoked, try to describe for each of your examples how the preposed information relates to previously evoked information. Remember that for inversions, it's possible that all of the information will be new and that there won't be such a relation. (If you have trouble collecting preposings and inversions, try looking at fables or children's stories, where they appear very commonly.)

2. Collect 10-15 instances of informative-presupposition *it*-clefts. You might try searching online for phrases like *It was later that evening that…, It was in Cleveland that…,* or *It was in 1945 that…,* substituting different times, places, and dates. Can you make any generalizations about when this structure appears, or how it seems to function? To what extent is this an artifact of the kinds of examples you searched for? Can you think of other types of examples (e.g., *It was without thinking that I…*), and does broadening your search change your generalizations?

3. Plug *there was a* and *there was the* into the Google Books Ngram Viewer (clicking 'case-insensitive' to get the best results). What do you make of the results, particularly with respect to the claim that there's a Definiteness Effect? Do these results make sense given the explanation of this 'effect' given earlier in the chapter? Now plug *"There was the"* (with the quotation marks) into a search engine, skip ahead some number of pages to get past the less helpful results (song names and the like), and look at a couple dozen results. Do you see any patterns? Do these results make sense in light of our hypotheses about the constraints on definiteness and on existentials?

Answers to self-test:

1. b
2. a
3. b
4. c
5. d
6. b
7. d
8. a
9. b
10. d

CHAPTER 9

Meaning and human cognition

> **KEY CONCEPTS:**
>
> - central, peripheral nervous systems
> - cerebrum, cerebral cortex, cerebellum, brain stem, corpus callosum
> - left and right hemispheres
> - frontal, parietal, temporal, and occipital lobes
> - neurons: axon, dendrite, soma, nucleus, terminal buttons
> - neurotransmitter, synapse
> - Broca's area, Broca's aphasia
> - Wernicke's area, Wernicke's aphasia
> - Sapir-Whorf Hypothesis
> - linguistic relativity, linguistic determinism
> - propaganda
> - language and prejudice
> - cognitive science

We've talked a lot in this book about the way meaning works at an interpersonal level: the sorts of inferences we make about each other, the expectations we have about each other's linguistic knowledge and world knowledge, and what specific sorts of shared rules and understandings make communication possible. But we haven't talked about the nuts and bolts that make it all work within an individual – that is, the architecture of the human brain that makes it all possible. That's where this chapter will start off; we'll look not only at the brain and how it handles language, but also at what can go wrong when the brain is injured or diseased. From there we'll go on to consider the relationship between language and thought, and whether the language we speak can influence the way we see the world (an intriguing prospect that people have been arguing over for the better part of a century now). We'll finish by briefly discussing cognitive science – an exciting and growing interdisciplinary field that brings together a wide range of perspectives on the human mind.

DOI: 10.4324/9781003351214-9

LANGUAGE AND THE BRAIN

Your brain weighs a little less than three pounds, but accounts for a great deal of what you think of as 'you'. The rest of your body can move in space, affect other entities, sense its environment, and keep you alive through its various processes, but your brain is the major player in terms of your emotions, beliefs, thoughts, and decisions. You may move in space, but it is usually your brain that tells your body to do so. (But there are some automatic reactions – for example, to pain – that actually occur without the brain's contribution, with sensory information traveling only as far as the spinal cord before triggering a motor response, such as pulling your hand off a hot stove.) Your heart may beat and your lungs may keep air moving in and out, but only because your brain tells them to (assuming you're not on, say, a ventilator). And your eyes can scan your environment, but the information they pick up doesn't do you any good until it's been interpreted by your brain. And it will come as absolutely no surprise that your brain plays a central role both in the production and reception of human language – that is, both in producing speech and in processing and understanding the speech of others. For this reason, any discussion of meaning in human language merits a consideration of the brain, the organ that makes meaning, and the interpretation of meaning, possible.

Brain structure

Your brain is part of your nervous system, which in turn is made up of the **central nervous system** (the brain and spinal cord) and the **peripheral nervous system** (all the nerve cells, or **neurons**, that branch out from the central nervous system). The peripheral neurons come in two types – **afferent** neurons that carry sensory information from the body to the brain, and **efferent** neurons that carry motor information from the brain to the body. The sensory information carried by afferent neurons is the usual information from your five senses (touch, smell, sight, hearing, taste), and the motor information carried by the efferent neurons tells your body what to do and how to move.

The largest area of your brain is the **cerebrum**, which is the wrinkly structure that makes up most of what you see in a photo of the brain. The wrinkly stuff itself is the **cerebral cortex**, which is essentially the outer surface of the brain. If the brain were an orange, the cerebral cortex would be its peel. The handy thing about all those wrinkles is that they greatly increase the area of the cortex: If you peeled off the cortex and spread it out flat on a table, it would cover vastly more area than if it were smooth and you did the same thing. The reason this is handy is that the cerebral cortex is where all of your 'higher thought' occurs – so the more area it's got, the more of this higher thought a creature is capable of. As it happens, human have an especially wrinkly brain, which largely accounts for our especially great brainpower.

At the bottom rear of the brain you'll find the **cerebellum**, which handles a lot of automatic functions like coordination, timing, and keeping you stable in space. (How hard do you have to think about staying vertical when you're standing up? Thank your cerebellum for taking that off your to-do list!) At the bottom of the brain is the **brain stem**, which extends downward to become your spinal cord – a bundle of neurons from which the peripheral nervous system's neurons extend outward.

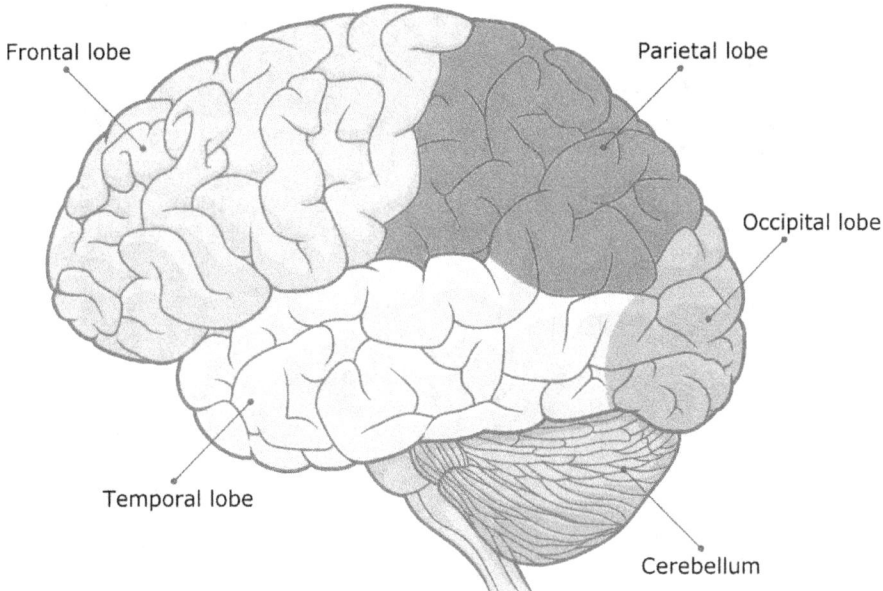

FIGURE 9.1 The brain and its lobes. Refluo/Shutterstock.com.

The brain is made up of two **hemispheres**, the left hemisphere and the right hemisphere. Each hemisphere, in turn, is composed of four **lobes**: the **frontal, parietal, temporal**, and **occipital** lobes. The two hemispheres are mostly separate, with the wrinkles of the cortex extending down into the fissure between them; but there's a thick band of neurons, the **corpus callosum**, that connects the two hemispheres and allows them to communicate with each other.

The brain is, to some extent, **lateralized** for different tasks – but no, this isn't what you've heard about 'left-brained' and 'right-brained' people. That's mostly nonsense. It's not the case that half of the brain is devoted to analytic tasks and the other half to artistic tasks, and that different people are stronger on one side or the other. What is true, and to my mind just as interesting, is that sensation and body control are **contralateral**, which means that each hemisphere of the brain is responsible for the **opposite** side of the body: Your left hemisphere tells your right arm how to move and processes what your right hand feels, while your right hemisphere tells your left arm how to move and processes what your left hand feels.

Language, meanwhile, is to a large extent housed in the left hemisphere, which results in some fascinating effects in people in whom doctors have had to sever the corpus callosum for medical reasons in rare instances. Remember that the corpus callosum allows the two halves of the brain to talk to each other, so in these people the two hemispheres cannot share information. Surprisingly, these people do remarkably well. But in a lab setting, you can see the effects of this inability to share information across the hemispheres. To take just one example: Suppose you seat such a person at a desk with their hands and various items under a barrier, so that they can't see what their hand is grasping. Now you hand them a key. If they're holding it in their right hand, all is well; they can tell you they're holding a key. This is because their left

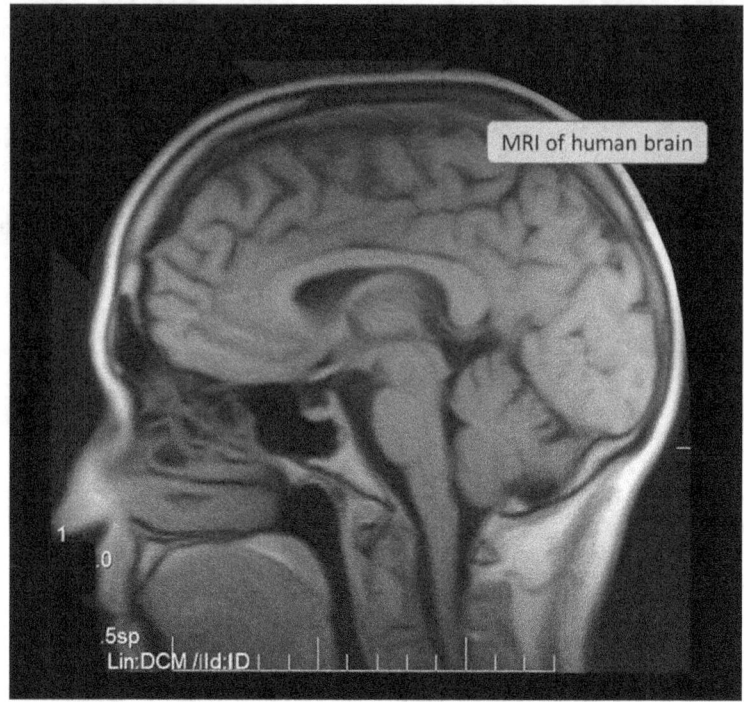

FIGURE 9.2 MRI of a human brain. Image supplied by the author.

hemisphere knows what their right hand is holding, and their left hemisphere also contains their speech centers, so they can say *key*.

But now suppose instead that you place the key in their left hand. They still know what it is; they can, for example, open a lock with it. But they can't tell you what they're holding. Why? Because their right brain is the hemisphere that knows what they're holding in their left hand, and it can't convey that information to the left hemisphere because the corpus callosum isn't intact. And since the left hemisphere can't get the information, the speech center (located in the left hemisphere) can't say what's in the left hand. You get similar effects if you present a written word to just one visual field: If the word is shown to their right visual field, no problem; the left brain can say what the word is. Present it to the left visual field, and only the right brain knows what it is, and has no way of telling the left brain, so the person can't say the word.

Just as specific functions may be lateralized on one side of the brain or the other, functions may also be **localized** in one area or another within that hemisphere. Now, you'll want to take this with a grain of salt, because the functions of the brain generally involve a great deal of interaction across different areas. So to say that language is lateralized in the left hemisphere doesn't mean the right hemisphere is dormant while we're speaking; quite the contrary. But we do know something about the areas that are especially active in producing and understanding language.

Language production relies heavily on an area in the left frontal cortex called **Broca's area** (named for Paul Broca, the 19th-century neurologist who discovered it). And language comprehension relies heavily on an area in the left temporal cortex called **Wernicke's area** (again, named for Carl Wernicke, the 19th-century neurologist who discovered it). Broca's area is conveniently located near the area responsible for controlling the movements of the articulators (lips, tongue, vocal tract). Broca's area is largely responsible for grammar – things like getting the words in the right order and adding inflectional affixes and function words – and for working with the nearby motor areas to get the articulators to form the words and sentences. Wernicke's area is heavily involved in comprehension and meaning, and it's conveniently located near the auditory cortex, where sounds come in and are interpreted. Wernicke's area seems to be where we store the meanings of words and where we work out the interpretation of other people's speech. Broca's and Wernicke's areas are connected by the **arcuate fasciculus**, a band of neurons that run between them so that they can communicate information to each other.

Neurons

Now that we've gotten a general idea of the architecture of the brain, let's zero in to where the real action happens, at the level of the individual nerve cell, or neuron. A neuron consists of a **soma**, or cell body, that contains a central **nucleus**. Branching out from the soma are a long **axon** and a number of **dendrites**. The axon sends signals out to other neurons; the dendrites receive signals from other neurons. The dendrites branch out repeatedly, making it possible for a single cell to receive signals from up to tens of thousands of other cells. The axon can be much longer, but it too branches out at the end, where it ends in a number of **terminal buttons**. This is where the action is – where the **synapse** occurs.

The synapse is how one neuron communicates with another. Each neuron has a threshold at which it will 'fire' (more about the threshold in a minute). When it fires, an electrical impulse called an **action potential** travels down the axon toward the terminal buttons. The terminal buttons release **neurotransmitters**, which are chemical messengers of a sort. There's a small

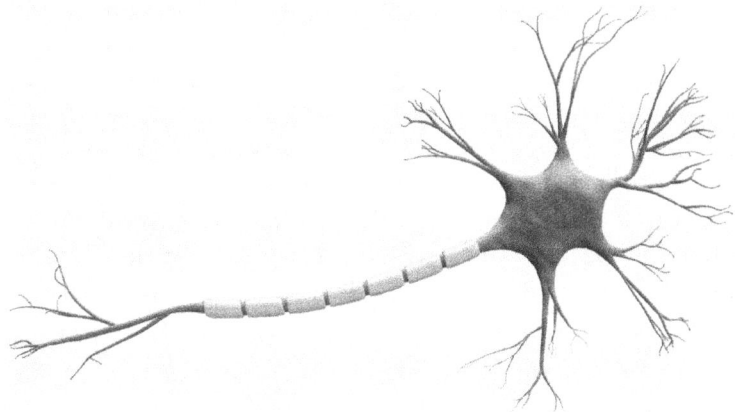

FIGURE 9.3 Neuron. MattLphotography/Shutterstock.com.

FIGURE 9.4 Synapse. KateStudio/Shutterstock.com.

gap between one neuron's terminal button and the next neuron's dendrite; this gap is called the **synaptic cleft**. When a neuron fires, the action potential travels down the axon to the terminal buttons, releasing the neurotransmitters into the synaptic cleft, where they are picked up by the dendrite of the next neuron.

These neurotransmitters can either **excite** or **inhibit** the next neuron. Any given neuron may be getting excited and/or inhibited by a vast number of other neurons at any given moment. Remember that threshold I mentioned above? If the neuron's total level of excitation hits that threshold, the neuron will fire, sending an action potential down its axon, and the whole process starts again. So in a way, the neuron is in a constant state of working on a math problem: If I add together all the excitatory impulses I'm being hit by, and subtract all the inhibitory impulses, have I reached my threshold for firing?

A human brain contains 86 billion neurons – and remember, any given neuron can be subject to thousands, or even tens of thousands, of connections to other neurons. This gives you a rough idea of how many neural connections are possible – an enormous number!

The interesting thing is that humans don't have the largest number of neurons in the animal kingdom. For example, the African elephant has about three times as many neurons as you do, at 257 billion (Jabr 2017). But the real difference is in the number of cortical neurons ('cortical' is the adjective form of 'cortex', so these are the neurons in the cortex). Remember that the cortex is where higher thought is located, and humans have more cortical neurons than any other known animal, thanks largely to all those wrinkles. We've got 16 billion cortical neurons, while the elephant only has 5.6 billion cortical neurons. This, apparently, is what makes all the difference.

Aphasia

How did we learn what parts of the brain serve what functions? Today we find out a lot through a variety of high-tech ways of scanning the brain and seeing what areas 'light up' (meaning, where the neurons are firing) during various tasks. But that wasn't always possible. A lot of what we know comes from patients who suffered damage to the brain, typically due to injury or a stroke: A neurologist could see what sorts of deficits their patient had, and correlate it with the area that was injured. That's how we came to know about the two most prevalent types of **aphasia**. Aphasia is language loss due to injury to the brain. Recall that Broca's area and Wernicke's area are named for neurologists Paul Broca and Carl Wernicke, who identified areas of the brain largely responsible for language. In each case they had a patient with a language deficit. Broca's patient had issues with language production, and his injury was to what is now known as Broca's area; Wernicke's patient had issues with language comprehension, and his injury was to what is now known as Wernicke's area.

In Broca's aphasia (also known as 'expressive aphasia'), Broca's area is damaged, and as a result, the patient typically has difficulty with speech production and grammar. Their speech is slow and labored, with little or very basic grammar. This all makes sense, given the location of Broca's area near the area of the motor cortex that handles movement of the articulators, and given that Broca's area is also responsible for speech production and grammar. You can see patients with Broca's aphasia at www.youtube.com/watch?v=f2IiMEbMnPM (a quite old but still useful video) and www.youtube.com/watch?v=1aplTvEQ6ew (a newer video of a teenage patient). Notice the patients' difficulty in finding words, their slow and labored speech, the lack of function words or varied syntax, the long pauses, and the reliance on a small number of content words like nouns and verbs. But notice also what these people are able to do: Since Wernicke's area is undamaged, they comprehend others' speech, and they manage to express their own meanings pretty well. If you're talking with someone who has Broca's aphasia, you may need to be patient, but you can understand what they're talking about.

In Wernicke's aphasia (also called 'fluent aphasia'), Wernicke's area is damaged, and as a result, the patient typically has difficulty comprehending the speech of others and with producing meaningful content words. Wernicke's area seems to be where semantic content, roughly speaking, is stored: The person with Wernicke's aphasia has a hard time not only accessing the meanings of other people's words, but also accessing the words to express their own meanings. If you're talking with someone who has Wernicke's aphasia, you'll have a hard time following what they're talking about – but notice that since Broca's area is undamaged, they talk fluently, with plenty of function words and complete syntax. You can see patients with Wernicke's aphasia at www.youtube.com/watch?v=aVhYN7NTIKU (again, an old but useful video) and www.youtube.com/watch?v=3oef68YabD0 (a newer video). Notice the fluency of their speech, but also their difficulty in comprehending what is said to them and responding appropriately. They have trouble accessing content words, so they tend to rely on the same words over and over, with frequent use of words whose meaning is vague or unclear. A person with Wernicke's aphasia will also frequently rely on **neologisms**, or invented words. For example, my friend's father, after suffering a stroke, once stated *I'm gonna spathe on the lenitex* to report that he was going to go to the bathroom.

One interesting result of these differences is that the person with Broca's aphasia will feel frustrated at their own inability to communicate clearly. Because their comprehension is unhampered, they can recognize their own deficits in speech production. The person with Wernicke's aphasia, on the other hand, has comprehension deficits, and so they may not be able to detect the unclarity of their own speech production; instead, this person may become frustrated with others, who for some reason seem unable to understand them and they just don't know why. The ironic thing is that it's the person with Broca's aphasia who is more likely to be able to make themselves understood, while the person with Wernicke's aphasia is less likely to be understandable.

Despite all that I've said above, it's important to remember that these are only broad-brush descriptions. For one thing, all areas of the brain are interconnected in various ways and work together; it's hardly the case, for example, that only Broca's area is active when a person is speaking. And there aren't strict delineations separating one area from another. When a person's brain is damaged by injury or stroke, it's not the case that the injury will occur to a distinct area that tidily maps onto either Broca's or Wernicke's area. It's obviously far more likely that the damage will cover part of one of these areas along with some portion of the adjacent brain areas.

LANGUAGE AND THOUGHT

One of the questions I'm most frequently asked as a linguist has to do with whether our language influences our world view – that is, whether a speaker of, say, Mandarin Chinese sees reality in a fundamentally different way from a speaker of Hindi or Portuguese or Swahili or English. It's a question that seems to take hold of our imaginations and curiosity in a unique way, and it's one that has been under serious investigation by linguists since at least the 1930s. Many linguists have discarded the notion altogether; others accept a carefully qualified view of it. Movies and novels have often accepted it with an unexamined enthusiasm. So it's worth taking a look at the issue: Does the language we speak affect the way we see the world?

Does the language I speak affect my view of reality?

The notion that what language you speak affects your world view is generally known as the **Sapir-Whorf Hypothesis**, after Edward Sapir and Benjamin Lee Whorf, two of its earliest and most enthusiastic modern proponents (though it traces back to Wilhelm von Humboldt before them).

Whorf was a student of Sapir's in the 1930s, and it was from Sapir that he got (and then developed) the idea that language influences world view. To get an idea of Sapir's view, consider this quote from one of his works:

> Human beings do not live in the objective world alone, nor alone in the world of social activity as ordinarily understood, but are very much at the mercy of the particular language which has become the medium of expression for their society. It is quite an illusion to imagine that one adjusts to reality essentially without the use of language and that language is merely an incidental means of solving specific problems of communication or reflection. The fact of the matter is that the 'real world' is to a large extent unconsciously built up on the language habits of the group.... We see and hear and otherwise experience very largely as we do because the language habits of our community predispose certain choices of interpretation.
>
> (Sapir 1929)

For Sapir, people are 'at the mercy' of their language; what we think of as reality is 'unconsciously built up on the language habits of the group'. That's a pretty extreme claim – that our language essentially constructs our reality for us. Whorf bought into this belief and took it further.

Interestingly, Whorf himself wasn't a professional linguist. Rather, he was a fire inspector for an insurance company and studied linguistics in his spare time. The two – his vocation and his avocation – intersected occasionally, for example when there was a warehouse fire in which some 'empty' drums had ignited. The drums had previously contained gasoline, and in this particular warehouse the 'full' drums and the 'empty' drums were stored separately. The workers smoked near the 'empty' drums, believing them to be safe because they were empty. But the 'empty' drums, which had previously contained gasoline, were now actually full of highly flammable fumes, which ignited due to the proximity of the cigarettes. In Whorf's view, language was the culprit: Because the workers thought of the drums as 'empty', they failed to see the risk in smoking near them.

When he wasn't busy working as a fire inspector, Whorf studied Native American languages, including Hopi, and he noticed some interesting differences between Hopi and English. For one thing, some words that are nouns in English are verbs in Hopi, including words like *lightning, wave, noise, spark, meteor, storm*, and *flame*. He suspected that the difference in syntactic category corresponded to a perceptual difference, and in fact that the syntactic difference caused the perceptual difference: He believed that English speakers viewed these as 'things' because they were represented by nouns in English, but that Hopi speakers viewed them as events or processes because they were represented by verbs in Hopi. In short, for an English speaker (he believed), lightning is a thing that can exist – likewise a noise, a spark, etc. – whereas for a Hopi speaker, it might 'lightning' outside, or something might 'noise'. (We do get a bit of this in English; something can spark or flame, but the primary sense of these words is their noun sense.)

There are two ways of thinking about this supposed difference in perception: You might say that the syntactic difference simply corresponds to a perceptual difference, or you might say that the syntactic difference **causes** the perceptual difference. The first view is **linguistic relativity** – the notion that different languages cut up reality differently, and that this correlates with the way their speakers experience the world. The second is **linguistic determinism** – the notion that these differences in language are the **cause** of differences in the way their speakers perceive reality. And of course you can also take the view that there's no difference at all – that is, that both linguistic relativity and linguistic determinism are false and that all human beings see reality essentially alike, since we are using the same organs of perception.

Here's another example: In English, just about every sentence we utter has to be marked for tense – past or present – so Whorf would say that we as English speakers get used to paying attention to the time of an event. In Hopi, tense-marking isn't required, but they do have a different set of obligatory markers. As Baker (1992) describes it, "the first is used to express timeless truths, as in 'The sun is round'; the second is used in connection with events which are either known or presumed to be known, as in 'Paris is the capital of France'; and the third is used for events which are in the realm of uncertainty, as in 'They will arrive tomorrow'" (1992:110). From Whorf's point of view, having to mark each sentence in this way causes the Hopi to pay extra-close attention to the source or validity of a given piece of information.

But now consider colors. Different languages have different sets of 'basic' color words. English, for example, has eleven: black, white, yellow, red, blue, green, purple, orange, gray, pink, and brown. (We also have terms like 'teal' and 'fuchsia', but those aren't basic terms that everyone knows.) Some cultures, like the Dani of New Guinea, have only two basic color terms, one for 'warm' colors like yellow, white, and red (Dani *mola*) and one for 'cool' colors like blue, green, and brown (Dani *mili*). Now, if language **forced** a world view on us, you'd expect people speaking such a language to only be able to perceive two colors. But obviously (and if it's not obvious, there's plenty of research to show it) Dani speakers can distinguish between a yellow flower and a red flower as well as you or I can – just as you and I can distinguish between a light, bright shade of red and a deep, dark shade of red, despite calling them both *red*.

Okay, so the strongest form of linguistic determinism seems to be a nonstarter. After all, if my language forced a world view on me, how could anyone have discovered that fact – since they could never step outside their own world view to see that others perceive reality differently? For that matter, how could anyone ever learn a second language?

But then there's the milder view – linguistic relativity. Going back to colors: English speakers tend to think of pink and red as different colors, even though pink is essentially a light shade of red; but we think of light blue and dark blue as different shades of the 'same' color. Is this because we have two words for pink and red but only one word for blue? In Russian, there are two different words for what we call 'blue': light blue (*goluboy*) and dark blue (*siniy*), and there's some evidence to show that Russian speakers are slightly better at distinguishing between light blues and dark blues than English speakers are. Anecdotally, I've had students who were native speakers of Russian, and they reported that they thought of light and dark blue as distinct colors.

In other studies, people have categorized objects based on the categories given to them by their native languages; for example, when their language has 'classifier' affixes for different classes of nouns, if they're asked to sort a pile of objects they tend to sort them into those classes. Another example: Some languages have no words corresponding to our *right* and *left*, which are 'relative' directions (what counts as 'left' is relative to what direction I'm facing), but instead have only 'absolute' directions like *north, south, east,* and *west*. So where I might tell you to turn left at the corner, a speaker of such a language would tell you to turn east. What's interesting is that if I line up several objects in front of you and tell you to remember the setup, and then turn you around 180 degrees and ask you to duplicate the setup, an English speaker will generally duplicate it right-to-left, whereas a speaker of an absolute-direction language will duplicate it, say, north-to-south. That is, for the English speaker, what was on their left in the first array will be on their left in the second, so that the two arrays are NOT mirror images of each other; for the absolute-direction speaker, what was at the north end of the first array will be at the north end of the second, so that the two arrays ARE mirror images.

So it seems that there is a mild effect of language on how we categorize things and what we think of as the 'same'. But it doesn't seem to force a view on us; it certainly doesn't prevent us from seeing that there are other ways of looking at things.

Way back in Chapter 1, we talked about the Conduit Metaphor and Michael Reddy's argument that English speakers talk about communication as though it were a matter of putting meaning 'into' words and 'conveying' them from one person to another. Recall that Reddy found this to be a particularly pernicious way of thinking about language because it misleads us into thinking that successful communication should be easy and automatic rather than a complicated and difficult matter of making inferences and trying to build up mental models of each other's cognitive worlds. Reddy's argument reflects a mild form of linguistic determinism: He is arguing that the language we speak influences our world view – specifically, that the way we talk about communication influences the way we think about it.

So where does that leave us? Again, it seems clear that a strong linguistic determinism is just wrong: First off, we all have the same perceptual faculties, and they're not overridden by our language. If your eyes and my eyes have the same structure (likewise similarly structured neurons that carry the perceptual information back to the similarly structured occipital lobes of our similar-structured brains), there's every reason to assume that we both see the same thing when we look at a red flower, regardless of the color terms our language provides.

But there does seem to be something of interest here – perhaps a mild effect of linguistic relativity – influencing what we consider 'the same' based on the categories given to us by our language. Lakoff and Johnson (1980) have shown that English speakers consistently follow a metaphor in which 'happy is up': I feel my spirits rising, I'm feeling high, etc., but I feel low, I'm down in the dumps, etc. And where time is concerned, English speakers consistently treat it as a series of objects that can be counted (minutes, hours, etc.) as well as saved, spent, given, taken, lost, etc. (you can take my time, I can give you some of my time, I can have time or lose time or not have enough time). Does all of this affect the way we think about happiness, or about time?

BOX 9.1

Whorf in fiction: From *1984* to chatting with aliens

The notion that language influences thought has had quite a run in fiction. Most prominently, in *1984* George Orwell's then-future world featured 'Newspeak', a language imposed by the government that prevented undesirable thoughts (such as, of course, thoughts opposing the government) by eliminating any words for them. The idea was that if you couldn't frame it in words, you couldn't think it; hence, controlling the language was tantamount to controlling thought. Consider this quote from a character in the book who is working on the newest edition of the Newspeak dictionary:

> "Don't you see that the whole aim of Newspeak is to narrow the range of thought? In the end we shall make thoughtcrime literally impossible, because there will be no words in which to express it. [...] Every year fewer and fewer words, and the range of consciousness always a little smaller. Even now, of course, there's no reason or excuse for committing thoughtcrime. It's merely a question of self-discipline, reality-control. But in the end there won't be any need even for that. The Revolution will be complete when the language is perfect."

This is clearly a Whorfian perspective on how language affects thought. You may be rolling your eyes thinking how naïve and silly such an idea is – and yeah, it's true that you can develop concepts you have no words for; otherwise how could we ever create anything new? But clearly the government does use language to try to control our opinions, as we'll see below in the discussion of politics, with terms like The USA PATRIOT Act and The Affordable Care Act being developed to influence our opinion of the act in question.

Meanwhile, in more recent science fiction, we have the movie *Arrival*, based on the short story 'Story of Your Life' by Ted Chiang. (For a fun interview I did with Slate.com about the movie, see Martinelli 2016, https://slate.com/culture/2016/11/a-linguist-on-arrival-s-alien-language.html.) This is the only movie I've ever seen – and quite possibly the only science fiction movie ever – to feature characters talking about the Sapir-Whorf Hypothesis as part of the plot. (Spoiler alert! If you haven't seen the movie and plan to, don't read the rest of this paragraph!) The main character is a linguist who is able, by learning an alien language that's holistic rather than linear, to essentially change the way she perceives time, giving her the ability to see into the past, present, and future. It takes Whorf to the point of absurdity (it's fiction, after all), but for a linguist like me, it was great fun.

And for a more recent case of science fiction aliens and their language, consider Andy Weir's novel *Project Hail Mary*, which is being made into a movie that will almost certainly have come out by the time you read this. (And again, for a fun interview I did with *Ars Technica* about this excellent book, see Hutchinson 2021, https://arstechnica.com/gaming/2021/05/andy-weirs-project-hail-mary-and-the-soft-squishy-science-of-language/.) This story involves a person who finds himself alone on a spaceship, with the task of single-handedly saving the human race. In the process (spoiler alert!), he encounters an alien with whom he needs to communicate. Here we have another instance of a human being learning an alien's language and vice versa, although the Whorfian implications aren't as deeply plumbed. But as the human and alien work to understand each other, the question still lies just below the surface: How much of their mutual understanding depends on language, and how much depends on a shared world view?

For one thing, the difficulty of learning an alien language goes beyond just 'What's your word for this thing I'm pointing to?' First, you'd need to establish that their minds are like ours in basic ways – consciousness, free will, self-awareness, etc. And then you'd need to establish that communication is actually a thing for these aliens, and that labeling objects is also a thing. And of course that they observe the Cooperative Principle – but that seems like a given for any species that communicates, since without it communication is pointless.

If you've managed all of that, you could then probably exchange a bunch of labels. But then, how do you jump from words for *tooth* or *chair* to labels for abstractions like *gift* or *friend* or *grace* (all of which arise in either *Arrival* or *Project Hail Mary*)? (Again, for a more detailed discussion of this stuff, see the

> *Ars Technica* interview!) Before we can even worry about the labels for these concepts, we need to establish that the aliens share the concepts – and how can we do that without a shared language?
>
> As always, there's a complex web of interconnections among culture, language, and world view. Whorf may have gone a bit overboard in assigning all of the power to language, but if we ever do end up needing to talk to aliens, it'll be interesting to see how their linguistic resources and associated concepts differ from ours, and what that tells us about the relationship between language and thought. Maybe the two species can work together on it.

Linguists continue to argue the point, in ever finer detail. Consider the titles of two recent books: Guy Deutscher's 2011 *Through the Language Glass: Why the World Looks Different in Other Languages* and John McWhorter's 2014 *The Language Hoax: Why the World Looks the Same in Any Language*. Clearly they're talking to each other. But what's striking is that they don't really disagree about the research; instead, they disagree about its significance. In a nutshell, one could say that Deutscher's argument is that the effects of language are minor but real, whereas McWhorter's argument is that the effects of language are real but minor.

McWhorter does make one very important point, however, which is that the minor effects of language on categorization behaviors and so on do NOT mean that the members of these

FIGURE 9.5 Saturday Morning Breakfast Cereal, courtesy of Zach Weinersmith.

language groups perceive reality differently in any meaningful way – and the reason this is important is that speakers of different languages are generally members of different social/racial/ethnic groups. Which means that our fascination with linguistic relativity brings us perilously close to arguing that different racial and ethnic groups see reality differently, which is emphatically NOT the case. Pondering small effects of language on our default choices for categorizing piles or ordering arrays of objects is fun, but that shouldn't blind us to the fact that all human beings are fundamentally alike in our cognition and perception.

LANGUAGE USE AND WORLD VIEW

The Sapir-Whorf Hypothesis asks the question: Does the language I speak affect the way I see reality? And as we've seen, the answer is something like 'mostly not, but it's complicated'. A much easier question to answer is: Does my language use, and that of other people, affect the way I see reality? And here, the answer is a resounding yes – in fact, it's a resounding 'Duh', because obviously I wouldn't bother giving lectures if I didn't think that what I'm saying could affect what my students believed. In the next few sections I'll expand on this notion to consider how other people use language to influence the way you see reality in three areas: advertising, politics, and prejudice.

Advertising

The most obvious area in which people use language to change your world view is advertising. If advertising didn't succeed in affecting your world view, companies wouldn't be spending billions of dollars on it (or trillions, depending how you count). They use many of the pragmatic tools we've already discussed in this book: For example, as we've seen, it's possible to get people to accept something as fact merely by presupposing it. If an ad promotes a product as being effective on 'your dry skin', you're more likely to assume you have dry skin than if the ad merely says it's effective on 'dry skin'. Similarly, if you want someone to buy a product, you tell the consumer what the product **will** do, not what it **would** do. The use of the word *would* suggests a conditional: here's what it would do if you used it. The use of the word *will* presupposes that you will use it, and tells you what will happen when you do.

One technique is to give a name to something that didn't previously have a name. I can market a new drink called SweetBomb that's sweetened with a mix of 10% sugar, 10% aspartame, and 80% high-fructose corn syrup; and I can name that particular mixture *Flibbertine*. (I assume I could also trademark it as such.) Now I can run ads saying *Only SweetBomb contains Flibbertine!* Other drinks may contain that same mix, but if I've done my trademarking right, none of them will be able to say they contain Flibbertine.

Another, similar tactic frequently used in ads for medications is to say that no other product is more effective at what it does. So suppose I market a drug for the prevention of ingrown toenails, and suppose there are currently a dozen other drugs on the market for that same purpose. (As far as I know, there aren't any, but just humor me here.) Now suppose that they all contain exactly the same active ingredient, and therefore they are all equally effective. I can nonetheless market my product *InGroan* by saying *No other product is more effective at preventing ingrown toenails!* In fact, I can say this even if there's no product, including mine, that is even remotely effective at preventing ingrown toenails. The crucial thing is that the word *more* invokes a scale, and the claim sets an upper limit: No other product is more effective than this. Now, the Gricean maxim of Relation tells us that the claim must have relevance – must be telling us something new and interesting. So there's a strong implicature that not only is InGroan at least as effective as all the others; it must in fact be more effective.

Advertising is one form of **propaganda**, defined as communication (language, images, etc.) that is intended to influence you, often by misleading means. Propaganda uses a wide range of techniques, such as appeals to authority (e.g., an actor portraying a doctor in order to sell medications), the bandwagon (presenting their product as something that everyone else is buying, suggesting that you should too), presupposition and implicature (as discussed above), and even shaming. One well-known TV commercial from a few decades ago showed a group of women entering another woman's home and immediately sniffing the air and saying something like "Fish again last night?" You might never have worried about whether your home had a smell, but the ad is designed to make you start. One thing ads do well is to create (or presuppose!) a problem so that they can provide the solution.

Politics and public policy

Another obvious area where propaganda plays a major role is in politics and public policy. Here you'll find a range of sources of propaganda, from those who deeply believe in and care about their chosen issue and therefore really want you to believe what they say about it to those who have crass financial interests at heart and are frankly trying to mislead you. Unfortunately, we live in an era of 'fake news', a label thrown around by both political sides in an effort to discredit the other. Just as unfortunately, some of what is peddled as news actually **is** fake, and it's important to be able to tell the difference.

One common strategy is to try to discredit legitimate science by casting doubt on its findings. We see this, for example, in the areas of vaccines and climate change. There is absolutely no doubt that vaccines are valuable and that their effects are wildly, overwhelmingly positive (when's the last time you saw anyone with polio or smallpox?); in fact, they're a primary reason why our life expectancy has roughly doubled from what it was a couple hundred years ago. But some people were misled by a 1998 paper in the respected medical journal *The Lancet* that suggested, based on a study of 12 children, that there might be a connection between vaccines and autism. That research was eventually shown to be invalid, and the paper was retracted by the journal. Later studies have shown that there is, in fact, zero connection between vaccines and autism. Let me say that once more for the folks in the back: **Later research has shown that there is no connection between vaccines and autism. None.** Nonetheless, the damage has been done, and now large numbers of people reject vaccines – including, at the time of this writing, the life-saving COVID-19 vaccine – because the doubt lingers. No matter how clear the scientific evidence, once a dissenting claim is out there, it's extremely difficult to stamp it out – and one of the reasons is that the media continue to present it as a controversy, in an effort to be 'balanced' in their presentation. Clearly 'balance' isn't an inherently good thing if it means 'balancing' a scientifically supported view with one having no empirical support.

A similar case in which 'casting doubt' works against the scientific consensus is climate change. The overwhelming scientific consensus is that climate change is real and dangerous and caused by human activity; and that the results of inaction will be disastrous. There's no real scientific question about any of that. But there is a controversy, largely because a handful of individuals are widely presented as 'experts' who dispute this scientific consensus (Oreskes and Conway 2010). Once these few individuals' views have been presented in the media and believed by a significant share of the population, media outlets feel compelled to present a 'balanced' view of the issue, presenting the scientific consensus and the manufactured controversy together. Interestingly, the same organization that is largely responsible for casting doubt on the dangers of climate change (in the interests of saving corporate dollars) was also responsible for casting doubt on the dangers of second-hand smoke (in collaboration with tobacco companies). The same strategy has been used, by some of the same people, to cast doubt on the dangers of acid rain, the hole in the ozone layer, and DDT. In each case, having an 'expert' say that the verdict is not yet in results, ironically, in the verdict not being in, even when the data are clear. The result is that people wait for clarity, believing the issue is still undecided. (For more on this tactic, see Oreskes and Conway 2010.)

Naming is also a standard tactic for affecting people's views on public policy issues. You need look no farther than the terms *pro-life* and *pro-choice*; each side of the debate wants to emphasize the positive value that they're in favor of. And just consider the names of bills and proposed policies: The USA PATRIOT Act of 2001 may have been an acronym for 'Uniting and Strengthening America by Providing Appropriate Tools Required to Intercept and Obstruct Terrorism', but more to the point, the name was designed to suggest that it was patriotic to support the act (which, among many other things, gave the government broad new powers of surveillance of civilians in the name of national security). Similarly, the Affordable Care Act is so titled in order to sound appealing; Republicans' use of the name 'Obamacare' was an effort to thwart this appeal – until President Obama in turn thwarted THAT effort by announcing that he was proud to have his name attached to the act.

Similarly, in November 2020 Illinois voters were offered a proposed amendment to the state constitution that would have made it possible for the state to adopt a graduated income tax, in effect making it possible to charge the wealthy a higher tax rate (for their earnings above a certain level) than the poor and middle-class. Proponents of this amendment called it the *Fair Tax Amendment*. Opponents called it the *Tax Hike Amendment*. Needless to say, everybody likes a fair tax, and nobody wants a tax hike – and also needless to say, most people didn't look into the issue much beyond the names given to it. (The amendment failed at the ballot box.)

BOX 9.2

Forbidden language

One interesting aspect of language and culture has to do with what words are considered forbidden – or (as in America) are 'sort of' forbidden, so that using them carries additional force. Here's something I would never say in front of my mother:

(a) That movie was fucking GREAT.

Is the word *fucking* forbidden? It certainly was in the family I grew up in, but it clearly isn't in the culture at large. And just as obviously, it's considered fine in some subcultures and not at all fine in others (hip-hop, yes; church, no). And cultures across the world vary with respect to what sorts of words are forbidden. The history of forbidden language in the English-speaking world is particularly interesting.

The first thing to notice is that in America, there are two main categories of forbidden words, which Melissa Mohr calls the 'holy' and the 'shit', in her delightfully named 2013 book *Holy Sh*t: A Brief History of Swearing*. The holy includes words like *God, hell, damn,* and *goddamn*, while the shit includes words referring to sex and body functions like *shit, fuck, piss,* and *crap.*

According to Mohr, the relative 'badness' of words for the holy and the shit has varied over the centuries. In the Middle Ages, for example, people were concerned about the holy, but not the shit; in the Renaissance there was a balance between the two, and since then the shit has been rising (so to speak). Today it's considered worse to say *fuck* than to say *damn,* but it hasn't always been that way. And even *fuck* is starting to lose its force.

Why the variation in strength between the holy and the shit? As Mohr puts it, "people swear about what they care about" (2013: 14) – so the history of swearing gives us a window into what people throughout history have cared about. There's a connection between what's shameful to show and what's shameful to name. So what was shameful to show in the Middle Ages?

Frankly, not much. Nudity was no big deal, and bodily functions like urination, defecation, and sex could take place in front of others. Bodily excretions were pretty much left all over the place. There wasn't much of a notion of privacy, largely because there wasn't anywhere to go to experience it. Correspondingly, Mohr says, there was a "low threshold of shame and repugnance" (2013: 106). People didn't care much about nudity and bodily functions, so they didn't swear much about them. Instead, if you wanted to be shocking, you'd swear an oath *by God* or on God's body parts. (Because the Roman Catholic Mass made God's actual body available to people, these oaths on God's body had particular

> resonance: You could **hurt** God.) Contracts didn't exist yet; instead, you'd swear an oath before God and let God dole out the punishments.
>
> In the Renaissance, Mohr argues, oaths were replaced by contracts; meanwhile, the invention of the fireplace made it possible for houses to have a number of different rooms for different functions. Privacy became possible, which in turn made it possible to defecate, urinate, and have sex privately. Over time, people hid these functions away, along with hiding their nakedness – and the language followed suit. By the Victorian age, it had become so forbidden to mention certain body parts that pianos had *limbs* rather than *legs,* and people eating a chicken dinner would ask for *white meat* or *dark meat* to avoid having to utter such salacious words as *breast* and *thigh.* Words considered 'obscene' took on the shock potential that oaths previously had.
>
> Today, the 'holy' continues to decline in force (along with the prominence of the church in society), while the 'shit' holds more force (but is also declining; *fuck* isn't as shocking a word as it once was). Currently, the most shocking words are epithets, such as racial or gender-based slurs. That is, what counts as forbidden language these days is language that's specifically designed to hurt people. And I think we can agree that that's appropriate: These are the words that **should** be forbidden. I'd rather hear *shit* and *fuck* all day long than a single racial slur, and I hope you would too.

Just as with advertising, we also see implicature and presupposition used to influence your political views. For example, in any given election year, I receive huge numbers of surveys in the mail. The fascinating thing about these surveys is that they're not designed to actually find out what I think; instead, they're designed to **tell** me what to think. And both sides of the political aisle do this. Consider a few survey questions from the 2020 election cycle:

(1)   a   What do you hope a Democratic president and Democratic Senate will do to repair the damage done by Donald Trump? (Check all that apply.)
      b   Which legislative priorities are you most excited about when Democrats take back the Senate in November? (Select your top 3)
      c   Which of Trump's actions do you think have been most damaging to our country? (Select your top 3)

(2)   a   Do you believe the national media has a strong bias against all things Donald Trump and Republican and fails to tell America's voters the real facts about Republican policies, principles, goals, and accomplishments?
      b   Do you think that Nancy Pelosi and the Democrat-controlled House are holding President Trump's agenda hostage and putting their political interests ahead of the good of our country?
      c   Do you approve or disapprove of the Democrats' agenda to raise taxes, provide free health care and college tuition for all, open our borders to all immigrants, enact dangerous abortion policies, pack the Supreme Court, allow inmates to vote, and abolish the Electoral College?

It goes without saying that the questions in (1) were drawn from a Democratic survey and those in (2) were drawn from a Republican survey. The question in (1a) presupposes that Donald Trump has done damage; (1b) presupposes both that Democrats will take back the Senate **and** that you're excited about their legislative priorities. In (1c) we see again the presupposition that Trump's actions have been damaging to our country – and in the list of options it offers, there are more and more and more presuppositions; these options include 'undermining the free press', 'lies and dishonesty', 'corruption and nepotism', and so on.

Meanwhile, the questions in (2a) and (2b) are clearly not designed to actually find out whether you believe these things (your options, incidentally, are 'yes', 'no', and 'unsure'), but rather to use the interaction of the maxims of Quantity and Relation to tell you **should** believe them (because if they weren't true, why would we be presenting them at such length and in such detail?). The same is true in (2c), but here again we have presupposition – the presupposition in this case being that this is in fact the Democrats' agenda. Note that no Democrat on earth would agree that their agenda includes enacting 'dangerous abortion policies'; that's clearly a Republican talking point. (And most Democrats would obviously contest most of the other points as well.) But by presupposing it in their survey question, under the guise of an innocent question designed to collect data, the survey designers are able to affect the world view of less-than-careful readers, influencing them to believe that this list does in fact represent the Democratic agenda.

I could obviously go on for chapter after chapter listing tactics used to affect your views on public-policy issues, but let me give just one more, which is the use of correlation to suggest that one thing caused another. As any scientist will tell you, **correlation does not imply causation**. It's practically a mantra among scientists. What does it mean? Well, suppose I tell you that the average temperature of the earth has gone way up over the same period of time in which life expectancy has gone way up. That's a correlation. Does that mean that the rising temperature has **caused** the increase in life expectancy – that is, that climate change makes people live longer? **Absolutely not.** Because during those same years, lots of other things have happened as well – cars were invented, and industry has grown, and we've gone to space, and we've developed vaccines, and the world population has skyrocketed, and the number of bicycles in the U.S. has increased, and the passenger pigeon has gone extinct. The fact that any two of these events are correlated (in that they've happened during the same time frame) does not in itself mean that one has caused the other. I think it's fair to say that the increase of bicycles in the U.S. isn't responsible for the increase in life expectancy either; nor is the fact that we've gone to space. Correlation is easy to show; causation is hard. (There's a wonderful website at http://tylervigen.com/spurious-correlations that shows lots and lots of correlations between events that have nothing to do with one another.)

Not all uses of correlation to imply causation are ill-intentioned or careless. Consider 3:

(3) Fifty years ago, the biologist Robert Payne first eavesdropped on a humpback whale community and heard whale song. He spread the word about their ethereal, beautiful forms of communication, and the world looked at whales differently. Since that time, whaling has sharply declined.

(Horowitz 2020)

Here, the writer clearly intends for the reader to believe that Payne's work is at least part of the reason that the world looked at whales differently and whaling has declined. With your Gricean toolkit, you can see this as an effect of the maxim of Relation; the reader wants to believe that each clause is related to the one that preceded it. Payne's work may or may not have had this effect; I'm in no position to judge (and I have no reason to doubt it). But the point is clear: Not all use of language to affect your views is insidious; but it's well worth your effort to be aware of it, because sometimes it is.

Language and prejudice

This is a topic that could (and does) fill books, and I'll have to be unfortunately brief here. To some extent, you can see the interplay of this topic with the Sapir-Whorf Hypothesis: 'Race' is a cultural construct that doesn't really correspond to any cleanly delineated set of distinct categories; so the prejudices we hold toward a group of people will have their origins in the categories we've created for these groups. This can be seen in the fact that on forms asking you to identify your race, the options given will differ from form to form. It's instructive, also, to see how the options given on the U.S. census have changed over the centuries. In 1800, your options were 'white' and 'black' (though the exact terminology changed over the years); in 1860 'American Indian' was added, and by 2010, 'Asian', 'Hawaiian/Pacific Islander', 'Hispanic', and 'other' were also options (Pew Research Center 2010), and people could also choose more than one category.

Just as the labels we have for people affects how we categorize them, these categories also affect the labels we have for them, including unkind labels. The groups that are currently subject to racial slurs in America aren't exactly the same groups that were subject to slurs in previous centuries, but many of the same issues drive the racism behind them.

Interestingly, however, it has been shown repeatedly that even when the groups are formed arbitrarily, prejudices arise and we favor 'our' group over 'their' group. Jane Elliott, a third-grade teacher, became famous for her experiment showing this among her students: She divided them into those with blue eyes and those with brown eyes and watched as the groups formed, developed animosities, treated each other badly, and easily incorporated the false stereotypes she fed them (e.g., kids with brown eyes are smarter than kids with blue eyes). Likewise, labels can provide a basis for believing that certain groups of people share characteristics, and a basis for believing that people categorized into different groups will differ in these characteristics (for whatever arbitrary characteristics you choose – intelligence, motivation, work ethic, morality, and so on).

And why am I not giving any examples in this section, unlike most sections in this book? Because recent research suggests that slurs themselves can serve to 'prime' negative associations (Herbert 2017). Priming is when making one concept salient has the side effect of making another salient as well; for example, if I utter the word *doctor*, it raises the salience of the word *nurse* for my hearer, even when *nurse* itself hasn't been uttered – and this has been shown experimentally by showing that those for whom a word has been 'primed' in this way are subsequently able to identify it more quickly than those for whom it has not been primed. Similarly, research shows that uttering a racial slur raises the salience of all those negative associations that come along with it. For example, Greenberg and Pyszczynski (1985) found that when they asked subjects to rate the skill of two debators, one black and one white, subjects who heard a racial slur used during their discussion of the debate ended up rating the target of the slur more poorly than when no such comment was heard. Worse yet, Herbert (2017) found that merely hearing the slur – not hearing it used toward anyone, but just hearing the word, even when only presented subliminally – was still enough to elicit negative associations toward the group targeted by the slur.

In short, labels help to reinforce stereotypes by giving us a way to organize our perceptions of others; and by reinforcing those stereotypes, they make them harder to change (as Whorf would predict). So next time you feel grumpy about a sports team changing the name of its mascot, consider the possibility that the change may in fact make a real difference in how a group of people is perceived.

> **BOX 9.3**
>
> ### Would you rather be someone's master or their mistress?
>
> In talking about language and prejudice, I've mentioned the way labels serve to reinforce stereotypes, but I haven't said much about language and gender – yet gender is an area in which language use absolutely serves to reinforce stereotypes. Recall that one way in which stereotypes are reinforced is the creation and perpetuation of category labels, which make it easier to put people in 'boxes' and believe that everyone subject to label A shares one set of properties and everyone subject to label B shares another set. And I also talked in Chapter 6 about singular *they*, which provides a way to escape the binary *he* and *she*, which helps to avoid this stereotyping and also offers a way to avoid forcing people into a male/female binary that may not fit them.
>
> If you're wondering where language has helped to perpetuate gender stereotypes, you need look no further than what Muriel Schulz (1975) has called the 'semantic derogation of woman'. Remember, first, that language is always changing and evolving. Moreover, it both affects and reflects the cultural beliefs of the society that uses it. With that in mind, consider these pairs of words:
>
> (a) master   mistress
>   governor   governess
>   lord   lady
>   sir   madam
>   wizard   witch
>   bachelor   spinster
>
> In each pair, the two terms are in some sense parallel – either in terms of their original meaning, or their historical root, or both. And at one time, of course,

they **were** parallel: *Governor* and *governess* differ only in their endings, and once denoted the male and female versions of similar roles. But the pairs of terms have clearly shifted from having parallel meanings to having meanings that aren't at all parallel.

This is the phenomenon that Schulz termed 'the semantic derogation of women'. The term *derogation* means a process of becoming more negative; it shares its root with the word *derogatory*. And what we see here is that over the course of history, terms for women have become derogatory in a way that isn't true of terms for men. To be a master at chess is one thing; to be someone's mistress, quite another. A *governor* is someone who has authority over a state, but a *governess* has authority only over children. And similarly throughout: *Lord* indicates a position of power, while *lady* does not; *sir* continues to be a term of respect, while a *madam* runs a brothel; to be acclaimed as a *wizard* is a compliment ('he's a wizard at math!'), but a *witch,* not so much; and *bachelor* is a much more neutral word than the derogatory *spinster.*

So what has happened? It's both simple and obvious: Our cultural views affect the connotations of terms applied to men and women, with the female terms 'derogating' or taking on a negative connotation. In cases where terms for high-ranking females are at odds with societal prejudices, no problem – we simply derogate the terms so that they reflect our stereotype of women as lower-status.

It's true that some of these still retain a meaning reflecting their original sense – it's still possible to use the word *lady* to refer to British royalty, or *madam* as a term of respect – but note that the male terms have no derogatory sense corresponding to those of the female terms. Can you think of a single pair of terms for men and women that were once parallel but in which the male version has derogated? And what does it say about our society that our terms for women have so consistently added a derogatory meaning while our terms for men have not?

Even our efforts to be neutral have often failed: For many years, prescriptivists insisted that *man* had a reading that included everybody, regardless of gender, as in 'Man is the only animal capable of language'. But that's not true, as shown in examples like this one from Horn and McConnell-Ginet 2018:

(b) Man's vital interests…life, food, access to females, etc.

(Fromm 1972)

But it's not a problem only with the word *man,* of course; the problem is that we see the default human being as male, as in this example, also from Horn and McConnell-Ginet:

(c) We must somehow become witnesses to the everyday speech which the informant will use as soon as the door is closed behind us: the style in which he argues with his wife, scolds his children, or passes the time of day with his friends.

(Labov 1972)

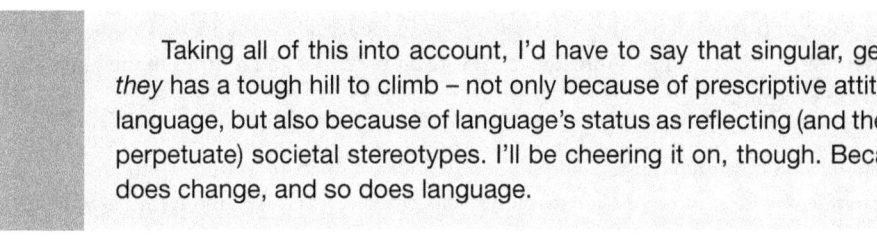

Taking all of this into account, I'd have to say that singular, gender-neutral *they* has a tough hill to climb – not only because of prescriptive attitudes toward language, but also because of language's status as reflecting (and then helping to perpetuate) societal stereotypes. I'll be cheering it on, though. Because society does change, and so does language.

CONNECTING THE DOTS

As we near the end of this chapter, you may feel that it's been a bit of a hodgepodge: What on earth do brain structure, language, world view, advertising, politics, and prejudice have to do with each other?

The answer touches on the complex academic field of **cognitive science**, which deals with human cognition from the perspective of a bunch of different disciplines, including neurology, linguistics, computer science, philosophy, anthropology, and psychology, among others. Cognitive science deals with the question of what human thought is, how it takes place, and how it is related to human interactions and human communities – as well as the intriguing question of how it is related to NON-human interactions and communities. (For that, hold on for the next chapter.) You can see how this set of questions can be addressed by the various disciplines listed above, and the kinds of questions they ask about human cognition:

- Neurology: What is the relationship between brain and mind? How does the brain work, and how does it give rise to thought, personality, will, and consciousness?
- Linguistics: How does the brain create language? What do we know when we know a language? How much of our linguistic knowledge is innate, and how much is acquired from our environment?
- Computer science: Can a computer think? What does it mean to 'think', anyway? If we duplicate the workings of a human brain on a computer, would that computer become conscious? Is artificial intelligence possible? How can we go about creating machines that mimic human thought, or are even smarter than humans – or would we even want to?
- Philosophy: Perhaps surprisingly, you get some of the same questions here that you get in computer science and neurology: What is the nature of the human mind, and how does it relate to the hardwired structure of the brain? What would it mean to say we could duplicate consciousness on a machine? Is there such a thing as free will – and if so, could a machine ever have it?
- Anthropology: How are human societies and cultures built up, and how is our cultural knowledge structured and acquired? What is the relationship between human minds, human language, and human culture? How is human culture reflected in language, and to what extent does language influence cultural knowledge and cultural categories?
- Psychology: How does thought happen, and how do our mental processes affect our behavior? What is perception? How do we sense the world around us, and how does our

personality and sense of identity develop? How do we learn? What are emotions, and how does memory work? What is intelligence? How do processes and injuries in the brain affect a person's cognition?

I could go on for much longer, but you get the idea: Human cognition – human thought – is a wild, tangled web of interconnected abilities and processes, and is of interest to a wide range of academic fields, some of which we've discussed at length in previous chapters. Granted, we've focused heavily on linguistics, this being a book on linguistic meaning, but the topic has tentacles (so to speak) that reach out into a lot of other academic areas that we've barely touched on. Cognitive science is the interdisciplinary field that touches on them all, and brings them all together in conversation with each other.

EXERCISES

Self-test:

1 Neurotransmitters can either
   a fire an action potential or remain in the soma.
   b travel down the axon or down the dendrite.
   c excite or inhibit the next neuron.
   d adapt to damage or cause aphasia.
2 The human brain contains about 86 billion
   a neurons.
   b synapses.
   c dendrites.
   d neurotransmitters.
3 The two hemispheres of the brain are connected by the
   a occipital lobe.
   b arcuate fasciculus.
   c peripheral nervous system.
   d corpus callosum.
4 A stroke victim who is able to speak fluently but whose words seem empty and who uses a lot of invented words probably has
   a Broca's aphasia.
   b Wernicke's aphasia.
   c Conduction aphasia.
   d Fascicular aphasia.
5 A stroke victim who finds it hard to pronounce words and omits function words like *the* and *a* is probably suffering from
   a Broca's aphasia.
   b Wernicke's aphasia.
   c Conduction aphasia.
   d Bloomfield's aphasia.

6 Benjamin Lee Whorf became famous for claiming that
   a your language affects your world view.
   b your world view affects your culture.
   c your perceptions affect your language.
   d your culture affects your language.
7 Which of the following is NOT a quote from an article by Whorf?
   a "The observable properties of the world cause speakers of a language to develop a particular set of habits and patterns in their grammar and in their word choices."
   b "Concepts of 'time' and 'matter' are not given in substantially the same form by experience to all men, but depend upon the nature of the language or languages through the use of which they have been developed."
   c "The background linguistic system … of each language is not merely a reproducing instrument for voicing ideas but rather is itself the shaper of ideas."
   d "We dissect nature along lines laid down by our native languages."
8 Whorf would say that because English treats time as countable units (e.g., hours, minutes),
   a English speakers are unable to use validity markers.
   b English speakers tend to be late for scheduled events.
   c English speakers think of units of time as objects.
   d English speakers are unable to translate the word 'time' into other languages.
9 One common propaganda technique is to
   a argue that language affects our world view.
   b engage in neuroscience.
   c prevent neurotransmitters from crossing the synaptic cleft.
   d try to sow doubt about legitimate scientific findings.
10 The interdisciplinary study of the human mind is called
   a neuroscience.
   b cognitive science.
   c linguistics.
   d pragmatics.

Comprehension questions:

1 What are the symptoms of Broca's aphasia, and why does damage to Broca's area cause those specific symptoms?
2 What are the symptoms of Wernicke's aphasia, and why does damage to Wernicke's area cause those specific symptoms?
3 Argue against someone who claims that the language you speak forces a world view on you, giving examples beyond those that appear in the text.
4 Imagine you're a political strategist, and you've been hired to influence people to support a bill that would outlaw avocados. What strategies for propaganda might you adopt? How will you make the best use of language to get people to support this (clearly bad) idea? What will you call the bill? Outline the campaign you'll propose to your funding agency.

Opinion questions:

1. If you had a choice, would you rather be stricken with Broca's aphasia or Wernicke's aphasia? Explain your choice.
2. Lakoff and Johnson (1980) point out that in our culture, we have a pervasive 'conceptual metaphor' to the effect that 'happy is up' and 'sad is down': So we say that we're flying high or down in the dumps, or that our spirits are rising, or that we're feeling low, and so on. Do you think this is evidence for Whorf (i.e., that speaking in this way affects how we view our emotions)? Explain your reasoning. (And if you're interested, Lakoff and Johnson 1980 makes for fascinating reading on this topic.)
3. Do you think the Sapir-Whorf Hypothesis is correct? If there's a correlation between language and world view, what direction(s) do you see the causation going: Does our language influence our world view, does our world view influence the way we talk about reality, or do the two develop together?
4. If you believe the language you speak does have an effect on the way you categorize the world, what do you think are the pros and cons of acknowledging and discussing that effect? If not, what are the pros and cons of defeating this pervasive notion? Where does our view of this relationship intersect with our social views and behaviors, if at all?

Discussion questions:

1. Have you ever known someone who had aphasia? What sort of aphasia did they have, and what were the symptoms? Since it's extremely unlikely that **only** Broca's or Wernicke's area would be affected while leaving the surrounding areas untouched, it's likely that even people with the 'same' aphasia will differ. Discuss with classmates who've known others with aphasia how their aphasic friends or family members differed in their language use and comprehension.
2. How would you design a new experiment to test the Sapir-Whorf Hypothesis? Would it test for the weaker version (linguistic relativity) or the stronger version (linguistic determinism)? If the weaker, how could you change it to test for the stronger version – and if the stronger, how could you change it to test for the weaker version?
3. Do you think that you personally are affected by propaganda? Develop a list together of as many ways as you can think of in which propaganda is used to influence you.
4. The U.S. government has asked you to help communicate with a newly encountered alien from a distant solar system. You need to outline for them what approach you will take and why. What do you tell them?
5. Do you use the word *fuck*? If not, why not? If so, when? Are there words you would never utter under any circumstances whatsoever?

Data collection and analysis questions:

1. Using the videos listed in this chapter or others you find online, give specific examples from the speech of a person with Broca's aphasia and a person with Wernicke's aphasia to illustrate the typical symptoms of these aphasias. List at least five specific examples for each.

2   Using Google's Ngram Viewer, find a socially 'forbidden' term whose use has either noticeably increased or noticeably decreased over the past couple of centuries. When did the change occur, and what forces do you suppose may have influenced it? In forming your ideas, keep in mind that the Ngram Viewer draws only from books, not spoken language. What difference does that fact make in your ideas about these influences?
3   Collect 5-10 ads, either in print or videos, and examine how they use language to influence the viewer. What specific techniques do you see?

Answers to self-test:

1   c
2   a
3   d
4   b
5   a
6   a
7   a
8   c
9   d
10 b

CHAPTER 10

Meaning, minds, and machines

KEY CONCEPTS:

- connectionism
- artificial neural networks
- parallel distributed processing
- natural-language processing
- artificial intelligence
- Turing Test, Chinese Room
- strong vs. weak AI
- data mining
- deep learning
- mind/body problem
- dualism, physicalism, functionalism
- emergent phenomena
- qualia
- the 'hard problem' of consciousness
- theory of mind

Can machines think?

We started out in Chapter 1 by talking about philosophical issues in language, and in a sense we're going to wrap up by heading right back to philosophy. But whereas in Chapter 1 we were talking about what 'meaning' is and how human language works, in this chapter we'll be looking at machines and whether it makes any sense to talk about 'meaning' for them, and likewise what role language plays in human/machine interaction. And we'll see plenty of places where the two discussions intersect. Obviously there are pretty major differences between humans and machines as well; for one thing, we as people (you ARE a person and not a computer, I hope) have bodies that can move about in the world and sense our environment and learn from that information. But computers are catching up fast. Should we be worried? We'll talk about that, too.

THE NUTS AND BOLTS

In Chapter 9 we talked about the nuts and bolts of the human brain. Since this isn't a computer science textbook, I don't plan to give a similar overview of how computers work (nor is it my area of expertise). But it's worth taking a moment to consider the structure of modern computers as compared with human minds.

Historically, there have been two views of how the human brain processes information. The classical view considered minds to operate by means of serial symbol manipulation. That is, you've got a set of neurons that stand for some concept, and another set that stand for another concept, and so on, and the brain performs operations on combinations of these symbols, resulting in new symbols that can then be subject to further processing.

A newer way of looking at the brain is called **connectionism**. In a connectionist model, cognition isn't a matter of operations performed on distinct sets of neurons, but rather occurs through patterns of neural activation throughout the brain. Instead of serial processing of concepts, the brain is seen as performing **parallel distributed processing** – parallel because many operations are occurring at once, and distributed because the activation is distributed throughout the brain rather than occurring in one spot within a relatively small set of neurons. The brain doesn't contain discrete symbols that are dealt with sequentially; instead, cognition is a network of interactions distributed throughout the brain and happening in parallel. In this sense, meanings aren't symbols at all, but rather are complex patterns of neural activation.

In a connectionist computer model of the brain, an **artificial neural network** replicates the way neurons work together in actual brains. You'll recall that in order to fire, a neuron has to add up excitatory and inhibitory stimuli coming from other neurons, and when it reaches a certain threshold, it fires, which adds its excitatory or inhibitory influence on other neurons. In an artificial neural network, the units are similarly weighted and interconnected. Although we don't know the structure of the brain anywhere near well enough to precisely duplicate its structure down to the neural level, neural networks like these are able to do a pretty good job at many of the tasks human brains achieve – things like calculating, problem-solving, language processing, and even learning (which we'll talk about a little later in this chapter).

In a one-layer neural network, you'd have one set of neurons lined up as inputs, and then another set lined up as outputs, and you'd be done. The input neurons that fired would determine which output neurons fired, and that would be that. But of course that's not how the brain works: You don't, for example, have one set of neurons that take in varying types and amounts of light and a second set that takes that information and outputs a decision about what you've seen. You couldn't possibly line up enough neurons to get enough combinations for cognition to work that way, with one set of firings counting as 'grand piano' and another counting as 'Mom' and another counting as 'Chicago skyline' and so on, for every conceivable concept.

Instead, the brain requires many, many layers of neurons – and so do the computer-based neural networks that model it. The initial layer of neurons may take in information about incoming sensations, but that information is built up through a complex pattern of multiple layers that represent ever more complex information. So instead of having a specific set of visual neurons that fire to directly represent Grandma, you might instead have an initial layer of neurons that take in the raw visual perceptions, followed by intermediate layers that combine to

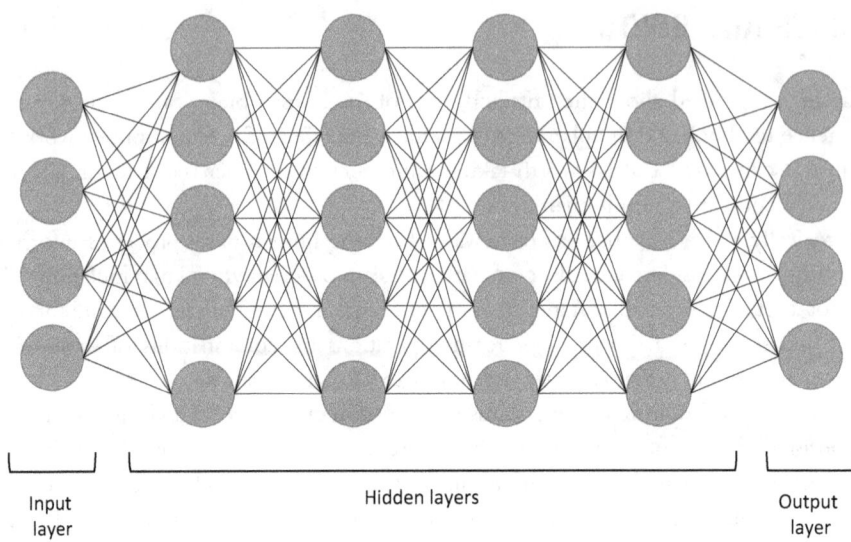

FIGURE 10.1 Hidden layers. Image by the author.

represent things like light patterns, curves, straight lines, shadows, etc., which in turn interact to result in ever higher-level concepts until the whole process results in a recognition of Grandma. And those intermediate light patterns, curves, etc., aren't specific to Grandma; the patterns that cause us to recognize a given set of inputs as, say, a person are likely to overlap considerably between Grandma and Grandpa.

The intermediate layers in a neural network are called 'hidden layers', because their activity is generally invisible to us: In a human brain, we may know the inputs and we may know the outputs (I see Grandma, I recognize Grandma), but – so far, anyway – what happens in between isn't something we can watch. We know a fair amount about the neurons that do the initial perceiving (e.g., taking in light), and we know when we've recognized Grandma, but we don't know much about how we get from one to the other. That's what the hidden layers do.

The interesting thing is that when we build artificial neural nets to model the brain, the same may be true; we now have systems that can automatically alter the weightings and connections of these 'hidden layers' to get ever-better results, but with the result that the original programmer no longer has control over, or even a clear understanding of, how the network is working and what's governing the machine's actions and decisions.

The upshot is that information isn't located in any one place, but rather is distributed throughout the system, in a way that the observer can't pinpoint. But all of that complexity is presumably what makes higher thought possible – including the higher thought that's right now letting you think about higher thought itself.

NATURAL-LANGUAGE PROCESSING

Most of this book has dealt with how language processing works within and between human beings, and the previous section touched on how processing occurs within a machine. One obvious next question is: What happens when a human and a machine need to communicate with each other? One solution is for the human to use a computer language to program the machine. But the more interesting question has to do with what happens in the other direction: How do machines deal with human language?

The 'natural' in 'natural-language processing' (or NLP) means human language, as opposed to artificial languages. And as we've seen, there is an awful lot going on in human language – phonology, morphology, syntax, semantics, and pragmatics. Some of these, of course, are harder to deal with than others, but none are easy. In NLP, the computer's task is to be able to 'understand' human language – or at least to be able to behave as though it has understood it. (More on that shortly.) The goal is for the computer to be able to determine the intended meaning of the utterance, update its knowledge base with any new information in the utterance, and respond appropriately.

Say you've logged onto a web page for a company, and a virtual assistant pops up and offers to help. You type in a request, asking whether the 'assistant' can help you with a problem. Because this example involves only written language, we've already bypassed one huge hurdle, which is the difficulty of understanding a spoken phrase when the pitch, vocal quality, accent, etc., of different people's voices are so different. So, great – and to make things even easier, we'll assume your spelling and grammar are good, where by 'good' I mean they match whatever the computer has in its NLP programming. You've typed:

(1) Can you help me with a problem?

Let's say the computer is programmed to know the difference between *you* and *me*, and knows that the referents for these deictics change depending on who's producing the utterances – that is, that *me* refers to me when I say it but refers to you when you say it. And conveniently, the word *problem* is reasonably unambiguous; there aren't a bunch of different meanings to deal with (as there would be if I asked for help finding a *light table*, which could be either one that illuminates or one that isn't heavy). But there's still some polysemy to worry about: A 'problem' can be anything from a medical issue to a complaint to a math problem to a life issue in need of solving.

Fortunately, there's no messy morphology to deal with. And the syntax of the question is pretty straightforward. And let's say that the program is even pragmatically savvy enough to know that *Can you X?* is frequently a request to do X. But when is it? How does the computer know whether this particular *Can you X?* counts as a request for help or a query about its abilities? In this case, it's especially tricky, because the question could go either way: The user might be requesting help, or might be asking whether helping with problems is the sort of thing the assistant is programmed to do. Fortunately, in either case the answer here is the same, but will the computer have been programmed to compare the optimal answers for the two readings, recognize that they're the same, and respond accordingly?

Worse, how does the computer know what it means to *help me with a problem*? You and I know that the user wants help **solving** a problem, but linguistically, it could be otherwise. A teacher writing up a math exam who asks a colleague for help with a problem might in fact want help **creating** a (math) problem. And help solving a problem could take many forms: Is the computer being asked for advice or being asked to do something that will resolve the problem? For that matter, how does the computer know that the user has a specific problem in mind, one that hasn't yet been specified, and that **that** is the problem they need help with? That is, they're not just saying 'please select some random problem and help me with it', but rather, 'please wait for me to explain the problem I have in mind and then help me with that'.

In short, even the simplest linguistic task is rife with opportunities for missteps, particularly in the area of pragmatics. And this comes as no surprise: When you and I interact linguistically, our understanding of each other's utterances requires (as we've seen) a great deal of knowledge of, and assumptions and inferences about, each other's discourse models, knowledge states, goals, likely inferential abilities, and so on. That's an awful lot to expect of a machine.

That makes it especially impressive when you consider just how much we actually have accomplished. Current NLP systems are used for a huge range of purposes, including machine translation (i.e., from one document to another), data mining (extraction of information from large sets of data such as your online behavior), customer service, personal assistants like Siri and Alexa, speech production and comprehension (e.g., when you call a medical facility and you're asked to 'describe your problem in a few words'), online search services (like Google), question-answering systems, and much much more.

ARTIFICIAL INTELLIGENCE

You may already be quite familiar with artificial intelligence, or AI, in at least two senses: First, you might know in general what it is and what sorts of things it encompasses, and second, you're familiar with it in the sense that you interact with it regularly in the course of your day-to-day life. AI can be defined roughly as machine systems that have been programmed to do what humans do, particularly in the areas that we think of as 'cognition'. AI systems give at least the impression of being able to think. (Whether they **actually** think depends on how you define the word *think*, which is a nontrivial issue, as we'll see shortly.)

Since we don't yet know exactly how the brain works, we can't (yet!) program a machine to do what we do in exactly the same way that we do it. But we're coming closer, in that connectionist AI systems, as discussed above, more closely mimic the brain's neural structure than did the systems of the past. But strictly speaking, we're mostly still in the era of imitating the results of human cognition rather than its precise mechanisms.

So when we ask whether machines are 'intelligent', it's hard to respond with anything but a shrug, since there's no universal agreement on precisely what 'intelligence' is, even for human beings. And so people differ on what they expect of a machine before they're willing to consider it 'intelligent': Do they need to simply get the results that a human would get? Or to do it in the same way that a human would? Or do they need to (in some sense) **know** what they're doing, and that they exist? Intelligence in humans includes a wide range of activities, from simple memory to learning to creativity, problem solving, and 'physical intelligence' – the sort of embodiment-in-space problem-solving capacity that lets my hand effortlessly reach out and grasp a spoon.

Mathematician and philosopher Alan Turing famously argued that in order to count as 'intelligent', a machine needed to be able to behave in a way that's indistinguishable from a human being. His famous **Turing Test** worked essentially like this: Imagine you're seated at a laptop computer. (Laptop computers didn't exist in Turing's day (1912-1954), but they'll work for our purposes.) You're told that you'll be conversing electronically (by typing) with either a person in another room or with a computer program. Turing's test was simple: Can you tell the difference? If you're conversing with a computer but you mistake it for a human being, that computer has passed the Turing Test, and according to Turing, it counts as intelligent.

Philosopher John Searle begs to differ, however. He argues that Turing's test doesn't identify intelligence in a machine at all. As a counterargument, he offers what is known as his **Chinese Room** argument. It goes like this: Imagine that you don't know Chinese. And assume you're in a closed room with an infinitely long book. (It's a thought experiment, so you can have things like infinitely long books.) This book lists every grammatical string of Chinese characters that you might encounter, matched with a reasonable response (again, in Chinese characters).

Let's say that the book is so thorough and you follow its instructions so well that a native speaker of Chinese who is outside the room, sending you written comments in Chinese and receiving your responses, cannot tell that you don't know Chinese. This, Searle argues, is NOT the same as your actually knowing Chinese. That is, the fact that your responses are indistinguishable from those of a native Chinese speaker does not count as proof that you know Chinese. You may be able to behave like someone who knows Chinese, but you don't **understand** Chinese, and that makes a big difference.

He argues that the Turing Test is similar: A computer that has been programmed to give appropriate responses is not – at least not on that basis – necessarily a computer that is intelligent. Just as the person in the Chinese Room still doesn't understand Chinese, the computer in the Turing Test still doesn't understand what it's doing, and without that understanding, it doesn't count as intelligent. Searle uses this argument to distinguish between what he calls **Strong AI**, in which the computer would actually understand what it's doing, and **Weak AI**, in which it's merely mimicking human behavior. And you won't be surprised to learn that Searle's counterargument has itself been subject to counterarguments. For example, if a computer could be embodied and use senses like ours to learn about the world and was THEN asked to interact with humans, perhaps that would give it a fairer opportunity to create what might count as 'meaning' and 'understanding'. That is, maybe it's just an unfair test if the computer can't possibly be imagined as intelligent without the sensory inputs that contribute to intelligence in human beings.

And maybe behaving indistinguishably from a human being isn't the goal, anyway. Human beings are famously flawed. What if a machine's cognitive behavior doesn't reliably mimic a human's because the machine is in fact better? If we want computers to emulate human thought, do we want to be sure to program errors and weakness and fatigue into the system? How do we feel about machines that end up better and smarter than we are? We're already there, in some areas. Computers long ago proved that they could beat the greatest chess masters, and more recently they have also beaten the best players of *Go*. They're obviously much better at complex mathematical calculations and far less error-prone.

But there are still areas in which humans are better. We're embodied, for one thing, which gives us huge sensory advantages. We're conscious, too, which is pretty handy; and we're wildly creative. And we're empathetic and terrific at nonlogical inferences. As I illustrated in (1) above, computers are still pretty lousy at pragmatic inferences. And they'll never be able to have a

Theory of Mind – that is, an understanding that others have a complex mental world that might differ from their own – until they have some sense that they have a mental world, which in turn will require them to have a sense of self. And it's hard to imagine that happening anytime soon. (But see below, where we'll talk about language and the self.)

So where do you see AI? In our current world, it's everywhere. Here's a small partial list of tasks and systems that use AI:

- speech recognition
- machine learning
- data mining
- face recognition
- route-finding (e.g., GPS systems)
- parsers
- video games
- smart phones
- targeted ads
- predictive text (as when your phone auto-completes words as you type)
- speech synthesis
- recommendations (books, music, etc.)
- self-driving cars
- machine translation
- Alexa and similar systems
- smart TVs
- smart appliances
- 'smart' everything
- …and tons more

Discussing all of these individually would take us far beyond the scope of this book, but let's take a minute to talk about one area that uses linguistics in AI systems to extract information from large data sets.

Data mining

Have you ever answered a Facebook quiz? Or needed to pass a 'CAPTCHA' test to prove you're not a robot in order to get into a website? If the answer is 'yes', you've almost certainly been subject to data mining. For that matter, even if the answer is 'no', you've almost certainly been subject to data mining. In data mining, a machine gathers information about you without your intentionally providing it. Sometimes this happens with giant data breaches that make the headlines, and sometimes information about you is included in enormous data sets that are sold by one company to another. Have you ever received a company's Privacy Policy in the mail and tossed it away unread? Of course you have; we all do. But if you read through it, you'll usually find that the company reserves the right to sell your contact information – and possibly other information about you – to other companies so that those other companies can contact you and try to sell you stuff.

In many cases, you hand over information about yourself without even realizing you're doing so. Take those Facebook quizzes – or, better yet, **don't** take them. Because in many cases, that harmless-looking quiz to find out 'Which Disney princess are you?' or 'Which Dr. Seuss character are you?' or 'What's your superpower?' (etc., etc., etc.) are just sneaky ways of getting information from you about your preferences and habits. While you're supposedly finding out which kind of tree you are (whatever that means), you're handing over information about what you like and don't like, how you live your daily life, and what sort of temperament you have.

Okay, you think – so let them know that I don't consider it a hot dog unless it has celery salt and that I prefer colorful socks to white socks. What's the big deal?

Well, there are two issues here. One is that they may also sneak in questions that can give away important security information. If a site gives you your 'hippie name' (or whatever) by telling you to combine the month you were born and your eye color, and then you post in the comments that your hippie name is 'September Blue', well, now you've revealed your birth month. (And it's just as bad if they ask you to consult a chart to determine what 'September' corresponds to as a first name, since they can effortlessly do a reverse look-up to retrieve 'September'.) Massive data-gathering operations can combine that with another quiz that retrieves the year in which you were born, etc., and the next thing you know, they've got all sorts of handy identifying information, along with the kind of information that is frequently asked about in the security questions that get you into your accounts when you've forgotten the password. ('What was your childhood pet's name?', for example.) You see the problem.

But that's not the worst of it. Remember Cambridge Analytica? To refresh your memory: "[i]n 2014 contractors and employees of Cambridge Analytica, eager to sell psychological profiles of American voters to political campaigns, acquired the private Facebook data of tens of millions of users — the largest known leak in Facebook history" (Confessore 2018).

Now **there's** a problem: Enormous corporations are taking your private social-media data and building psychological profiles of voters to sell to political campaigns so that those campaigns will know how best to sell their message to you. You answer a bunch of harmless-looking and kind of fun quizzes about your preferences, some massive corporation acquires the aggregate preferences of millions of people, they build up psychological profiles of voters, and then they develop propaganda to send to carefully targeted individuals, using techniques and rhetoric that those individuals will be especially susceptible to. Think you wouldn't fall for carefully targeted propaganda? Well, remember that advertising isn't a gazillion-dollar industry for nothing: It's ubiquitous because it works. Yup, even on you. And me.

Deep learning

Teaching a computer is easy; you program information into it. Teaching a computer to teach **itself** is hard. Deep learning involves teaching a computer to iteratively extract information from a set of data and then use that information to help it extract new information, etc. And all the while, it's refining the weightings of those 'hidden layers' we talked about earlier to make it better and better at its task.

For example: Maybe you'd like to teach a computer to play backgammon. You give it the rules of backgammon, along with some basic strategies. These rules and strategies take the form of a complex neural net, complete with hidden layers that have some preliminary weightings. Now you set it loose to play thousands of games against human players (or against more advanced backgammon-playing computers). Based on its wins and losses, it can determine which moves were good ones (leading to wins) and which ones were bad ones (leading to losses); and it'll adjust its weightings accordingly, so that it does a better job the next time. Over the course of thousands – or millions – of games, it will become better and better at backgammon.

That's great – but there's an interesting two-pronged hitch. Prong one is that eventually it may well exceed the backgammon-playing skill of the person who programmed it. Prong two is that it will at that point be playing backgammon with a neural net that wasn't directly programmed by the programmer – a neural net whose details are no longer known to the programmer. Ultimately, the computer ends up with a 'reasoning' process that the programmer doesn't know and can't work out. The computer has taught itself, and nobody knows precisely what it has learned. In effect, you've taught the program to program itself, and you're out of the loop.

To take another example: You've all seen the CAPTCHA screens that ask you to prove you're not a robot by reading squiggly text or clicking on squares that contain crosswalks or motorcycles or whatever. What you may not have realized is that these are Turing Tests. Remember that a Turing Test is designed to distinguish between genuine intelligence and a simulation of intelligence. In fact, CAPTCHA stands for 'Completely Automated Public Turing test to tell Computers and Humans Apart'. Fair enough; the system wants to know whether you're a machine, and by clicking on the correct squares, you're proving that you're not, because unlike a machine, you can distinguish between squares with a motorcycle and squares without a motorcycle.

The interesting part comes in when you discover that you're simultaneously teaching the **computer** what does and doesn't count as a motorcycle. Suppose you're given a 3×3 grid – nine squares total, and you have to identify the ones containing motorcycles. Let's say eight of those squares are being used for the stated purpose: The system knows whether each of those squares contains a motorcycle or not, and it's going to see whether you get the answers right. The ninth (randomly positioned) square, though, is one whose status the computer doesn't know. By either clicking or not clicking on it, you're giving the computer your opinion as a human being; and by combining your vote with those of hundreds or thousands of others, it will ultimately learn whether that picture is a motorcycle, and over time it will refine its understanding of what counts as a motorcycle. You're helping the company that creates the test to develop ever-smarter algorithms, which it can use in other systems for whatever purpose it might have (self-driving cars? GPS travel-time predictions? motorcycle sales?). Whatever the purpose, you're part of the learning process, providing a 'correct' answer against which the computer can compare its current 'neural' weightings and change them as appropriate. You're helping to teach the computer what counts as a motorcycle – or, in the squiggly-writing version, what counts as an 'm' or an 'a'. You're helping the computer learn to pass its own Turing Test.

BOX 10.1

Learners of all kinds

Many years ago, I took my daughter trick-or-treating with a few neighbors and friends. One little girl's mother came with us, as did one little boy's father. These families had never met before. Throughout the trick-or-treating, the little girl called the little boy's father 'Daddy'. While this sort of error can make for lots of joking (what don't we know about this kid's parentage??), it's actually very common in young children. Imagine it from the girl's point of view: The adult male I encounter every day is called a *daddy*; I guess adult males are called *daddies.* And since she would never have encountered evidence to the contrary (given that negative evidence in general is hard to come by), and she might even have heard other kids calling adult males *daddy*, well, you can understand her mistake.

Young children do this sort of thing all the time, and in both directions: While they might overextend a term like *daddy* to cover too much semantic territory (applying it to all men rather than only their own father(s)), they might on the other hand underextend a term like *doggie*, applying it to, say, cocker spaniels (if that's what their own dog happens to be) but failing to realize it also applies to the neighbor's St. Bernard. Of course, over- and underextension can apply to the same terms: One child might only call cocker spaniels *doggie*, while another might call a much wider range of animals *doggie*, including everything from hamsters to lions.

The interesting thing to notice here is how similar this is to what the computer is doing when it's engaged in deep learning. The task of a child acquiring language – well, one of their tasks, at least – is to determine how wide a range is covered by each term. That round thing with the chocolate chips in it is a *cookie;* but what about this other round thing that's just as delicious but has no chocolate chips and is covered in frosting? What about that much larger, softer round thing that gets covered in frosting and cut into wedges? Occasionally the child might ask explicitly whether the cake is a *cookie,* but mostly they just need to hear the word *cookie* used over and over and over, and keep track of what is and isn't called a *cookie*, until they've adjusted the word's range to match the way the rest of their speech community uses the word. (And even then, they may find that other speech communities differ – for example, they may eventually discover that something they call a *cookie* in their American speech community is called a *biscuit* in England.)

This is not unlike what a computer must do in deep learning, except that since it cannot move through its world encountering language naturally, as a child does, it has to use what it's given. So, to take the example of CAPTCHAs discussed in the text, it will encounter users' judgments of what counts as a *motorcycle* over and over and over, until its understanding of the word *motorcycle* matches that of the rest of the speech community. And perfection isn't the goal here, since it's unattainable in both cases: Recall our discussion of prototype theory in Chapter 2, where we found that even for relatively homogeneous communities of English-speaking adults, what counts as, say, a *sandwich* may differ widely from one person to another. And likewise for other words: Does a two-person love seat count as a *chair*? Does a stool count as a *chair*? Is a rectangular table a *desk* if it's covered in books and papers and a laptop? Where does the territory of *flatbread* end and that of *pizza* begin? Throughout our lives, we keep refining our language use to match those of our interlocutors – and meanwhile, the language itself slightly shifts, until what used to be a *hound* and what used to be a *dog* have now more or less switched places. (*Hound* used to denote all domesticated canines, and *dog* was a subclass; now *dog* denotes all domesticated canines, and *hound* is a subclass. Go figure.)

So what the deep-learning computer is doing by running through a huge database of language use to learn how various words and phrases are used isn't all that different from what a child does in acquiring language. Just as the machine's neural nets represent an attempt to mimic the human brain, its deep-learning algorithms represent an attempt to mimic the way a child learns about their world, including, importantly, their language. It's a system that's been shown, throughout the history of the human species, to work pretty well.

MEANING AND THE SELF

In thinking about meaning and machines, we will necessarily have to address the question of those of us who are **not** machines. There's not enough space here (or maybe anywhere) to fully address the question of what it means to be human, but throughout this book there's been an implicit assumption that by 'meaning' we're talking about meaning **for humans**. We've addressed human language, human interaction, human inference, human interpretations, and so on, right up until this chapter, where we have veered very briefly into the question of meaning and machines. But in that connection, it makes sense to compare machines, which can simulate meanings, with humans, who can actually have them. What do I mean by that?

Let's take *meaning* in this case to mean roughly 'intention' or an intended understanding. Back in Chapter 1, we distinguished between **natural** and **nonnatural** meaning in Grice's sense. Remember that for Grice, for a speaker A to have 'meant' something by saying *x* in the nonnatural sense "is (roughly) equivalent to '*A* intended the utterance of *x* to produce some effect in an audience by means of the recognition of this intention'" (Grice 1957). That is, when a human being 'means' something intentionally, they intend for the listener to realize that they mean something, and for that recognition of their intention to have some effect. You say *Hi!*, and I recognize that you intend this as a greeting, and so I feel validated, or friendly toward you, or inclined to respond, or whatever. And for Grice the **recognition** of the intention is crucial: It's not enough for me to simply recognize that *Hi!* is a greeting; I need to recognize that you **intended** it as a greeting. Otherwise it doesn't count as meaning; you may have greeted me, but you didn't 'mean' to greet me.

Why do I mention this here? Because it's a crucial difference between humans and machines. Human meaning has intention: When I attach a meaning to an utterance, I intend for you to recognize the semantics of that utterance and for it to produce a response in you – but also, crucially, that the response will result from your recognizing my intention. And that's the link that's missing (so far) in communication between humans and machines: When I communicate with a machine (whether it can pass a Turing Test or not), I don't recognize any intention on the part of the machine, nor is it able to recognize an intention on my part. There's something about intention that we attribute to humans and (to some extent) to other animals, but generally not to, say, fungi and plants, and not to machines, no matter how closely they may resemble us in their computational processes. And this brings us to the question of the **mind/body problem**: What is the relationship between mind and body – and to what extent would replicating our physical structure (in, say, a machine) entail that we have replicated our intentions, our meanings, our consciousness… our 'selves'?

Bodies and minds

In referring to the 'mind/body problem', I mean the whole issue of the relationship between our experiences and the brain that (presumably) gives rise to them. The basic question at the heart of the problem is: Can our 'mind' – whatever that is – be reduced to the physical brain, or is there something else or something more complicated going on? Or, to put it another way, is there anything to **you** besides the physical matter that makes you up?

Historically, there have been a whole pile of approaches to the question, and we really don't have space here to do them justice. But there are a few broad categories into which these approaches fall:

- **Dualism:** Body and mind are distinct things.
- **Physicalism:** Body and mind are a single thing.
- **Functionalism:** Body and mind are different types of things.

For much of history, dualism reigned. Body and mind were considered distinct, and the question was merely which of them controlled the other and how. These days, it's more common for cognitive scientists to take a physicalist view – and more specifically a **reductionist** view, in which the mind can be reduced to the brain. In this view, the mind essentially **is** the brain, or is the way in which we experience the brain. One reductionist view sees the mind as an **emergent** property of the brain – a phenomenon that emerges from the particular structure of the brain. Emergent phenomena are typically described using the example of water: A hydrogen atom isn't wet, and an oxygen atom isn't wet, but when you put them together in a certain configuration and in a certain amount, wetness emerges. The mind is similar, in this view; what we experience as the mind is a property that emerges from having a certain type of brain constructed in a certain way.

Functionalism tries to sidestep the mind/brain problem by defining it away: Here, the mind isn't a thing, but rather a set of processes. Those processes can run on a brain, but there's no reason in principle that they couldn't run on any other appropriately built structure. And that's where we get to the issue of minds and machines: If we were able to build a machine that had precisely the same material structure as a human brain, and could somehow also have the same sensory inputs (or have the equivalent programmed in), on a reductionist or functionalist view such a machine must necessarily have a mind that would have the same subjective experience of reality (what philosophers call **qualia**, the subjective quality of what it's like to be 'you') that humans have. And if you don't buy it – if you're convinced that having a brain that's identical to the human brain wouldn't be enough to endow a machine with a mind – then you're presumably a dualist, believing that there is something more to the human mind than simply the structure of the brain. But if so, then what is that 'something more'? And why does injury to the brain so obviously affect the workings of the mind?

One way to get at the mind/body problem is to try to simulate a human mind on a machine, since if the mind is made up entirely of physical matter, it should at least in principle be possible to build a new mind out of physical matter, resulting in a machine that could experience itself as we do. One tiny problem, though, is that we haven't yet figured out the precise structure of the human brain, so the question of whether duplicating it on a machine would allow us to create a mind is still just a philosophical one.

Language and consciousness

We are fast approaching a time when the Turing Test will be easy to pass. Deep learning has made it possible for machines to get better and better at human language, in a way that mimics child language acquisition. For decades, AI efforts at teaching language to machines proceeded in a pretty obvious way: Figure out the rules of a human language (such as English), and then build those same rules into the machine. And one obvious limit on the progress of this approach was the fact that human languages are so complex that we haven't fully worked out the rules for any of them. What we don't know, we can't teach the computer. And so we end up with computer systems that can mimic human language users, but not perfectly.

With deep learning, we have a new approach. We can give the computer some basic rules, and then give it access to massive databases of natural language, and let it teach itself English – not by setting up symbolic systems with noun phrases, phrase structure rules, and so on, but by fiddling with the weightings of its 'neurons' in such a way as to more and more closely approximate the sorts of things that human language users say, including idioms like *kick the bucket* and *because science*, and new words like *lol* and *COVID*. And the machine doesn't need to worry about the precise linguistic rules for why (2a) and (2b) below are both okay to say, but whereas (3a) is okay, (3b) isn't:

(2) a It's likely that John is smart.
  b It seems that John is smart.
(3) a That John is smart is likely.
  b *That John is smart seems.

We **could** program in a bunch of rules to allow the first three and disallow the fourth, but doing that for every subtle and complex rule of English would be (and has proven to be) a daunting task. And the computer really doesn't need to know why (3b) is bad; all it needs to know is that the first three sentences are the sorts of things that appear in its massive database of natural language, whereas the fourth one isn't – and then to adjust its neural net accordingly. In this way the computer is very much like a human child, encountering a barrage of natural language and needing to work out what is and isn't possible. But remember Chomsky's argument that the only way the child is able to succeed at this task is because they've got an innate Universal Grammar to work with. The computer isn't so lucky – at least until such time as the contents of UG (if it exists at all) are worked out.

But let's assume that linguistic and computational research solves these knotty problems, and we end up with a computer that can use language in a way that's indistinguishable from the language use of a human being. Given everything we said about the mind/body problem above, at what point does that computer count as conscious – and how would we even know whether we've reached that point? If it's passing the Turing Test for language (its use is indistinguishable from a human's), it will be able to tell me that it's conscious. Suppose it does. Now what? How do we distinguish between a nonconscious machine that is able to tell me, in beautiful colloquial English, that it's conscious, and an actually conscious machine that does the exact same thing? Once a machine has passed the Turing Test for language, what more – if anything – is required for it to pass the Turing Test for consciousness?

There's some relevant research being done on zombies. Yes, you read that right. Bear with me. A zombie, in philosophical terms, is an imaginary being that is physiologically and behaviorally identical to a human being, but lacks qualia – that subjective sense of 'what it's like' to exist. Now here's the question: Is such a being **logically** possible? If so, that suggests that the physical world could logically have developed without consciousness being part of it – as philosophers tend to put it, that God had to do 'extra work' to add consciousness. (Dualism!) If such a being is logically impossible – well, why? What is it about the brain that entails consciousness? Or to put it another way, what rules out a purely physical but nonconscious world? According to David Chalmers, a leading zombie researcher (and who wouldn't like THAT job?), there are at least three questions in play (see also http://consc.net/zombies-on-the-web/):

- Is the existence of zombies logically possible?
- If so, why aren't **we** zombies?
- Why did evolution do the extra work of producing conscious beings if zombies would have survived just as well?

To take a simple example, all evolution needs is for me to run away from a lion; it doesn't benefit from my **also** feeling fear. And presumably evolving a creature that runs away from lions is vastly easier than evolving one that has conscious experiences. (For some high-level discussion of this question, see the wonderful online *Stanford Encyclopedia of Philosophy* and its entry on zombies: https://plato.stanford.edu/entries/zombies/.)

As Chalmers states: "[E]ven when we have explained the performance of all the cognitive and behavioral functions in the vicinity of experience – perceptual discrimination, categorization, internal access, verbal report – there may still remain a further unanswered question: *Why is the performance of these functions accompanied by experience?*" (Chalmers 1995). This is what's known as the 'hard problem' of consciousness. The easy problem (although even Chalmers recognizes that it's not easy at all) is understanding why we think and behave as we do. The hard problem is understanding why we experience as we do.

> **BOX 10.2**
>
> ### Our new overlords?
>
> Almost longer than there have been computers and robots, there have been science fiction books and movies premised on the fear of what will happen if and when these machines become intelligent, sentient, and/or conscious. The usual fear is that they will surpass humans in these areas, and ultimately will take over, making us their servants or eliminating us altogether. Good thing science fiction is just fiction, right? Whew!
>
> Except that some very smart people are worried that this future may not be fictional. Recall that one of the great features of deep learning is that computers can carry it out without the aid of humans: They can keep on refining and learning and improving, faster than humans can, and ultimately ending up better than humans at all kinds of tasks (such as playing intricate games like chess and *Go*). And since they've learned without our help, we don't know what precisely they've learned (and at that point looking at a bunch of internal circuits and weightings sure won't help). In short, we end up with a computer that's super-reliable in its reasoning process – but it's a reasoning process that the programmer doesn't know and can't work out.
>
> Is this something we should worry about? Stephen Hawking, Bill Gates, and Elon Musk have all expressed concerns:
>
>> Stephen Hawking told the BBC, "I think the development of full artificial intelligence could spell the end of the human race."
>>
>> Bill Gates told Charlie Rose that A.I. was potentially more dangerous than a nuclear catastrophe.
>>
>> (Dowd 2017)
>
> In short, deep learning offers really, genuinely huge benefits – but the potential cost is currently unknown. So the question isn't only 'what is intelligence/consciousness/free will/etc.?' or even 'how will we know when or whether machines have it?', but also, and maybe more importantly, 'do we want them to?'
>
> The *Washington Post* quotes Elon Musk as calling AI our "biggest existential threat":

> "I think we should be very careful about artificial intelligence. If I were to guess like what our biggest existential threat is, it's probably that. [...] With artificial intelligence we are summoning the demon."
>
> (McFarland 2014)
>
> Maureen Dowd, in the *New York Times*, notes that the question of whether AI will control us may have already been answered: Social media are being used to manipulate our self-image (and the depression level of countless teens) and influence our elections. She interviewed Eric Schmidt, who has been (among other things) the CEO of Google as well as the chair of the National Security Commission on Artificial Intelligence. Schmidt noted that the commission had been most worried about AI-enabled nuclear weapons that, he said, "may be able to adapt and learn well beyond their intended targets" (Dowd 2021).
>
> So, should we be worried? Should we empower government agencies to prevent AI from getting out of hand? Or, alternatively, should we be making sure our own AI outstrips the AI of other countries in order to ensure our own survival – essentially running a new AI-based arms race? Should we be empowering AI to improve our lives and to win the AI race? Or should we be putting on the brakes before it's too late? To all these questions, I can confidently say "I have no idea." All I know for sure is that when I get too stressed out about questions like this, I can turn to my ever-smarter phone and tablets and laptops, which will show me soothing pictures of kittens. And those kittens are adorable.

This discussion may seem to have taken us far afield, but here's the rub: We can't tell whether a machine is having experiences, except by virtue of its linguistic report that it is doing so. (Recall that our understanding that others have mental worlds just as we do is known as **theory of mind**.) And right now, even if we've got a machine that's programmed to tell us that it has experiences, we wouldn't believe it. What we need is Grice's notion of meaning: Recall again that for Grice, for a speaker A to have 'meant' something by saying x in the nonnatural sense "is (roughly) equivalent to 'A intended the utterance of x to produce some effect in an audience by means of the recognition of this intention'" (Grice 1957). A machine can report itself as having intentions, and therefore as having meanings; but until it can actually have such intentions, it won't have intentional meanings in this Gricean sense.

And that's why all of this discussion of artificial intelligence, philosophy, and zombies is relevant to meaning. As you'll already have realized, the basic question in AI is whether machines will ultimately develop consciousness, or whether they will remain zombies, the structural equivalent of the human brain but without its qualia, forever mimicking us structurally and behaviorally but lacking our consciousness and our intentionality… our meaning.

FIGURE 10.2 Phonlamai Photo/Shutterstock.com.

EXERCISES

Self-test:

1 People are much better than computers at
   a pragmatics.
   b calculations.
   c data mining.
   d playing games.
2 Functionalism tries to get around the mind/body problem by
   a arguing that our bodies don't exist.
   b arguing that mental processes don't exist.
   c adopting a religious perspective.
   d defining a mind in terms of its function rather than what it's made of.
3 The word 'qualia' refers to
   a the reality of the world.
   b our decision-making abilities.
   c our subjective experience.
   d the physical properties of an object.
4 Data mining is being used to
   a develop systems that can beat humans at games like chess and *Go*.
   b create psychological profiles of users in order to influence us.
   c develop systems with physical intelligence.
   d prevent the development of computers with free will.
5 Deep learning involves
   a the computer teaching itself.
   b learning that happens at a lower level.

c   learning that is conscious.
d   learning that mimics an adult's physical abilities.

6   One feature of deep learning is that it results in
    a   the programmer retaining tight control over what the computer knows.
    b   physical movement and perception.
    c   the programmer not knowing exactly how or what the computer is learning.
    d   the existence of new computer chips.

7   In AI applications such as deep learning, neural networks make use of
    a   consciousness.
    b   symbols and rules.
    c   top-down processing.
    d   hidden layers.

8   The 'hard problem' of consciousness is
    a   why we experience our existence.
    b   how to get computers to behave like humans.
    c   why humans behave as we do.
    d   why human beings haven't developed consciousness.

9   The Turing Test and the Chinese Room argument involve
    a   how to know whether a machine is intelligent.
    b   how to know whether a machine is embodied.
    c   how to know whether a human being is intelligent.
    d   how to know whether a human being is embodied.

10 One question raised by philosophical zombies is
    a   whether they really exist.
    b   why we bothered to evolve qualia.
    c   whether the human mind controls the brain.
    d   how we represent them in our discourse model.

Comprehension questions:

1   How do hidden layers improve the functioning of AI, and why are they called 'hidden'?
2   How does the philosophical notion of a zombie help to clarify the mind/body problem?
3   List six common situations (other than social-media quizzes and CAPTCHAs, which are discussed in the text) in which you could be subject to data mining. For each, state how that information might be used without your knowledge.

Opinion questions:

1   How would you define 'intelligence'?
2   Do you think 'strong AI' will ever be attained? Why or why not?
3   List three games that you think no existing computer could beat you at, and three games that you think a sufficiently advanced, currently existing computer could easily beat you at.
4   Would you consider yourself a dualist, a physicalist, a functionalist, or none of these? What's your stance on the relationship between mind and body?

Discussion questions:

1. To what extent do you think machines these days can pass the Turing Test for language? That is, do you think you're ever fooled into thinking you're communicating with a human being when it's actually a computer?
2. Are the advantages of deep learning worth the fact that the programmer loses control over the learning process? Why or why not?
3. How do you feel about data mining? Is this something you worry about, or not at all?
4. More generally, do you think the dangers of AI are real or overblown? How do you see the balance between the benefits and drawbacks of AI?

Data collection and analysis:

1. From *lol* to *tl;dr* and beyond, computer-mediated communication (CMC) has affected, and continues to affect, our language. Spend a few days watching your own online interactions, and collect terms that you first encountered online or which are specific to CMC. How would you define them (without checking a dictionary)? Which ones do you think will still be in active use 50 years from now, which ones do you think won't be, and (in both cases) why?
2. Collect at least six examples of data-mining efforts (or what you think might be data-mining efforts) that you encounter over a span of a few days on social media, on websites, in email, etc. Describe what sorts of data are being surreptitiously collected and how they might be used.
3. Many online retailers use chatbots as virtual assistants, to help answer your questions, etc. Conduct a brief conversation with one of these assistants or with another chatbot you find online, and then write a page analyzing the interaction. How natural did the conversation seem? Could it pass the Turing Test? What features distinguished this conversation from one that you might have with a human being? (You might have to pretend to be a customer, and you'll definitely want to use a different browser from your usual one and clear your cookies afterward, or you'll be hearing from this company forever.)

Answers to self-test:

1. a
2. d
3. c
4. b
5. a
6. c
7. d
8. a
9. a
10. b

References

Acton, Eric K. 2019. Pragmatics and the social life of the English definite article. *Language* 95.1:37-65.
Bach, Kent. 1994. Conversational impliciture. *Mind & Language* 9.2:124-162.
Baker, Mona. 1992. *In Other Words: A Coursebook on Translation*. Routledge.
Banks, Lynn Reid. 1980. *The Indian in the Cupboard*. Doubleday.
Bergner, Daniel. 2019. The struggles of rejecting the gender binary. *New York Times Magazine* 6/4/2019.
Birner, Betty J. 1994. Information status and word order: An analysis of English inversion. *Language* 70:233-259.
Birner, Betty J. 1996. *The Discourse Function of Inversion in English*. Garland Publishing.
Birner, Betty J. 2006. Inferential relations and noncanonical word order. In Betty J. Birner and Gregory Ward, eds., *Drawing the Boundaries of Meaning: Neo-Gricean Studies in Pragmatics and Semantics in Honor of Laurence R. Horn*. John Benjamins. 31-51.
Birner, Betty J. 2018. On constructions as a pragmatic category. *Language* 94.2:e158-e179.
Birner, Betty J. and Gregory Ward. 1998. *Information Status and Noncanonical Word Order in English*. John Benjamins.
Blake, Aaron. 2017. Henry Kissinger's lukewarm non-endorsement of Jared Kushner is even more damning than it seems. *Washington Post* 4/20/2017. www.washingtonpost.com/news/the-fix/wp/2017/04/20/henry-kissingers-lukewarm-non-endorsement-of-jared-kushner/?noredirect=on&utm_term=.4664600c96e3.
Bloomberg News. 1996. Bre-X Minerals told to split gold find. *New York Times* 11/28/1996.
Bradner, Eric and Maegan Vazquez. 2018. Stormy Daniels says she was threatened to keep quiet about Trump. *CNN* 3/26/2018. www.cnn.com/2018/03/25/politics/60-minutes-stormy-daniels-interview-main/index.html.
Bromfield, Louis. 1933. *The Farm*. Grosset & Dunlap.
Brontë, Charlotte. 1847. *Jane Eyre*. Smith, Elder & Co.
Brown, Penelope and Stephen C. Levinson. 1978. *Politeness: Some Universals in Language Usage*. Cambridge University Press.
Carston, Robyn. 2002. *Thoughts and Utterances: The Pragmatics of Explicit Communication*. Wiley-Blackwell.
Chalmers, David J. 1995. Facing up to the problem of consciousness. *Journal of Consciousness Studies* 2:200-219.
Chiang, Ted. 2016. Story of your life. In Ted Chiang, *Stories of Your Life and Others*. Vintage.
Clancy, Tom. 1984. *The Hunt for Red October*. Naval Institute Press.
Clark, Herbert H. 1977. Bridging. In Philip Nicholas Johnson-Laird and Peter Cathcart Wason, eds., *Thinking: Readings in Cognitive Science*. Cambridge University Press. 411-420.
Coleman, Linda and Paul Kay. 1981. Prototype semantics: The English word *lie*. *Language* 57.1:26-44.
Confessore, Nicholas. 2018. Cambridge Analytica and Facebook: The scandal and the fallout so far. *New York Times* 4/4/2018.

Conley, Sean P. 2020. White House memorandum. www.politico.com/f/?id=00000172-2a4e-d930-a77f-abff75a10000.
Dahl, Roald. 1961. *James and the Giant Peach*. Alfred A. Knopf.
Dahl, Roald. 1964. *Charlie and the Chocolate Factory*. Allen & Unwin.
Dahl, Roald. 1970. *Fantastic Mr Fox*. Allen & Unwin.
Deutscher, Guy. 2011. *Through the Language Glass: Why the World Looks Different in Other Languages*. Metropolitan Books.
Donnellan, Keith S. 1966. Reference and definite descriptions. *Philosophical Review* 75:281-304.
Dowd, Maureen. 2017. Elon Musk's future shock. *Vanity Fair*. April.
Dowd, Maureen. 2021. A.I. is not A-OK. *New York Times* 10/30/2021.
Enger, Leif. 2018. *Virgil Wander*. Grove Press.
Fillmore, Charles J. 1970. The grammar of hitting and breaking. In R.A. Jacobs and P.A. Rosenbaum, eds., *Readings in English Transformational Grammar*. Ginn. 120-133.
Fillmore, Charles J., Paul Kay, and Mary Catherine O'Connor. 1988. Regularity and idiomaticity in grammatical constructions: The case of *let alone*. *Language* 64:501–538.
Foer, Jonathan Safran. 2019. *We Are the Weather: Saving the Planet Begins at Breakfast*. Farrar, Straus and Giroux.
Fraser, Caroline. 2021. Enraptured. *New York Times Book Review* 2/21/2021.
Frege, Gottlob. 1892. Über Sinn und Bedeutung. *Zeitschrift für Philosophie und Philosophische Kritik* 100:25-50.
Fromm, Erich. 1972. The Erich Fromm theory of aggression. *New York Times* 2/27/1972.
Goffman, Erving. 1955. On face-work: An analysis of ritual elements in social interaction. *Psychiatry: Journal of Interpersonal Relations* 18.3:213–231.
Goldberg, Adele E. 1995. *Constructions: A Construction Grammar Approach to Argument Structure*. University of Chicago Press.
Greenberg, Jeff and Tom Pyszczynski. 1985. The effect of an overheard ethnic slur on evaluations of the target: How to spread a social disease. *Journal of Experimental Social Psychology* 21.1:61–72.
Grice, H. Paul. 1957. Meaning. *The Philosophical Review* 64:377-388.
Grice, H. Paul. 1975. Logic and conversation. In Peter Cole and Jerry Morgan, eds., *Syntax and Semantics 3: Speech Acts*. Academic Press. 41-58.
Guterson, David. 1994. *Snow Falling on Cedars*. Harcourt, Brace.
Haberman, Clyde. 1988. Some Japanese (one) urge plain speaking. *New York Times* 3/27/1988.
Halliday, Michael A.K. 1967. Notes on transitivity and theme in English, Part 2. *Journal of Linguistics* 3:199-244.
Halliday, Michael A.K. and Ruqaiya Hasan. 1976. *Cohesion in English*. Longman.
Hankamer, Jorge. 1971. *Constraints on Deletion in Syntax*. Doctoral dissertation, Yale University.
Harris, Joanne. 2000. *Chocolat*. Penguin Books.
Haviland, Susan E. and Herbert H. Clark. 1974. What's new? Acquiring new information as a process in comprehension. *Journal of Verbal Learning & Verbal Behavior* 13:512-521.
Herbert, Cassie. 2017. *Exclusionary Speech and Constructions of Community*. Doctoral dissertation, Georgetown University.
Hirschberg, Julia. 1991. *A Theory of Scalar Implicature*. Garland Publishing.
Horn, Laurence R. 1984. Toward a new taxonomy for pragmatic inference: Q-based and R-based implicature. In D. Schiffrin, ed., *Meaning, Form, and Use in Context: Linguistic Applications*. Georgetown University Press. 11-42.
Horn, Laurence R. 1989. *A Natural History of Negation*. University of Chicago Press.
Horn, Laurence R. and Sally McConnell-Ginet. 2018. Ceteris paribusiness: Salience and CP-override. Fourth International Conference of the American Pragmatics Association. Albany NY. November 3.
Horowitz, Alexandra. 2020. Talk to the animals. *New York Times Book Review* 5/17/2020. muse.jhu.edu/article/697195/pdf.

Hutchinson, Lee. 2021. Andy Weir's *Project Hail Mary* and the soft, squishy science of language. *Ars Technica*. arstechnica.com/gaming/2021/05/andy-weirs-project-hail-mary-and-the-soft-squishy-science-of-language/.
Irving, John. 1985. *The Cider House Rules*. William Morrow.
Jabr, Ferris. 2017. To unlock the brain's mysteries, puree it. *New York Times Magazine* 12/14/2017.
Johnson, Steven. 2021. The living century. *New York Times* 5/2/2021.
Kamp, Hans and Barbara Partee. 1995. Prototype theory and compositionality. *Cognition* 57.2:129-191.
Karmel, Annabel. 2007. *Lunch Boxes and Snacks: Over 120 Healthy Recipes from Delicious Sandwiches and Salads to Hot Soups and Sweet Treats*. Atria Books.
Kay, Paul. 1997. *Words and the Grammar of Context*. CSLI Publications.
Kissinger, Henry. 2017. Jared Kushner. *Time: The 100 most influential people*. *Time* magazine.
Konigsburg, E.L. 2004. *The Outcasts of 19 Schuyler Place*. Atheneum Books.
Krumpelmann, John T. 1939. West Virginia peculiarities. *American Speech* 14:155–156.
Kummer, Corby. 2019. Food for thought. *New York Times Book Review* 7/7/2019.
Kurtzleben, Danielle. 2017. With 'fake news,' Trump moves from alternative facts to alternative language. *NPR WBEZ Chicago* 2/17/2017. www.npr.org/2017/02/17/515630467/with-fake-news-trump-moves-from-alternative-facts-to-alternative-language.
Labov, William. 1972. *Sociolinguistic Patterns*. University of Pennsylvania Press.
Lakoff, George. 1971. Presuppositions and relative well-formedness. In Steinberg and Jakobovits, eds., *Semantics: An Interdisciplinary Reader in Philosophy, Linguistics, and Psychology*. Cambridge University Press. 329-340.
Lakoff, George and Mark Johnson. 1980. *Metaphors We Live By*. University of Chicago Press.
Lakoff, Robin. 1973. The logic of politeness; or minding your p's and q's. *Papers from the 9th Regional Meeting*. Chicago Linguistics Society.
Lane, Anthony. 2017. Trump vs. Comey: Hope against hope. *New Yorker* 6/9/2017.
L'Engle, Madeleine. 1962. *A Wrinkle in Time*. Newbery.
Levin, Beth. 1993. *English Verb Classes and Alternations: A Preliminary Investigation*. University of Chicago Press.
Levinson, Stephen C. 2000. *Presumptive Meanings: The Theory of Generalized Conversational Implicature*. MIT Press.
Lewis, David. 1979. Scorekeeping in a language game. *Journal of Philosophical Language* 8:339-359.
Loftus, Elizabeth F. and Guido Zanni. 1975. Eyewitness testimony: The influence of the wording of a question. *Bulletin of the Psychonomic Society* 5.1:86-88.
Maher, Zach and Tom McCoy. 2011. Positive *anymore*. *Yale Grammatical Diversity Project: English in North America*. http://ygdp.yale.edu/phenomena/positive-anymore. Updated by Katie Martin, 2018.
Mahootian, Shahrzad. 1997. *Persian*. Routledge.
Maleckar, Dave. 2019. 100 word rant. *Funny Times*, August 2019.
Martinelli, Marissa. 2016. How realistic is the way Amy Adams' character hacks the alien language in *Arrival*? We asked a linguist. Slate.com 11/22/2016. https://slate.com/culture/2016/11/a-linguist-on-arrival-s-alien-language.html.
McCarthy, John J. 1982. Prosodic structure and expletive infixation. *Language* 58.3:574–590.
McCawley, James. 1978. Conversational implicature and the lexicon. In Peter Cole, ed., *Syntax and Semantics 9: Pragmatics*. Academic Press. 245-259.
McFarland, Matt. 2014. Elon Musk: 'With artificial intelligence we are summoning the demon.' *Washington Post* 10/24/2014.
McGinn, Colin. 2015. *Philosophy of Language: The Classics Explained*. MIT Press.
McWhorter, John H. 2014. *The Language Hoax: Why the World Looks the Same in Any Language*. Oxford.
Miller, Philip. 2001. Discourse constraints on (non)-extraposition from subject in English. *Linguistics* 39.4:683-701.
Mohr, Melissa. 2013. *Holy Shit: A Brief History of Swearing*. Oxford University Press.
Morris, Michael. 2007. *An Introduction to the Philosophy of Language*. Cambridge University Press.

Neale, Stephen. 1992. Paul Grice and the philosophy of language. *Linguistics and Philosophy* 15:509-559.
New Yorker. 2017. Constabulary notes from all over. 12/4/2017.
Ohio State University Department of Linguistics. 2016. *Language Files*, 12th ed. OSU Press.
Okrand, Mark. 1992. *The Klingon Dictionary.* Gallery Books.
Oreskes, Naomi and Erik M. Conway. 2010. *Merchants of Doubt: How a Handful of Scientists Obscured the Truth on Issues from Tobacco Smoke to Global Warming.* Bloomsbury Press.
Orwell, George. 1949. *1984.* Secker & Warburg.
Pausch, Randy and Jeffrey Zaslow. 2008. *The Last Lecture.* Hyperion.
Petri, Alexandra. 2018. A ranking of 100 – yes, 100 – Christmas songs. *Washington Post* 12/7/2018. www.washingtonpost.com/opinions/2018/12/07/100-best-christmas-songs-ranking/
Pew Research Center. 2010. What census calls us. 2/6/2020. www.pewresearch.org/interactives/what-census-calls-us/.
Phillips, Kristine. 2018. 'Truth isn't truth': Rudy Giuliani's flub tops 2018's quotes of the year. *Washington Post* 12/11/2018. www.washingtonpost.com/politics/2018/12/11/truth-isnt-truth-rudy-giulianis-flub-tops-s-quotes-year/
Pinker, Steven. 2019. A linguist's guide to quid pro quo. *New York Times* 10/7/2019.
Polizzotti, Mark. 2018. Why mistranslation matters. *New York Times* 7/28/2018. www.nytimes.com/2018/07/28/opinion/sunday/why-mistranslation-matters.html
Pollan, Michael. 2019. *How to Change Your Mind: What the New Science of Psychedelics Teaches Us About Consciousness, Dying, Addiction, Depression, and Transcendence.* Penguin Books.
Pramuk, Jacob and John W. Schoen. 2017. Comey: I took it as an order when Trump told me to drop Flynn investigation. CNBC 6/8/2017. www.cnbc.com/2017/06/08/comey-to-senate-committee-trump-wanted-me-to-drop-flynn-probe.html.
Prince, Ellen F. 1978. A comparison of *wh*-clefts and *it*-clefts in discourse. *Language* 54:883-906.
Prince, Ellen F. 1981. Toward a taxonomy of given-new information. In Peter Cole, ed., *Radical Pragmatics.* Academic Press. 223-254.
Prince, Ellen F. 1988. On pragmatic change: The borrowing of discourse functions. *Journal of Pragmatics* 12.5-6:505-518.
Prince, Ellen F. 1992. The ZPG letter: Subjects, definiteness, and information-status. In S. Thompson and W. Mann, eds., *Discourse Description: Diverse Analyses of a Fundraising Text.* John Benjamins. 295-325.
Proulx, Annie. 2005. *Brokeback Mountain.* Scribner.
Pullum, Geoffrey K. 2018. *Linguistics: Why It Matters.* Polity.
Punske, Jeffrey and Andrew Barss. 2010. It's not just positive, anymore. Paper presented at Arizona Linguistics Circle 4, Tucson, October 16.
Reddy, Michael J. 1979. The Conduit Metaphor: A case of frame conflict in our language about language. In A. Ortony, ed., *Metaphor and Thought.* Cambridge University Press. 284-324.
Roberts, Craige. 2012. Information structure in discourse: Towards an integrated formal theory of pragmatics. *Semantics & Pragmatics* 5.6:1-69. http://dx.doi.org/10.3765/sp.5.6.
Rombauer, Irma S. and Marion Rombauer Becker. 1931. *Joy of Cooking.* Scribner.
Rosch, Eleanor H. 1973. Natural categories. *Cognitive Psychology* 4:328-350.
Rosch, Eleanor H. 1975. Cognitive representations of semantic categories. *Journal of Experimental Psychology: General*, 104.3:192-233.
Ross, John R. 1967. *Constraints on Variables in Syntax.* Doctoral dissertation, MIT.
Royko, Mike. 1999. *One More Time: The Best of Mike Royko.* University of Chicago Press.
Russell, Bertrand. 1905. On denoting. *Mind* 14.56:479-493.
Sadock, Jerrold M. 1978. On testing for conversational implicature. In Peter Cole, ed., *Syntax and Semantics 9: Pragmatics.* Academic Press. 281-297.
Sapir, Edward. 1929. The status of linguistics as a science. In D. G. Mandelbaum, ed., 1958, *Culture, Language and* Personality. University of California Press.
Schulz, Muriel R. 1975. The semantic derogation of women. In Barrie Thorne and Nancy Henley, eds., *Language and Sex: Difference and Dominance.* Newbury House. 64-75.

Searle, John R. 1969. *Speech Acts*. Cambridge.
Searle, John R. 1975. Indirect speech acts. In Peter Cole and Jerry L. Morgan, eds., *Syntax and Semantics*, vol. 3: *Speech Acts*. 59-82.
Seow, C. L. 1995. *A Grammar for Biblical Hebrew*. Abingdon.
Sigma Iota Beta. 2018. *The Torch*. Hope College, April.
Skinner, B. F. 1957. *Verbal Behavior*. Appleton-Century-Crofts.
Solan, Lawrence M. and Peter M. Tiersma. 2005. *Speaking of Crime: The Language of Criminal Justice*. University of Chicago Press.
Sperber, Dan and Deirdre Wilson. 1986. *Relevance: Communication and Cognition*. Harvard University Press.
Steinbeck, John. 1952. *East of Eden*. Viking Press.
Strawson, Peter F. 1950. On referring. *Mind* 59:320-344.
Upfield, Arthur W. 1950. *The Widows of Broome*. Reprint 1985, Scribner.
Walker, Matthew. 2018. *Why We Sleep: The New Science of Sleep and Dreams*. Scribner.
Ward, Gregory. 1988. *The Semantics and Pragmatics of Preposing*. Garland Publishing.
Ward, Gregory and Betty J. Birner. 1995. Definiteness and the English existential. *Language* 71:722-742.
Washington Post. 2019. Transcript: Night 2 of the second Democratic debate. www.washingtonpost.com/politics/2019/08/01/transcript-night-second-democratic-debate/.
Waters, Alice. 2021. By the book. *New York Times Book Review* 6/6/2021.
Waugh, Evelyn. 1945. *Brideshead Revisited*. Chapman and Hall.
Weiland, Noah. 2019. Impeachment briefing: How Republicans are using hearings. *New York Times* 11/22/2019. www.nytimes.com/2019/10/02/briefing/impeachment-briefing-what-happened-today.html
Weir, Andy. 2021. *Project Hail Mary*. Ballantine.
Wierzbicka, Anna. 2001. *What Did Jesus Mean?: Explaining the Sermon on the Mount and the Parables in Simple and Universal Human Concepts*. Oxford University Press.
Wilson, Deirdre and Dan Sperber. 2004. Relevance Theory. In Laurence R. Horn and Gregory Ward, eds., *Handbook of Pragmatics*. Blackwell. 607-632.
Wolfram, Walt and Donna Christian. 1976. Appalachian speech. Center for Applied Linguistics.
Zimmer, Ben. 2010. Crash blossoms. *New York Times* 1/27/2010. www.nytimes.com/2010/01/31/magazine/31FOB-onlanguage-t.html
Zimmer, Ben. 2019. Hospitals named after sandwiches kill five. *Language Log* 10/14/2019. https://languagelog.ldc.upenn.edu/nll/?p=44683.

Index

1984 253–254

AAVE 173–175
abuse 127–129
accent 147, 223–224
accommodation 209–212, 233
acronym 35, 161, 258
action potential 247–248
Acton, Eric K. 196, 214
adjective 31, 36–37, 56, 59, 70, 153–158, 162, 170–171, 195
adjunct 176
advertising 210–211, 256–257, 277
afferent neuron 244
affix 31–35, 58, 159–160, 164, 188, 247, 252
agent (semantic role) 218–219, 229, 234
agreement 145–146, 159, 174
alloform 236–237
allomorph 151, 237–238
allophone 148–151, 236–238
ambiguity 17, 19, 50–59, 74–76, 86, 96, 158, 161–165, 175–177, 193, 218, 236, 273
American Dialect Society 154
analytic statement 54, 66–67
anaphora 187–188, 192–195
animal communication 5, 34
anomaly 57
antecedent 64, 192, 194
anthropology 265
antonym 36–39
aphasia 248–250

apology 119–123, 129–130, 132–133
arbitrariness 9–10, 32, 34, 104
arcuate fasciculus 247
argument 71, 217–221, 228–230
argument reversal 228–229
argument structure 219–221
Arrival 254
art 11–13
artificial intelligence 274–280, 284–285
artificial neural network 271–272
aspiration 148–150, 238
assertion 17–19, 131, 198, 203–207, 210
assimilation 34
atomic proposition 71
attributive reading 18–19
axon 247–248

Bach, Kent 106–107
backformation 35, 161
Baker, Mona 251
Barss, Andrew 7
Becker, Marion Rombauer 234
behaviorism 145
biconditional 65–66, 83, 98–99
Birner, Betty J. 222, 226–231, 235–236
bivalence 198, 206
Blake, Aaron 117
blend 35, 161
borrowing 30–31, 161, 223–224
bound morpheme 151, 156
bound variable 72–73

boundary, semantic/pragmatic 112–114, 183–185
brain 244–250, 265–266, 271–274, 281–283
brain stem 244
bridging inference 230–231
Broca, Paul 246, 249
Broca's aphasia 249–250
Broca's area 246–247, 249–250
Brontë, Charlotte 155, 194
Brown, Penelope 137

calculability 100–102, 131
Cambridge Analytica 277
cancellability 100–105, 131, 207
canonical word order 221–222, 225, 229
CAPTCHAs 276, 278–279
Carston, Robyn 106
cataphora 193–195
cerebellum 244
cerebral cortex 244
cerebrum 244
Chalmers, David J. 283–284
change-of-state verb 204–205
Chaucer, Geoffrey 155
Chiang, Ted 254
Chinese Room 275
Chomsky, Noam 145–147, 165, 172, 176–178, 186, 283
Christian, Donna 7
Clark, Herbert H. 230
classifiers 252
cleft (construction) 204–205, 208, 212, 223, 232–233
cleft (synaptic) 248
Clinton, Bill 28, 48, 95, 116, 117, 132–133
clipping 35, 161
closed proposition 72
Cognitive Principle of Relevance 110
cognitive science 243, 265–266
coinage 36, 161
Coleman, Linda 45, 91–92
collocation 49
color terms 41, 252–253
Comey, James 133–134, 137
common ground 207, 211–212
Communicative Principle of Relevance 110

comparative suffix 32, 36, 58
competence 3–4, 8–9, 34, 39, 147, 156
complement 164–165, 170–172, 176, 178, 205, 221–222, 235
complementary antonym 36–37
complementary distribution 149, 236
complex proposition 54, 62, 68–71
componential analysis 40–44
compositionality 15–16
compound 29–31, 152–153
computer science 265
conditional 64, 74, 83, 98–99, 102
conditional strengthening 83, 98–99
conditioning by environment 149, 151
Conduit Metaphor 9, 252–253
conjunction 62–63, 67, 97, 102–103
connectionism 271, 274
consciousness 265, 275, 281–5
consequent 64
constancy under negation 203–204
constant 70–72
constative 121–124
constituency, constituent structure 159, 161–165, 175–177
construction 7, 204–205, 208–209, 221, 224, 228, 232–238
Construction Grammar 237
context-dependence 20, 112
contradiction 54, 58, 66–69, 101–102
contranym 37–38
conventional implicature 102–104, 112–113
conventional meaning 10–11, 15, 20, 28, 32, 84, 100–104, 112–113, 134–135, 184
conversational implicature 100–105, 112–114, 131
conversion 31, 161
Conway, Erik M. 258
Cooperative Principle 83–102, 107–108, 111, 119, 129–131, 135–136, 183, 210, 234, 254
copula 173–175, 227, 235–237
coreference 14–16, 19, 187, 195
corpus callosum 245–246
corpus/corpora 8–9, 49, 196, 227
correlation vs. causation 261

crash blossom 59–60
Critical Period Hypothesis 146

Dahl, Roald 199, 221, 222
Dani 252
Daniels, Stormy 125
data mining 274, 276–277
declarative 123–125, 134
deep learning 277–284
defeasibility 101
definiteness 16–19, 28, 184–185, 196–206, 212, 221, 227–228, 230
Definiteness Effect 227–228
deictic center
deictics, deixis 187–192, 196, 273; discourse deixis 192; personal deixis 188–190; spatial deixis 190–191; temporal deixis 188, 191–192; *see also* distal deictic; proximal deictic
dendrite 247–248
derivation 31, 159, 161
descent 30–31, 163
descriptive approach 2–3, 9, 84, 173
determiner 169–170, 234
determinism 251–253
Deutscher, Guy 255
dialect 4–8, 36, 147, 163, 173–175, 205, 223–224
direct speech act 124–125, 133, 138
discourse entity 186
discourse model 20–22, 186, 192, 198, 209–210, 233, 274
discourse-status 222–226, 229–237
discreteness 5, 144, 147, 271
disjunction 63–64, 73, 98
distal deictic 190–191
Division of Pragmatic Labor 108–109
Donnellan, Keith S. 18–19
double negative 2–3, 147
Dowd, Maureen 284–285
dualism 281–283

efferent neuron 244
elaborating inference 231
elicitation 8, 211, 263
Eliot, George 155

Elliott, Jane 262
embodiment 274–275
emergent properties 281
empirical study 8, 257
entailment 23, 55–57, 101–102, 198, 202–206, 231, 281, 283
eponym 35–36, 161
Esperanto 164
essential condition 128, 132–133
exclusive *or* 64, 80, 83, 98, 102
existential commitment 73
existential (postposing) 225–231, 234, 237
existential quantifier 72–75
experiencer (semantic role) 218
explicature 105–107, 112–114, 187
explicit performative 122, 125, 129–130, 133, 138

face 137–139
Facebook 276–277
factive 204–205
fake news 56–57, 257
familiarity 138–139, 199–201, 228
felicity conditions 121, 126–132
figurative meaning 20
Fillmore, Charles 219, 237
first person 120, 160, 234
flouting (a maxim) 86, 88, 90–96, 100–101
fluent aphasia 249
Flynn, Michael 133–134
focus 205, 232
Fodor, Jerry 42
Foer, Jonathan Safran 192
forbidden language 137, 259–260
free morpheme 151–152
free will 254, 265, 284
Frege, Gottlob 15–19, 73, 204, 206
French 11, 30–31
frontal lobe 245–246
fuck, fucking 33–35, 259–260
fulfilling (a maxim) 86–91
functionalism 281–282
fuzzy logic 43
fuzzy set 43–45, 91

Gates, Bill 284
generalized conversational implicature 104–105, 112, 114, 131
German 31, 54, 138–139, 159–160, 223
given information 207, 221, 225–232
Given-New Contract 221, 225–226, 231–232
goal (semantic role) 218, 220
Goffman, Erving 137
Goldberg, Adele E. 237
gradable antonym 36
grammar 3–4, 8, 145–147, 165, 169, 174, 178, 237, 247, 249, 283
Greenberg, Jeff 263
Grice, H. Paul 10–11, 19, 83–91, 97–105, 109–114, 131, 136, 183, 280, 285

Haberman, Clyde 52
Halliday, Michael A.K. 221
Hankamer, Jorge 223
'hard problem' of consciousness 284
Hasan, Ruqaiya 221
Haviland, Susan E. 230
Hawking, Stephen 284
head (of a phrase) 164–165, 170–172, 176–178, 229
head-first/head-final language 172
hearer-status 226–232, 237
Hebrew, Classical 52, 160–161
hemispheres (of the brain) 245–246
Herbert, Cassie 262–263
hereby test 119–123, 128–129, 138
hidden layers 272, 277–278
hierarchy 5, 144–145, 157–159
Hirschberg, Julia 105
homograph 38–39
homonym 38–39, 58, 157–158, 161
homophone 38–39
honorific 137–139
Hopi 154, 251
Horn, Laurence R. 13, 50, 108–109, 131, 199, 207, 264
House of Representatives 38, 196
Hutchinson, Lee 254
hypernym 40
hyponym 39–40, 55–57

identifiability 198–201
idiolect 9
I-heuristic 109
illocutionary force 134–136
imperative 123–124
implication 64
implicature 85–114, 131, 136, 199, 257, 260
implicit performative 122, 125, 129
impliciture 106–107
inclusive *or* 64, 98
indexical 187–188
indirect speech act 119, 124–125, 130–134, 138
inferential relation 222, 229, 231
inferrable information 215, 222–223, 229–231
infix 32–34
inflection 31–32, 159–161, 188, 247
information packaging 221
information status 221
information structure 220–238, 234–236
informative-presupposition *it*-cleft 208, 233
innateness 145–147, 165, 265, 283
instrument (semantic role) 218–219
intentional meaning 1, 11, 20, 104, 125, 280–281, 285
interrogative 123–124
intersective adjective 56–57
inversion 221–222, 229, 235–237
is, meaning of 95
island 29, 152
Italian 163
iterative 205

Jabr, Ferris 248
Johnson, Mark 253

Kamp, Hans 56
Kavanaugh, Brett 89–90
Kay, Paul 45, 91–92, 237
King of France, the 15–19, 184, 197–198, 203–207
Kissinger, Henry 117
Klingon 164
Kurtzleben, Danielle 57
Kushner, Jared 117

Lakoff, George 57, 193, 253
Lakoff, Robin 137
language acquisition 43, 45, 145–147, 152, 165, 172, 178, 197, 236, 265, 279–280, 282
language and thought 250–256
language change 6–8
language invention 163–165
language of thought 42
language processing 271–274
language universals 145
lateralization (of brain) 245–246
Latin 30, 163
letter of recommendation, Gricean 90, 94, 96, 100–101, 111
Levin, Beth 219–220
Levinson, Stephen C. 105, 109–110, 114, 137
Lewinsky, Monica 48, 95, 116–117, 132
Lewis, David 209–210
lexical ambiguity 58, 161
lexical relations 36, 40, 51, 55
lexicon 6, 30
Liberman, Mark 155
licensing (an inference) 88, 93, 100, 108–109, 111
lie, meaning of 45, 64, 89, 91–94
linguistic determinism 251–256
linguistic relativity 251–256
literal meaning 1, 11, 19–21, 45, 52, 84, 91, 95, 104–105, 188
localization (within brain) 246
location (semantic role) 218
locutionary force 134
Loftus, Elizabeth F. 211
logical connective, logical operator 61–66, 70, 82–83, 97–99, 102–103
long passive 229, 235

Magritte, René 11–13
Maher, Zach 7
Mahootian, Shahrzad 179
manner, maxim of 86, 96–98, 108
marked term 36, 108–110, 138, 251
Martinelli, Marissa 254
material implication 64

maxim 85–91, 107, 109–111, 136; *see also* manner; quality; quantity; relation
maxim clash 86, 88–91
McCarthy, John J. 33
McCawley, James 110
McConnell-Ginet, Sally 264
McCoy, Tom 7
McFarland, Matt 285
McGinn, Colin 11
McWhorter, John H. 255–256
memory 29, 195, 210–211, 266, 274
mentalism 14, 186
metalanguage 41, 51, 53, 61–62, 74
metalinguistic negation 207
M-heuristic 109–110
Miller, Philip 240
mind/body problem 281–283
minimal pair 148–149
miscommunication 9–10
misfire 127–129
Mnuchin, Steven 135–136
Mohr, Melissa 259–260
morpheme 28, 150–152, 156–161, 164, 237–238
Morris, Michael 11
Munroe, Randall 41
Musk, Elon 284–285
mutual entailment 55–56
mutual hyponymy 55–56
mutual knowledge 207, 209, 234–235

narrow scope 75
native-speaker intuitions 8, 33, 147, 165, 252
natural-language processing 272–274
natural meaning 10–11, 32, 104, 112–113, 280
natural observation 8
naturally occurring data 8, 227, 279
Neale, Stephen 112
negation 17, 61–62, 67, 203, 205–207
negative face 137–139
neo-Gricean theory 107–114, 137, 198
neologism 249
nervous system 244–250
neural network 271–272, 278, 280, 283
neurology 244–250, 265

neuron 244–249, 253, 271–272, 282
neurotransmitter 247–248
new information 208, 221, 225–235, 273, 277
noncanonical word order 221–229, 232, 235
nonconventionality 100, 102, 112–113, 136
nonnatural meaning 10–11, 32, 104, 112–113, 280, 285
nonsubsective adjective 56–57
non-truth-conditionality 20, 22, 104–105, 112–113, 184
noun 31, 37, 56, 59, 70, 153–161, 165–170, 176, 188, 195, 249, 251–252
noun phrase 18, 58, 145, 147, 166, 169–170, 184, 195–197
nucleus (of neuron) 247

oath 126–129, 185, 259–260
Obama, Barack 126–129, 258
occipital lobe 245, 253
O'Connor, Mary Catherine 237
Okrand, Mark 164
Old English 30, 163
one-place predicate 71, 217
onomatopoeia 34, 161
opaque context 15–16, 207
open proposition 72, 223–224, 232–233
opting out (of a maxim) 86–88
Oreskes, Naomi 258
orthography 165
Orwell, George 253–254

parallel distributed processing 271
paraphrase 55–56, 200
parietal lobe 245
Partee, Barbara 56
particularized conversational implicature 104–105, 112–114
parts of speech 153–157, 169
passive 167, 217, 229, 234–237
patient (semantic role) 218
performance 3–4, 9, 147
performative 120–125, 128–130, 133
perlocutionary effect/force 134–136
Pew Research Center 262

phoneme 148–152, 237–238
phonemic sound 149
phrase structure tree 157, 163, 165–169, 173, 177
physicalism 281
Pinker, Steven 100
Politeness theory 123, 136–139
Polizzotti, Mark 51
polysemy 38–39, 273
positive *anymore* 7–8
positive cognitive effect 110–111
positive face 137–139
possible human language 145–146
possible world 20, 22, 53–54, 61–62, 65–69, 74, 121, 202
post-Gricean theory 110
postposing 225–231, 236–237
poverty of the stimulus 146
predicate 70–73, 76, 217
predicate logic 70, 76, 197
prejudice 262–265
preparatory condition 128, 132–133
preposing 221–230, 235–237
preposition 2, 59, 145, 147, 153, 166, 170, 195, 219
prescriptive approach 2–3, 6, 84, 154–156, 173–174, 264–265
presentational (postposing) 225–226, 237
presupposition 17, 19, 184–185, 198, 202–212, 232–233, 256–257, 260–261
Prince, Ellen F. 208, 222–224, 229–230, 232–235
pro-form 195; *see also* pronoun
productivity 5, 33
Project Hail Mary 254
pronoun 6, 138, 145, 154–156, 187, 190–195
propaganda 257–258, 277
proper name 204–205
propositional attitude 15
propositional content condition 128, 132–133
propositional logic 66–70
Proto-Indo-European 30–31
prototype theory 42–45, 91, 280
proximal deictic 190–191
psychic continuity 186
psychology 265, 277
Pullum, Geoffrey 5, 174

Punske, Jeffrey 7
Pyszczynski, Tom 263

Q-heuristic 109
Q-inference 109
Q-principle 108–110
qualia 282–285
quality, maxim of 86–88, 91–93, 107–109
quantifier 72–76
quantity, maxim of 85, 87–90, 94–96, 98, 100–101, 107–109, 131, 261
question under discussion (QUD) 233

race 28, 262
recursion 169, 176
Reddy, Michael J. 9, 252–253
reductionism 281–282
redundancy 57–58, 101–102
reference resolution 193–194
referent 14–19, 185–188, 192–195, 199–201, 206, 209, 222, 273
referential reading 18–19
referentialism 14, 16, 186
relation, maxim of 86, 88, 93–95, 98–100, 102, 108–109, 131, 257, 261–262
relational antonym 36–37
relativity 251–256
Relevance theory 107, 110–114
request 100, 119–125, 128, 130–131, 134–135, 138–139, 145, 273
R-inference 109
Roberts, Craige 233
Roberts, John 126–127
Rombauer, Irma S. 234
Rosch, Eleanor H. 43
Rose, Charlie 284
Ross, John R. 193, 223
Royko, Mike 142
R-principle 108–109
rule-governed nature of language 4, 9, 32–33, 144, 149, 152, 160–161, 173–174
Russell, Bertrand 16–19, 197–198, 206
Russian 252

Sadock, Jerrold M. 101
sandwich, meaning of 35, 42–45, 161, 280
Sapir, Edward 250–251
Sapir-Whorf Hypothesis 250–256, 262
scalar implicature 87–88, 90, 98, 101, 104, 109, 114, 199
Schmidt, Eric 285
Schulz, Muriel R. 263–264
scope 74–75
Searle, John R. 128–132, 275
Second Amendment 185
semantic derogation of woman 263–264
semantic primitive 41–42
semantic role 217–220
semiotics 11
Senate Intelligence Committee 133
sense 15–16, 19
sentence meaning 11, 19–20, 50–76
sentence structure 161–178
sentential ambiguity 58
sentential relations 55–58
Seow, C.L. 160
Shakespeare, William 9, 90, 155
sincerity condition 126, 128, 132–133
Skinner, B.F. 145
Solan, Lawrence M. 88, 185
soma 247
sound structure 147–150
source (semantic role) 218
sources of new words 30–36, 39, 159–161
Spanish 32, 163
speaker meaning 11, 19–20
speech act 119–139, 145
Sperber, Dan 106, 110
spinal cord 244
Standard English 6, 173–175, 224
Star Trek 164
stem 157
'Story of Your Life' 254
Strawson, Peter F. 17–19, 198, 206
strong vs. weak AI 275
structural ambiguity 58, 161, 175–177
structure dependency 159
submaxim 85, 96–98, 107–108

subsective adjective 56–57
superordinate 40, 55
Supreme Court 48, 89, 127, 185, 202
surveys 8, 33, 260–261
Swahili 28, 152, 250
Swift, Jonathan 155
synapse 247–248
synaptic cleft 248
synonym 36–40, 55–56, 216
synthetic statement 54, 67–69

tautology 54, 66–67, 69–70, 121
taxonomy 39–40, 125, 237
temporal lobe 245–247
tense 28, 32, 38, 70–71, 95, 120, 146, 156, 159–160, 172, 174, 187–188, 251
terminal button 247–248
tests for conversational implicature 100–102
theme (semantic role) 218–219
theory of mind 276, 285
there, dummy 225
they, singular 154–156, 263
three-place predicate 71, 217
Tiersma, Peter M. 88, 185
Tolkien, J.R.R. 163
translation 51–53, 164, 224, 274
tree, phrase structure 157, 163–169
tree, word structure 157–159
trigger, presupposition 204–206, 210–211, 232
Trump, Donald J. 25, 92–93, 99–100, 117, 124–125, 128–129, 134, 137, 141–142, 199, 260–261
Trump, Donald Jr. 134
truth table 61–69, 74, 103, 183
truth-conditions 20, 22–23, 37, 54, 68, 72–73, 84, 102–107, 112–113, 121, 183–185, 187, 218
truth-functional operator 61, 64
truth-value 16–18, 23, 54, 61, 67, 69, 72, 107, 198, 204, 206
Turing, Alan 274–275
Turing Test 274–275, 278, 281–283
two-place predicate 71, 217
type/token 9, 181, 228, 237–238

unbound variable 72
uniqueness 16–17, 197–201, 227–228
Universal Grammar 145–146, 165, 178, 283
universal quantifier 72–76
unmarked term 36, 108–110

vaccines 257, 261
validity markers 251
variable 61–62, 68, 72–73, 76, 171
verb 31–32, 70, 145–146, 153–166, 170–176, 204–205, 217–222, 225, 229, 234–235, 249, 251
verb phrase 58, 145, 166, 170, 173, 195
violation (of a maxim) 85–97, 100, 108–109
voicing 148–151

Ward, Gregory 194, 222, 226–227
Washington Post 3, 284
Waters, Maxine 135–136
Weir, Andy 225, 254
Wernicke, Carl 247, 249
Wernicke's aphasia 249–250
Wernicke's area 247, 249–250
what is meant 20, 106
what is said 20, 104–105, 112–113
Whorf, Benjamin Lee 250–255, 263
wide scope 75
Wierzbicka, Anna 41
Wilson, Deirdre 106, 110
Wolfram, Walt 7
word meaning 27–45, 53, 149, 159
Word of the Year 154–156
word structure 150–161, 163
word structure tree 157–159

X-bar schema 172, 176

Yiddish 223–224

Zamenhof, Ludwik 164
Zanni, Guido 211
Zelensky, Volodymyr 99–100, 124
zero copula 174–175
Zimmer, Ben 2, 59–60
zombies 283–285

For Product Safety Concerns and Information please contact our EU
representative GPSR@taylorandfrancis.com
Taylor & Francis Verlag GmbH, Kaufingerstraße 24, 80331 München, Germany

www.ingramcontent.com/pod-product-compliance
Lightning Source LLC
Chambersburg PA
CBHW051147290426
44108CB00019B/2631